THE ILLUSTRATED ENCYCLOPEDIA OF

SIGNS & SYMBOLS

THE ILLUSTRATED ENCYCLOPEDIA OF
SIGNS & SYMBOLS

**Identification and analysis of the visual vocabulary that formulates
our thoughts and dictates our reactions to the world around us**

MARK O'CONNELL
AND RAJE AIREY

LORENZ BOOKS

CONTENTS

Introduction   6

PART ONE:
SIGNS OF LIFE 8

ANCIENT SYMBOLS
Primordial Beginnings 10
The Cradle of Civilization 12
Ancient Egypt 14
The Classical Age 16
Pagan Europe 20
The Middle East 22
Tribal Africa 24
South and South-east Asia 26
Oceanic Traditions 28
Central and South America 30
Native North Americans 32
Arctic Traditions 34

SYMBOLS OF SPIRITUALITY
Shamanism 36
Taoism 38

Hinduism 40
Buddhism 42
Judaism 44
Christianity 46
Islam 48

SYMBOLS AND THE MIND
Freud and Jung 50
Archetypal Symbols 52
Process-oriented Psychology 54
The Symbolic Life Path 56
Dream Symbolism 58
Symbols in Synchronicity 60

SYMBOLISM IN SOCIETY
Meaning and Connection 62
Roles and Relationships 64
Taboos 66
Group Identity 68
Traditional Storytelling 70
Art 74
Advertising 76
Symbolism and Science 78

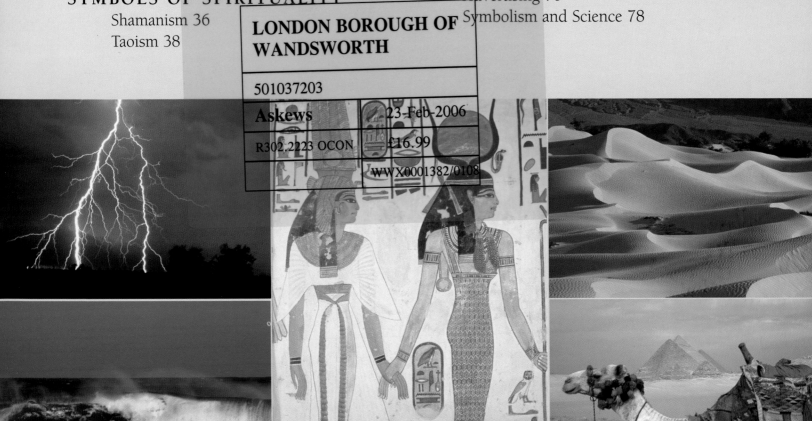

PART TWO:
SYMBOLS WE LIVE BY 80

EVERYDAY LIVING
Common Themes 82
Dwellings as Symbols 84
The Gateway 86
Travelling and Journeys 88
The Garden 90
The Home 92
Status and Wealth 94
Alphabets and Writing 96
Body Language 100
Body Art 102

PATTERNS AND GRAPHICS
Numbers 104
Dots and Lines 106
The Cross 108
Spirals and Circles 110
Triangles and Squares 112
Colour 114

MYTH AND THE COSMOS
The Creative Process 116
The Sun 118
The Moon 120
The Stars 122
The Zodiac 124
Gods and Goddesses 126
Heaven and Hell 130
Demons and Angels 132
Fairies and Nature Spirits 134
Fantastic Creatures 136
The Dragon 140

CONNECTING WITH SPIRIT
Sacred Objects 142
Altars and Sacred Places 144
Alchemical Transumation 146

Labyrinths and Mazes 148
Mandalas and Yantras 150
Oracles and Divination 152

THE CYCLE OF LIFE
The Human Body 154
Birth and Death 158
Sex and Fertility 160
Love and Kinship 162
Rites of Passage 164
Childhood and Games 166
The Wheel 168

FLORA AND FAUNA
Trees 170
Plants, Herbs and Spices 172
Flowers 174
Fruit 176
Animals 178
Birds 180
Aquatic Creatures 182
Insects 184
The Snake or Serpent 186

THE LIVING PLANET
Seasons and Time 188
The Earth 190
Maps and Direction 192
The Land 194
Water 196
Air and Sky 198
Fire 200
The Rainbow 202

PART THREE:
DIRECTORY OF SIGNS 204

ACKNOWLEDGEMENTS 250

INDEX 251

INTRODUCTION

ABOVE The ancient Egyptian ankh is an early manifestation of the cross symbol.

The word "symbol" is derived from the ancient Greek *symballein*, meaning to throw together. Its figurative use originated in the custom of breaking a clay tablet to mark the conclusion of a contract or agreement: each party to the agreement would be given one of the broken pieces, so that when they reconvened the pieces could be fitted together like a jigsaw. The pieces, each of which identified one of the people involved, were known as *symbola*, so that a symbol not only represents something else but also hints at a missing "something", an invisible part that is needed to achieve completion or wholeness. Whether consciously or unconsciously, the symbol carries the sense of joining things together to create a whole greater than the sum of its parts, as shades of meaning accrue to produce a complex idea.

A sign, on the other hand, may be understood as something that stands for, or points to, something else in a more literal way. A sign exists to convey information about a specific object or idea, while a symbol tends to trigger a series of perceptions, beliefs and emotional responses. For example, as a sign, the word "tree" means a particular type of plant that develops a permanent woody structure with a trunk and branches, roots and leaves. As a symbol, the tree may have many meanings: it can represent fruitfulness and the bounty of nature, endurance and longevity or the web of family relationships; as a Christian symbol it can refer to the cross, and in many traditions it represents the "tree of life" that links the everyday world with the world of spirit.

Neither signs nor symbols have intrinsic meaning. The same tree can be described by many different words in different languages, and its meanings as a symbol are formed through human interaction with it. Both signs and symbols have become part of human social and cultural identity, changing and evolving as we do. They are vehicles for information and meaning, operating on many different levels – the universal and particular, intellectual and emotional, spatial and temporal, spiritual and material. They are a way of making sense of experience. If we could not classify the world using symbolic codes and structures we would be overwhelmed by sensory data. We need a way of describing what happens to us in order to understand it.

As well as being an essential part of human society, signs and symbols appear in nature, and may refer to pre-conscious information, as in the case of smoke signifying a fire nearby, or tracks signposting the presence of a particular animal. This book is primarily concerned with signs that have a conscious or unconscious meaning for humans, but as we are rooted in nature, we will see that there may be deeper connections between natural phenomena and the symbols that are meaningful to us.

While signs and symbols can serve as maps or pointers in everyday, or consensus, reality, the symbols of the dream or spirit worlds can help us to navigate the psychospiritual terrain of non-consensus reality. Spirits and dream figures are understood to guide us or compensate for some part of our wholeness as yet unlived. The significance of such symbols and signs fundamentally depends on our freedom to respond to them.

The ability to give meaning to signs and symbols led to the possibility of communication and reflection, and has enabled human beings to pass down their histories, mythologies and worldviews by means of storytelling, art and the written word. Signs and symbols have played a crucial part in furthering our scientific understanding of the world and have helped us to develop increasingly complex technologies, advancing from the invention of primitive tools to computers and spacecraft. Religious and spiritual traditions have used symbolism to help on the journey towards an understanding and experience of the divine and towards "right living". In psychology, approaches have been developed that use symbolism to work towards the alignment of mind, body and nature.

ABOUT THIS BOOK

This book explores the use and power of symbols, whether they are exploited for individual or social well-being, or towards divisive or manipulative ends. It is divided into three sections. Part One provides an overview of the uses, meaning and development of signs and symbols as seen from a number of different perspectives: historical, cross-cultural, sociological and psychological. Part Two looks at the applications of symbols in many areas of life, and includes chapters on culture and communication, abstract symbols, myth and the cosmos, plants and animals, the human life cycle, and the earth. Finally, Part Three, the reference directory, contains more than 1,000 signs and symbols, each with its own ideograph and a brief explanation of its meaning and application.

It is hoped that the information in this book will stimulate readers' interest in this profound and complex subject, prompting them to look beyond the superficial meaning of everyday objects and ideas to arrive at a greater understanding of the ways in which so much of daily life, and the way we communicate with each other, is informed by the richness of signs and symbols.

ABOVE The pyramids of Ancient Egypt symbolized for their architects the creative power of the sun and the immortality of the pharoahs who were buried inside them.

LEFT Mermaids, or sirens, are symbols of the alluring aspect of the female which has a powerful hold on the male.

BELOW The six-pointed star has great symbolic significance in many cultures, but is perhaps best known as the Star of David, an important symbol in the Jewish faith.

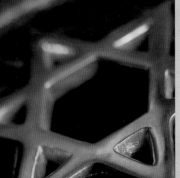

ABOVE Space, the planetary system of which Earth is a part, has had great symbolic meaning over the centuries. This is subject to change as science finds out more about the universe we exist in.

PART ONE

SIGNS OF LIFE

Symbols are at the heart of cultural identity, informing every aspect of life. They draw on all sources – animate and inanimate – for their inspiration and appear in every conceivable form: as pictures, metaphors, sounds and gestures, as personifications in myth and legend, or enacted through ritual and custom.

Since the earliest times, the concept of symbolism has appeared in every human culture, social structure and religious system, contributing to every worldview and informing human understanding of the cosmos and our place in it. The great power of symbols has long been recognized: the ancient Chinese sage Confucius is said to have asserted that, "Signs and symbols rule the world, not words or laws."

RIGHT The monolithic statues on Easter Island have a life-like presence that symbolizes the steadfastness of the human spirit.

ANCIENT SYMBOLS

THE POWER AND MEANING OF SOME OF THE WORLD'S OLDEST SYMBOLS ARE STILL AVAILABLE TO US TODAY. FOUND IN THE SURVIVING ART AND ARTEFACTS OF THE WORLD'S EARLY CIVILIZATIONS, THEY SPEAK CLEARLY OF OUR ANCESTORS' PHYSICAL, SOCIAL AND SPIRITUAL CONCERNS, AND REPRESENT IDEAS THAT REMAIN FUNDAMENTALLY IMPORTANT TO MODERN HUMANITY.

PRIMORDIAL BEGINNINGS

ABOVE This Palaeolithic cave painting in Lascaux, France, was probably intended to create a symbolic link between the hunter and the bison, connecting him with the spirit of the animal.

BELOW The San Bushmen of the Kalahari desert still create rock paintings as symbolic visualizations of successful hunts.

Between the era of *Australopithecus*, the "Southern Ape" (from about 3.6 million BC) to *Homo sapiens sapiens* (25,000–10,000 BC), humans began to make tools, learned to use and then make fire, and constructed homes with hearths. They also began to use language, ritual and symbols.

What we know of our early ancestors comes from archaeological evidence such as cave paintings, artefacts and the traces of possible ritual practices, as well as comparisons with primitive peoples of later eras. Evidence of the development of symbol and ritual comes mainly from the Paleolithic people who emerged about two million years ago. They were hunters, and much of their industry involved working with chipped stone. During this era, the mythic imagination was stirred, and art began to be created.

The dawn of mythology and symbolism meant that people were beginning to relate to concepts deeper than just their daily existence. It is easy to imagine that their relationship with nature, the seasons and weather, the animals they hunted, the birth of their children and the inevitability of death led them to ponder the source and meaning of events in their lives. The primitive symbols of the cave, fire, the hand-axe, and the representation of animal figures, may serve as foundation metaphors for the complex human mythologies that have subsequently evolved. The symbols and rituals of primordial human beings may have served to align these people with the rhythms of their bodies and in nature, and to honour the forces influencing them.

THE MAKING OF FIRE

The ability to make fire and harness its energy was a highly significant development, achieved by *Homo erectus* (around 1.6 million–300,000 BC), and gave fire important symbolic qualities. The act of making fire represents the spark of imagination and creativity, and the energy of fire is in itself a symbol of power: harnessing and using nature to control other aspects of the natural world, bringing life-sustaining warmth, and frightening away threatening animals. Fire enabled people to extend the day after dark, creating a social time around a campfire or hearth, sharing myths and stories. At this early stage fire also became a symbol of transformation through the process of cooking.

CAVES AND CAVE ART

To primitive humans, caves were sacred places. People appear to have lived around or just inside the entrance, but ventured deeper into a cave only for religious or magical purposes.

Painting animals on the walls of caves may have been a means of connecting with their spiritual qualities. Boys were taken into the caves to be initiated as hunters – a rite that probably involved a symbolic death and rebirth, and which must have been a powerful experience, deep within a dimly lit, womb-like place surrounded by animal images.

To early humans a cave may have symbolized the leaving of everyday reality, as they went inside to find where their deeper

THE HAND-AXE

The stone-age hand-axe appears wherever early humans existed (except the very far east of Asia) and has been the most popular form of tool during the last two million years. It is a multi-purpose tool used for scraping animal skins, cutting meat, digging holes, cutting wood, and possibly as a weapon of self-defence against animals or other humans. The making of these tools involved chipping flakes from a "core" stone, signifying spiritual and psychological renewal of the core essence. Early two-faced axes are also thought to represent the repairing of interpersonal conflict.

nature connected with and honoured the spirits of other animals; a place of transformation where they ritually died and were reborn in a new form.

Many early cave paintings, such as those of the Trois Frères cavern, in southern France, depict beings who are part-animal and part-human in form. A bearded male figure, with the ears of a bull, antlers and a horse's tail, may have represented either a divinity or a magician.

It is hard to differentiate between images of human magicians and divine figures in Palaeolithic art, as both appear to share this mixture of human and animal features. The magician was an important member of the community, and was probably considered a god in human form, with influence upon the gods and animal spirits.

HUNTING MAGIC

Palaeolithic humans certainly used magic to help in hunting animals. The principal form of magic was mimetic: they would imitate an animal they were hunting to connect to its spirit and ensure success. However, they also used sympathetic or homeopathic magic, in the belief that an act upon an object representing the animal would literally have an effect on the animal itself. Thus clay figures and drawings of animals that have been cut and slashed have been found, which were presumably to aid success in hunting.

A constant supply of game for the hunt was crucial, and fertility magic was performed to ensure it.

This usually involved depicting a mating pair of animals, or females with offspring. Clay models of bison in couples and a bull following a cow have been found in France; at La Madeleine a drawing shows a doe with a fawn.

MAKING OFFERINGS

The earliest evidence of probable offerings to supernatural powers was found in the Drachenloch, in the Tamina Valley, in Switzerland. Bear bones had been placed there with some flesh still attached to the skulls, brains intact, and some leg bones, in a state as if to be eaten. They are thought to have been offerings to appease the animal spirits, to thank them for a successful hunt, and to seek favour with them for future hunting expeditions.

BURIAL

Palaeolithic finds include the first evidence of burial for sacred purposes. The dead were believed to gain supernatural powers, and would have been respected and referred to for guidance. Red ochre was sprinkled over the bodies; this may have represented blood and symbolized life and strength for the journey into the other world.

In Les Hoteaux, in Ain, France, a late Palaeolithic skeleton was found in a small trench, covered with red ochre. There was a large stone behind its head, and buried

with it were flint tools and the staff of a chieftain made from horn and engraved with a stag. Numerous other examples of bodies have been found in stone tombs or shallow graves, together with valuable jewellery, tools and other ritual objects. It seems the dead were being given food and tools, perhaps symbolically, to equip them for their existence in the next world.

Sometimes buried bodies have been found to have been tied up in a doubled-up position. This may have been intended to stop the dead from returning and tormenting their living descendants. In China the remains of human beings at an evolutionary stage halfway between *Pithecanthropus* and Neanderthal humans were found: apart from their skulls and lower jawbones, the other bones of the bodies had been placed to represent the animals they would have eaten. Did this ancient funerary ritual mean "You are what you eat"?

ABOVE Depictions of the sun and moon are centred on a human figure in this Venezualan engraving.

ABOVE Early people made ritual use of red ochre, used to stain this stone found in Bevoc, Bohemia, from 250,000 years ago.

BELOW As a symbol, fire is associated with creativity, destruction and imagination.

THE CRADLE OF CIVILIZATION

ABOVE We can only imagine what the early cities of ancient Mesopotamia looked like. This artist's impression shows a city's towering ziggurat to the left of the picture.

BELOW The law code of Hammurabi, 18th century BC, is an example of cuneiform script, the first written signs to replace pictorial representations.

fairly simple mud-brick constructions, decorated with cone geometrical mosaics and frescoes with human and animal figures. A rectangular shrine, known as a "cella", had a brick altar or offering table in front of a statue of the temple's deity. Public rituals, food sacrifices and libations took place on a daily basis, as well as monthly feasts and annual celebrations of the New Year.

As early hunter-gatherer societies found ways to work the land, more permanent settlements began to appear, particularly in areas where crops would flourish. One such area was in Mesopotamia, the "Fertile Crescent" of land between the Tigris and Euphrates rivers in what is now southern Iraq. From around 5000 BC small farming villages in the region were gradually developing into towns and cities, giving birth to some of the earliest civilizations – the word "civilization" comes from the Latin *civis*, which means "citizen of a city". People were inventing written languages, building temples, palaces and dwellings, and creating complex societies in which signs and symbols were interwoven with the fabric of daily life.

RECORD KEEPING

The ancient civilization of Sumer had thriving agriculture, trade and industry and was one of the first civilizations to develop a system of writing. Initially pictographs or icons were used, with one of the earliest dictionaries containing about 2,000 graphic symbols, each one meant to resemble that which it represented. However, as society developed and the need to record complex matters increased, the limitations of pictorial representation became apparent. Gradually people realized that written signs could be used to represent sounds rather than things, and so pictures were replaced by cuneiform script, a written code based on a series of wedge-shaped characters, usually inscribed on to a soft surface, such as clay.

RELIGIOUS LIFE

The flooding of the Tigris and Euphrates was violent and unpredictable: from one day to the next, life-giving rain could change into an agent of devastation. It was believed the gods controlled these powerful forces, with humans little more than slave subjects to the whims of fate. This put religion firmly at the centre of daily life, with a temple dedicated to one of the major gods at the heart of each town or city. Initially these were

ZIGGURATS

These early temple complexes gradually evolved into ziggurats, towering pyramid-like structures, some reaching as high as 90m (300ft). One of the earliest examples from the region is the White Temple of Uruk (Erech in the Old Testament), dedicated to the Sumerian god An, lord of the heavens, dating back to the late 3000s BC.

Mesopotamian ziggurats were built in a series of three, five or seven increasingly narrow terraces, with steps for climbing to the next level. The seven terraces are said to correspond to the seven planetary Heavens. According to a Sumerian tradition, the bottom level was linked with Saturn and was painted black; the second level was white and corresponded to Jupiter; the third was brick-red and symbolized Mercury, while the fourth, blue level was associated with Venus. The sixth level, Mars, was yellow, while the seventh level was grey or silver to represent the moon, upon which the golden light of the sun would shine. Sacrifices were usually

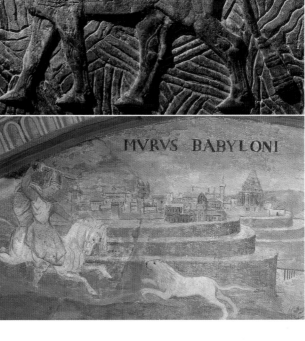

RIGHT A winged bull with a human head, one of the hybrid mythological creatures known as lamassu that were carved into important public buildings in Assyrian cities.

made at the top level. The symbolism of the ziggurat has also been compared with the cosmic mountain alleged to lie at the centre of the world, as well as with temples built in the shape of mountain. Symbolically, ziggurats are similar to ladders, joining Heaven and Earth and creating a passageway for mortals to ascend and the gods to descend. Ziggurats were allegedly the inspiration for the Tower of Babel, which in the Old Testament was interpeted as a symbol of pride built by humans attempting to equal God's splendour.

THE GODDESS ISHTAR

Arguably the most important deity in ancient Mesopotamia was the moon goddess, Ishtar, also known as Inanna, Astarte or Ashtar (and later, in ancient Egypt, as Isis). Ishtar personifies the forces of nature that can give and destroy life, and, like the moon, her form is ever-changing. Sometimes she was represented as a large-breasted, round-bellied fertility goddess. She is the goddess of sexual love, and in the homes of ancient Babylon little shrines containing her image showed her nude, seated in a window frame – the typical pose of the prostitute.

Ishtar is also the goddess of war, and in this aspect she could be depicted standing on a lion (symbolizing ferocity) and with the talons and wings of an owl. She was also shown wearing a three-tiered crown of stars, blue lapis lazuli stones and a rainbow necklace, symbolizing her connection with the sky. As queen

of the heavens, each night she rides across the sky in a chariot drawn by lions or goats. The zodiacal constellations were known to the ancient Arabs as the Houses of the Moon, and the whole zodiacal belt was known as the "girdle of Ishtar", a term that referred to the moon calendar of the ancients.

BABYLON

In ancient Babylon, the lion was a popular symbol of royal power, while the dragon was associated with the supreme god, Marduk. The laws and customs of the land were unified under Hammurabi (r.1792–1750 BC), and the city of Babylon became a renowned centre for learning, especially in science, mathematics and astronomy. Babylonian scholars developed a numbering system, based on groups of 60, which led to our 60-minute hour and 360-degree circle. The ancient Greek historian Herodotus declared that Babylon "is so splendid, that no city on earth may be compared with it". Its walls and famous hanging gardens were among the seven wonders of the ancient world, and Babylon became synonymous with excellence and attainment. In the Judaeo-Christian tradition, however, it became the antithesis of paradise and the heavenly Jerusalem, and symbolized the profane.

LAMASSU

Symbols of power and protection, massive winged sphinxes, or lamassu, have their roots in Babylonian magical traditions, although they are more usually

associated with Assyrian culture (c.1000–600 BC). With the body of a bull or lion, sometimes with five legs, winged, and with bearded human heads, these sculptures were incorporated into important civic structures, such as the royal palace or city gateways. Some stood as high as 5m (16ft) and weighed as much as 30 tons. The lion and the bull symbolized masculine power, virility and sovereignty, although both animals were also associated with the moon goddess: the spectacular Ishtar Gate that led into the city of Babylon was decorated with lions, while the bull's horns on Ishtar's headdress denoted the crescent moon. The head of the lamassu symbolized the power of the sovereign to protect his people, the wings denoted the ability to fly, while the legs represented vigilance against both human and supernatural enemies who could attack from any direction.

ABOVE This artist's impression of Babylon shows the popular sport of lion hunting. The lion was a symbol of royal authority and power for the Babylonions.

BELOW An impression of one of the towers of the Ishtar Gate of the city of Babylon, which was elaborately decorated with golden lions.

ANCIENT EGYPT

ABOVE The Egyptian pyramids hold a wealth of symbolism.

ABOVE MIDDLE The Double Crown of ancient Egypt had many symbolic associations, linking the two kingdoms of Upper and Lower Egypt.

PYRAMIDS

The pyramid is a symbol of ascension: erected in alignment with the sun and stars to create a passageway between Earth and the Heavens by which the dead pharaoh could cross to the afterlife. In the Western hermetic tradition, the pyramid combines the symbolism of the square with the triangle. The symbolism of the pyramid is also linked with the mound (and cosmic mountain), thought to resemble the hill that emerged from the primeval waters when the earth was created, so a symbol of the power of life over death.

In its prime, the civilization of ancient Egypt was arguably the most spectacular on earth. It emerged about 5,000 years ago and continued to flourish for three millennia, giving us a fascinating array of symbols, many of which were rooted in the land and nature. Ancient Egypt existed in a landscape of extremes, referred to in symbolic terms as Red and Black. The Red Land (Deshret) was the Saharan side of the country, made scorched and barren by the fierce heat of the sun; the Black Land (Kemet) was the fertile area in the Nile valley, darkened by the river's seasonal floods and shaded by its vegetation. In this way, the land of Egypt came to symbolize a marriage of opposites, a synthesis. This view informed the Egyptians' belief systems and lay at the heart of their culture.

ORDER AND CHAOS

The relationship between order (*maat*) and chaos (*isfet*) was at the crux of ancient Egyptian thought. The god Horus was associated with all that was right and ordered, and Seth with chaos, as well as infertility and aridity.

Similarly Kemet was a place of order – at the same time each year the Nile, Egypt's lifeblood, flooded the land, ensuring bountiful harvests – while Deshret was associated with infertility and disorder. Harmony was achieved when these two forces were held in equilibrium, neither gaining control at the expense of the other, and was personified by the goddess Maat, daughter of Re, the creator god and pre-eminent solar deity.

Maat was represented wearing an ostrich feather, symbol of truth and an ideogram of her name, on her head. She maintained order on Earth and in Heaven, ruling over the seasons, day and night and the movement of the stars, she also decided the fate of the dead in the underworld, weighing the deceased's heart against the feather of truth in her scales of justice. When the scales balanced, paradise was the reward; when they tipped, the deceased was devoured by a monster, part-lion, part-hippopotamus, part-crocodile. Maat also presided over decrees, legal acts and social relationships, and regulated religious rites.

ABOVE The Nile symbolized the lifeblood of Egypt, as the land's fertility was, and is, dependent upon its seasonal floods.

DIVISION AND UNIFICATION

Politically, the kingdom was divided into two parts: Upper and Lower Egypt, with Upper Egypt being in the south, and Lower Egypt in the north in the Nile Delta region – a division represented by the white and red crowns. The red crown of Lower Egypt had a tall, thin back and a narrow coil at the front, while the white crown of Upper Egypt was shaped like a tall cone with a bulbous tip. It was sometimes adorned with two plumes in a form called the atef-crown, which was associated with Osiris, lord of the underworld. Sometimes both crowns were combined to form the Double Crown.

It was believed that the origins of the state of Egypt could be traced to an act of unification of Upper and Lower Egypt by a ruler named Menes (for whom there is no actual archaeological evidence), around 3100 BC. The hieroglyphic sign used to express this notion of unification was a

THE ANKH

Formed by a loop over a T-cross, the ankh was the ancient Egyptian hieroglyph for life and immortality and was often used in the iconography of opposites. The loop, a form of circle, may stand for the universe (the macrocosm), and the T-cross for man (the microcosm). Alternatively, it combines the male and female symbols of the god Osiris (the T-cross), and the mother goddess Isis (the oval), sister and wife of Osiris, and symbolizes the union of Heaven and Earth. In Egyptian wall paintings, gods (particularly Isis) and kings are depicted holding the ankh, to symbolize their powers over life and death. The ankh is also associated with death and funerary rites: carried by the dead, it signals a safe passage between this world and the next, while held upside down, it is the key that unlocks the gates of death into eternity. Sometimes it is seen placed on the forehead between the eyes, linking it with clairvoyance.

stylized rendering of a pair of lungs, with a windpipe extending straight upwards from between them. In artistic representations, this emblem might be flanked by two deities, sometimes Horus and Seth, or on other occasions two Nile gods, one with a papyrus plant (the heraldic emblem of the Delta) on his head, and the other with the lotus (or waterlily) plant (the emblem of the Nile Valley). The figures on each side are often depicted tying the papyrus and lotus stems in a knot around the hieroglyph. It was the role of the king, or pharaoh, to unite these two lands, with his titles of "Lord of the Two Lands" and "King of Upper and Lower Egypt".

THE PHARAOH

The term pharaoh (*per-aa*) literally means "great house". In the New Kingdom period (c.1550–c.1069 BC) it was used to describe the king, but before that time it referred to the king's palace or the royal court. In ancient Egypt the king, or pharaoh, was believed to be a living manifestation of divinity, associated with both Horus, the falcon-headed sky god, and Re,

sometimes represented as a winged sun disc. This god-like status gave the pharaoh absolute power, having control over the army and all civil appointments, as well as the priesthood. Everywhere they went, ordinary people were reminded of the pharaoh's status, symbolized by massive stone statues of the king in the guise of Re, as well as the majestic pyramids – the funerary monuments of the kings and queens of ancient Egypt.

THE AFTERLIFE

Death and burial had many symbolic associations in ancient Egypt, where the existence of an afterlife was at the heart of religious belief. The practice of mummification reveals the strongly held belief that the body was required to be intact for life after death, while funerary texts show that the dead were believed to ascend to the heavens, the realm of the sun and place of the afterlife. There were several methods of ascent, including riding on the back of a falcon, goose or other bird; being wafted upwards with burning incense; or travelling on a reed float or barque that was sailed, rowed or towed. The journey was hazardous, and spells and recitations were uttered to help

the deceased on their way, while protective funerary amulets were positioned on the dead body.

Two of the most widely used amulets were the protective Eye of Horus (also known as the udjat or wadjat eye), which in one version of the myth of Osiris is used by Osiris's son, Horus, to bring his father back to life, and the scarab, which was placed over the heart. The scarab beetle was associated with Khepri (an aspect of the solar deity, Re) and was therefore a symbol of new life and resurrection. Sometimes scarabs were depicted with falcon's wings, as a symbol of transcendence and protection.

ABOVE The practice and ritualistic elements of mummification were full of symbolic meaning.

BELOW The Eye of Horus (wadjat) gives protection to a funerary barge on its way to the afterlife.

THE CLASSICAL AGE

ABOVE The Acropolis symbolizes the glory of the classical world.

ABOVE In antiquity, a laurel wreath was a symbol for victory, as well as a sign of status worn by the ruling classes.

Both the classical Greek civilization and the mighty Roman Empire have had an enormous impact on Western society, influencing its laws and customs, its art and science, its philosophy and way of life. The belief systems of these Mediterranean peoples can be seen in their mythologies, which were characterized by a vivid, dramatic vitality that enshrined the moral principles, natural laws and the great contrasts and transformations that determine both cosmic and human life. The gods and goddesses of the Greco-Roman pantheon acted out archetypal themes such as birth, death and renewal, war and peace, love and marriage, and governed all aspects of daily life.

The highest peak in the landscape of ancient Greece was Mount Olympus, home to the gods. From here they presided over the world and helped or hindered humans according to their whims. All the gods were thought to be descendants of Gaia (the Earth) and Uranus (the sky), and their lives were thought of in human terms – they fell in love, had children, played music, quarrelled and had affairs. Each of the gods had their own sphere of influence – Aphrodite (Roman Venus) governed love, and Ares (Mars) war, for example – and all the major deities had temples and sanctuaries dedicated to them.

CENTRE OF THE WORLD

One of the most important sanctuaries was the main shrine of Apollo at Delphi on the slopes of Mount Parnassus. Apollo, who in one of his aspects was associated with the sun, had the power of prophecy and divination, and at Delphi he would reply to questions about the future through his priestess. Delphi was thought to be the centre of the world, the point where two birds flying from opposite ends of the earth met. A huge stone, known as the *omphalos* or navel-stone, was placed there to symbolize this.

THE SUPREME GOD

The greatest god was Zeus (Jupiter to the Romans), who was the supreme ruler of Heaven and Earth as well as dominating the lesser Olympian gods. He was married to his sister Hera, but had many other sexual liaisons, fathering offspring of both goddesses and mortal women, typically while in disguise – taking such forms as a swan, a bull, a horse or a shower of gold. His symbols were the thunderbolt and eagle, although he was also depicted in human form wearing a crown of laurel leaves, seated on a throne and holding a sceptre.

TEMPLES

The earthly homes of the gods were their temples, and no expense was spared in their construction. Early wooden structures gave way to stone, especially marble, and they were decorated with brightly painted friezes showing the exploits of gods, goddesses and heroes. Most temples were dedicated to a particular deity, whose cult was centred on the location.

One of the most famous temples of ancient Greece, the Parthenon, was built on the Acropolis ("the high city") in Athens between 447 and 432 BC. It was dedicated to the city's patron deity, Athene, goddess of wisdom and warfare, and housed a huge gold and ivory statue of her. The owl, symbolizing wisdom, was her emblem and can be found on silver coins issued in Athens after the Greeks won decisive victories against the Persians in 479 BC.

The Romans' custom of deifying dead emperors meant that many temples were built to worship them, including that of Augustus and his wife Livia, which still stands in Vienne, France. Such temples were symbols of both divine and worldly power, testimony to the cultural and political achievements of the Romans.

SEASONS AND CYCLES

Greek life was dominated by religion, and this was inherently bound up with nature's cycles. The annual death and rebirth of the Earth's vegetation took symbolic form in the myth of Persephone (whom the Romans called Proserpine), the virgin daughter of Zeus (Jupiter) and Demeter (Ceres) the Earth Goddess. According to the myth of Persephone, Hades (Pluto, lord of the underworld) spied the beautiful maiden picking poppies and abducted her to be his queen in the realm of the dead. Consumed by grief, Demeter neglected the land while she searched for her daughter. The earth became barren as crops withered and died, and the result was perpetual winter.

To help humanity, Zeus intervened and sent Hermes (Mercury), the messenger god, to bring Persephone back. Meanwhile, however, she had eaten the food of the dead (in the form of six pomegranate seeds) and so was bound to Hades: she could be restored to Demeter for only part of the year. Her annual arrival is marked by the rebirth of spring but at the end of summer, she must return to Hades and the earth once again becomes barren.

GAMES

Not just for entertainment, sport was a way of training for warfare and of honouring the gods. National festivals attracted athletes from all over the Greek world, the most important being the Olympic Games, held every four years in honour of Zeus.

The Games were so important that wars were suspended to allow people to travel in safety to and from Olympia. The first Olympics were held in 776 BC and continued into Roman times, coming to an end in the late 4th century AD. They were revived in the modern era in 1896. One of the symbols associated with the Olympic Games is a runner bearing a torch, harking back to the time when relay races took place after dark, and the runners carried torches to light the way. The winning team used them to light fires on altars dedicated to Zeus or Athene. Winners wore laurel wreaths sacred to Apollo and a symbol of victory.

ABOVE The five rings that make up the symbol for the modern Olympic Games represent the five continents of the world.

BELOW Triptoleme, a prince of Eleusis, being initiated into the Eleusian Mysteries by Demeter and Persephone.

LAUREL

Through its association with Apollo, the aromatic leaves of laurel, or bay, were the crowning emblem of the Greco-Roman world for both warriors and poets. It was a symbol of truce, victory, peace, divination and purification.

BELOW The caduceus, a rod or staff entwined by two serpents, is a symbol of the god Hermes. It is used as an emblem for homeopathic medicine.

BELOW A she-wolf suckling the twins, Romulus and Remus, is one of the symbols for the ancient city of Rome.

MEDICINE AND HEALING

To the ancient Greeks, illness was seen as a punishment sent by the gods, to whom they also prayed for a cure. Sanctuaries dedicated to Asclepius (a Greek physician deified as the god of medicine) were set up all over the Greek world, the most famous being at Epidaurus. The sick made pilgrimages to such temples, where they practised a healing process known as incubation. They slept in the temple and used their dreams as a channel for communication with Asclepius, in the hope that he could show them how to get well. The priest would then carry out the recommended treatment. It was customary to leave some kind of symbolic representation of the afflicted part of the body, both when asking for healing and as an offering of thanks afterwards.

The emblem of Asclepius was his staff, a rough-hewn branch entwined with a serpent, whose shedding of skin symbolizes the renewal of youth. The staff is still a familiar symbol of healing, and is used by medical bodies such as the World Health Organization.

The Romans also believed that illness could be caused by the gods, as well as by witchcraft and curses, and also left offerings to the gods in the shape of body parts. This practice continues in churches in some Mediterranean countries today, where embossed metal tokens are used.

THE FOUNDING OF ROME

According to legend, Rome was founded in 753 BC by the twin brothers, Romulus and Remus, sons of the Roman war god Mars. As babies, the twins were thrown into the river Tiber and left to die but were carried ashore and cared for by a female wolf. When they grew up, they decided to build a city on the Tiber. To decide where to build the city, each brother climbed a hill (Remus the Aventine and Romulus the Palatine) and sought omens from the gods. In the Greco-Roman tradition, the vulture was sacred to Apollo and was a bird of augury. So when Romulus saw 12 vultures, while Remus saw only 6, the Palatine hill was chosen, and Romulus ploughed a furrow to mark out the city's limits. When Remus tried to take the initiative from his brother, Romulus killed him. Once Rome was established, Mars carried Romulus away in his chariot to become a god.

With its valour and predatory nature, the wolf was held sacred to Mars and became a totem symbol of Rome, one of the world's greatest superpowers. The Roman empire was built on the strength of its army.

POWER AND VICTORY

Based on rigorous discipline, iron will and courage, the Roman army became synonymous with the might of Rome. The army not only extended the empire's frontiers but also was responsible for its protection, building impenetrable hilltop fortresses to defend Roman gains. The goddess Nike, a winged aspect of Athene, became the symbol of military

victory. She was often shown with a globe and a victor's wreath, and sacrifices were made to her before and after battles to ensure victory and give thanks for success.

The eagle was adopted as the Roman standard. Known as the *aquila*, the standard itself became an emblem of imperial power. The eagle's wings sheltered the peace of the empire, while the bird's capacity to fell its victim in one deadly swoop was a reminder of Rome's warrior-like virtues.

Slaves were one of the spoils of war, and some (including women) trained as gladiators, who fought each other, often to death, in amphitheatres erected all over the empire. Public architecture of this kind, a powerful symbol of Roman domination, culminated in the building of the spectacular Colosseum in Rome. Opened in AD 80, it held about 50,000 people, and it has been estimated that 500,000 combatants died there. Gladiatorial fights had a religious origin, having been held at funerals to honour the dead, but by the time of the emperors

they were a bloodsport. The victors could win their freedom, and some gladiators achieved celebrity status – a graffiti inscription at Pompeii describes one called Celadus as "the man the girls sigh for". When a gladiator was wounded he could appeal for mercy. If the crowd (and the emperor) favoured him, the thumbs-up sign spared his life, while a thumbs-down sign signified a brutal death.

THE CULT OF MITHRAS

Originally a Persian sun god, Mithras achieved cult status with the Roman army, which spread his worship throughout Roman society and the empire. As creator and controller of the cosmos, Mithras was usually depicted slaying a bull, symbolizing man's victory over his animal nature, as well as Rome's political power over her enemies. Mithras was

RIGHT In the ancient Roman empire, the cult of Mithras was open to men only. This frieze depicts the god slaying a white bull, symbolizing male sexual potency and power in its purest form.

worshipped in subterranean temples where the *taurobolium* (ritual sacrifice of a bull) took place, and initiates into the cult were baptized in its blood. Sometimes Mithras is depicted spanned by the circle of the zodiac, possibly alluding to the end of the age of Taurus and the beginning of the age of Aries pertinent to the time.

ABOVE Winged Victory – or Nike, an aspect of Athena to the Greeks – holds two of the most important Roman symbols of power and victory, a staff with an eagle on top and a wreath made of laurel leaves.

ABOVE LEFT The standard of a Roman legion was the ultimate symbol of its pride and military honour.

PAGAN EUROPE

ABOVE An instrument of the soul, the Celtic harp was said to have inspired three responses: happy laughter, tears of sadness, and serenity or sleep.

THE CELTIC SWORD

To the Celts, the sword symbolized power, protection, courage, authority, truth and justice. The sword is also a phallic symbol. Some swords were thought to possess magic qualities. The image of Arthur drawing the sword from the stone after others had failed was a sign of his royalty.

When Rome and its western empire fell to barbarian invaders in AD 476, northern Europe entered a period of instability. The influence of Roman civilization receded, though classical learning was preserved in Christian monasteries, and the old Celtic culture was interwoven with the Germanic and Scandinavian traditions of the incoming forces.

In the 6th century the Anglo-Saxons reached Britain from Scandinavia and Germany, displacing Roman, Celtic and Christian culture from what now became the "land of the Angles", or England. Later, between 800 and 900, the Vikings raided mainland Europe and Britain. By the 11th century, however, the new cultures had been assimilated and Europe rose re-formed out of the Dark Ages into the Middle Ages, with the flourishing Roman Christianity as the dominant faith, blended with elements of the older, pre-Christian cultures.

THE CELTS

Celtic myths and symbols were passed down by the bards, who blended the roles of priest, teacher and entertainer and kept the culture alive. The Celts had a deep affinity to nature, and natural patterns feature strongly in Celtic art.

In County Galway in Ireland stands an ancient standing stone, known as the Turoe stone. It is carved with stylized patterns suggestive of plants and animals, and is a symbol of regeneration. It may have been a place where ageing kings were sacrificed for cultural renewal.

The Celtic cauldron was an important symbol of abundance, rebirth and sacrifice: an unending supply of food or knowledge, often associated with the supreme Celtic god Dagda. The dead, thrown into the cauldron, were said to be reborn the next day. The Celtic cauldron may be a precursor of the Holy Grail of the Arthurian legends. A magnificent gilded silver and copper cauldron of the 1st or 2nd century BC, the Gundestrup cauldron depicts Kernunnos, the "Horned God", a male animal deity, in a sacred marriage with Mother Earth, or nature. He bears the antlers of a stag, symbolizing renewal (as stags shed their antlers and grow new ones). He appears also with a boar, which the Celts admired for its speed and willingness to fight; they believed it had magical qualities and direct links to the underworld. Kernunnos holds a ram-headed serpent, symbol of sexuality and regeneration.

There are many examples in Celtic art of the triple goddess, appearing in her three aspects: maiden, mother and crone. Brigid was the triple goddess commonly associated with the Celtic spring festival of Imbolc, celebrated at the time of lambing. She inspired

ABOVE The Gundestrup cauldron displays a magnificent array of Celtic nature symbolism, including the horned god Kernunnos, an animal deity.

the bards and was a deity of healing who also protected women in childbirth.

Another triple goddess was Morrigan, who was associated with the crow. The consort of Dagda, she was a goddess of battle, strife and fertility. She had the power to make men completely helpless, in particular when they did not recognize their feminine qualities. Dagda's name means "the all-powerful god". He was a protective father-figure, often pictured holding a club, or with an erect penis, symbolizing virility and the creation of life.

The Celts worshipped their gods in sacred groves of trees. They began to build temples only when influenced by the Romans. The oak tree symbolized power and protection, and oak groves were sacred spaces.

THE ANGLO-SAXONS

Around AD 450 the Anglo-Saxons began their migration to Britain from Denmark and northern Germany. They were a proud warrior society, with polytheistic beliefs, and worshipped animals such as the boar, horse and stag.

The Anglo-Saxons believed in a fixed destiny or fate, known as *wyrd*. The concept was embodied in the three Wyrd Sisters, or Norns, who wove the web of fate (rather like the Greek Fates who were believed to spin, measure and cut the thread of each human life).

Horses were sacred to the Anglo-Saxons, and represented great wealth and rank. Legends tell of Hengist ("stallion") and Horsa ("horse"), the twin gods who were said to have led the invasion of Britain. Huge chalk horses carved into the hillsides of southern England, such as those at Uffington and Westbury in Wiltshire, are thought to be Anglo-Saxon in origin.

The boar was an Anglo-Saxon symbol of protection and royalty. It was associated with Frô, a god of kingship and fertility. Warriors bore its image on their helmets, in the belief that this would make the power of the boar accessible to the wearer. At Yuletide, to mark the shortest day of the year, solemn vows were made over the

Yule Boar, which was then sacrificed: it was thought to go straight to the gods, taking the vows with it, while its carcass was roasted and served with an apple in its mouth, symbolizing the rebirth of the sun goddess.

The stag was a noble symbol for the Anglo-Saxon king and his leadership. A stag-pole, mounted with the head of a stag facing the sun, was customarily erected to curse or insult an enemy.

The festival of the fertility goddess Eostre was celebrated in spring, and she gave her name to the Christian festival of Easter. Her animal was the hare or rabbit – the origin of the modern Easter Bunny: according to one legend she transformed a bird frozen in a winter storm into a rabbit, which continued to lay eggs each spring in gratitude.

THE VIKINGS

The Norse people of Scandinavia, worshipped a pantheon of gods and goddesses led by Odin. The Vikings were seafaring Norse warriors and traders who flourished from the 8th to the 11th centuries, raiding Europe

from the sea in their mighty, longships, taking first belongings, and then territory, from the native Saxons.

Odin, or Wotan, the chief Norse deity, was the god of thought and memory, two mental faculties esteemed by the Norse peoples. Thor was the god of lightning and thunder, and thus of power, wielding a mighty hammer to protect humans and gods from giants. Freya was the goddess of love and beauty, but was also a warrior goddess; her sacred animal was the cat. Freya's twin brother was Freyr, a horned fertility god, god of success, and also a warrior god, fighting with a horn or an elk.

BELOW Viking longships were symbols of terror and ferocity to the unfortunate people who suffered the incursions of the Norsemen.

ABOVE The Anglo-Saxons associated the boar with kingship, plenty and protection in battle.

VIKING SHIPS

The Vikings were master ship builders and saw their sea vessel ("horse of the waves") as a symbol of power and speed. The ships were also potent symbols for safe passage to the afterlife, with ships used in burials, securely moored and anchored, protecting the corpse's body.

HELM OF AWE

Thought to make the wearer magically invincible and terrifying to his enemies, the Helm of Awe is a Viking symbol of protection. As well as being a physical helmet worn between the eyes, the Helm of Awe also probably refers to a form of magic practice used to create delusions in the minds of others.

THE MIDDLE EAST

FARAVAHAR

The supreme god of the Persians, Ahura Mazda was personified by the *faravahar*, an image of a kingly figure rising out of a winged disc, which represents human aspiration to form a union with the god. The figure symbolizes free will: its pointing hand stands for the aspirations of the human soul while the other hand holds a ring, symbolizing kingship, and the cycle of birth, death and rebirth.

Sometimes referred to as the crossroads of history – the meeting point of East and West – the Middle East saw the beginnings of civilization and was the birthplace of Judaism, Islam and Christianity. Its cultural complexity reflects its long history of human migration, conquest and trade.

THE PERSIAN EMPIRE

From the late 6th century BC the Persian Empire, the largest and best-organized empire the ancient world had hitherto seen, dominated the Middle East, embracing lands from the Mediterranean coast to the borders of India. The Persians unified for the first time the Iranian plateau, which became the new power centre of the region – an area that had been dominated culturally and politically by Mesopotamia and Egypt for most of the preceding 2,500 years.

A vast and mountainous area, the Persian empire contained many different peoples who often rebelled against Persian control. To keep order, the Persians had a very effective army of 10,000 specially trained men, bodyguards to the king and keepers of law and order who were feared wherever they went, moving quickly to put down rebellions. The members of this elite warrior force were known as the "immortals" because when one

soldier died, he was immediately replaced. Mosaics of the immortals carrying spears decorated the royal palace at Susa, the capital city.

ZOROASTRIANISM

In AD 247, the Sassanid dynasty established Zoroastrianism as the official religion of the Persian Empire, and it is still practised in Iran and other parts of the world. It is founded upon the teachings of the prophet Zarathustra (called Zoroaster by the Greeks), in which the opposing forces of good and evil are symbolized by Ahura Mazda, the supreme deity responsible for truth and light, and the evil Ahriman. The two represent the duality of the cosmos: unlike Satan, Ahriman is not a creation of the supreme god but his equal.

The universal conflict between good spirits (*ahuras*) and bad ones (*daevas*) will ultimately result in the triumph of Ahura Mazda, and the faithful are encouraged to follow Ahura Mazda through "good thoughts, good words and good deeds".

These three ideals are represented by the three wing feathers of the *faravahar*, a central Zoroastrian symbol. Zoroastrians believe that the first animal to be created was a white bull, the progenitor of all other animals and plants, while the focal point of the religion is fire, seen as the purest manifestation of Ahura Mazda. Perpetual fires were set up all over Persia, some in the open air, others enclosed in fire temples, and tended by priests known as magi (from which comes the word "magic"). Depictions of fire altars are found on ancient coins.

Because Zoroastrians consider fire to be sacred, cremation is disallowed because it would contaminate it; instead, bodies are exposed at the top of "towers of silence" for their bones to be picked clean by scavengers.

THE BEDOUIN

The Bedouin are the desert-dwelling nomads of the Middle East, many of whom preserve their traditional lifestyle to this day. Their name comes from an Arabic word meaning "inhabitant

BELOW The camel is central to the survival of the Bedouin, and is celebrated by Arab poets as the "ship of the desert", transporting people and goods across vast oceans of sand.

RIGHT This winged device is the *faravahar*, a symbol of the human desire to achieve union with Ahura Mazda, the supreme deity of the Zoroastrian faith.

CARPETS

Throughout the Middle East, carpets are much more than functional objects, being used to symbolize important elements of tribal, family and personal life. Their patterns are rich in symbolic meaning. For instance, camels, the wealth of the Bedouin, signify happiness and riches for the weaver and owner of the carpet, while the peacock's wheel-like tail is a symbol of the sun and the cosmic cycle. It is customary for a carpet to contain a deliberate flaw, as only God can create perfection.

of the desert". They wear long, flowing robes to stay cool, but probably the most important aspect of a Bedouin man's attire is his headgear. This consists of a cloth held in position by the *agal* (rope), which indicates the wearer's ability to uphold his honour and fulfil the obligations and responsibilities of manhood. Bedouin women also signify their status with their headgear – married women, for instance, wear a black cloth, known as *asaba*, about their foreheads.

Traditionally the Bedouin are divided into related tribes, each led by a sheikh. Moving from place to place according to the seasons, and living in tents, they herd camels, sheep and goats, riding highly prized horses, famous for their grace and speed.

In such a harsh environment, any violation of territorial rights is viewed with severe disfavour:

BELOW Incense resins are precious substances with many different symbolic properties. Frankincense is used for purification.

small piles of stones are traditionally used to mark property boundaries. On the other hand, in the silence and solitude of the desert, encountering another person can be an unusual and noteworthy event. This has led Bedouin culture to place great value on hospitality and social etiquette: visitors are greeted with music, poetry and dance. Throwing frankincense pellets on the fire is a traditional greeting.

PRECIOUS INCENSE

One of the best-kept secrets of antiquity was the location of the trees that produced myrrh and frankincense, valued more highly than gold. Fantastic stories surrounded their whereabouts: the Greek historian Herodotus wrote that they were guarded by winged serpents who would kill any who tried to take their resins, and the wealth of the legendary Queen of Sheba was said to have been built on these substances. In the desert lands of Arabia,

frankincense and myrrh were rich in symbolic associations. Together with gold, they have always been associated with royalty and divinity. Incense has a long tradition of use in sacred ceremonies, its swirls of fragrant smoke viewed as a flight path for prayers and communion with the gods. Frankincense is associated with masculinity and the spirit of the heavens myrrh is feminine and linked with the earth.

ABOVE The black head-cloth worn by Bedouin women is a sign of their married state.

TOP Many of the everyday trappings of Bedouin life have symbolic meaning, including this man's tent and clothes.

TRADITIONAL TENTS

The tent is the abode of the desert nomad and has many symbolic associations. In the Old Testament, the wandering tribes of Israel set aside a tent (or tabernacle) for God, which became the prototype for the temple. Like the temple, the tent is a place to which the godhead is summoned to make itself manifest. In many traditions, the tent's pole is linked with the symbolism of the pillar and column (as well as the tree), representing the connection between Heaven and earth. Bedouin tents symbolize the duality of male and female. They are usually divided into two sections, one for men, one for women, by a curtain known as a *ma'nad*. The men's area is called the *mag'ad* (sitting place) and is for the reception of most guests. The *maharama* (place of the women) is where the women cook and receive female visitors.

TRIBAL AFRICA

ABOVE A Tongan shaman from Zambia sits in his grass hut with various gourds, animal horns, and other symbolic items spread before him.

FETISHES

A fetish is a symbol of divine energy encapsulated into an object. Natural fetishes, such as pieces of wood, shells, pebbles and feathers, are believed to owe their magical properties to the spiritual forces that dwell in them. Carvings or statuettes can also become permeated with this power when activated through the rites and incantations of the *nganga*.

A land of deserts, savannah, high mountain ranges and dense, equatorial rainforests, Africa is a vast and diverse continent. It is home to many different social systems, where more than 1,000 languages are spoken and where myths and cosmologies are interlinked with moral codes and ways of seeing the world.

Although it is impossible to come up with a homogeneous view of African culture, it is fair to say that for thousands of years, the way of life for many Africans has changed less than in more industrialized parts of the world, and that traditionally people have made their living by herding, hunting or farming. Symbols in African religion, art and culture reflect this social and historical continuity, and in most African societies the spiritual world and natural world is reflected in everyday life.

SPIRITUAL BELIEFS

In many traditional African societies the spiritual world and the everyday world are one and the same, with all aspects of life permeated by a strong power or vital force. In some societies this is seen to emanate from a supreme creator spirit – the Masai of Kenya call him Ngai, while the Nupe in Nigeria say that their god Soko is in the sky, for instance. There is often a hierarchy of spirits, from the nature spirits of rivers, rocks, trees and animals, through ancestor spirits of the dead, to divinities who derive their power from the creator spirit. The Lugbara of Uganda have a cult centred on the spirits of the dead, in which the living are considered to belong to the "outside" world while the dead belong "in the earth". If the ancestors are neglected, the dead punish their descendants by inflicting misfortune and sickness.

It is widely believed that spiritual power can be manipulated for good or bad. Positive mystical power is productive, can cure illnesses, and is protective, while negative power eats the health and souls of its victims and causes misfortune. A variety of specialists such as witch doctors, medicine men and women (known as *nganga* in most Bantu languages), diviners and rainmakers possess knowledge of this power and use it in the making of "medicines". Medicines may be used to encourage or prevent rain from falling, to aid hunting, for protection against malign spirits, for success in love affairs, or to find stolen property.

They may also be used for treating illnesses. Medicines can be made from almost any material, but natural materials such as trees, plants and animal skins or feathers are common, and are fashioned into amulets and charms with symbolism that varies according to the materials used and the purpose for which it was created.

MASQUERADE

Among traditional African societies, masks are used for many different social events and rituals, particularly those surrounding initiation ceremonies and rites of passage. Combined with a costume to hide the identity of the wearer, the role of the mask has many functions, both spiritual and temporal. Masks are worn to inform or educate, discipline or lend authority, to give the wearer access to special powers, or simply to entertain. The role of the mask is communicated through movement and dance – masquerade – where the complete costume becomes a powerful and energetic force that represents both the human and spiritual world. Masquerade is often performed by men who are members of secret societies: among the Dogon of Mali, for instance, the men's secret society or *Awa*, organizes all funeral events, with masked dancers in funeral processions. The masks have strong symbolic meaning, and the dancers represent figures of male and female powers and figures from the animal world, and the afterworld.

In traditional Yoruba society, women are considered to have two distinct sides to their nature, the power to create and nurture life, coupled with the potential for great destruction. Among the Yoruba, the Gelede masquerade, danced in either male or female pairs, is supposed to ensure that women's power is channelled for the benefit of the community. Gelede masks come in many different designs and are usually worn on top of the head, adding greatly to the wearer's height.

Whatever their purpose, all costumes and masks are highly stylized creations, their symbolism varying depending on the context. Among the Ogoni of

Nigeria, many masks are designed to look like animals, with the wearer assuming the spirit or character of the mask and performing athletic displays in imitation of the animal he represents. Many masks are highly elaborate constructions: the Sande female initiation society of the Mende of Sierra Leone have a wooden mask decorated with carvings that represent ancestors who preside over the initiates.

ADINKRA SYMBOLS

The art of adinkra – symbols hand-printed on cloth – is characterized by symbolic motifs, graphically rendered in stylized geometric shapes. The symbols relate to the history, philosophy and religious beliefs of the Ashanti people of Ghana and the Ivory Coast and are grouped into

various categories, including creatures, plant life, celestial bodies, the human body and non-figurative shapes. Initially used for funerals, the cloth is now worn for many other occasions, providing the symbols are appropriate, and is itself seen as a symbol of the Ghanain culture.

ABOVE LEFT Akoben, the adinkra symbol for vigilance and wariness.

ABOVE RIGHT Gye Name ,meaning "except for God", is the most popular adinkra symbol of Ghana.

BELOW Adinkra cloth was originally specially made for funerals. Its name translates as "saying goodbye to one another".

BELOW The masks of the Dogon form a line, symbolizing connection between the sun and Earth through the conduit of the dancer's body.

THE UNIVERSAL CALABASH

A calabash is a gourd that has a hard rind, which makes it a useful container once the flesh has been scooped out. It can be used as a water pot or else filled with seeds, as a rattle. When cut in half horizontally, a round calabash is often used as a container for offerings or symbolic objects in temples, and is usually decorated with carvings or paintings of geometric patterns, as well as pictures of humans and animals. In Abomey, in Benin, the universe is likened to a round calabash, the line of the horizon being where the two halves of a divided calabash meet. The sun, moon and stars are said to move in the upper part of the calabash, while the Earth is flat, floating inside the sphere in the same way that a small calabash may float in a big one.

SOUTH AND SOUTH-EAST ASIA

ABOVE The Chinese emperor, dressed in symbolic yellow, in front of a dragon-motif screen.

ABOVE The Japanese Flag, showing the "sincere" red sun on a "pure" white background.

KOI CARP

The Japanese Koi carp found swimming in many Japanese water gardens are symbols of the patience, courage and strength required to achieve big goals in business and life.

The cultural, political and spiritual history of East Asia has been rich and dramatic, and it is a huge reserve of symbolism, stretching from the ancient traditions to modern times. Great civilizations had been established in India by 2500 BC and in China by 2000 BC. Japan viewed itself as the "third kingdom", equal to China and India, and by tradition was founded in the 7th century BC by the Emperor Jimmu, whose imperial dynasty continues unbroken to this day.

EMPERORS

Far Eastern emperors have long associated themselves with elemental and mythical sources of power. Nippon, the Japanese name for Japan, means "the land of the rising sun", and the imperial family emphasized its central role in the country – and its authority – through the use of solar symbolism. Japanese emperors, through their legendary ancestor Jimmu, traced their ancestry back in a direct line to the great sun goddess, Amaterasu,

the central deity of the Shinto pantheon. The imperial seal was the chrysanthemum, a symbol of the sun and the national flower of Japan. In modern Japan the emperor continues to occupy the chrysanthemum throne: the long unbroken dynasty symbolizes continuity with the past, and the emperor is constitutionally defined as the symbol of the state.

Emperors in China were the rulers of the Middle Kingdom (the everyday world) and the Four Directions, maintaining harmony between Heaven and Earth. They had nine insignia: the dragon, mountains, the pheasant, rice grains, the axe, flames, pondweed, the sacrificial bowl, and patterns symbolizing justice.

The dragon is symbolic of imperial power and the emperor's role in mediating between Heaven and earth. It appeared on the Chinese national flag during the Qing dynasty, and was embroidered on court robes. The Chinese believed themselves to be the direct descendants of the Yellow Emperor, who was said to have the head of a man and the body of a dragon. Yellow, symbolic of the Earth and therefore of farming, remained the imperial colour. From the Han dynasty (206 BC–AD 220) onwards, dragons were also depicted in other colours, each with different symbolism: the turquoise dragon became the symbol of the emperor, connected with the East and the rising sun.

In 1950 the Indian government adopted, as a national symbol, a sculpture from the reign of Emperor Ashoka (r.272–232 BC).

This pillar of carved stone depicts four lions, an elephant, a horse, a bull, and another lion, all separated by a lotus at the base with the inscription "truth alone triumphs". The sculpture is founded upon the wheel of law or dharmachakra, which symbolizes the teachings of the Buddha.

ARCHITECTURE

The Great Wall of China is a universal visual symbol for China. It snakes its way across the country's entire northern boundary and was completed by the Qin emperor Qin Shi Hang as a means of defence against barbarian tribes from the north. Thousands of slaves died during the building of the wall, which led to it becoming a symbol of tyrannical oppression.

During the Ming dynasty (1368–1644 BC) the wall was refortified in the grand style seen today, and it is considered one of the seven great wonders of the world. From various perspectives it can be seen as a symbol of power, division, closed attitudes and oppression.

In India near the city of Agra, the Taj Mahal is an enduring and profound symbol of love. Completed in 1652, this magnificent tomb was built by the Mogul emperor Shah Jahan, in memory of Mumtaz Mahal, his favourite wife, who had died in childbirth. Centrally sited among canals and tranquil gardens, the tomb is built of shimmering white marble, embellished with semi-precious stones. The four canals in the gardens symbolize the four rivers of Paradise described in the

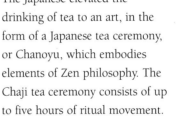

Qur'an, while the gardens represent the final resting place for the souls of the dead.

The Taj Mahal was erected as a symbol of love, but perhaps also as a demonstration of Shah Jahan's greatness. It is said that he planned a second mausoleum for himself, built in black marble on the opposite side of the Jamuna river and connected to the first by a silver bridge, but he died before his plan could be carried out and was buried in the Taj Mahal.

RICE AND TEA

Throughout Asia, rice is a staple food, generally associated with abundance, prosperity and fecundity, a symbol of life. The Balinese, who eat rice at every meal, refer to it as *nasi*, meaning "nostril": in other words, eating rice is seen to be as important as breathing. In China, girls with poor appetites have been told that every grain of rice they do not eat will be a pockmark on their husband's face.

In Japan rice is seen as sacred, and the eating of rice as a sacred ritual. Offerings are made to the Shinto deity Inari, the bearer of rice. The Japanese believe that soaking rice prior to cooking releases life energy, which can bring peace to the soul. Sometimes rice grains are referred to as "little Buddhas" to encourage children to eat them.

In India, rice is considered an auspicious food. The new crop is celebrated as part of the festival of Pongal, when it is cooked in pots until they overflow. People decorate the ground in front of their homes with coloured rice

flour and make offerings to the gods. It is said that grains of rice should be like two brothers, close but not stuck together. At Hindu weddings the couple hold rice, oats and leaves, symbolizing health, wealth and happiness.

In China, tea is served to a guest as a symbol of respect and goodwill, and refusing a cup of tea is considered rude. The teacup is filled only seven-tenths full, the other three-tenths being filled with friendship and affection. According to legend, tea drinking began when the emperor Shen Nung rested one day in the shade of a tea plant, and several leaves tumbled into his cup of hot water. Upon drinking the golden liquid a wonderful sense of well-being came over him.

Green tea was taken from China to Japan by Zen Buddhist monks, who drank it to keep

them awake while meditating. The Japanese elevated the drinking of tea to an art, in the form of a Japanese tea ceremony, or Chanoyu, which embodies elements of Zen philosophy. The Chaji tea ceremony consists of up to five hours of ritual movement.

THE LOTUS

Although it grows in the mud, the lotus maintains its beauty. As India's national flower it is a symbol of pure spirit rooted in mundane reality. The Buddhist mantra "Om mane padme" refers to enlightenment, the "jewel in the lotus".

OCEANIC TRADITIONS

ABOVE A mask from the Malay Archipelago (New Guinea) using elements that link the human world with the natural one.

TOP Polynesian canoes are intricately carved, symbolizing spiritual power and prestige.

The thousands of islands in the central and southern Pacific Ocean, including Australia, New Zealand, Polynesian Hawaii and the Malay Archipelago, together make up Oceania. There are three major cultural groupings: Polynesia, Melanesia and Micronesia. The indigenous people of Australia are another important cultural grouping from this area.

INDIGENOUS AUSTRALIANS

"Aborigine" is a Western term used to describe indigenous people who have been conquered or colonized by Europeans. The indigenous people of Australia have occupied the country for over 60,000 years, probably coming originally from the Malay Peninsula. Their spirituality is intimately linked with their relationship with the land through the "Dreamtime".

The Dreaming is a vital concept of creation. It refers to the creation of the earth, humans and animals, but at the same time it is eternally present on a mythical level. All life is believed to be imbued with the Dreaming. Dreamtime stories portray the Ancestors moving through the earth, shaping the land, and giving life to plants and animals. Through the Dreamtime the Aboriginal people and the earth are part of one another. The individual tries to live his or her life according to the law laid down by the Ancestors.

As the Spirit Ancestors journeyed through the land, they created dreaming tracks, often called "songlines", as they sang the land into life. The aboriginal peoples believe that by singing specific songs, at key points on the land, they directly connect with the Dreaming.

Totem animals play an important part in aboriginal society. Clans have a totemic relationship with a specific animal, and it is taboo for them to eat the meat of that animal, as it would be like eating a close relation. The characteristics and qualities of the totem animal become accessible to the clan. Some Australian Aboriginals still adhere closely to the Dreaming of their totem. One man whose totem was the cockatiel was allowed to travel the world because the nature of the cockatiel was to fly over borders.

POLYNESIA

Encompassing much of the eastern area of the South Pacific, with the major islands of Hawaii and New Zealand, Polynesia was one of the very last areas in the world to have been populated, mostly in waves of migration.

Although the islands are widely separated, Polynesian societies have a thread of unity running through their belief systems and social structures. These are aristrocratic societies, led by chiefs. The nobility are thought to have spiritual power, known as "mana", which is brought out through ritual and art.

The Polynesian sculptor brings out the mana in his or her art by revealing the beauty and essential qualities in the wood or stone. Ornamental carvings appear on spears, canoes, jewellery, house beams and on many other kinds of domestic and spiritual objects. Tiki Man is a male figure found throughout Polynesia, in wood sculptures, carved in stone, and in tattoo and clothing designs. He is believed by Polynesians to be their first ancestor or the original human, and symbolizes the phallus or procreative power.

Carvings made by the Maori of New Zealand, in bone, shell, jade and wood, depict important mythological themes and patterns in nature. The *koru* represents the fern frond, a symbol of new life and purity coming into the world. The twist is a vertical form in which two spirals interweave. This represents eternity and the eternal relationships of couples or cultures. *Hei-matau* is a stylized fish-hook, representing prosperity and abundance and a deep respect for the ocean. It is a symbol of power and authority and is said to give the wearer protection when travelling at sea.

The huge Easter Island statues are carved in stone, and probably represent guardian gods, facing inwards towards the island peoples. The oversized head in Polynesian sculptures highlights the sacred attributes of the head.

POLYNESIAN TATTOOS

There are two kinds of Polynesian tattoo. *Enata* are natural symbols that refer to the individual's life, origin and social rank. They also protect the wearer: a fisherman would have designs that would protect him against sharks, while a warrior's tattoos would defend him against attack. *Etua* are

mystical symbols referring to past ancestors – a lineage of shamans, chiefs and divinities. These symbols showed mana, which was passed down the lineages.

MELANESIA AND MICRONESIA

There are many cultures and over a thousand languages in Melanesia and Micronesia. The Papuans were the first inhabitants of Melanesia, arriving at least 40,000 years ago. Traditional society is based upon agriculture, the domestication of pigs, hunting and trade.

Melanesian religious art usually displays brilliant colours and is made from a broad range of materials. Much religious artwork honours and placates the powerful influences of animal and nature spirits, as well as showing respect for the ancestors. It often consists of a network of human, animal and natural images. Effigies of the totem animal of a

BELOW The Rainbow Serpent appears in aboriginal paintings up to 6,000 years old.

clan, such as a fish, snake or crocodile, sometimes show the animal devouring a clan father. Although this looks sinister, it probably indicates the spiritual identification of the people with their totem animals. For the Latumul people of New Guinea, the saltwater crocodile is the creator of all things. It is said that Crocodile, who was the first human being, mated with a crack in the ground (the first woman) to engender life. The lower jaw of Crocodile became the earth and the upper jaw the sky. The people believe that, during initiation, boys are swallowed by Crocodile and regurgitated as men.

Respect for the ancestors is important for the Melanesians, as they are thought to influence the living relatives. Much symbolic art is aimed at maintaining a good

relationship between the earthly and the spiritual realms. The wearing of masks is one important way of honouring and depicting the ancestors. The masks of north central New Guinea depict supernatural spirits and ancestors. Made from an array of shells, animal skins, seeds, flowers, wood and feathers, these masks are understood to be a dwelling-place for the spirit, and a great source of strength in business and in warfare.

In traditional Vanuatuan society the human–pig relationship is of intense importance, to the extent that when a pig is slaughtered it is sung to and caressed before and during its death. Pigs are believed to have souls and may be considered family members. The number of pigs owned relates to the leadership status of the owner, as does the length of their tusks. When pigs feed naturally the tusks wear down and, to avoid this owners feed them by hand. The pig is also a sexual symbol, embodying the relationship between men and women.

ABOVE The Easter Island statues are symbols of religious and political power, and are believed to be repositories for sacred spirits.

ABOVE The *koru*, a Maori fern spiral, represents the unfolding of new life.

BELOW The crocodile is an honoured totem animal in many Oceanic cultures.

RAINBOW SERPENT

The Rainbow Serpent is central to the beliefs of the people of Arnhem Land, but is found in aboriginal art throughout Australia. It is a large snake-like creature associated with the waterways of Australia. It represents the source of life and protects the people and the land, but if not respected it becomes destructive.

ABOVE RIGHT A temple relief shows the Mayan Jaguar god conducting a blood-letting ritual with his wife, Lady Xoc.

ABOVE The jaguar is a central motif throughout Central and South America, frequently associated with deities.

BELOW The markings on the ancient giant Sun Stone are symbols linked to Aztec cosmology.

At the time of the Spanish conquest in 1519, great urban civilizations existed in Mesoamerica – controlled by the Maya and Aztecs – and the central Andes region – under Inca rule. The foundations of these civilizations were laid by earlier cultures such as the Olmec, Chavin, Nazca and Toltec, and shared many features: monumental architecture, ceremonial centres with pyramid and plaza complexes, complex calendrical computations and – for the Maya – hieroglyphic writing. The art and culture of these civilizations was rich in symbolism, linked especially to the natural world.

THE JAGUAR

Once known as the people of the jaguar, the Olmec worshipped gods that were half-human and half-animal. The jaguar was their most favoured and feared deity. Admired for its strength, ferocity and hunting ability, the jaguar was one of the most powerful symbols in both Mesoamerica and South America, and its stylized form appears on artefacts throughout the region. Gods were often portrayed wearing the jaguar's skin as a sacred costume, and the cat was venerated as the divine protector of royalty by both Maya and Aztec rulers. The supreme Aztec god and patron deity of royalty, Tezcatlipoca (Lord of the Smoking Mirror), was said to possess an animal alter-ego in the form of a jaguar, which inhabited mountain summits and cave entrances. According to Maya mythology, copal resin, one of the most important and sacred incense-burning substances of the ancient American cultures, was a gift of three different jaguars, white, golden and dark, corresponding to the three different colours of the resin.

CALENDARS

A calendar is a symbolic representation of time. It is a way of pinpointing the regular recurrence of natural phenomena – such as the rising and setting of the sun – against which human events can be set. The Maya used two calendars of different lengths,

one sacred, one secular; dates were calculated on the two planes of existence concurrently. The two calendars were so complex that the same juxtaposition could not recur for 374,440 years.

The great Aztec calendar stone (also known as the Sun Stone) is the largest Aztec sculpture ever found. Measuring 4m (13ft) in diameter, its markings were more symbolic than practical and relate to Aztec cosmology. The Aztecs believed that the world had passed through four creations, which had been destroyed by jaguars, fire, wind and water. The sun, moon and human beings were created at the beginning of the fifth and current creation, which is predicted to be destroyed by earthquakes. The calendar stone was used to calculate such danger periods. At its centre is the face of the Earth Monster, surrounded by symbols of previous creations. Twenty glyphs representing the names of each day in the Aztec month occupy the innermost circular

ABOVE This Aztec carving of their ritual ballgame shows a decapitated player (right): the blood streaming from his neck is shown in the form of snakes, which were symbols of fertility.

band. Each day the sun god had to be fed with human hearts and blood to give him strength to survive the night and rise again.

HUMAN SACRIFICE

Religious rituals involving human sacrifice formed part of the Inca, Aztec and Maya traditions. Human sacrifice was a symbol of communion with the gods, particularly the sun, rain and Earth deities. For the Aztecs and Incas, these bloody acts took place in temples or on mountains, while the Maya sometimes sacrificed their victims in wells. The Aztecs usually sacrificed their captured enemies, and it is said that in one four-day period of great celebration, some 20,000 victims were killed. Men, women and children could all be chosen.

The Aztecs preferred to stretch out their victims over a sacrificial stone and pluck out the still-beating heart; this symbolized the most precious organ that could be offered to the gods and replicas

were sometimes made in jade.

Prized more highly than gold, jade was a symbol for life and agriculture. Ritual vessels thought to be for the blood or hearts of sacrificial victims were often decorated with skulls, a symbol for fame and glory, or else defeat, depending on the situation. Human skulls were sometimes made into masks and used in ritual performances.

THE BALL COURT

For the Mayas and Aztecs every aspect of life, including sports, revolved around religion. In particular, the Mesoamerican ball game *ulama* had a sacred symbolism. Only nobles could play the game, in which two teams of two or three players aimed to propel a small, solid rubber ball through rings in order to score points. The rings were variously decorated, sometimes with snakes and monkeys. The ball-court represented the world, and the ball itself stood for the moon and the sun. The game was fiercely competitive, as the losing team was often sacrificed; it represented the battle between darkness and light, or the death and rebirth of the sun. It was also

AZTEC NAMES OF DAYS
This Aztec codex of days shows the 20 names for days from the farmers' calendar. The symbols were combined with a number from one to 13 to give the date, such as Three Vulture.

alligator   wind   house   lizard   serpent

death's head   deer   rabbit   water   dog

monkey   grass   reed   jaguar   eagle

vulture   motion   flint knife   rain   flower

believed that the more the game was played, the better the harvest would be.

NAZCA LINES

More than 1,000 years ago perfectly depicted giant figures, including animals such as a hummingbird, a whale, a monkey and a spider, were carved into the coastal desert floor near Nazca in southern Peru. Some are so large that they can be appreciated only from the air. It seems likely that they had some kind of sacred significance, perhaps as offerings to the mountain and sky gods.

ABOVE Maya numbers, from top, left to right: 0, 1, 4, 5, 11 and 18. The Maya number system used 3 signs – a dot for 1, a bar for 5 and the shell for 0. Other numbers were made by combinations of these signs.

HUACAS
The Incas' sacred sites were known as huacas, often natural spots in the landscape, such as caves, springs and boulders. The term *huaca* was also applied to portable objects such as amulets and figurines. These symbolic objects were thought to offer protection and were regarded as sacred.

NATIVE NORTH AMERICANS

ABOVE White sage is a sacred herb that symbolizes purification, and is often used in North American rituals.

MIDDLE The eagle stands for power and vision.

TOP The quadrated circle of the Medicine Wheel, symbol of the earth.

FAR RIGHT Many Native American peoples revered the bison as a symbol of power and good fortune.

BELOW The bear represents both power and healing to the Native Americans.

The indigenous peoples of North America probably came from Asia 12,000–25,000 years ago via the Bering Strait. Waves of migration from Alaska to the east and south led to a large number of different tribes or linguistic families populating seven major cultural areas: the Arctic, the North-west Coast, the Plains, the Plateau, the Eastern Woodlands, the North and the South-west. A commonly understood sign language was developed among these people, who were often on the move and sometimes at war. The arrival of Europeans, from the 15th century, led to huge population collapses from imported diseases to which the indigenous people had no immunity. Many wars also took place between the Native Americans and the expanding white community.

The Native Americans were shamanic societies who lived in a close spiritual relationship with the land. Their lifestyle was adapted to various ecosystems, sometimes sedentary and sometimes nomadic, with an emphasis on hunting, gathering, fishing or agriculture. Their history and relationship with nature inform the mythologies and symbol systems that appear in the art, music and rituals of these peoples.

THE MEDICINE WHEEL

Sometimes known as the Sacred Hoop, the Medicine Wheel is an important representation of Native American spirituality, but is also conceived as a living entity in which humans and nature are interrelated. The Medicine Wheel

is a circular model in which the individual or culture orientates itself with all aspects of nature on the journey through life.

The Native Americans believe that the Great Spirit created nature in the round. The sun and moon are round, circling around us and marking circular time. The sky is a circle and the horizon is the edge of Mother Earth, from where the four winds blow. Each year is a circle divided by seasons, and the life and death of an individual is also seen as a circle.

The wheel is a quadrated circle, with the four directions and the four sacred colours marked upon it. Each direction represents particular natural and animal powers and the qualities that go with them. The eagle is found flying in the east and is a symbol of vision, endurance and strength. The mouse and innocence may be found to the south, the bear and introspection to the west and the buffalo and wisdom to the north. In addition to these four are three more directions: Father Sky (above), providing rain and warmth for things to grow; Mother Earth (below) the source of life-sustaining plants and animals; and the sacred fire at the

centre, where the people are attached to the Great Spirit.

To the Native American, "medicine" means power, a vital energy force in all forms of nature. The individual is placed on the wheel at birth, with certain perceptions and medicine powers, and as they walk their path on the wheel they acquire medicine power or wisdom from new perceptions and aspects of nature.

ANIMAL MEDICINE

Bison medicine was often seen as a representation of the feminine principle of the nourishing and life-giving force of the earth. The bison was considered to be the chief over all animals of the earth. Bear medicine has male aspects of strength and power, as well as more feminine aspects associated with knowledge of healing using roots and herbs, and introspective qualities related to hibernation.

The eagle is the lord of all birds and holds the greatest power. Eagles, and birds in general, are thought to have a very similar spirit to humans, as they fly in circles, with circular nests, and are not bound to the earth like four-legged animals. The eagle embodies great vision and

overview, and a tremendous power to overcome all enemies and to strike with impeccable intent. When worn, the eagle feather is a reminder that the Great Spirit is present: the eagle is associated with the sun and its feathers with the sun's rays.

TOTEM POLE

The Algonquin word *totem* means a person's personal guardian, usually an animal or plant by which the Native American is adopted through a rite of passage at adolescence.

The totem pole is carved, often out of cedar, and is both a family or clan emblem and a reminder of their ancestors. It is a symbol of dignity and accomplishment, the historical and spiritual rank of the people. Many of the symbolic meanings and stories associated with the images are known only to the people of the clan. For example, the stories of the North-west Pacific Coast tribes tell of the transformation of animals into humans as wel as humans into animals. The salmon or whale people are said to live in great happiness in cities beneath the waves. Thunderbirds are said to dive from the sky, snatching huge whales for their dinner. Wolves, becoming tired of hunting on the land, become killer whales and hunt in the sea.

THE CORN GODDESS

Corn, or maize, originated from a wild grass called *teosinte*, which grew in southern Mexico 7,000 years ago. The Native Americans selectively cultivated corn, and once the Europeans arrived, corn

RIGHT Eagle feathers on the headdresses of Native American chiefs symbolize the sun's rays.

agriculture quickly spread to the rest of the world. As a staple food, corn has inspired many important myths. It is said to be one of three sisters, Corn Woman, Squash Woman and Bean Woman, goddesses of fertility.

The Iroquois corn goddess (Onatah) is the daughter of Mother Earth (Eithinoha). Onatah is caught by spirits from the underworld, and must be rescued by the sun so that the crops can grow. Similar stories relating to the seasons are found in many agricultural societies.

THE VISION QUEST

An individual seeking guidance or answers to questions may embark on a vision quest, a ritual practice through which helpful signs may be given, which can be interpreted as guidance from the spirits. Vision quests occur when an adolescent makes the transition to the path of adulthood. The seeker asks the shaman for help. A remote site in nature is found and marked out with a rectangle or circle, where the seeker waits for a vision. Sacred offerings such as tobacco (which blesses the earth) are placed within this area for the Great Spirit. Sometimes sage, the purification herb, is laid on the ground as a bed for the seeker. The seeker stays in the sacred area for one night or several, praying and awaiting signs from the world around. The Great Spirit might speak through any experience, even insignificant encounters with animals and birds or other forces in nature. Eventually thanks are given to the

Great Spirit for what has been given, and the seeker shares the experience with the shaman to gain understanding.

THE GIVE-AWAY

Potlatch is a Chinook word for a "give-away" ceremony in which prominent people give a feast and give away their possessions, redistributing them among the tribe. Sometimes at the end of the ceremony they burn down their house and become poor, until they build up their wealth again.

Giving is important to the Native American, who considers it a great honour on the part of the one who gives and for the one who receives. One should share one's wealth and never hold on to more than is needed. The turkey is thought of as the give-away or earth eagle. The turkey is a free-spirited bird of sacrifice, opening the channels to others.

ABOVE The totem pole is carved with figures and faces placed on top of each other. They represent ancestors or supernatural beings encountered by clan members, or who have given them special gifts.

ARCTIC TRADITIONS

ABOVE The Arctic is known as the land of the midnight sun.

ABOVE For the Innuit the igloo is a symbol of home and family life. In Canada it is a registered trademark for the Inuit.

BELOW Some of the symbolic tools of the Inuit: the box top, *kepun* axe and the *cavik*, a curved knife.

Within the Arctic Circle, a large ocean is surrounded by land, with tundra at its fringe and animal, human and plant life throughout the area. The Arctic includes Siberia and other parts of northern Russia, Alaska in the United States, northern Canada, Greenland, Lappland in Finland, northern Norway and Sweden. It is peopled mainly by the Inuit of Alaska, Canada and Greenland, and the Finno-Ugrians of northern Scandinavia and Siberia, which include the Saami.

The ecology, climate and geology of the Arctic influence the signs and symbols of its peoples. The Arctic is known by the people who live there as the "land of the midnight sun": in the summer the sun never sets, and in the winter it never rises. The taiga and tundra are featureless landscapes with wide horizons, a good home for reindeer or caribou, and thus suit nomadic cultures that rely on reindeer for food. Seal hunting, whaling and saltwater fishing are also important to human survival.

INUIT SPIRITS

The name "Inuit" means "the real people": the Algonquin named them "Eskimos", meaning "raw flesh eaters". Inuit spirituality is concerned with conciliating the gods and nature spirits, to help humans survive in harsh conditions. Unseen forces in nature are called *innua*, and they can be found in the air, water, stones and animals. The *innua* can become totemic guardians of men, known as *torngak*.

Stone and bear spirits are considered particularly powerful. When a bear spirit becomes a man's *torngak*, he is symbolically eaten by the bear and reborn as a sorcerer or *angakok*.

The *innua* of animals are thought to be very sensitive to the craftsmanship of the weapons by which they are killed. If they were killed by a poorly made tool they would report this to the spirit world, and the animal spirit might not return to earth in another animal body. To avoid this the Inuit take great pride in their craftsmanship.

THE IGLOO

The word igloo means "dwelling", and the *igluvigaq* is the ice dwelling used by the Central Inuit in the winter. Constructed from upward spiralling blocks of ice, the igloo walls curve inwards, creating an ice dome with a hole for ventilation in the top.

The igloo is a symbolic extension of those who built it and their relationship with their surroundings. The igloo is built from within, and once the "keystone" has been placed at the top, the igloo and its builder become one. The igloo enables the Inuit to survive harsh conditions, and is built from the very elements of that extreme environment.

In Inuit mythology, Aningan is a moon god and a proficient hunter who has an igloo where he can rest in the sky, when not being chased through the sky by his brother the sun. He shares the igloo with Irdlirvirissong, his demon cousin, who sometimes comes out to dance in the sky making people laugh.

The igloo symbolizes a resting-place and psychic home for different facets of human nature. In 1958 the Canadian government registered the image of the igloo as a trademark to protect the work of Inuit artists and woodcarvers.

SYMBOLIC TOOLS

Two other important items in Inuit culture are the *inuksuk* and the *ulu*. A common symbol in northern Canada, the *inuksuk*, means the "likeness of a person" in Inuktitut. It is a signpost guiding the Inuit through the featureless tundra. Made from rock, *inuksuk* appear as human forms with their legs outstretched, and often serve the purpose of guiding caribou into places where they can easily be captured. The longer arm of an *inuksuk* points the hunter in the appropriate direction. If an *inuksuk* points towards a lake, it is an indication that fish can be found in the lake at the same distance the *inuksuk* stands from the edge of the lake.

The *ulu* is a woman's knife with a crescent-shaped blade, used for cutting out clothing, preparing skins, and in cooking. The *ulu* is a symbol of femininity and the woman's role in Inuit society.

THE COSMIC TENT OF THE SAAMI

Formerly known as Lapps, the Saami are part of the Finno-Ugric race, a large group of tribes speaking many different dialects of one parent language. The Saami were traditionally hunters and fishermen, who also farmed domesticated reindeer; since the reindeer have been dying out, they have become more nomadic.

As an essentially shamanic culture, the Saami conceive of a world with different levels of reality: the lower world, the middle world and the upper world. The world is imagined to have been constructed as a kind of cosmic tent, with the central pole of the World Tree reaching up from its roots in the lower world, through the middle world of everyday life, to the upper world constellation of the Great Bear at its top. The central pole is also described as a four-sided world pillar.

The sky is thought to have been fixed in place by the "north nail", the Pole Star, and prayers ensure it stays in place so that the sky does not fall down. The Saami are concerned that the Pole Star might one day move, leading to the destruction of the earth.

The traditional Saami dwelling is a conical compound tent or *kata*, a predecessor of the yurt, capable of withstanding very strong winds and snow. It is a symbolic map of the cosmos, with the hearth at the centre, the skin of the tent representing the sky, held up by wooden supports equivalent to the world pillar.

Within the *kata* there is a sacred area where the sacred drum is kept. The Saami also believe that when a member of the family dies the body should be taken out of the tent through the *boasso* (or kitchen) side, otherwise someone else will die.

REINDEER

The reindeer has central importance within Saami culture, and reindeer herding is a symbol of personal, group and cultural identity. Saami children are often given a "first tooth" reindeer and a "name day" reindeer, and more reindeer are given to them at their wedding, so that a new household is usually equipped with a small herd of reindeer with which a couple can start their new life together. The reindeer is also often associated with moon symbolism and with funerary ritual and passage.

ABOVE The reindeer is an all-encompassing, multi-faceted Saami symbol of life and death. It is believed to conduct the soul of a dead person to the upper world.

KALEVALA

Elias Lönnrot, a Finnish scholar, collected the mythic and magical songs passed down orally by generations of peasants, and published the *Kalevala*, the Finnish national epic, in 1835. Its poems and sagas offer important insights into the beliefs and traditions of the Saami peoples.

SACRED DRUM

The sacred drum is important to the Saami. Constructed from birch, with a drum head of reindeer skin, the drum is commonly painted in alder juice or blood with figures of people, the nature spirits and the four directions around a central symbol of the sun. A series of small rings moves as the drum is beaten, and where they eventually come to rest leads to shamanic predictions and divinations. The Saami use their drum as a guide in daily life, to find things that have been lost, and for healing purposes

SYMBOLS OF SPIRITUALITY

BOTH SIGNS AND SYMBOLS PLAY A VITAL ROLE IN ALL THE WORLD'S RELIGIONS AS OBJECTS ON WHICH THOUGHTS AND PRAYERS CAN BE FOCUSED. THEY POINT A WAY THROUGH THE NUMINOUS WORLD OF THE SPIRIT, ACTING AS BADGES OF FAITH, TEACHING TOOLS AND AIDS ON THE JOURNEY TOWARDS AN UNDERSTANDING OF COMPLEX PHILOSOPHIES.

SHAMANISM

ABOVE Seedpods are commonly used for making shamanic rattles.

BELOW A North American shaman, holding a drum and spear, "shape-shifts" into a wolf .

The ancient tradition of shamanism involves the individual entering altered states of consciousness to visit other levels of reality, from which teaching, healing or visions may come for his or her community. With its origins in the Palaeolithic period, shamanism may be found at the roots of many of the world's major religions, and at the fringes of many others.

The word *saman* comes from the Tungus of Siberia, and means "one who knows". Shamans are adepts of trance, an ecstatic and altered state in which they are thought to leave their bodies, ascending into the sky in "magical flight" or descending into the underworld, to meet with the ancestors and commune with nature spirits. Many of the symbols of shamanism represent transcendence or release from one way of being into another.

Traditional shamanism is now little practised, but a wave of interest has developed in the West, inspired by Jung's linkage of it with his ideas about the "collective unconscious", and a growing recognition of the importance of travelling between different worlds or states.

THE CALL OF A SHAMAN

Shamans may inherit their role, but more often they experience a spontaneous vocation in which they are called or elected by nature. The shamanic calling is itself a symbolic occurrence. Often an initiate is called by a near-death experience, such as being struck by lightning or surviving a life-threatening illness. Some have a lucid dream-like experience of dismemberment, whereby they metaphorically die and are then reborn.

Other shamans may be "called" by meeting a divine or semi-divine figure in a dream. Often these dream figures are the dead ancestors of the shaman who inform him that he is being elected. Some shamans have celestial wives by whom they are called to their path.

Facing your own death, or journeying into death, is powerfully symbolic of the shamanic ability to transcend the everyday self and to live impeccably in the face of the attacks and challenges of life. It is said that some shamanic warriors have become so centred that they can walk across a firing range without harm. Psychologically, the deathwalk is the ability to drop personal history and identity, so there is nothing to be attacked.

SHAMANIC FLIGHT

The shaman is said to be able to take magical flight in the form of an animal, or as a spirit detached from the body. In this way shamans can fly about the universe bridging Earth and the heavens, and many symbols reflect this.

Palaeolithic cave paintings at Lascaux, in France, show the shaman in a bird mask, and Siberian shamanic priestesses still wear bird costumes. In rock art of the San (Bushmen) of southern Africa, the *ales*, or "trance buck" is an antelope-like creature, with its legs raised in flight. It probably symbolizes the shamanic ability to commune with the ancestors, since in San mythology the dead are transformed into elands. Similar flying animals occur in Siberian shamanic mythology (and may be the source of the flying reindeer of Santa Claus).

PARALLEL WORLDS

The basic shamanic cosmology consists of three levels or worlds – the upperworld, middle earth and the underworld – but some traditions describe as many as seven or nine different worlds.

The role of the shaman is to make links or travel between these worlds, and many symbols refer to the connection between them. In Native American traditions the smoke rising through the smoke hole of a tipi refers to the passage of spirit between earth and sky. The world tree is a shamanic symbol that occurs in many cosmologies – the Norse god Odin, who hangs himself on the world tree Yggdrasil, achieves knowledge through the altered state that results from his suffering. The ladder is a similar symbol, seen in the seven-notched birch trees of Siberian shamanism, but also in other traditions, such as in the Egyptian Book of the Dead and the Old Testament.

For many shamans there is a direct relationship between themselves and the natural world. A Romany shaman speaks of the earth as his grandmother, and the plants, animals, sun, moon and stars as his relatives, with whom he communicates for guidance. All of nature thus becomes a form of living symbolism. Some

RIGHT A Tungus shaman of Siberia wears the skin and antlers of his spirit ally, the reindeer, to deepen his relationship with the animal.

psychologists see a direct connection between the parallel realities of the shaman and the relationship between dreaming and everyday reality. From this perspective signs and symbols from the unconscious, or in nature, are doorways calling us into another level of reality. A dream about an eagle, for example, may invite us to take a detached overview, with sharp-focused attention.

THE DRUM

Used to induce a shamanic trance, the drum has particular symbolic significance as a vehicle into altered states or otherworlds. The repetitive rhythm played upon the drum, and sometimes on rattles or other instruments, blocks out other sensory information, enabling the shaman to enter a different state of consciousness. The drumbeat relates to the primal sound sometimes thought of as the heartbeat of the earth.

For the shamans of the Altai of central Asia, the drum skin stands for the division between the upperworld and the lowerworld. In all shamanic cultures the drum is symbolic of the relationship between the upperworld, often associated with the male, and the underworld or womb, associated with the female.

THE SHAMAN'S ALLY

A shaman has an ally or teacher in the form of an ancestor, a dead shaman, or often an animal or nature spirit, who helps them reach altered states and their deepest nature. It is through this

relationship that the shaman eventually encounters their double or individuated self. The shaman may imitate the actions and voice of an animal ally as a way of sharing their perceptions, gifts and intelligence. Saami shamans are said to become wolves, bears, reindeer or fish. The Tungus shaman of Siberia has a snake as a helping spirit and during the shamanic trance replicates its reptilian movements.

SHAMANIC JOURNEYS

The symbolic world of the shaman can be meaningful to people who suffer breakdowns or near-death experiences. The shaman can leave the present reality in order to find wisdom or knowledge in alternative realities. The helpful spirits of animals and ancestors may be seen as aspects of a person's unconscious, encountered on life's journey.

BELOW A shamanic drum with a stylized image of a running horse painted on its surface.

TAOISM

ABOVE The "all-powerful" seal of Lao-tzu, a Taoist magic diagram harnessing cosmic *chi*.

BELOW According to legend, Lao-tzu, saddened by people's inability to accept the "way" he proposed, departed from civilization and rode into the desert on a water buffalo. At the last gate of the kingdom he was persuaded to leave a record of his teachings, and wrote the *Tao Te Ching*.

Taoism is a religious and philosophical system, said to have been founded in China by the sage Lao-tzu (or "the old one") in the 6th century BC. Taoism was influential in China and Japan, and in modern times interest in it has also spread to the West.

According to tradition, Lao-tzu was the author of the *Tao Te Ching*, or "Book of the Way", a collection of aphorisms concerned with the nature of the world and the alignment of humanity to this nature. Its central principle is non-action – not passivity but an active responsiveness to the nature of life, an appreciation of life as it is, rather than striving to fulfil a succession of desires.

Both Taoism and Confucianism have been highly influential upon Chinese culture and history. Confucianism is an ethical approach to living and government based on fixed principles, rooted in the belief that civilization can build a better society, while Taoism is more concerned with living in accordance with the nature of things as they are.

THE TAO

Both a personal and a cosmological principle, the Tao (or the "way") describes the origins of the universe and creation. It refers to the source of nature's patterns and the ebb and flow of natural forces. At the same time, the Tao is a mystical path that can be followed by living in a state of simplicity, in accordance with nature's rhythms.

Whereas in the West the heart is seen as a source of courage or love, to the Chinese it is the source of sensation, the seat of the five senses. Discovering the Tao depends on "emptying" the heart of the ever-changing illusions of the senses, so that it is true and eternal. Lao-tzu is commonly quoted as stating that "the Tao which can be spoken is not the eternal Tao". This means that the Tao refers to that which precedes all manifest things (or "myriad things") in nature.

Whereas many religious systems view heaven as a state outside of the human earthly existence, Taoism, and much Chinese thinking, is more concerned with oneness, in which a person lives in and identifies with the Tao. Thus living according to the Tao means to be guided by the deepest path in nature, which lies between earthly and heavenly existence.

YIN AND YANG

For Lao-tzu there was no such thing as a fixed definition of good or evil, in that as soon as a state of "goodness" is described it immediately and inevitably invokes a balancing state of "non-goodness" as an opposing force. The yin/yang symbol is indicative of the balancing natural law or cycle of change, in which every movement contains or eventually turns into its opposite: strength leads to weakness, life to death, and male to female.

Yin, the female principle, is associated with coldness, darkness and the earth; yang, the male principle, with light, warmth and heaven. The symbol shows that life must be viewed as a whole and cannot truly exist in isolated parts. The dark and light parts of the symbol are directly opposed yet interlocking and mutually dependent; the two small spots in the symbol show that each opposing force contains the seed of the other. Together the two shapes form a perfect circle, symbolizing the wholeness of nature.

A contemporary example of this principle is evident in humankind's relationship with the ecology of the planet. Our ability to harness power, resources and information has grown enormously, but if we fail to recognize our dependence on the greater whole – the animals and forces of nature around us – our strengths will eventually bring about our demise. The yin/yang symbol shows how each force, when at its most powerful, gives rise to its opposite.

LEFT The Bixia Temple on Tai Shan, the sacred mountain of the east, is reached by climbing the 7,000-step "Stairway to Heaven".

DIVINE FIGURES

Originally, Taoism had no static religious doctrines, nor was it involved in deity worship, but over time, as it became popular, it was mixed with older Chinese beliefs such as the theory of the five elements and the veneration of the ancestors. It became something more akin to a folk religion, and a whole pantheon of divinities was worshipped, including the mythical Jade Emperor. Lao-tzu himself was deified and became one of the most important Taoist gods.

The Taoist pantheon mirrors the imperial hierarchy in Heaven and Hell, and Taoist priests relate to these divinities through meditation and visualization. Sometimes for the general public, metaphysical or symbolic theatrical rituals have been devised to portray the meaning and workings of the divine hierarchy. Many Taoists pray to these divinities or make offerings at shrines devoted to them.

Lao-tzu is said to be one of the reincarnations of the Great Supreme Venerable Lord, or T'ai-shang Lao-chun. He is symbolic of one who has become one with the Tao, thus succeeding in the creation of an immortal body that separates from the physical body at death.

Yu-huang, the Jade Emperor, also known as the Lord of Heaven, is said to be the supreme ruler of the heavens and of the underworld. For the Chinese, jade symbolizes nobility, perfection and immortality, and is considered the "stone of heaven". The Jade Emperor is the chief administrator of moral justice and also the protector of humanity. In Chinese tradition, the heavenly administration was regarded as a replica of the emperor's government on Earth, and the Jade Emperor was in direct communication with the emperor of China.

P'AN-KU AND THE FIVE SACRED MOUNTAINS

Another important Taoist figure is the mythical P'an-ku, who is said to be the first created being. Upon the creation of the universe, in which Chaos was divided into the forces of yin and yang, the interaction of these opposing principles led to the creation of P'an-ku, who thereupon picked up a chisel and a mallet and began to carve the rest of creation, and in particular the space that lies between Heaven and Earth. P'an-ku lived for 18,000 years, growing every day, and when, on completion of his task he lay down and died, his body became the world, the extent of which was marked by the five sacred mountains of China. Symbolically linked to the five elements, these stood at the four cardinal points and in the centre of the empire, and were believed to support the heavens.

Lao-tzu advised his followers to "be still like a mountain and flow like a great river", and many have sought the Tao by retreating to live alone in the mountains. In Taoist belief, mountains are a medium of communication with the immortals and with nature. Like the image of the world tree, they link the worlds above and below. The sacred mountains are sites of pilgrimage. They have been worshipped as deities in their own right, monasteries cling to their slopes, and the emperor himself climbed annually to the summit of the holiest peak, Tai Shan, the mountain of the east, to offer a sacrifice.

ABOVE The Jade Emperor was revered as the divine head of the hierarchy of heaven and hell.

TOP The yin/yang symbol represents the endless interplay of opposing qualities in nature.

THE TAO AND THE MOON
According to some texts, the earliest Taoists were shamans who flew to the moon and there learned all the secrets of change. In contrast, the Taoist view of the sun was of some-thing constant. These early Taoists were far more interested in what could be learned from the moon and its phases.

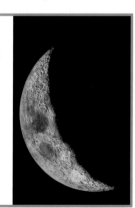

HINDUISM

ABOVE The four heads of Brahma represent the four directions.

TOP Ganesh, the elephant-headed god, symbolizes sacred wisdom and abundance.

With no single historical founder, no set of creeds or dogmas and no one source of authority, Hinduism encompasses a huge variety of beliefs and rituals, intricately woven into the land and culture of India. Of the world's major religions, Hinduism has the third largest number of followers (the majority of whom live in India and Nepal). Many Hindus, however, do not recognize the term Hinduism as a description of their religion, referring instead to *sanatana dharma* – the eternal religion or law. The complex Sanskrit word *dharma* refers to the natural unchanging laws that sustain the universe and keep it in balance, a similar concept to the Tao. It translates in daily life as an obligation to follow certain laws and to fulfil social and ethical responsibilities, so that for many Hindus there is no division between secular and religious life.

BRAHMAN

In Hindu thought, there is one ultimate Supreme Being – Brahman – who is infinite and eternal. Brahman is the source of life, the world soul, and is present in all things as the *atman*, the true self or the unchanging essence of the individual living being.

Just as all living beings represent tiny parts of the universe, so Brahman takes different forms, representing certain aspects of the divine. Consequently there are many gods and goddesses in the Hindu pantheon, including the elephant-headed Ganesh, god of good fortune and wisdom; Hanuman, the monkey god, representing loyalty, courage and devotion; and Lakshmi, the four-armed goddess of fortune.

THE TRIMURTI

The word *trimurti* means "having three forms" in Sanskrit, and is the term used to describe the supreme trinity of Hinduism: Brahma (the Creator), Vishnu (the Preserver) and Shiva (the Destroyer). Brahma the Creator (sometimes depicted with four heads facing in four directions) is the balancing force that links Vishnu, the agent of light, and Shiva, lord of darkness, together. Although Brahma is important, there are only two known temples dedicated exclusively to his worship, while both Shiva and Vishnu are worshipped extensively as principal deities.

LEFT Vishnu and his consort, Lakshmi, ride upon Garuda, the eagle who symbolizes the wisdom attained by an open mind.

VISHNU

Also called the Preserver, Vishnu maintains the harmony of the universe and is a manifestation of the sun as it crosses the heavens each day with three great strides, at dawn, noon and sunset. As preserver of the world, he is said to have assumed ten incarnations, referred to as "avatars" (literally "one who descends"); these include Rama, Krishna and the Buddha. As Lord of the Universe, Vishnu floats on the primeval waters, asleep on the serpent Ananta. His four main symbols are the *shanka* (or conch shell), used to dispel demons, the *gaddha* (or club) to represent power, the *chakra* (or discus) used against evil forces, and the *padma* (or lotus) symbolizing reincarnation. *Tulasi* (sweet basil) is sacred to Vishnu and is kept in temples dedicated to him, its leaves used in sacred ceremonies.

SHIVA

A deity of contrasting and often contradictory characteristics, Shiva represents not only destruction, but also regeneration, just as order arises out of chaos, and new life emerges after death. As Nataraja, he is lord of the universal dance of creation and destruction through which he maintains the balance of the cosmos. The dancing Shiva is usually depicted with four hands surrounded by a circle of flames, representing the sun disc and the creation and continuation of the cosmos. Shiva is also the supreme god of masculine virility, symbolized by the phallus-shaped linga (the counterpart of the

female yoni), as well as an ascetic yogi, clad in ashes and animal skins. His third eye (the chakra in the middle of the forehead) can destroy with fire all those who look upon it, while also granting transcendent wisdom. Shiva is sometimes depicted riding the white bull, Nandi, symbol of power and virility, who often appears at shrines to the god.

SHAKTI

The concept of Shakti is another important aspect of the divine. Shakti is the feminine principle, the dynamic life-giving energy of the universe that activates creativity; without Shakti, the other gods remain passive and lacking in motivation. Shakti is often shown embracing Shiva and has two sides to her nature, one gentle and serene, the other fierce and formidable. The goddess Kali, usually shown with a black tongue, rolling eyes, pointed teeth and a garland of skulls, is a personification of the latter, while Parvati, consort of Shiva, represents the former.

THE SOUND OF OM

In Sanskrit calligraphy, the mystic syllable *om* is the symbolic representation of Brahman. It is described in the Upanishads (one of the sacred texts of Hinduism) as the sound that creates and sustains the cosmos, and it is thought that through its utterance, the whole universe (past, present and future) is encapsulated. The sound contains the three sounds of A, U and M, representing the three gods (Brahma, Vishnu and Shiva) who

control life. They also symbolize the three human states of dreaming, sleeping and waking, and the three capacities of desire, knowledge and action. Om is used as a mantra in meditation as well as in sacred ceremony.

DAILY WORSHIP

Puja, or daily worship, is usually carried out in the home and is the main form of Hindu worship, although worship led by a priest also occurs twice a day at the *mandir* (temple). At home, worship is held at a shrine, where the family's chosen deities are represented in the form of pictures or statues, known as *murtis*. At the mandir, a highly ritualized ceremony known as the *arti* takes place. This involves the lighting of five divas by the priest, who circles the lamps in front of the central deity, while the worshippers sing a devotional scriptural verse. At the end of the ceremony, a symbolic offering of food (such as fruit, nuts or sweets) is presented to the deity for blessing and then shared among the congregation.

FESTIVALS

The Hindu year contains many festivals to mark events in the lives of deities or to celebrate the changing seasons. They are lively, colourful affairs involving music, dance and drama and provide an opportunity for families and friends to come together. Held in honour of the goddess Lakshmi, Diwali, the festival of lights, is the most widely celebrated festival in India, symbolizing the triumph of good over evil. In some regions,

Diwali (in October or November) marks the new year; it augurs a fresh start, and is a time when debts are paid, and homes are cleaned, repainted and lit with an array of lights. The festival of Holi, in March, celebrates the grain harvest and is very high-spirited, with bonfires, tricks (such as showering people with coloured dyes) and dancing.

THE GANGES

In a land of heat and dust, the great rivers of India are an important source of life and energy and unsurprisingly are revered as holy. The most important is the Ganges, worshipped as the goddess Ganga, which flows across India from its source in the Himalayas, also held sacred. Pilgrimages are made to Varanasi (associated with Shiva) on the Ganges' banks to wash in the river's sacred waters. It is believed that Ganga offers liberation from *samsara*, the cycle of rebirth, and Varanasi is considered an auspicious site for cremation and for scattering the ashes of the deceased. Pilgrimages are also made to holy sites in the Himalayas, particularly to Mount Kailas, where it is said that Shiva sits in meditation.

ABOVE The Om symbol represents the sacred sound of creation.

BELOW Shiva, dancing in a circle of flames, is a cosmic symbol of life, death and rebirth.

THE COW

In Hinduism, the cow is held sacred, and slaughtering one is considered a terrible crime. Symbols of fertility and plenty, cows are central to Indian agriculture, their milk is an important food source, while oxen are used to pull the plough, allowing the planting of grain.

BUDDHISM

ABOVE When the Buddha cut off his hair he was using the act as a symbol of his decision to renounce the world.

BELOW A Buddha's footprint decorated with Buddhist symbols, including the reversed swastika, an ancient symbol that predates the German Nazis.

Some 2,500 years ago, Siddhartha Gautama, the founder of Buddhism, was born on the border between Nepal and northern India. The Buddha – or Awakened One – is the title he was given after he achieved spiritual self-realization, or "enlightenment", becoming the embodiment of perfect wisdom and compassion. Buddhism is not based on a belief in God, nor does it have a set creed, a central authority, or a universally accepted sacred scripture. Never demanding sole allegiance from its followers, Buddhism has coexisted with local religious traditions and has given us a rich tradition with a diversity of symbols and mythic thinking.

LIFE OF THE BUDDHA

Siddhartha Gautama's life story is fundamental to Buddhism, symbolizing many of its basic teachings, including the need for great effort, complete detachment and boundless compassion. Raised as a prince, Gautama renounced his riches and abandoned his family in search of the cause of life's suffering. After many years as a wandering ascetic, he concluded that neither indulgence nor extreme austerity held the answer and sat down to meditate on the problem under a bodhi tree in the village of Bodhgaya, India. It was here that he became enlightened and experienced nirvana – a blissful state of perfect peace, knowledge and truth. Though no longer bound to the physical world, the Buddha decided, out of compassion, to spend the rest of his life teaching. He gave his first sermon to a small group of disciples at Sarnath, where he taught the Four Noble Truths and the Eightfold Path, teachings which explain the nature of suffering and how to end it. The path involves discipline of thought and action and endorses a way of life that seeks to harm no one. The monastic sangha (assembly) was inaugurated by the Buddha to preserve and spread his teaching.

THE BODHISATTVAS

While some forms of Buddhism focus upon personal salvation, there is also a way to Buddhahood referred to as "the path of the bodhisattva". A bodhisattva is a disciple of Buddhism (either male or female) who is capable of attaining nirvana – and hence freedom from samsara (the rebirth cycle) – but chooses to remain in the physical world in order to help others. In Pali (a language derivative of Sanskrit), the word bodhisattva means "one who is the essence of truth and wisdom". Bodhisattvas are differentiated from the Buddha by their relaxed pose, often depicted seated or lying down to show their continuing relationship with humankind. Among the most important bodhisattvas are Maitreya (Mili in China), a benevolent figure of the future, an awaited messiah of Buddhism, usually shown seated in the Western style; and Avalokiteshvara (Guan-Yin in China), the embodiment of compassion and mercy.

BUDDHIST COSMOLOGY

Unlike the Western view of a cosmos that proceeds from beginning to end, Buddhist cosmology is cyclical. This not only applies to human life (the endless birth, death, rebirth cycle) but also to world systems. These will come into being, pass away and be succeeded by a new order. Some Buddhists also believe that there are countless world systems in existence simultaneously, each having its own Buddha, some of whom have names and can be interacted with. Thus buddha icons do not always represent the historical Buddha Gautama, (also referred to as Shakyamuni Buddha), but may depict buddhas in different incarnations. One such is Amitabha, the Buddha of Infinite Light and guardian of the West, who is often shown holding a lotus flower and accompanied by a peacock.

THE STUPA

One of the most important and easily recognizable symbols of Buddhism is the stupa. In ancient texts, the word stupa meant "summit", and originally stupas were burial mounds containing sacred relics of the Buddha, or else of his main disciples (some of whom also attained enlightenment). As well as being a symbol of the Buddha and his final release from samsara, the stupa is also a cosmic symbol. Although there are many architectural variations, typically it consists of a dome (*anda*), symbolizing both the "world egg" (an archetypal symbol of creation) and the womb, while the relics it houses represent the seeds of life. Usually the dome rests on a square pedestal, which is typically aligned with the four cardinal points, signifying the dome of Heaven resting upon the earth. Stupas later developed into places of worship, and have sometimes been built to commemorate important events.

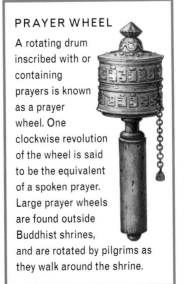

PRAYER WHEEL

A rotating drum inscribed with or containing prayers is known as a prayer wheel. One clockwise revolution of the wheel is said to be the equivalent of a spoken prayer. Large prayer wheels are found outside Buddhist shrines, and are rotated by pilgrims as they walk around the shrine.

BUDDHA'S FOOTPRINT

In Buddhism (and also Hinduism) footprints can represent the presence of a holy person or deity, encapsulating all their qualities and attributes. Many Buddhist temples contain carvings of copies of the Buddha's footprint, often with auspicious Buddhist symbols such as the eight-spoked wheel, symbolizing the Buddha's law. The Buddha's footprints are also decorated with symbols such as the fish, swastika, diamond mace, conch shell, flower vase and crown. It is thought that if devotees follow in the Buddha's footsteps, they too may attain enlightenment or Buddhahood.

TIBETAN BUDDHISM

Buddhism has tended to adapt itself to the different countries and cultures to which it has spread. Sometimes referred to as the Vajrayana (Diamond or Thunderbolt vehicle), Tibetan Buddhism is characterized by a pantheon of Buddhas and bodhisattvas, and many colourful rituals, artefacts and works of art. The importance of living teachers is stressed; some (known as lamas) are believed to be reincarnations of holy teachers from earlier times, living on earth as bodhisattvas. Ritual practices involve making mandalas (abstract, wheel-like designs), chanting mantras and performing mudras (symbolic hand gestures). Statues and mandalas are used to focus the mind in meditation.

ZEN BUDDHISM

Space and simplicity characterize Zen Buddhism. Developed in China, Korea and Japan, the Zen tradition has influenced Sino-Japanese art forms, such as calligraphy, painting and poetry, as well as the arrangement of flowers and gardens, the tea ceremony, and even martial arts, all of which share order, simplicity and set procedures.

ABOVE A golden Dharma-chakra, an 8-spoked wheel that symbolizes the teachings of the Buddha, stands between two statues of deer, representing the Buddha's first sermon at Deer Park, Sarnath. Jokhang Temple, Lhasa, Tibet.

ABOVE The many-layered symbol for the stupa.

THE ELEPHANT AND THE BUDDHA

The story of the Buddha's birth is surrounded by portents of his greatness. While pregnant, his mother dreamed of giving birth to a white bull-elephant with six tusks. The arrival of a chosen one had long been predicted, and interpreters took this dream as an announcement of his impending arrival. In Indian culture, the white elephant is the mount of Indra, king of the gods, and elephants are called "the removers of obstacles", an attribute given to the Hindu elephant-headed god, Ganesh. In Buddhism the elephant is sometimes used as a symbol of the Buddha, representing his serenity and power.

JUDAISM

ABOVE The eastern wall of every synagogue contains the Torah scrolls, which are read from a raised platform to signify respect. A lamp burns perpetually as a symbol of the Jewish people's covenant with God.

ABOVE The Ark of the Covenant is a symbol of the Exodus.

The world's oldest monotheistic religion, Judaism has a continuity of tradition covering some 4,000 years. The name "Judaism" is derived from the tribe of Judah, one of the twelve tribes of Israel, but it is the life of Abraham – known as the father of the Jewish people – and his relationship with God that is fundamental to Judaism. The Jewish scriptures tell how God made a covenant, or agreement, with Abraham: that his descendants would be God's chosen people, in return for which the people should keep God's laws. These laws were given to Moses on Mount Sinai as he led the Jewish people out of captivity in Egypt (the Exodus) to Canaan (Israel), the land God had promised to Abraham.

THE PROMISED LAND

Judaism's history is rooted in Israel, the promised land. More than just a place, it is one of Judaism's most important symbols, part of the Jewish people's ethnic identity. Jerusalem, city of David, Israel's greatest king, is particularly important. It was here that David's son, Solomon, built a temple, a symbol of communion between man and God. The temple was rebuilt many times until its final destruction by the Roman emperor Titus in AD 70. The Wailing (or Western) Wall is the last remnant of the temple and is a place of pilgrimage and prayer for Jews from all over the world.

THE TORAH

Study of the holy scriptures is one of the most important aspects of the Jewish faith. The first five books of the Hebrew Bible are known as the Pentateuch, or Torah, believed to contain all of God's teaching as revealed to Moses on Mount Sinai.

More than a repository of laws and stories, the Torah is seen as the inner, or spiritual, dimension of the world itself, the medium through which the individual may gain access to higher realms. Every synagogue has a set of parchment scrolls (the Sefer Torah) on which the Torah is handwritten in Hebrew by a specialist scribe; it can take a year to complete. Each scroll has a belt to hold it when rolled, a breastplate and a crown, together with a silver pointer used when reading, to avoid finger contact with the parchment. One of the most sacred symbols of Judaism, the Torah scrolls are kept in a special cupboard or alcove (known as the Holy Ark, after the Ark of the Covenant) in the wall that faces Jerusalem.

THE SYNAGOGUE

After the destruction of the temple, the Jews were scattered throughout the Roman Empire, and the synagogue became the centre of Jewish community life. The synagogue has three main functions: it is a house of

BELOW The *shofar* is a ram's horn trumpet used in Jewish rituals. It recalls the story of Abraham and Isaac and is a sign of God's grace.

JEWISH MYSTICISM

The Torah is said to comprise four levels of meaning: the literal, the allegorical, the homiletical (teaching or preaching) and the secret or mystical. Mystical interpretations view the Torah as a means of understanding the nature of God. The Kabbalah, the most influential strand of Jewish mysticism, conceives of God's attributes as a series of ten spheres (or sephiroth), through which the individual must pass in order to reach the divine source. All aspects of human life are ultimately expressions of the sephiroth, which constitutes the deepest reality, our contact with God. The Kabbalah's central text is the Zohar (Book of Splendour), which was first circulated in Spain in the 13th century. Symbols associated with the Kabbalah include the Star of David and the Tetragrammaton.

assembly where the Jewish community can meet for any purpose; a house of study, where the scriptures are studied and children learn Hebrew and study the Torah; and a house of prayer, where services are held on the Sabbath (Shabbat). Men and women occupy separate areas, and in obedience to the Second Commandment, there are not usually any images of people or animals. Every synagogue also has a perpetually burning lamp before the Ark – a symbol of God's eternal light, illuminating the darkness of ignorance.

TETRAGRAMMATON

According to tradition, God's name was revealed to Moses, but was so sacred that it could never be spoken aloud. The tetragrammaton comprises the four letters, Y, H, W, H, which spell the true name of God in Hebrew, referred to as "the name" (*ha shem*), or Adonai ("My Lord"). When vowels are added, the letters spell the name Yahweh, which some Christians translate as Jehovah.

The tetragrammaton was engraved on the rod of Aaron and the ring of Solomon, both emblems of authority. The rod was also believed to have miracle-working properties (like the wand, common to many traditions), and Solomon's ring was said to give him powers of divination. In Kabbalism, the tetragrammaton was believed to signify life and to possess magical and healing powers. It is often written on amulets and on plaques displayed in the

synagogue, as well as in Jewish homes, a constant reminder of God's omnipresence.

LAWS AND CUSTOMS

It is said that the law was given to Moses at Mount Sinai on two stones, known as the Tablets of the Decalogue (the Ten Commandments), engraved by the finger of God. At the heart of Jewish belief is the Shema, the first commandment – love of God. The words of the Shema are written on tiny scrolls and placed in small boxes (tefillin), with straps or tapes attached to them. During weekday prayers, Orthodox Jewish males wear the tefillin bound to their foreheads, left arm and hands. Shema scrolls are also put into small boxes called "mezuzah", which are nailed to the doorways of the home (usually outside every room, except the bathroom and toilet), harking back to the time when the words of the Shema were carved into doorposts.

Typically, Orthodox Jewish men wear a small cap (yarmulke) to show their submission to God. The tallit is a fringed garment – usually a cloak or shawl – worn by male Jews. This refers to a passage from Numbers (15:38–39), which instructs that tassels with a blue cord should be attached to undergarments as a reminder of the commandments of God. Orthodox Jewish women are required to cover their hair in the presence of men other than their husband, as a sign that he alone may enjoy their sexuality; most achieve this by wearing a wig in public.

FESTIVALS

Jewish history and teaching is embodied in its festivals, in which traditions are passed on by means of stories, actions, symbolic food, and singing. There are five major festivals, or Days of Awe, laid down in the Torah: Rosh Hashanah (Jewish New Year), Yom Kippur (Day of Atonement), Pesach (Passover), Shavuot (Pentecost) and Sukkoth (the Feast of the Tabernacles), with many symbols connected to each.

Laws governing the consumption of food are a central part of the Jewish faith. During Pesach only unleavened bread (matzah) is eaten, as a reminder of the Exodus, when the Israelites had to leave Egypt in a hurry, with no time to bake ordinary bread. Bitter herbs symbolize slavery in Egypt, and a lamb bone symbolizes the Pesach offerings that would have been brought to the temple in Jerusalem.

The *shofar*, a ram's horn trumpet, is blown during Rosh Hashanah, a call for people to repent and start the new year afresh. This horn is a reminder of God's grace when he allowed Abraham to sacrifice a ram instead of Isaac. There are three main sounds blown on the *shofar*, and during Rosh Hashanah, they are repeated 100 times.

STAR OF DAVID

One of the most widely recognized signs of Judaism, today the Star of David is a symbol of the State of Israel, appearing since 1948 on its national flag. A six-pointed star formed from two interlocking triangles, it is said to derive from the hexagrammic shield that David carried against Goliath. The white of the upper triangle and the black of the lower triangle symbolize the union of opposites.

CHRISTIANITY

ABOVE The labarurm, or Chi-Rho cross

ABOVE Jesus crucified on the cross is a central Christian motif.

ABOVE One of the oldest secret symbols for Christ.

Together with Islam, Christianity is the most widespread of the world's religions. Emerging out of Judaism, it has many different traditions, but its central tenet is that the Jewish-born Jesus of Nazareth is the Son of God, the long-awaited Messiah whose coming was foretold by the Old Testament prophets. The life of Jesus, from his humble birth to the Virgin Mary to his crucifixion, death and resurrection, form the basis of Christian theology as told in the Gospels (meaning "good news") of the New Testament.

SYMBOLS OF CHRIST

Christianity takes its name from the Greek translation of the Hebrew "Messiah" (the Anointed One). Christ is the title Jesus was given by his followers and is symbolized in many ways.

The fish is one of the earliest Christian symbols, found on graves in the Roman catacombs – an ancient, secret meeting place when the Christians were persecuted by the Romans for their faith. It is based on an acrostic: the initial letters of the Greek words for Jesus Christ, Son of God and Saviour spell out ichthus, the Greek word for fish. Christ also referred to his apostles as "fishers of men", while the early Christian fathers called the faithful pisculi (fish).

Another of the earliest symbols for Christ is the labarurm, a monogram composed of the first Greek letters of Christ's name, X (chi) and P (rho). Also known as the Chi-Rho cross, the letters are usually inscribed one over the other, sometimes enclosed within a circle, becoming both a cosmic and a solar symbol. It is said that the Roman emperor Constantine I had a vision of the Chi-Rho cross promising victory to his army, after which he converted to Christianity. Byzantium, the capital of the Eastern Roman Empire, was renamed Constantinople (Istanbul) and became the centre of the Eastern Orthodox Christian Church.

Other symbols associated with Christ are objects linked to the Passion (or crucifixion). These include the cross on which he died, a crown of thorns, a scourge or whip, the hammer and nails used to fix him to the cross, a spear that the Roman soldiers used to pierce his side, and the ladder by which he was lowered from the cross. From the 14th century, these objects became the

BELOW Jesus the Good Shepherd carries a lamb back to the fold, a symbol of Christ as Saviour.

ABOVE The crown of thorns is a Christian symbol of the crucifixion.

focus of intense devotion among some Christians, designed to arouse an emotional response to Jesus' suffering.

SHEEP AND SHEPHERDS

Jesus drew heavily on his native land and culture for symbols to use in his teachings. For instance, many people in the region would have kept sheep, and the comparison between Jesus as a shepherd and his followers as his flock is a key metaphor.

In John's Gospel, Jesus is referred to as the Good Shepherd who will lead those who have gone astray back to a proper relationship with God, while he is also referred to as "the lamb of God", symbolizing the sacrifice he made, dying in order that humanity's sins may be forgiven. In Christian iconography, Jesus is often shown with a lamb draped over his shoulders, symbolizing his ability to save lost souls. He also carries a shepherd's crook, or crozier, which has been adopted by bishops of the Church and has become a symbol of their pastoral authority over their congregation, as well as a reminder of Jesus.

THE DOVE

In Judaic and Christian cultures, the dove holding an olive branch symbolizes God's grace. As punishment for humanity's wickedness, God had sent a great flood, symbol of destruction and also purification and cleansing. The righteous Noah was warned, and built an ark in which his family and a pair of every animal were saved. After the rain stopped, Noah sent out a dove to search for dry land. It returned, carrying an olive branch from the Mount of Olives, a symbol of God's forgiveness. In Christian iconography the dove is used to represent the Holy Spirit, with seven doves signifying the Holy Spirit's seven gifts.

ABOVE An image of the Virgin Mary, showing her with a halo in which there are twelve stars. This picture depicts the immaculate conception, and Mary stands on a crescent moon, a symbol of chastity. She also wears the blue robes that link her with heaven.

THE TRINITY

Although Christianity is monotheistic, Christians believe that God shows himself in three different and distinct ways – as Father, Son and Holy Spirit. This threefold nature of God is known as the Trinity. Although each aspect of the Trinity is whole in itself, each is also part of God and the one Godhead. In the 5th century, Saint Patrick used the shamrock, a plant with one stem and three leaves, to try to explain the concept: just as each leaf is distinct, so each is also an integral part of the plant. According to John the Baptist, the Trinity was present at the baptism of Jesus: the Son in the water, the Father speaking words of approval from the heavens, and the Holy Spirit descending to Earth in the form of a dove.

THE VIRGIN MARY

Also known as the Madonna (Italian for "my lady"), the Virgin Mary is honoured as the chosen mother for God's holy son, particularly by the Roman Catholic Church. Mary is represented by a great variety of symbols, including the Madonna lily and white rose, which represent her purity, and the red rose (the Passion of Christ), as well as the sun, moon and a halo of twelve stars, which appear to be linked to the apocalyptic vision described in Revelation (12:1) of a woman "robed with the sun, beneath her feet the moon, and on her head a crown of twelve stars". Other symbols of her sanctity and virginity include an enclosed garden, a closed gate and a mirror. She is usually shown with a halo (a symbol in Christian iconography for divinity and majesty) and wearing a blue cloak, the cloak signifying protection and its colour linking her with the skies and the heavenly realm, as well as with the waters of baptism. The Virgin also became a symbol herself, worshipped as the Divine Mother.

THE CHURCH

Although we use the word "church" to describe a building where Christian worship takes place, strictly speaking it means "group of believers", or those who gather together in the name of Jesus. Traditionally churches are built in the shape of a cross, the universal symbol of Christianity, a reminder of Jesus' death.

THE EUCHARIST

Most churches hold a service known as the Eucharist, also known as Mass or Holy Communion, to commemorate the Last Supper. This is the meal that Jesus shared with his twelve disciples the night before his arrest. Like the Last Supper, the Eucharist involves sharing bread and wine, representations of the flesh and blood of Christ, to symbolize taking Christ's body, or essence, within.

THE FOUR EVANGELISTS

The writers of the first four books of the New Testament – Matthew, Mark, Luke and John – are known collectively as the four Evangelists. Apocalyptic visions in the Book of Revelation, as well as those of the Old Testament prophets Daniel and Ezekiel, associate Matthew with an angel, Mark with a lion, Luke with an ox and John with an eagle. In the Western Hermetic tradition, they are linked respectively with the Zodiac signs of Aquarius, Leo, Taurus and Scorpio, the four points of the compass, the four directions and the four elements, as well as the Archangels Raphael, Michael, Gabriel and Uriel.

ISLAM

ABOVE A detail from the Qur'an, the words themselves of which are believed to signify the divine presence.

ABOVE The star and crescent moon symbol is an emblem of the Islamic world.

THE MINARET

The word "minaret" is derived from the Arabic *manara*, meaning "giving off light", alluding perhaps to its symbolic function as a beacon of illumination to the surrounding community. A minaret is a slim tower with a balcony from which the muezzin (caller) calls the faithful to prayer, a constant reminder of Allah's presence. The minaret itself suggests mediation between the people assembled in the mosque below and the heavens above to which it points. The crescent moon, one of the symbols of Islam, is sometimes positioned at the top of the minaret.

The name Islam is from an Arabic word meaning "to submit", with a Muslim being "one who submits" – that is, one who lives in the way intended by Allah (God). As Allah is One, there is no division between the sacred and the secular, with every aspect of life governed by Islamic moral principles. The central tenet of Islam is that it is the original religion, the faith revealed to all the prophets, including Adam, Abraham, Moses and Jesus, but culminating with Mohammed, the last and most important of Allah's divine messengers. Mohammed (or "the Prophet") was born in Makkah, Arabia (now in Saudi Arabia), in the 6th century AD. He is believed to have restored the purity of the teachings of Allah, so bringing Allah's message of guidance to the world to completion and perfection.

FIVE PILLARS OF ISLAM

Islam is built on five main beliefs: belief in Allah, in the Qur'an, in the angels, in Mohammed and the prophets who went before him, and in the Last Day. Muslims also believe that faith alone is meaningless but must be backed up by action in everyday life. These actions are known as "the five pillars of Islam" (a pillar symbolizing support) and are faith, prayer, fasting, pilgrimage and charity.

THE QUR'AN

The sacred text of Islam is known as the Qur'an (derived from the Arab word for "recite"). Muslims believe that this is Allah's own Word, not that of any human being, as directly transmitted to Mohammed over a period of 23 years through the Angel Jibril (Gabriel) in a series of visions. As Mohammed received each portion of the text, he learned it by heart, with Allah teaching him how to recite it.

The actual words of the Qur'an are seen to signify the divine presence of Allah, and so must be written clearly and carefully in the original Arabic; translations are never used in worship. Qur'anic calligraphy has developed as a devotional art, with passages from the Qur'an used to decorate buildings and artefacts – figurative representations are not encouraged in Islam as they are considered tantamount to idolatry. Copies of the Qur'an are always handled with great care, and are kept on a high shelf, wrapped in a clean cloth. A stand is used to hold the book open while reading, and before handling the book, Muslims always make sure that their hands are clean.

THE MOSQUE

Muslims worship Allah in the mosque, or masjid (place of prostration), oriented towards Mecca – with its direction indicated by a mihrab, or niche in the wall. As Islamic sacred art is non-figurative, mosques are decorated with arabesques and geometric patterns, as well as calligraphy from the Qur'an. The patterns reflect the fundamental harmony of the universe and the natural world, derived from the Islamic belief that Allah is One. Although styles of mosque architecture and decoration vary according to local custom and period, many mosques have a domed roof representing the heavenly sky, the universe and creation, usually crowned by a minaret. Other characteristic features include an enclosing courtyard, walkways, and fountains (or showers) for the ablutions required by Islam. Shoes are not worn in the mosque, as they are regarded as unclean. Because Allah is

THE HAND OF FATIMA

Fatima was the daughter of Mohammed and his beloved wife Aisha. Although she is not mentioned in the Qur'an, the Shiite Muslim tradition gives her similar attributes to the Virgin Mary, referring to her as the "Mistress of the Women of the Worlds", the "Virgin" and the "Pure and Holy", and says that she was created from the light of Allah's greatness, or from the food of paradise. In popular religion, the faithful rely on Fatima, who takes the part of the oppressed in the struggle against injustice begun by her father. Shiite women travel to shrines dedicated to Fatima, where they pray for her help with their problems. Amulets known as "the hand of Fatima" are sacred and are worn for protection. The five fingers of the hand also symbolize the five pillars of Islam.

ANGELS

In Islam, angels are creatures of light who praise Allah and carry out his instructions. Jibril, chief of the angels, was responsible for bringing Allah's guidance to all the prophets, including Mohammed. Angels pray for human beings, especially believers, and support the faithful. Muslims believe that everyone has two angels whose task is to record that person's deeds for the Last Day.

everywhere, Islam teaches that the whole world is a mosque, so that the mosque itself can be thought of as a world symbol. The mosque is also regarded as a centre for education, and some of the great mosques of history have had schools and libraries attached to them.

RITUALS AND CUSTOMS

Mohammed decreed that "Cleanliness is part of faith", so before *salah* (prayer), worshippers must wash. This ritual cleansing, or *wadu*, is a symbolic act, the water not only washing the physical body but also cleansing the soul from sin. If water is unavailable, dry ablution using dust or sand is permissible.

In communal worship, Muslims stand side by side, symbolizing the equality of all in Allah's eyes. Men and women are separate, however, and the Iman, who leads the prayers, is in front. Parts of the Qur'an are recited, followed by a series of formal actions that include bowing and prostrating, (signs of submission to Allah). Special mats are used for prayer, and they are always rolled, not folded, after use.

Fasting plays an important part in Islam, and involves abstaining from food, drink and sex during the daytime. Muslims believe that fasting increases their awareness that they are always in Allah's presence, and many Muslims fast regularly on certain days all the year round. It is, however, essential for the whole month of Ramadan, the ninth month of the (lunar) Muslim calendar, which commemorates the time when the first words of the Qur'an were revealed to Mohammed. The end of Ramadan is marked by the new moon, when Muslims break their fast with a family feast.

PILGRIMAGE

Every year, millions of Muslims make their pilgrimage (*hajj*) to Mecca, Islam's holy city, a place so sacred that non-Muslims are not allowed to enter. The pilgrims stay in a huge encampment, and before entering the city, they set aside their normal clothes and put on a simple white garment, a sign of equality with others and humility before Allah.

When in Mecca, they pay homage to Islam's most holy structure, the Ka'aba (cube), the central focus of Muslim worship throughout the world. Standing in the courtyard of the Great Mosque in Makkah, the Ka'aba is a simple cube-shaped stone building that, according to tradition, is the first ever house built for the worship of Allah, rebuilt by Abraham and his son Ishmael. The Ka'aba symbolizes Allah's presence and is covered by a black velvet cloth called the *kiswah*, which is replaced each year. The cloth is a sign of humility and respect, because to gaze on the Ka'aba directly would be akin to looking at Allah, which is forbidden. It is embroidered in gold with passages from the Qur'an, especially on the part over the door – leading to the sacred interior. Reciting prayers, the pilgrims circle the Ka'aba seven times (a mystical number). Walking anticlockwise, they begin at the corner where the sacred Black Stone is embedded in a silver frame. The stone is believed to be a meteorite, a symbol of divine grace and power fallen from Heaven.

BELOW The Ka'aba in the courtyard of the Great Mosque at Mecca is one of Islam's most sacred and profound symbols.

SYMBOLS AND THE MIND

MODERN WESTERN THEORIES ABOUT THE MEANING AND USE OF SYMBOLS HAVE BEEN GREATLY INFLUENCED BY PSYCHOLOGY, THE SCIENTIFIC STUDY OF THE HUMAN MIND. SYMBOLISM IN DREAMS HAS BEEN A SUBJECT OF FASCINATION SINCE ANCIENT TIMES, BUT IN THE 19TH CENTURY PIONEERING PSYCHOLOGISTS BEGAN TO EXPLORE ITS USE AS A PSYCHOANALYTIC TOOL.

FREUD AND JUNG

ABOVE Sigmund Freud believed that symbols are products of the unconscious mind and can contain meaningful information.

ABOVE According to Jung, male and female are also psychological states, known as the *animus* and *anima*.

Sigmund Freud (1856–1939), who is often referred to as the "father of psychoanalysis", differentiated between the conscious and unconscious mind. His seminal work, *The Interpretation of Dreams* (1900), postulates that symbols are a product of the unconscious, typically produced while in the dreaming state as a way of communicating with the conscious self, or ego. A one-time pupil of Freud's, Carl Gustav Jung (1875–1961) broke away from his mentor, developing his theory of the "collective unconscious", a mythical level of the unconscious whose symbolism is archetypal rather than personal.

EROS AND THANATOS
Freud identified two coinciding and conflicting instinctual drives: *eros* and *thanatos*. Eros, or sexuality, is the drive of life, love and creativity; thanatos, or death, is the drive of aggression and destruction. The struggle between them is central to human life, with neuroses occurring when instinctual urges are denied (because they are painful or anti-social) and repressed in the unconscious mind. As products of the unconscious, symbols are a way of finding out more about these repressions.

SEXUAL SYMBOLISM
Put simply, anything that is erect or can penetrate, or resembles a phallus in any way, is a symbol of male sexuality. Freud remarks: "All elongated objects, such as sticks, tree trunks and umbrellas (the opening of these last being comparable to an erection), may stand for the male organ." Other examples could include mountains, tall buildings, trains, pens or bananas. Conversely, anything that can be entered, that is concealed, or resembles the vulva and/or vagina in any way is a symbol of female sexuality: for instance, valleys, caves, doorways, boxes, drawers, cupboards, fruit such as figs, or flowers such as roses. Female breasts are suggested by curving or round shapes, for instance domed buildings, rolling hills or any round fruit such as gourds or melons. However, Freud himself recognized that such things are not inevitably sexual symbols, and is reputed to have said: "Sometimes a cigar is just a cigar."

ANIMA AND ANIMUS
For Jung, male and female sexuality were expressions of deeper creative forces, referred to by him as the "animus" and "anima". The animus represents the male, or rational, side of the psyche and the anima the female, intuitive, side; the way they are symbolized varies. If one or the other is repressed, it can become destructive: a "negative animus" could lead to a rigid, controlled or controlling personality. It could also be experienced symbolically in dreams as a threatening male figure, or in waking life as fear of a male authority figure.

COMPENSATION
Jung saw the psyche as self-adjusting: trying to compensate for areas that are out of balance to reconcile its opposing parts. When these are reconciled we are psychologically balanced and

SYMBOLIC STRUCTURES
Freud thought of the mind as having three conflicting internal tendencies: the *id* is the unconscious, seat of instinct and desire, the *ego* is the conscious self and the *superego* is an internalized self-critic. To avoid censorship by the superego, the id uses symbolic imagery to communicate with the ego. For Jung, the mind also has three main parts: the conscious mind; the personal unconscious, a storehouse of individual "memories"; and the collective unconscious.

LEFT From a Freudian perspective, the soft rolling contours of a hilly landscape can symbolize the curvy shape of the female form.

ABOVE Carl Jung developed the theory of the collective unconscious, a layer of the mind that uses symbols to express universal human themes.

achieve a state of wholeness. He believed symbols could be used to explore the boundaries between oppositions, and in his clinical work he analyzed the symbols in his patients' dreams, seeing them as clues to their state of mind and indicators of their rate of progress.

THE LIFE PROCESS
Organic growth is fundamental to Jung's thinking, with the human organism designed to develop to psychological as well as physical

BELOW An atomic explosion symbolizes Freud's concept of thanatos, or the death wish.

maturity. Jung referred to this as "the process of individuation", with the symbols arising from the unconscious providing clues to the individual's current stage of mental and emotional development. This process is not something that can be brought about by conscious willpower, but just as a seed grows into a plant, is something that happens involuntarily, according to a predetermined pattern. Jung also believed that there was an organizing intelligence in each person's psychic system, the inventor and source of symbols. He referred to this as the Self, and saw it as both the nucleus and the totality of the psyche. Other cultures have also expressed an awareness of an inner centre: for instance, the Greeks referred to it as a *daimon*.

SIGNS AND SYMBOLS
Jung differentiated between signs and symbols, saying that a sign was always linked to the

conscious thought behind it, and by implication was always less than the concept it represented. Symbols, on the other hand, always stood for more than their obvious and immediate meaning, hinting at something not yet known. He thought they were produced spontaneously in the unconscious, and were not something that could be created by conscious intent. He believed they occurred not only in dreams, but in all kinds of psychic manifestations, saying that thoughts and feelings, acts and situations can all be symbolic. He went so far as to say that even inanimate objects can appear to "cooperate" with the unconscious in the arrangement of symbolic patterns, citing examples of well-authenticated stories of clocks stopping, pictures falling, or mirrors shattering at the moment of their owner's death.

A MULTI-STOREYED HOUSE

Jung frequently used the symbols generated by his own dreams to further his understanding of the psyche. For instance, he referred to his dream of exploring a house with several floors to describe the layers of the mind.

The dream began in a first-floor (US second-floor) room, a pleasant sitting room from the 18th century; the surroundings felt comfortable and reasonably familiar. On the ground (US first) floor, the rooms became darker and the furnishings much older, dating back to the 16th century or before. Becoming curious about what was in the rest of the house, he came upon a heavy door. Opening it, he went down to the cellar and found himself in a beautifully vaulted room that looked very ancient. Feeling very excited, he saw an iron ring on a stone slab and pulled it. Beneath the slab was a flight of stairs leading down to a cave, which seemed like a prehistoric tomb, containing skulls, bones and shards of pottery.

Jung thought the first floor related to his conscious self, the ground floor to the personal unconscious, the cellar to the collective unconscious, and the cave to the most primitive layer of the unconscious, bordering on the "animal soul".

ARCHETYPAL SYMBOLS

ABOVE Batman's heroism arises from his ability to integrate his "bat" or Shadow nature with his human nature.

he belief that there are patterns or tendencies organizing nature and human experience has been commonly held throughout human history and across world cultures. The pagan notion of *wyrd* as a preordained web of fate, the Aboriginal Dreaming, and every other mythological system, pantheon of gods or single deity presupposes the idea of an unseen influence behind everyday life. Carl Jung took this principle and developed a psychological theory of deep organizing patterns, or archetypes, shedding light on the shared source of symbolism throughout the world.

BELOW Sir Galahad, from Arthurian legend, represents the ability to be true to our inner nature, thus fulfilling the Holy Grail quest.

THE COLLECTIVE UNCONSCIOUS

Contrary to Freud, Jung believed that the symbols produced by the unconscious did not relate to personal material only. He noted a recurrence of certain symbolic imagery, and a similarity between many of the images he found and the symbols that appear in myth, religion and art, and esoteric traditions such as alchemy. Jung argued that symbolism plays an important role in the psychic processes that influence human life, containing information about human emotions and expressing profound spiritual truths.

JUNG'S ARCHETYPES

An archetype is a basic underlying pattern that gives an event symbolic meaning. Archetypes are not exactly motifs or symbols themselves, but are rather the deep-rooted tendencies or trends that influence symbol formation. Jung understood archetypal images to be grounded in the biology of the body and its organs, connecting us to our evolutionary history and our animal natures. He gave them names such as Anima, Animus, Self, Eros, Mother and Shadow.

Jung considered archetypes, operating at the level of the collective unconscious, to be common to all humanity, beyond the diversities of race, place or history, though the symbolism that arises from archetypal patterns varies: the anima and animus, for example, may appear as fairies and elves or gods and goddesses that are specific to each tradition or mythology.

Archetypes help us to understand common human experiences, such as birth, death, change or transformation, wholeness, growth and development, achievement or failure, wisdom and love.

THE SELF

Jung defined the wholeness for which all humans strive as the Self; it is often symbolized by the circle or the square. The Self is the goal of the individuation process, through which we become our true selves.

The quest for the Holy Grail, in Arthurian legend, can be seen as representing the Self: Sir Galahad finds the Grail and ascends to heaven, or fulfilment of his true nature. The symbol of the car or chariot commonly represents the journey to the Self, demonstrating where a person is on their life path in relation to their wholeness. A house can represent the structure of the Self, and other symbols of the Self include the hero and the mountain.

THE SHADOW

Aspects of a person's nature that are unconscious or not integrated, and which they regard as inferior or bad, are represented by the archetype described by Jung as the Shadow. They include unacceptable desires, undeveloped feelings or ideas, and animal instincts. Lived unconsciously, the Shadow appears as bad or evil figures in dreams or myths. In a dream, the Shadow might appear as a burglar of the same sex as the dreamer.

In cultures with restrictive

RIGHT Demeter, the Greek earth
goddess, shown with a headdress
that is made from her symbols of
corn and harvest fruit.

FAR RIGHT The role of the jester is
to act as a mirror in which those in
authority see their own foolishness.

social codes, the Shadow
compensates through becoming
more prominent. Vampires are an
image of the Shadow. Having a
human appearance, they live in
the darkness, with hidden desires,
feeding on the blood of the living,
and drawing power from what we
call "normality".

THE MOTHER

Nurturing and protection are
embodied in the Mother
archetype. She gives life energy to
her children, friends and
community, and is also associated
with reproduction and abundant
growth in nature. The negative
mother is domineering,
interfering, jealous, and may take
or destroy life. Some Jungians
argue that a woman who is
strongly connected with the
Mother archetype must learn to
nurture herself and her own
creative life-force, in order to
avoid becoming destructive.

The Mother archetype is found
in goddesses of the earth and sky
and other Great Mother figures.
The Egyptian sky goddess, Nut, is
a figure of overarching maternal
protection. The Greek earth
goddess Demeter (Roman Ceres)
is associated with both
motherhood and the harvest, and
her principal symbols are barley
and corn, crops essential to life.
The maternal aspect of Mary is
found in her manifestation as
Queen of Earth.

The destructive aspect of the
Mother archetype is more obvious
in the Hindu goddess Kali, who is
a destroyer but also a mother
goddess of creation and
protection. Witches in dreams

and fairy tales can also represent
the negative aspect of the
archetypal Mother. A witch may
personify a jealous attitude that
resists another person changing or
developing for the better. She
casts spells on people to
hypnotize them, send them to
sleep or trap them in a certain
place, thus maintaining control.
We may dream of witches at a
time of transition, when it is hard
to leave a certain way of life or
belief system.

THE TRICKSTER

Wisdom within foolishness is
represented by the archetype of
the Trickster. He does not
conform to the laws of the
everyday world, and challenges
authority. Clown figures are
common to most cultures
throughout the world. In
Shakespearean drama, the fool, or
court jester, is a recurring
character, whose riddles and
humour counterbalance the rigid
authority of the ruler, indirectly
offering him wisdom.

In Nigerian mythology, Edshu
was a trickster god who took
great delight in provoking
arguments among members of a
community. He would wear a hat
that was red on one side and blue
on the other, so that the people
would argue about what colour
hat he had on. Thus, while
appearing to have a destructive
effect, through his mischief he
helped people to see that there
was more than one way of
looking at things.

TIMESPIRITS

The contemporary therapist Dr
Arnold Mindell has used the word
"timespirit" to describe the
concept of archetypal roles and
relationships that are not static
but evolving. It presupposes that
we live in a kind of field, like a
magnetic field, which both
organizes our experience and is
influenced by our actions.

Mindell envisages an archetypal
or mythical stream flowing
through the world, whose flow
and direction changes over time.
Particular roles that are relevant
to a culture, region and history
arise, make themselves known
within everyday life, then fall
away. We are said to be immersed
in this stream, and at one time or
another we are carried by
particular roles or spirits, which
touch us personally but are also
part of the greater stream.

The concept formalized in such
theories, of dreamlike or mythical
patterns underlying everyday life
experience, suggests that symbolic
processes are calling on us to be
lived consciously and with
awareness. One way of
understanding this is that behind
every human conflict there are
mythical stories trying to unfold.

THE ELDER AS A TIMESPIRIT

The figure of the
elder is important in
most cultures. As
wise figures with an
overview for their
community or world,
elders embody the
principle of
appreciating and
valuing all viewpoints
and perspectives. The
timespirit of the elder
often appears when
people need help, but
elders are not
infallible and they
sometimes become
stuck or rigid,
focusing on the use
of power, rules and
morality. The United
Nations is a symbolic
"circle of elders"
whose aim is to help
in conflict zones.

PROCESS ORIENTED PSYCHOLOGY

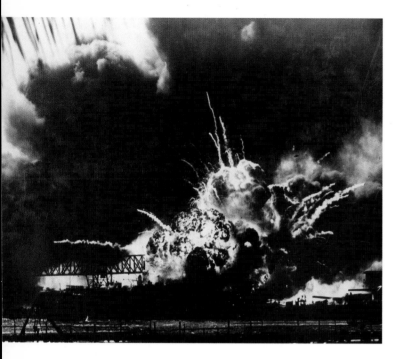

ABOVE An explosion occurring at the edge of awareness in a dream or in "explosive" physical symptoms may signify the need to be more emotionally expressive.

BELOW RIGHT Edges occur in nature where two environments meet. Psychological "edges" are where we meet the limit of what we know or believe we can understand.

BELOW A dream of mist or fog represents the obscuring of our usual perceptions, thus forcing us to use different senses to experience the world.

In the 1960s the psychological theorist and therapist Arnold Mindell founded dreambody work, later renamed Process Oriented Psychology or Process Work. Mindell found common ground in the theory and wisdom of quantum physics, Jungian psychology, shamanism and Taoism, together with other sociological and psychological approaches. Process work is a phenomenological approach, which seeks to increase people's awareness of the pattern, nature and flow of what they experience.

Process work contributes to the study of signs and symbols because it approaches even the most extreme or chaotic events on the basis that they are rooted in archetypal patterns. Bodily symptoms, difficult mental states, life transitions and relationship or global conflicts can all be understood as archetypal and symbolic manifestations, seeking to be unfolded and consciously lived through us in our day-to-day experiences.

PROCESS VERSUS STATES

Mindell points out that we have a tendency to view life in terms of states – fixed symbols, fixed meanings, fixed identities, states of mind – whereas we really live in a world of process – receiving a constant flow of signals and information. He makes the analogy of the process of life as being like a track along which a train moves, with stations representing temporary states. In process work symbols are seen not only as having fixed meanings, but also as being part of an ongoing fluid development requiring constant awareness.

Jung argued that some symbols have a fixed meaning, being archetypes that go beyond cultural and temporal differences. In process work the therapist is guided by a person's feedback to an interpretation rather than by the interpretation itself.

FEEDBACK AND SYMBOL INTERPRETATION

A central concept in process work, which is also inherent in Taoism and many other nature-oriented traditions, is that it is led by feedback. While a symbol can be interpreted by an expert or a professional, the best interpretations are mirrored and confirmed by the signals and responses of the inquirer.

Positive feedback is information that points or leads the way in a person's process. When a dream symbol is interpreted by the therapist, positive feedback may or may not be the verbal response to the interpretation, but can also be found in other signals and responses, such as unconscious movements, feelings or sensations, visual experiences or unintentional sounds.

PRIMARY AND SECONDARY PROCESS

From a process perspective, we might think of symbols as snapshots in a given time and place. Primary symbols are familiar things with which we identify. For example, the badges and uniforms worn by police officers, firefighters or doctors symbolize their identity with their role and professional body, and are primary symbols for them. The national flags and anthems of athletes at the Olympic Games are also primary symbols. When people are asleep, their primary process or identity will appear in dreams as symbolic figures that are familiar or known to them, or as aspects of their past. The dreamer will speak of recognizing

or knowing these figures easily. During the daytime, the primary process is found in the roles, body language, ways of behaving and any other signals close to a person's identity.

Secondary symbolism may inspire or disturb us: it represents aspects of ourselves with which we do not so easily identify, but points to our deeper process and evolution. A secondary process disturbs a person's personal identity, and is experienced as something "other". For example, when a group of people make jokes about another group, the qualities that they are ridiculing may be projected secondary qualities of the jokers themselves.

Secondary symbols in dreams are those symbols with which we are unfamiliar: the bears, gurus, leaders, mysterious flowers, shadowy figures, enemies, attackers and lovers in our dream world. Dreaming of a caged bear, for example, may represent a bearlike aspect of a person's identity – possibly rage, power or a connection with the earth – which has become locked away. Secondary information of this kind might appear in the daytime as a mood of depression, or as tension in the body. Secondary symbolism is commonly projected on to the "enemy" or, conversely, on to people whom we admire.

THE EDGE

Mindell defines the border between our primary identity and secondary processes as the "edge". The edge defines the limits of who we think we are. It is defined by the conscious or unconscious

beliefs we hold about ourselves, and fixes or colours our viewpoint and perspective.

The edge is our growing boundary and psychic "skin". Whenever we are confronted by the unknown, or something that disturbs our view of the world, then we are at an edge. Edge symbols are common in mythology, folklore and dreams.

The forest edge is the line between safety and terror, the conscious and the unconscious, and the human realms and nature. It is where we leave the known for the unknown. Like the forest, the edge between day and night represents that between the light of the conscious and the darkness of the unconscious, though it is a cyclical edge that recurs rhythmically. Many cultures regard the twilight hours or dusk, as a liminal (or transitional) time in which we are closest to the spirits of the dead, or as the time when fairies come out to play. Conversely, dawn symbolizes joy and awakening, a fresh perspective on things.

The cliff edge has connotations of fear and doom, but is simultaneously a symbol of abandon and exhilaration. Seen from the sea, cliffs can be a symbol of hope for the returning traveller and strength against enemies, but they are also places of suicide. The most significant edge of all is that between life and death, often represented by the grave. As a metaphor, death can symbolize a dead end, or a loss of joy or hope, but can also mean a transformation, or transition to a new level in life.

HOW DREAM FIGURES COMMUNICATE

When we consider our bodies as dreaming entities, it seems reasonable that the figures we dream about at night should also be expressed in our bodies during the day. For example, a man was identified with flexibility and an easy-going attitude, and he concentrated a great deal upon relaxing his body. However, he found to his surprise that people related to something intense and unyielding in his personality, communicated through his body posture. He became disturbed by tensions and a sense of rigidity in his posture, and developed headaches that felt like a helmet covering his head. With a slight shift of emphasis upon these symptoms, and by slightly amplifying the tensions within them, he found he stood and walked like a knight in black armour. He had discovered that he was too flexible and needed to stand up for his inner standards.

Process work invites us to revise our fixed approach to life and symbolic meaning, developing instead an awareness that we are part of the flow in a symbolic universe.

ABOVE Figures such as the "black knight" appear symbolically in dreams, and their characteristics may be reflected in our physical symptoms when we are awake.

SYMPTOMS

Mindell's original interest in the relationship between dream symbolism and the information held or channelled through the body led him to work with a man who had a large stomach tumour. Amplifying the experience in his tumour, the man felt that he was going to explode. He was supported to go further, and upon "exploding" found himself expressing feelings that he had held back for years. Afterwards he recalled that he had recently dreamed of a bomb exploding in the centre of the city where he lived.

The Symbolic Life Path

ECOLOGICAL SELF

The philosopher Arne Naess introduced the idea of the ecological self, through which people realize their deep identification with nature. The ecological self is known to many cultures that maintain a close connection to the natural world. A Navajo chant goes: "The mountains, I become part of it ... The herbs, the fire tree, I become part of it ..." The aboriginal people, through initiation, experience a fundamental identification with the land, seeing this not as symbolic, but as a basic reality.

How do we find our way in life? What makes a life path meaningful or fulfilling? Comparative mythologist Joseph Campbell used to tell his students to "follow your bliss", believing this to be the best way to discover an individual's true path. Mythology and symbolism from many cultures present life as a heroic journey, representing a path of self-realization through developing an awareness of, and a connection to, ourselves and the world around us.

THE HERO'S JOURNEY

Within the archetypal journey of the hero, symbolism concerns the human struggle to find identity and a sense of meaning and purpose. The heroic cycle can be described in three distinct parts: the call to adventure, initiation and the return.

At the beginning of the quest a calling invites the hero to cross a physical or psychological threshold and enter the unknown or realm of the unconscious. In the ancient Sumerian epic, the restless king Gilgamesh was called to adventure through meeting his helper Enkidu, eventually travelling through Iran to a forest to fight the demon Humbaba. In Homer's *Odyssey*, Odysseus was held captive on the island of Ogyia, perpetually resisting the nymph Calypso, who tried to win his heart. The god Hermes, messenger of Zeus, finally told Calypso to set him free, whereupon his quest began. King Arthur, with the help of Merlin, began his journey through his unique ability to draw a sword from a stone.

GUARDIANS

Helpers or guardian figures embody the qualities necessary to undertake a heroic journey. The hero is often initially weak or inexperienced, but gains the support of a guardian, who may be an older, wiser figure, an animal helper or a divinity.

In psychological terms, guardian figures symbolize the whole psyche of the individual. Mentors and guardians embody qualities such as love, trust, protection, faith, courage, power and magic. The Navajo guardian spirit, Spider Woman, protected the Twin-Warriors during their journey to the sun, the house of their father. She provided them with a protective hoop with eagle feathers to keep enemies at bay. The young Maori hero Hatupatu, who had been treated badly by his brothers and then murdered by them, was brought back to life by an *atua*, or supernatural being, in the form of a blowfly, sent by his parents.

THRESHOLDS

The heroic journey always involves crossing a threshold between civilization, or the known world, and the wilderness, or the unknown. In Stanley Kubrick's film *2001: A Space Odyssey*, the threshold is crossed by entering space, while for Homer's Odysseus it was sea travel. In the old sagas and heroic tales, the sea was portrayed as the vast unknown, full of mystery. In modern times, space has become the new symbol of the uncharted, unknown territory. In the *Star Trek* adventures, the captain's log referred to space as the "final frontier" in which the Enterprise was to seek out new civilizations, travelling "where no man has gone before".

INITIATION AND TESTS

Crossing the threshold implies being confronted by new challenges that are beyond everyday existence. This is the purpose of initiation in many cultures, through which individuals or groups are caused to extend their identities. Once the hero has embarked on his journey, a variety of powerful adversaries or initiatory tests are faced, involving all manner of challenges, battles and seductions, awakening the hero to his powers and weaknesses. Each heroic victory is truly a victory over the hero's own failings.

In Jungian terms, the Shadow, which embodies disavowed personal qualities such as egotism, laziness, pride, cowardice, possessiveness, jealousy and ambitiousness, must be confronted and conquered, or accepted and integrated. This may mean fighting an enemy figure, or being presented with some other challenge. One of the labours given to Heracles (Hercules) is to clean up, in one day, decades of dung deposited by hundreds of cattle in the Augean Stables, thus transforming a dirty place (or an undesirable part of himself) into something acceptable.

Heroic battles often involve the hero putting his or her life on the line for another person or ideal. The souls of the Aztec heroes were thought to be assigned to various heavens, depending on the kind of heroism they had shown. This would apply equally to warriors who died in battle and to women who died during childbirth. Many heroes have slain dragons to save damsels in distress, symbolically freeing or protecting their anima, or feminine aspect, from the ravages of jealousy or power.

In the late medieval story of *Don Quixote*, the knight rode out to fight giants, but instead met windmills, contemporary symbols of the new mechanistic world view that had replaced the monsters of old. Increasingly, modern heroes are required to wrestle with technologically advanced adversaries, symbols of our mechanistic nature.

The hero is often challenged with seduction or offers of power, or is held under a spell or trance. In the Arthurian story of *Gawain and the Green Knight*, Sir Gawain must resist the advances of the Green Knight's wife, Bercilak, to prove himself a true knight.

Gawain's hunting of the innocent deer, the wild boar and the cunning fox – each representing one of the qualities used by Bercilak in her attempts to seduce him – depicts his refusal to succumb to her enticements.

Heroes are commonly spellbound by witches, fairies and daemon lovers who try to overcome their willpower, or put them to sleep. Odysseus made his crew fill their ears with wax in order to save themselves from the seductive singing of the alluring Sirens. He himself could not bear to forgo the pleasure of hearing them, but ordered his sailors to tie him to the mast, to prevent him leaping on to the rocks.

The hero must often also journey beyond life into the realms of death. In the Sumerian legend of Inanna the sky goddess, she goes down to the underworld, experiencing death, in order to bring her lover back to life. Jonah, in the Old Testament, is taken into the belly of a whale and is later reborn with new powers. Many totemic cultures depict a tribal leader being eaten by a totem animal, thus becoming one with the animal.

Whatever the trial, the true qualities of the hero are brought out through these encounters during the heroic journey. Each adversary that presents itelf is a symbolic facet of the hero's wholeness, awaiting transformation and integration.

THE RETURN

Once the hero has realized the aims of the quest, he or she can return with a boon or vision for

the benefit of the community. This may be a great treasure hidden in a cave and guarded by a sleeping dragon. It might be a priceless commodity, such as the fire that Prometheus stole from the gods to make human life bearable. The treasures of the unconscious are rarely released until one has developed the ability to face one's deep fears.

Some heroes must be reconciled with their father, marking the point when they can take up their role in society. Some, having integrated all the experiences of the quest, achieve apotheosis – becoming a god. The hero now straddles the worlds of everyday reality and of the gods. Gilgamesh is tricked out of the secret of immortality, but returns home with the wisdom of his own mortality, and the ability to live and enjoy life.

ABOVE The heroic Prometheus bringing his gift of fire to humanity.

BELOW Don Quixote had an impulsive personality, and was determined to live his days fully as if he were about to die.

DREAM SYMBOLISM

According to Jung, the totality of a person's dream life represents their potential for individuation. As we respond to our personal world of symbolism, we travel along a path that leads to self-realization, or the Self, Jung's archetype of wholeness.

THE LIFE-MYTH

The Self has parallels in the inner *daimon* of the Greeks, the *genius* of the Romans and the ancient Egyptians' Ka (the spirit or life-force that was created with an individual, and reunited with them at death); in more primitive cultures the idea of a guiding or accompanying spirit is seen in the totemic animals and plants that protect members of a clan. The Naskapi Indians, from the Labrador peninsula, believe their soul is an inner companion called Mista'peo (or "Great Man"), who resides in their heart and after death is thought to reincarnate in another being. They find their way in life by following guidance given to them in dreams.

Childhood dreams are said to contain patterns that are symbolic of our life-myth or path. They commonly portray the everyday personality being threatened and overwhelmed by a powerful mythical figure such as a witch, a Yeti, or a wave, representing aspects of our wholeness that will be met during the course of our lives. For example, a girl may suffer frightening dreams in which she is pursued by a witch, but encouraging her to play at being a witch herself may help her conquer her fears by finding new feminine powers of her own.

The life-myth is the fundamental pattern, or mythic potential, that informs and organizes a person's life path. Dr Arnold Mindell refers to this mythic potential as the "Big You", which underpins the twists and turns of our lives. Every difficulty in life, such as a relationship break-up, chronic physical symptoms, addiction or the loss of a role or identity, would therefore be connected to the life myth. The challenge to the everyday self, or "Little You", is to take the heroic challenge and wrestle with the Big You until it becomes an ally and will give up its secrets.

AMPLIFICATION TECHNIQUES

A great deal of focus has been given to the interpretation of signs and symbols according to our rational understanding and knowledge of their meaning. But, approached more holistically, it becomes evident that a deeper understanding of the signs and symbols of the psyche will involve not only our minds but also the wisdom of our bodies and nature. Amplification refers to focusing on symbolic content, whether in dreams, the imagination, in our bodies or in nature, and strengthening the experience so that it can unfold, allowing its wisdom to flower.

JUNG'S ACTIVE IMAGINATION

Active imagination is a psychological tool that can help towards achieving wholeness or individuation. It involves direct contact or confrontation with the unconscious, without the need for tests and interpretations.

When a patient is in analysis, the first stage involves some degree of "symbol transference", in which the patient unconsciously transfers symbolic content on to the therapist, who holds these projections until the patient is ready to integrate them. For example, the therapist may represent a negative or positive mother, father or authority figure for the patient; through the therapeutic relationship, the patient can learn to integrate the qualities that have been projected.

Jung once said that stepping into dreams and using active imagination is the essential second half of analysis, and that without active imagination one could never become truly independent of a psychotherapist.

The basic approach of active imagination is to sit down alone as free as possible from disturbance, concentrating on whatever comes from the unconscious. Often an image or sound will arise in this situation, which must then be prevented from sinking back into the unconscious: this may be achieved by representing it in drawing or painting, writing it down, or possibly expressing it in movement or dance.

A more indirect approach to active imagination is to write stories about another person; this process inevitably brings the storyteller's unconscious into play. Jung also spoke of having conversations with the personified voices of the unconscious, as a later stage of active imagination. At a time when he was in a particularly low point in his life, and was feeling depressed, Jung said he had long and deep conversations with a wise inner figure called Philemon, from whom he felt he had received great insights.

Jung viewed active imagination in many respects as replacing the importance of dreaming, in that it was a direct contact with, and

amplification and expression of, the archetypes. In his latter years, Jung spent a great deal of time engaged in active imagination, playing in the sand and carving stone sculptures at his home in Böllingen, Switzerland.

PROCESS AMPLIFICATION

Inspired by Jung's approaches to amplification, Dr Arnold Mindell developed a more explicit approach to amplifying dreamlike information as it occurs in different channels of perception.

As individuals we have preferred, or "occupied", channels of perception (or senses), and less preferred, or "unoccupied", channels. Some people think and perceive physical sensations primarily in pictures, while others interpret the world in words. If a person tends to perceive the world through vision or through sound and words, then they have occupied visual or auditory channels. A person who naturally favours "feeling" or movement is said to occupy the proprioceptive or kinaesthetic channels of perception. In each case other

channels will be relatively unoccupied. The information that does occupy these channels tends to disturb us, and yet at the same time it can have meaningful symbolic content, pointing to less-known aspects of ourselves.

THE SENOI TEMIARS

For some cultures, the amplification of dream symbols is second nature. The Senoi Temiars of northern Malaysia place great value upon dream-life, and the exploration and expression of this dream-life is used to further the social life and projects of the community. They use a playful form of trance dance and community singing in order to connect with and amplify dream material.

The Senoi Temiars also encourage the telling of dreams at breakfast time, and if a child is fearful of a dream, for example a dream in which they are falling, the parents will help the child to learn to dream lucidly, so that they can control the course of the dream – they can then change the uncontrolled falling into controlled flight.

ABOVE The dreams of young adults and children, whether benign or malign, are believed to contain patterns that symbolize our life path.

THE JEWEL IN THE WOUND

Rose-Emily Rothenberg used active imagination to work with a serious skin disorder that she had had from childhood. She described how she remodelled herself through creative play. Initially she viewed the scars on her body as an inferior part of her, which she wished to have removed, however, over time she began to relate to the scars as "stars" or jewels, guides to parts of her that she felt were out of control and in pain.

SYMBOLS IN SYNCHRONICITY

FAR RIGHT A clock stopping at the moment of its owner's death is a good example of synchronicity. The theory of synchronicity uses symbols to relate the meaning of two otherwise disparate events, thus creating a "meaningful coincidence".

Jung coined the term "synchronicity" to describe coincidences of two or more events that he felt could not be due to chance alone. In his 1952 book *Synchronicity: an Acausal Connecting Principle*, he expounded his theory that this kind of "meaningful coincidence of inner and outer experience" was not governed by the principle of causality, but was a case of internal psychic states influencing external events. The concept has been used to explain otherwise unaccountable phenomena such as telepathy, astrology and the interpretation of the Tarot.

In cases of synchronicity, seemingly unrelated things are found to have a connection because, in Jung's view, they share the common ground of the *unus mundus*, or "one world", the mythical dimension behind all life. Such events carry meaningful symbols across the threshold between the unconscious and the conscious.

BELOW AND BELOW RIGHT Flashes of light and reflections in water are examples of the way movement and light can attract us, and "flirt" for our attention.

COINCIDENCES AT THE SAME TIME AND PLACE

Jung famously recounted one of his own experiences of synchronicity, in which a patient was telling him about her dream

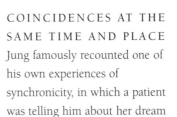

of having been given a golden scarab. Jung, who had his back to the window, in the same moment heard tapping against the glass and, to his surprise, turned to see a scarabaeid beetle (the common rose-chafer), a relative of the scarab, banging on the window. The scarab is an Egyptian symbol of the solar cycle and of rebirth (or transformation), and the patient's exclusively rational perspective on her situation was transformed by the episode.

Another of Jung's examples concerned the pendulum clock that was said to have stopped at the moment when Frederick the Great of Prussia died in 1786. The stopping of clocks at the moment of their owners' death is thought to be a common phenomenon, and may symbolize the ending of time, and the cessation of the heartbeat.

Similarly, there are many accounts of mirrors or pictures falling to the floor and breaking when there is a death, symbolic of the shattering of the earthly image.

COINCIDENCES AT THE SAME TIME IN DIFFERENT PLACES

Leaps of discovery sometimes occur simultaneously in different places; according to the biologist Rupert Sheldrake, this is due to archetypal patterns influencing structural development. The phenomenon was described by Ken Keyes in his book *The Hundredth Monkey* (1981). Japanese scientists had been studying the monkey *Macaca fuscata* for over 30 years, when in 1952 they observed a female monkey develop a new behaviour: she began to wash sweet potatoes in a stream before

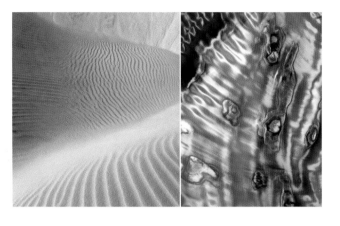

eating them. This new skill was learned by the mothers and young monkeys, though not by the older monkeys, but in 1958 there was a sudden expansion of the activity across the entire population of monkeys on the island. More surprisingly, it seemed that it also jumped simultaneously to monkey colonies on other islands, and to the monkeys on the mainland. Sheldrake has suggested that this phenomenon was connected to a change in the archetypal pattern when a critical mass was reached.

Having spent twenty years formulating his theory of the origin of species, in 1858 Charles Darwin received a letter from the naturalist Alfred Russel Wallace, containing a brief but very similar explanation of the way in which species evolved through natural selection. Wallace was working in the Malay Archipelago, and had come to his conclusions independently of Darwin's work.

COINCIDENCE AT DIFFERENT TIMES

As a persuasive example of the foreknowledge of dreams, Jung relates the dream of a student friend of his, whose father had offered him a trip to Spain if he passed his exams. He became so excited that he dreamed about Spain, seeing himself walking along a street leading to a square where he saw a Gothic cathedral. Upon turning a corner he saw an elegant horse-drawn carriage. When he awoke, he told his friends of the dream, and after passing his exams, he went to Spain, and was greatly surprised

to find the square, the cathedral and the carriage from his dream.

The first Neanderthal fossil bones were discovered in 1856 by quarry workers in the Neander Valley in Germany, and the early humans were named after the valley. By coincidence, the area had been named in the 17th century after a local pastor, Joachim Neumann, who adopted the Greek pseudonym Neander, meaning "new man".

THE FLIRT

Arnold Mindell uses the word "flirt" to describe the interchange and reflection of dreamlike signals between the observer and the observed, whereby it becomes impossible to determine which came first – the sense that an object is asking for attention or the observation itself. Mindell suggests that we have different kinds of attention and awareness. We pay most attention to a consensual reality, but at the edge of this experience many signals flirt for our "second attention". These "flirts" may be a signpost to another reality: a bird swooping, the glint of light on water, or an imagined tear in a friend's eye. Mindell sees flirts as coming from a sentient realm equivalent to Jung's collective unconscious, a pre-signal level where things exist as tendencies before they become manifest. He describes this realm as something like a root system between two trees that are so intertwined it is impossible to separate them.

The belief that the earth and people are deeply connected underpins all shamanic practice,

and is shared by many indigenous peoples. Mindell tells of an Australian Aborigine describing the mysterious power of a tree, which draws our attention, talking to us and telling us a story. A Romany shaman has described his initiation, lying in a field in order to connect to the earth and find his true path, and Native American vision quests are based upon the principle of synchronicities and flirts in nature coming to the inquirer.

The concepts of synchronicity and flirts presuppose that all life is fundamentally connected. This is not yet commonly accepted by mainstream science, and yet developments in quantum physics and field and process-oriented psychological research are pointing in this direction.

ABOVE The playfulness of nature shows itself in these iridescent shell patterns.

ABOVE LEFT Nature is full of rhythms and patterns. Modern science is showing that acausal connections exist through time and space.

BELOW A single falling leaf catching the light as it descends can flirt for our attention.

SYMBOLISM IN SOCIETY

A SYMBOL MAY BE NATURAL OR AN ARTEFACT, AND SYMBOLISM CAN ARISE THROUGH ACTIONS, GESTURES, THOUGHTS OR FEELINGS TO REPRESENT AN UNDERLYING CONCEPT. HOWEVER, THE MEANING OF A SYMBOL IS NOT INTRINSIC IN THE THING ITSELF, BUT RELIES ON ITS CULTURAL AND HISTORICAL CONTEXT AND CAN CHANGE OVER TIME AND SPACE.

MEANING AND CONNECTION

ABOVE Street signs use a "visual shorthand" of pictures, letters and numbers to convey practical information.

TOP For motorists throughout the world, a red traffic light is the universal symbol for "stop".

In the 20th century, theories began to be developed about the meaning and origins of signs and symbols in human society. The American philosopher Charles Sanders Pierce (1839–1914) and the Swiss linguist Ferdinand De Saussure (1857–1913) were the founding fathers of semiotics, the philosophical study of signs and sign systerms, and the way in which meaning is produced and exchanged within a culture.

SEMIOTICS
Pierce referred to three types of signs: "iconic" signs, or those that clearly represent the objects they depict (for instance, a road sign showing the silhouette of a car and a motorcycle); "indexical" signs, which represent concepts that we have learned to associate with a particular sign (for instance, smoke is an index of "fire"); and "symbolic" signs, whose meanings are determined by convention and do not resemble the original object to which they refer (for instance, the international symbol for nuclear waste – three black triangles in a circle on a yellow background – or a red traffic light to indicate "stop"). Pierce noted that as people view the world through the filter of personal and cultural experience, the same symbol can

hold different meanings for different people.

Pierce's contemporary, De Saussure, applied this theory more specifically to language, which is itself a system of signs that endeavours to communicate information and meaning. De Saussure identified two parts of a sign: the "signifier" (the actual sign itself) and the "signified" (the conceptual meaning ascribed to it, which is arrived at by cultural convention). For instance, the letter formation c-a-t (the signifier) in the English language describes a furry animal with four legs, a tail and whiskers, that purrs and miaows (the signified). The signifier is a symbolic sign: the same letter formation could just as easily be used to represent anything else, while to a non-English speaker, it may mean nothing at all.

CULTURAL CONVENTIONS
While this may seem obvious, for De Saussure the implications were profound, extending far beyond the reaches of simple word formations. He argued that the signs we use may appear to be arbitrary, but in fact embody

RIGHT There are many different words for "cat", each suggesting a slightly different meaning.

cultural ideologies and values that we then come to think of as "norms". This view shifted the emphasis away from the notion that there is some kind of objective reality "out there" to the idea that "reality" is always encoded, that the way we perceive and make sense of the world is through the codes of our own culture.

De Saussure also pointed out that meanings operate within a paradigm; we choose signs from a whole range of alternatives. To use the earlier example again, there are several alternative signifiers – puss, pussy, moggy, puss-cat, kitty – that we could use instead of "cat", each one of which confers a slightly different nuance of meaning. Semioticians such as De Saussure have argued that we live among and relate not to physical objects and events, but to systems of signs with

RIGHT Structuralism examines the language of fashion and how our perceptions are formed by sets of signals, this image of a punk rocker could signal either beauty or danger.

meanings. These meanings are not "natural" or inevitable but are embedded in our social structure and value systems.

STRUCTURALISM

De Saussure had examined language as a structure, arguing that this method could equally be applied to any system of making meaning: a set of signals or codes, such as the rules of a game; a tribal or community ritual (a wedding, a rain dance, a funeral); "fashion" (in clothes, food and possessions); and the visual arts, literature, advertising and cinema.

De Saussure's work had far-reaching implications, within not only linguistics, but also the study of all communication. It influenced sociology and was taken up by the leading proponents of the Structuralist movement, the anthropologist Claude Lévi-Strauss (b.1908) and the philosopher Roland Barthes (1915–80).

De Saussure had asserted that a signifying system is any structure or system or organization that creates meaning out of cultural signs. As an anthropologist, Lévi-Strauss applied these ideas to kinship systems, cultural organizations and myth, while Roland Barthes explored contemporary Western cultural "signs", particularly in the realms of food, advertising and clothing.

KINSHIP SYSTEMS

Lévi-Strauss came to the conclusion that regardless of content, all systems of cultural organization share the same

fundamental structures. One of these is kinship: every society has had some system for deciding who can marry whom, who can inherit what and from whom, and how these relationships are named. A kinship system is a structure that contains units (men, women and children) who are labelled (fathers, mothers, children), with rules for connecting them; this can be represented visually as a genealogical chart.

Kinship systems structure how goods, people and ideas are "exchanged" within a culture; for example, family groups may "give" women to another family in exchange for something of value (a dowry). Lévi-Strauss insisted that relationships within the structure occur in pairs, which are either similar or opposite. In his book *The Raw and the Cooked* (1964), Lévi-Strauss argues that binary pairs, particularly opposites, form the basic

structure of all human cultures (man and woman, for instance) and ways of thought (good and evil). He notes that in every pair, one term is favoured over the other – the "cooked" (culture and civilization) is better than the "raw" (natural and "primitive"), good is preferred to evil, light to dark, and male (in many cultures) to female.

Like Jung, Lévi-Strauss was also interested in explaining why myths from different cultures seemed so similar. Rather than looking at their content, he applied a structural analysis, arguing that structure is what they share. Like language, a myth is made of units that are put together according to certain rules or conventions (such as repetition, the telling of the story in layer after layer), and these units form relationships with each other, based on binary pairs or opposites, which provide the basis of the structure.

ABOVE A wedding, like any other ritual in any other society, has its own set of rules or signals that are similar to the rules or signals of a language.

BELOW Fast food is a hallmark of modern society, while fresh fruit and vegetables symbolize natural goodness and are associated with health.

MYTHOLOGIES

Between 1954 and 1956, Roland Barthes produced a series of 54 articles on a variety of subjects for a French left-wing magazine. Collectively entitled "Mythologies", they provide insights into Barthes' ideas about the construction of meaning, especially in popular culture – films, advertising, newspapers and magazines, photography, cars, children's toys and popular pastimes. Barthes was fascinated by the meaning of things that surround us in everyday life and wanted to challenge their seeming "innocence" and "naturalness". For instance, a sports car and an unpretentious family vehicle share the same functional utility – they are both means of transport – but they connote different things about their owners. It was these secondary signals that Barthes explored, concerned to analyse what he referred to as the "myths" that circulate in contemporary society and that construct the world and our place in it.

ROLES AND RELATIONSHIPS

ABOVE Cigarette smoking by western women in the early 20th century was associated with women's growing independence and equality.

BELOW The symbolism of the veil has varied in different times and places according to social, religious and political conditions.

Social-role theory of the 1960s showed that in any community various roles tend to arise. The successful functioning of the community relies upon the interactions of all these roles, and each one is defined in terms of its relation to all the other roles. Each role is a living symbol of the cultural values of the community.

As societies have become more complex, so too have the role structures within them. In modern societies it is increasingly that an individual will occupy true multiple roles, over time and even simultaneously. A great deal of symbolism is used in defining human roles and role changes, making use of such pointers as uniform, social behaviour or symbolic rites and rituals marking role transition.

Early role theory described roles as social constructs determined by social expectations and the values that needed to be fulfilled within a community. Culturally defined gender roles, particularly, were seen to govern family and occupational activities. More recent theories suggest that roles are also determined by field patterns in nature; they recognize "ghost roles", which, though not explicit, represent undercurrents of feeling in a community.

AGE AND GENDER

In societies where survival is not a given, roles tend to be fewer in number and clearly delineated by gender and age. In more complex societies there is more variation of roles, and more specialization. Complex societies tend to have a greater need of symbols such as uniforms, conventions or rules of conduct to frame the roles.

In the Native American Comanche society, a hunting and warrior people, a boy was expected to be aggressive and to seize what was his. But as he grew older his role changed towards eldership, and he was expected to settle disputes and avoid making enemies unnecessarily. His role became one of wisdom, gentleness and endurance.

In patriarchal societies throughout the world, women and children have held less privileged roles than men, with consequential fights for the rights of both women and children. The 19th-century American reformer Elizabeth Cady Stanton wore Turkish trousers instead of a restricting crinoline; they were taken up by, and named after, Amelia Bloomer, who promoted them as a symbol of the women's rights movement.

The emancipation of women in Iran has been a complex process in which clothing has also been a central symbol. Women came to the fore during the anti-Shah movement, during which their black veils became revolutionary symbols. Upon establishing an Islamic republic, the veil once again became a part of the state's definition of women. Modern Islamist feminists are now trying to differentiate between patriarchal tradition and the values of Islam, with the veil now a complex symbol, often meaning different things to different people, affected by religion, culture or gender.

Many North American tribes honoured the role of the *berdache*, a man or woman whose gender identity differed from his or her sex. Berdaches symbolized spiritual power, were natural "go-betweens" in gender disputes, and were consulted by tribal elders, as they were thought to be connected to the Great Spirit.

RANK AND PRIVILEGE

All societies have systems of rank and associated privileges that are related to the predominant values and beliefs of the culture. Among the Iban of Borneo, for example,

BOTTOM RIGHT A common theme in the discrimination against gypsies is that their differences make them inferior to settled societies.

RIGHT Michael Jordan has been an important role model for young black men, particularly in the United States of America.

the witch doctor works with the extremes of society, with life and death and the healing of the sick, interacting directly with the spirit world. His role gives him a high rank in the tribe, represented by his elegant feathered headdresses, jewellery and masks.

Sometimes ranking systems are in place for the good of the whole society, and at other times they represent biases within the society, in favour of some people and opposing others. Gypsies have suffered discrimination worldwide, and studies show how they have been subtly ranked as "other" and therefore inferior, by associating them with animals. In India, the Hindu caste system rigidly defines the roles and interactions in traditional society, prohibiting marriage, socialization or even physical contact between members of different castes.

ROLE PLAY AND ROLE MODELS

People need positive role models in order to find the path of their own development. Through role play and role modelling children are able to learn about the roles they are growing into by playing them out in games.

Social learning theory teaches that a major part of child development occurs through role models. The child observes that a role model, often of the same sex, is successful or rewarded in society for their behaviour. The child then adopts the characteristics of the model, and finally identifies more fully with the characteristics of the role, which become his or her own.

Public figures often serve as role models, usually for other people of the same sex, gender, race or physical ability. The outstanding basketball player Michael Jordan, for example, serves as a powerful role model to black boys in America. Celebrities may become legends or icons when they come to symbolize or model specific values for other people's lives. The role model symbolizes what a young person (or an adult) might aspire to. But while many role models are famous people, some of the most important role models may be found within our personal circle: they may be parents, older siblings or other family members, teachers or friends.

CHANGING ROLES

Roles and their symbolism change within the bounds of a culture as its values shift. In Western society, it has been traditional for a woman getting married to wear engagement and wedding rings, and adopt her husband's surname to indicate her changed role. In recent decades, however, these customs have ceased to be universal, and new symbols of marriage are emerging. Women no longer automatically change their surname and couples now wear matching rings as symbols of mutual and equal commitment.

Roles may change gradually, mirroring cultural trends, or their overturning may define an abrupt or violent change, such as the deposition of a monarch during a revolution, or the transformation of intellectuals into farm labourers during China's Cultural Revolution in the 1970s.

TABOOS

ABOVE In this 8th-century banner of the Buddha preaching, he is insulated from touching the ground, as if his spiritual energy would be drained away by contact with the earth.

BELOW Lot's daughters, believing that all other men had been destroyed, felt forced to disregard the taboo of incest and trick their father into having sex with them by getting him drunk.

The word "taboo" comes from the Polynesian *tabu*, which is a system of prohibiting actions or the use of objects because they are considered either sacred or dangerous, unclean or accursed. Taboos may emerge from a moral consciousness and motivate individual and collective moral conscience, but they may also be used to maintain social hierarchies and order.

In animist and nature-based societies, the origin of taboos probably relates to the likes and dislikes of the various levels of spirits in relation to one another. In later cultures, taboos relate more to the people's attempts to appease their gods and goddesses. Within contemporary society, the word taboo has less spiritual significance, and more generally refers to things that are not allowed or not done within society for various social reasons.

PROTECTING DIVINITY

In many cultures, royalty has been seen as divine, and royal individuals have been protected from mundane reality by never being required to touch the ground. They would be carried on the backs or shoulders of others, on an animal or in a carriage, or would walk on carpets specially laid for them.

Montezuma, the Aztec emperor of Mexico, was always carried by his noblemen and never once set foot on the ground. Early kings and queens of Uganda never set foot outside the beautiful enclosures within which they lived. The king of Persia walked on carpets upon which only he could tread. Even today there is a worldwide custom of rolling out a red carpet for royalty on ceremonial occasions.

INCEST TABOOS

Incest – having sexual relations with someone who is a close relation – is a form of taboo that is found worldwide, probably because of the genetic defects it often leads to. Native American and Chinese cultures extend the idea of incest to having relations with people with the same family name. However, gods and royalty are often exempt in order to keep the royal or divine blood pure. While Freud interpreted incest

literally, and sexuality as a potentially dangerous force requiring taboo to avoid its dangers, Jung viewed incest as a symbolic image referring to the attempt of the individual to return to the mother's womb to be reborn.

Incest is a common mythological theme among gods, goddesses and royalty, and particularly in societies that are focused on maintaining their supremacy. When rulers are seen as divine, marrying someone outside the family would sully the pure royal blood. The Egyptian goddess Isis married her brother Osiris. Queen Cleopatra herself was the result of seven generations of brother–sister marriages. In the Old Testament Lot's daughters have sex with their father because there is no other male available to impregnate them. Inca rulers were allowed to marry their sisters.

GENDER TABOOS

In the traditional Kung Bushman society of the Kalahari, where living conditions are very harsh, social roles are strongly divided according to gender. The men hunt, and make weapons and fire, and the woman build a shelter for the family, prepare food, keep the fire and keep the house in order. The separation of their roles is emphasized by assigning different sides of the fire for where men and women should sit. If a woman sits in a man's place, it is thought she will succumb to a mysterious illness, and if the man sits on the woman's side of the fire, his hunting powers might be

lessened. It is also thought that if women touch a man's weapons, his power will lessen.

TABOO FOOD AND ANIMALS

In many cultures it has been believed that spirits could enter or possess inanimate objects, which then become objects of worship, or fetishes. When edible fruits or plants became fetishes they became taboo as food. As an example, the Levantine peoples never ate apples because they believed them to be inhabited by a nature spirit. Animals that were capable of eating human flesh would become a fetish; thus the dog became a taboo animal for the Parsees. Eating apes and monkeys is taboo in many societies because their appearance is similar to that of humans. Both the Phoenicians and the Jews considered the serpent a channel for evil spirits.

In ancient Egypt, animals were worshipped and cared for as vessels of good or evil powers. Their gods were considered incarnate in particular species, which were then protected by taboo. Like Jews and Moslems, they considered the pig an unclean animal, possibly because of its habit of scavenging. It was thought that if a pig was touched in passing, the person should immediately plunge themself in water for purification. Egyptian swineherds were considered of low caste and were not allowed to enter temples.

The cow is considered sacred in Hindu India, where it is a living symbol of motherhood due to its ability to produce milk. The feeding of the cow is therefore an act of worship. The majority of Hindus are vegetarian, and it is particularly taboo to kill or eat cows. As a result they may commonly be seen wandering the streets undisturbed. Even the urine from a cow is seen as sacred, and is sometimes used in purification rituals for people who have transgressed a taboo.

In societies where animals take on the role of totems, there are taboos against people eating or killing animals to whose totem clans they belong. In identifying with the animal, a person becomes a relative or guardian of the animal. However, another member of the community with a different animal familiar may freely hunt and eat the animal. The Euahlayi people of New South Wales and southern Queensland believe that a child who eats their own animal familiar by accident will become sick: in the case of taboo plains bustard or turkey eggs, this could result in the loss of sight, while eating taboo kangaroo flesh could cause their skin to break out in sores and their limbs to wither. However, while it is taboo for the Euahlayi to eat their animal familiar, it is acceptable to eat the totem animal of their clan.

MENSTRUATION TABOOS

Within patriarchal societies, menstruation has commonly been taboo, both in the ancient and the modern world. However, in matriarchal societies, which revered the female body, menstruation was considered a

powerful and healing process. It has also been associated with great feminine powers. The menstrual cycle and the cycles of the moon were measured in pre-patriarchal times on wooden sticks that historians have called "calendar sticks". One possible origin of the menstruation taboo may be the fear that women could control the tides and seasonal changes through the monthly cycles of their bodies.

The Jews of the ancient world believed that menstrual blood had poisonous qualities. The Old Testament includes a prohibition against contact with it: Leviticus records that Moses received word from God that a man who sleeps with a menstruating woman should be cut off from his people, and that menstruating women are unclean for seven days.

Freud related the menstrual taboo to a negative view of women, whereas Bruno Bettelheim suggested that both the ability to bear children and to menstruate evoked intense envy in men, who created taboos in an attempt to make the sexes more equal. Feminists have called this "womb envy", partly as a protest against Freud's theory that women suffer "penis envy".

POST-PARTUM BLOOD

In many parts of the world the blood that accompanies childbirth has been seen as unclean, perhaps because a woman giving birth, and the new baby, were believed to be in close contact with spirits and other worlds. Some cultures have cleansing rituals for removing the blood.

ABOVE For Hindus it is taboo to kill or eat a cow.

TOP The apple, a Judaeo-Christian forbidden fruit.

GROUP IDENTITY

ABOVE Every detail of a flag is symbolic – its colour, pattern and design, and motifs.

FLEUR-DE-LYS

Most commonly associated with French royalty and the right to rule France, the fleur-de-lys (lily flower) has three petals, standing for both the Holy Trinity and the triple majesty of God, creation and royalty.

Symbolism has always been used to denote identity and to confirm adherence to social groups or "families", the basic units of society. Whether based on shared beliefs or common interests and activities, all organized groups – whether at a local, regional, national or international level – have their own symbols of identity. These may be in the shapes of totems, banners, flags or standards, or expressed through dress codes or through the observance of certain ritualized forms of behaviour. One of the important features of such symbolism is its visibility: it is designed to provide an instantly recognizable sign of group identity, a way of codifying and structuring social relations, of creating a distinction between who's "in" and who's "out", and to stir an emotional response, such as fear, respect, humility or pride, in all who see it.

LEADERSHIP
When people started to form large groups to live and hunt together, a leader was appointed to rule them and settle disputes.

As a mark of office, a leader might wear a ceremonial headdress and hold a long decorated staff, rod or spear, topped with an emblem. The staff was also used as a visible sign to rally around or to point out the direction of a march or attack. These early "flags" are known as vexilloids, and originally were made of wood, feathers and other animal pieces (bones, horns, skins). Aztec vexilloids, for instance, made extensive use of green quetzal feathers, and were decorated with precious metals such as gold, silver and copper, and precious stones. Today tribes in New Guinea use vexilloids that consist mostly of wood and dried grass, with emblems of painted wood, feathers and bits of cloth.

FLAGS
In China the invention of silk fabric led to the creation of banners, which were easier to carry and more visible from a distance than vexilloids. From China, the use of fabric flags spread to Europe, where they were first used as military and ceremonial signs, but later as a

way of identifying rulers, their domains and nationality at sea. The 17th century saw the introduction of standardized regimental colours, war ensigns, jacks (the square flags hoisted up the "jackstaff" on a ship) and the house flags of the trading companies (a precursor of the modern logo). The first national flags on land appeared in the last quarter of the 18th century. During the 19th and 20th centuries, a host of other flags also appeared: of government agencies and officials; provincial flags; rank flags in all branches of the armed forces; and flags of schools, universities, scientific institutions, organizations, political parties, trades unions and guerrilla movements. There are also flags of ethnic groups, business corporations and sporting clubs.

All the elements of a flag are symbolic – its colours, motifs and overall design – and there are many customs surrounding flag etiquette. For instance, in a military parade, flags are saluted when being hoisted, lowered or passed; flying a flag at half-mast is a sign of mourning; a pall flag laid over a coffin, used mainly at government and military funerals, is a symbol of national respect for the deceased; desecrating a flag is a punishable offence in most countries of the world.

TRIBE AND NATION
In traditional societies, clans and tribes have used a variety of symbolic devices to distinguish one group from another. For instance, among many Native

OCCUPATIONS AND PROFESSIONS

For many people, membership of a trade or profession is a symbol of identity, conferring rank and social status through belonging to that particular group. Many traditional occupations can be recognized by generic symbols – for instance a chef's hat, a barber's pole, a pawnbroker's three golden balls, a sailor's anchor – while almost every modern commercial enterprise has its own distinctive company logo. Many professions are also instantly recognizable by their dress codes – the formal uniforms of the armed forces, the blue overalls of a manual worker, the dark suit and tie of a city worker or the white coat of a laboratory technician – while special titles may be used to denote hierarchy within the group, such as doctor, professor, lieutenant, sergeant or chief executive officer (CEO).

Americans totems (natural objects, such as animals) are used to represent particular lodges and tribes, as well as individuals, while each clan of the Scottish Highlanders has its own tartan (a type of checked fabric) design. In medieval heraldry, most European rulers adopted coats of arms and armorial banners bearing one of the two most important heraldic figures: the lion (king of beasts) or the eagle (king of Heaven). The fleur-de-lys, another frequent heraldic motif, was particularly associated with the French court; it was later adopted by the international Boy Scout movement. Today many nations continue to be associated with a particular emblem: for instance, the USA with the bald-headed eagle, Canada with the maple leaf and England with the Tudor Rose.

There are also many nations without statehood (for instance in the USA there are more than 550 federally recognized nations and tribes) who have their own emblem of identity. For instance, eleven Sioux tribes living in South Dakota share a common white flag. The flag's central compass emblem symbolizes the Native

American Medicine Wheel (and the four directions, the four seasons and the four elements) and is surrounded by eleven tepees, representing the number of tribes. There are also many groups within mainstream society who have chosen a symbol to identify themselves. For instance, in the West, the colour pink has been adopted by gay people, black by some racial and political groups, and green by the environmental movement.

POLITICS AND REBELLION

Political groups, rebellions and revolutions have always been associated with particular symbols. At the end of the 15th century, German peasants rebelled under a white pennant with the emblem of a golden peasant shoe, the Bundschuh, which in contrast to the boots worn by the nobility was a symbol of peasantry. Communism and fascism, two of the most influential political movements of the 20th century, also both made use of symbols. The symbol of communism was the hammer and sickle, representing the alliance between

industrial and agricultural workers; for most of the 20th century, the hammer and sickle was the emblem of the Russian flag and the world's first communist state.

Fascism is a nationalist movement led by a dictator. It is named after the "fasces" symbol that was worn as a badge by the Italian dictator Benito Mussolini (1883–1945). The fasces comprised a bundle of birch or elm rods, bound by a red cord, sometimes wrapped around an axe, a symbol of justice, scourging and decapitation. It dates back to ancient Rome, when it was carried by lictors, officials who had the power to pronounce sentence. Hitler, however, used a different symbol for his fascist Nazi party: the swastika.

ABOVE The hammer and sickle is a communist symbol, standing for the union of industrial and agricultural workers.

TOP The word fascism is derived from "fasces", the bundle of rods carried by Roman officials.

TRADITIONAL STORYTELLING

THE ART OF LISTENING

In some South American storytelling traditions, it is said that humans are possessed of a gift of hearing that goes beyond the ordinary. This is the soul's way of paying attention and learning. The story-makers, or cantadoras, of old spun mythical tales of mystery in order to wake up the sleeping soul, wanting it to prick up its ears and tune in to the wisdom contained within the story's telling.

ABOVE The mermaid embodies a deep connection between woman and the sea.

BELOW Noah's Ark, a symbol of man's faith and hope when faced with life-destroying disaster.

From the earliest times, human beings have used stories to describe things they could not explain otherwise. Such stories attempt to answer some of the most fundamental questions about human existence – about why we are here and where we are going, about the nature of the world around us and how we fit into it.

Every culture has formulated its own poetic visions and sacred narratives – the metaphorical understandings that we refer to as myths. The word "myth" is derived from the Greek *mythos*, meaning word or story, but it has come to stand for a narrative that helps to explain the origin and character of a culture in symbolic terms. The meaning and content of such stories will vary across time and place, and from person to person, but one of the functions of myth is to celebrate the ambiguities and contradictions at the heart of human existence.

THE STORYTELLER

Long before myths were written down, they were transmitted by word of mouth. In order to survive the passage of time, they had to be presented as good, memorable stories, appealing to one generation after another, possibly evolving to adapt to new social needs. Storytelling could take place almost anywhere – in the home, in the marketplace or at the royal court – and traditionally the art of storytelling was highly valued, since it was the means by which a culture's social codes and values, its

ancestral lineage and history, and its connection to the divine were kept alive. The storyteller played a vital role in the community, sometimes as an official of a royal or noble court, sometimes as a wandering minstrel who travelled from place to place, delivering stories that were entertaining and instructive. Many religious figures, including Jesus and Mohammed, used storytelling as a vehicle for their teachings.

STORYTELLING RITUALS

The style or protocol of storytelling varies from culture to culture. In many traditional African societies, the audience feels free to interrupt, make criticisms or suggest improved versions to the storyteller. Throughout Africa, a common storytelling form is the "call and response", whereby a "caller" raises a "song" and the chorus in the community participate and respond to the call.

When the San people of the Kalahari tell stories about particular animals, they mimic the formation of the animals' mouths, pronouncing their words as the animals might, as a way of keeping in touch with and honouring the spirit of the animal. Smoking a pipe and passing it from person to person is often a part of storytelling rituals among Native American peoples, such as the Algonquin. According to the Algonquin, "if we cease sharing our stories, our knowledge becomes lost". In many parts of the world today, people are rediscovering the

THE VALKYRIE

In Norse myth, the Valkyries were supernatural women, death angels who hovered over the battlefields granting victory or defeat to warriors. After death, they took the spirits of the valiant slain to Odin's realm of Valhalla.

power of storytelling to make sense of their lives and to keep the connection with their cultural and ancestral lineage alive.

MYTHIC THEMES

Questions about life and death are explored through myth, and stories of the origins and the end of the world can be found in all cultures. Creation myths refer to a primal chaos, symbolized in many cultures as a watery, dark and mysterious place. Myths also anticipate the destruction of the world in a catastrophic event – such as the Norse cataclysm Ragnarok – while many refer to an earlier time when the world was nearly destroyed by a deluge. The Biblical story of Noah is the best-known example; in a similar Mesopotamian tale, Utnapishtim, a wise man who alone survived the flood, was made an immortal.

Typically, myths are tales of divine and semi-divine beings – gods and goddesses, heroes and heroines – archetypal figures who act out the struggle between good and evil, exploring moral conflicts and powerful human emotions such as desire and greed, jealousy and lust, ambition, love and hate. Notions of an underworld and an afterlife, as well as a magical otherworldly realm, are common, and animals with extraordinary powers helping humankind feature in many myths.

ANIMALS IN MYTH

Mythologies from around the world feature animals in one form or another, and they have often been deified. In ancient Egypt, shrines were set up for the worship of sacred beasts such as the Ram of Mendes and the Bull of Apis, while at one time, cobras and vultures were the prime deities of Lower and Upper Egypt respectively. In Africa, particular tribes and chiefs trace their ancestry back to an animal god. For instance, Haile Selassie (the "Lion of Judah"), founding father of the Rastafarian religion and one-time emperor of Ethiopia, traced his lineage back to the powerful god Simba the lion, while some Zulu chiefs claim descent from the python.

Creatures that are half-human and half-animal also appear in many cultures, such as Garuda, the eagle with the body of a man in Hindu mythology, or the centaurs and mermaids of classical myth. The hybrid man-horse centaur has been used to symbolize man trapped by his own sensual impulses, especially lust and violence.

In the stories of many other cultures, animals and humans enjoy a more symbiotic relationship: in Native American myths, animals are often addressed as "brother", while in the Arctic regions, there is a spiritual relationship between humans and the animals that are vital for the community's survival.

Animals sometimes appear as trickster figures in traditional stories; Coyote is the trickster god of the Native Americans and can change his form at will, while African stories feature Hare (Brer Rabbit in America) and Anansi, the spider. Such characters break the rules of nature, or the gods, though usually with positive results, and perhaps represent the irrepressibility and inventiveness of the human spirit.

MODELS OF SOCIETY

Mythology often reinforces and justifies relations of power and leadership. Typically this is explored through a pantheon with a hierarchical structure: a supreme god and/or goddess at the head (often associated with the heavens and the earth) followed by a host of greater and lesser deities. This structure follows that adopted by the human society. In China, for instance, Heaven was visualized as a bureaucracy, maintaining law and order in the same way as the imperial administration. In Japan, the tale of Izanagi and Izanami

ABOVE Odysseus's epic journey symbolizes individual endeavour, but also stands as a metaphor for the cycle of life.

ABOVE Centaurs are used to symbolize lust: the trap of animal sexual impulse.

ABOVE The cobra has a protective aspect in myth and sacred tradition.

ABOVE In some Native American traditions, the coyote is associated with evil, winter and death.

LEFT In Greek myth, a siren is a demonic figure, part woman part fish, which uses its song to enchant sailors and lure them to their death.

bad luck) – while rivalry between the gods is evident in Norse myth. In all these stories the gods exhibit character traits and behaviour that are entirely representative of human nature.

Veneration of the ancestors is an important part of the structure of many traditional societies, and thus features prominently in their mythologies; in Australian Aboriginal mythology, for example, it is the ancestors of the Dreamtime who are said to have shaped the landscape and determined the entire nature of the animal and human world.

HEROIC FIGURES

The exploits and journeys of heroic figures are frequently the subject of myth. Many owe their superhuman powers to some divine connection: Kintaro, the warrior hero of Japanese myth, was the son of a mountain spirit; Rama, in the Hindu epic the Ramayana, was an incarnation of the god Vishnu, while Heracles,

perhaps the greatest of the Greek heroes, was the son of Zeus. Through their actions and their personal qualities – such as bravery, persistence, patience and unconditional love – the heroes and heroines of myth offer a pattern on which people can model themselves.

Some myths show how humans can aspire to the divine: in China, Taoist myths of the Eight Immortals describe how, through their piety and devotion, the Immortals manage to earn everlasting life in Heaven; while Heracles, through his famous twelve labours (tasks given him as punishment for an early crime), became the only Greek hero to achieve immortality.

The medieval Celtic myth of King Arthur and his Knights of the Round Table was centred on the quest for the Holy Grail, said

BELOW The exploits of the divine hero, Rama and his wife Sita (an incarnation of Lakshmi) are told in the Ramayana.

CELTIC BARD

Responsibility for passing on Celtic tribal history, legend and folklore lay with the bard. The earliest bards on record include Aneirin and Taliesin from the 6th century AD. Stories were presented in the form of poems and songs as well as narratives, and the bard's skill was highly valued, in particular a quality called *hwyl* in Welsh – the passion that could inspire an audience. Today the Celtic bardic tradition is continued at Welsh cultural festivals called *eisteddfodau*.

(the first man and woman) served to justify women's alleged inferiority to men, although there are hints that originally Japan may have been organized on a matriarchal lineage, with the imperial family claiming descent from the sun goddess Amaterasu right up until the end of World War II in 1945.

The relationship of deities to one another is explained in human terms of kinship, love and hatred, competition and influence, with each deity responsible for a particular area of human life – fertility, childbirth, love and relationship, war and conflict, the arts, wealth and prosperity. Many stories of Greco-Roman myth concern the interactions of the gods – with humans often used as pawns in their power games (explaining the apparent randomness of good and

to be the chalice used by Christ at the Last Supper, or used to catch his blood at the Crucifixion (though it also had pre-Christian roots, in the Celtic theme of the magic cauldron). The Grail became a symbol of immortality and perfection, attainable only through great virtue.

Many heroic figures are also "culture heroes", the discoverers of secrets of nature or of the ideas and inventions on which a civilization depends. Examples include the Greek Prometheus, who stole fire from the gods and gave it to humans, and the Polynesian Maui, who "fished up" land from the ocean and stole fire from the underworld.

DANGEROUS WOMEN

Women in myth are often bad, dangerous or demonic, either because of their curiosity and disobedience or because of their beauty or magic powers. In Greek myth, Pandora disobeys the gods and opens a box that unleashes sickness and evil into the world, just as in the Judaeo-Christian tradition, Eve disobeys God and is held responsible for humans' expulsion from paradise. The Sirens of Greek myth, sea monsters with an insatiable appetite for blood, lured sailors to their death by shape-changing into beautiful maidens, while in China, demon spirits associated with violent death were also apt to disguise themselves as beautiful girls. In India, it was said that the true character of a rakshasi (female demon) could be recognized by the way her feet pointed backwards.

RIGHT As punishment for giving the divine energy of fire to humans, Zeus bound Prometheus to a rock for eternity.

MODERN MYTH-MAKING

The myths of the ancient storytellers continue to resonate in modern times because they symbolize aspects of human nature and interaction that remain relevant to us, and they are constantly being reworked and adapted in art, literature and popular culture.

Although the tradition of storytelling as a formal way of preserving group culture and myth has largely died out in the West, many people still use photograph albums and scrapbooks to record important life events through pictures and words. Psychologists now recognize this as therapeutic for people who have lost direct access to their past through their families, such as adopted children or survivors of traumatic events.

THE HERO GILGAMESH

The epic of Gilgamesh is one of the earliest known hero myths and contains many archetypal motifs. Gilgamesh, King of Uruk in Mesopotamia, was part-human, part-god. He was becoming so arrogant that the gods created the warrior Enkidu to challenge him. After fighting, the two men became close friends and together defeated the monster Humbaba. Impressed by his courage and manly beauty, the goddess Inanna desired Gilgamesh as her lover. When he spurned her, she exacted her revenge by sending the Bull of Heaven to terrorize Uruk, but together Enkidu and Gilgamesh struck it dead. The gods demanded that one of the heroes must pay with his life for the slaughter of the bull, and Enkidu died. Distraught, Gilgamesh set out on a journey to try to learn why men must die. He travelled to the underworld and was carried over the bitter waters of death by Urshanabi, ferryman of the gods. In the underworld he met Utnapishtim, the immortal ancestor of humankind and the only man to have survived the great flood, who told him that like sleep, death comes to us all and is not to be feared. On his way home, Gilgamesh found a plant that could restore youth, but as he stopped to drink at a pool, a snake ate the plant. This is why snakes shed their skins and become young again, while men age and die. Gilgamesh returned home sadly to tell his story to his people, forced to resign himself to acceptance of his fate. His story encapsulates the timeless themes of human ambition, attachment and loss, the restless questioning of existence and its purpose, and the inevitability of death.

ART

ABOVE Masks are a feature of tribal art, linked with ritual practices and carrying many layers of symbolic meaning.

ABOVE TOP The Venus of Willendorf, prehistoric Mother goddess.

RIGHT Chinese art contains many symbolic items, much of it linking landscape to the human body or offering spiritual or moral messages.

Since the earliest times, many of humanity's most profound and enduring symbols have been recorded through art. Whether the cave paintings, sculptures and artefacts of tribal art, the highly elaborate creations of the European Renaissance, or movements such as Surrealism, symbols in art have been used in a variety of different ways to express the beliefs and preoccupations of the day. For whether consciously executed or not, it has always been the role of the artist to act as instrument and spokesperson for the spirit of their age, giving form to the nature and values of the time.

TRIBAL ART

The carvings, paintings and compositions of the indigenous peoples of Africa, America, Australia and Oceania have little in common except that they all evolved – like nearly all major artistic forms – in intimate association with religion and magic. Seldom decorative in intention, they are expressions of humanity's common endeavour to live in harmony with, or to control, natural and supernatural forces. Take for instance Easter Island's monolithic heads and half-length figures, sculptures up to 18m (60ft) high that were carved over a long time period (AD 900–1500). These are thought to symbolize the power that throughout Polynesia, ruling chiefs were believed to inherit from the gods and retain after death, when they themselves were deified. Carved and painted wooden masks are a feature of

both African and North American cultures. Some have life-like human faces, others incorporate animal forms, many are mainly animal. Often these are linked with shamanic practices, designed to transform the wearer and connect them to the magic power of the spirit-world, and are used in ritual and ceremony.

Australian Aboriginal art has remained visible at sacred sites over the millennia and has a continuity of tradition, using the surface of the earth, rocks, caves and tree bark as well as the human body to express a world view in which there is no distinction between the secular and the sacred, the natural and the supernatural, past and present, or even the visible and the invisible.

RELIGIOUS SYMBOLISM

The intimate relationship between religion and symbolism is expressed in the art and artefacts of all civilizations. In prehistory, the iconic Venus of Willendorf, a limestone statuette of a

full-breasted nude (c. 24,000–22,000 BC), is believed to be at once a fertility symbol and an archetype of the Great Mother. Other figurines from this period, having similarly exaggerated sexual characteristics, have led to speculation that these early European hunter societies had a matriarchal sacred tradition, venerating the Mother archetype of the Great Goddess.

Thousands of years later in ancient Egypt, funerary art reveals preoccupations with the afterlife, while in medieval Europe, narrative paintings with a multi-layered symbolism were used to instruct the illiterate masses in the Christian Scriptures and to spell out people's relationship with God and the cosmos. Islamic art is non-figurative – representation of living creatures is forbidden, since this would mean representing an aspect of Allah, which is beyond human capability. The art is therefore characterized by repeating geometric patterns and designs. Its only specifically religious

RIGHT The works of Max Ernst, like those of his fellow surrealists, is full of Freudian sexual symbolism.

elements are its Qur'anic inscriptions, a reminder to the faithful that Allah is ever present and supersedes anything created by humans. Conversely, in both Buddhism and Hinduism, an emphasis is placed upon the visual power of symbols to elevate consciousness, and figurative symbolism appears in both traditions. Though the Buddha said he did not want to be worshipped, and early Buddhist art confined itself to representations of his footprint (to symbolize his presence) and of the wheel as a symbol of his teachings, people's desire for an image of the Buddha himself soon took over. One of the most impressive examples (dating from the 5th century AD) is a colossal carving, nearly 14m (45ft) high, cut into the cliff-face at the Longmen cave at Yungang, China, the site of a rock-cut temple.

CHINESE TRADITIONS

Highly stylized forms of symbolic expression are characteristic of Chinese art, which has always sought to inspire and educate the viewer, providing insights into the relationship between humans and the divine. Spiritual and moral messages were conveyed through certain set themes, particularly landscapes and the natural world. For instance, every part of the landscape was believed to symbolize an aspect of being human: water was blood, trees and grass were hair, clouds and mists were clothing, and a solitary wandering scholar was the soul. Bamboo, which can be bent without breaking, represented the

spirit of the scholar, while jade stood for purity. Japanese art also draws on nature for its symbolism: cherry blossom is a frequent motif, a herald of spring and token of good luck, and because of its transience a symbol of mortality.

THE RENAISSANCE

Beginning in 14th-century Italy, the Renaissance (French: "rebirth") represented a renewed interest in the art, architecture and literature of ancient Greece and Rome. Many artists looked to nature, the human body and Greco-Roman mythology for inspiration. For instance, the painting *Primavera* ("Spring") by Sandro Botticelli (1445–1510) recounts the story of the nymph Chloris, pursued by Zephyr, god of the wind, who transforms her into Flora, goddess of spring. At the centre of the painting is the goddess Venus, symbol of the season's fertility, while spring itself is also a metaphor for the Renaissance period, the return of an appreciation for the arts, science and learning.

Biblical themes were also invested with classical symbolism; for instance, in his painting *The Last Judgement*, Michelangelo (1475–1564) glorifies Christ as resplendent Apollo, the Greek sun-god, rather than portraying him as a crucified and suffering saviour. Raphael (1483–1520), who was commissioned to decorate the Vatican, combines the more traditional symbolism of God as a grey-bearded patriarch with mythical satyrs and nymphs in his Loggia.

SURREALISM

Beginning as a literary movement, Surrealism was strongly influenced by Freud's ideas about sexuality, free association, dreams and the subconscious. Sexual symbolism – phallic noses, pubic hair in unexpected places – pervades Surrealist imagery, as painters such as Max Ernst (1891 –1976), René Magritte (1898– 1967) and Salvador Dali (1904–89) tried to represent and liberate the workings of the irrational, subconscious mind, challenging the conventions of artistic Realism and polite society. Magritte intentionally mislabelled his paintings, Ernst created strange landscapes inhabited by extraordinary animals and organic forms, while Dali built up a new language of symbolic imagery of melting watches, spindle-legged creatures, flowers hatching out of eggs and other bizarre images.

POP ART

Emerging in Britain and the United States during the mid-20th century, pop art used the imagery of commercial art and other mass media sources. With a background in commercial art, Andy Warhol (1928–97) represented pop art at its most extreme and subversive, praising mechanical repetition and making a cult of the banal and superficial. His poster style paintings, which repeat the same image over and over again, can be viewed as powerful symbols of our modern consumer society.

ADVERTISING

ABOVE Steve McQueen in *Bullitt* with his 1968 Ford Mustang. Both the man and the car became icons representing rebellious male power.

BELOW Sexual imagery has long been used to sell products. Images of women as sex symbols may be targeted at both men and women, as epitomized in this advertisement for a bra.

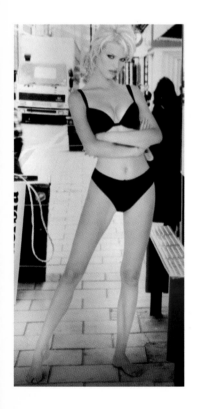

Using the powers of persuasion to promote a product is an ancient practice. The symbolism used to persuade or influence people must appeal to the central concerns and beliefs of the consumer. In the modern advertising industry, successful advertisers relate to what people consciously or unconsciously respond to or want to be associated with, and design and package products to ride trends in cultural and personal taste.

While the intrinsic quality of the product and the good reputation of its manufacturer were central factors in early marketing, large-scale mass-production and international trade have distanced the consumer from the product and the producer, and advertising has stepped in to fill the gap, becoming a role and an industry in its own right. Most modern advertising is aimed at promoting an entire brand rather than an individual product, creating a sense of allegiance in its customers by matching its image to them through symbolism.

PSYCHOLOGY IN ADVERTISING

Freudian psychology influenced 20th-century advertising with its ideas about unconscious desires. Advertisers began to use "subliminal persuasion" and "symbolic association" to such a degree that the image or brand name became more important than the product. The car is no longer merely a form of transport: while it is designed to be streamlined and functional, it is also enhanced with feminine curves or phallic frontage to appeal to its potential male buyers. It is advertised as a symbol of status and lifestyle.

In the 1920s Freud's nephew, Edward Bernays, used his uncle's ideas for the manipulation of American public opinion, and is often called "the father of public relations". He showed corporations how they could match people's unconscious desires to their products and turned consumer items into lifestyle symbols: for instance, in a famous stunt of 1929 for the American Tobacco Company, he hired models to parade through the streets of New York, smoking, under the banner of "the torch of freedom". By linking smoking with the drive towards women's liberation, he effectively broke the taboo against American women smoking in public.

SEX IN ADVERTISING

The saying that "sex sells" is equally true of any other imagery that appeals to human emotions, such as the use of people's instinctive response to babies to sell a product. But sexuality is probably the most commonly used "attractor", and is widely used in marketing, both subtly and blatantly. Most advertising uses conventional sex symbols, depicting women as objects of lust and men as dominant.

Both the film and advertising industries continually explore and push the limits of sexual explicitness. Sexual imagery generates the greatest impact, inducing excitement and outrage, when it tugs on the morals and taboos of a given culture.

ADVERTISING AND CINEMATIC INTERFACE

The worlds of advertising and film use symbolism to evoke powerful emotions appealing to the popular culture of the time. These two industries borrow strongly from one another in their use of symbolism and genre: films are used to sell fashion items through product placement, and movie icons are used in advertisements, so that sometimes there seems little difference between the two.

A good example of the interplay of film and advertising is the 1968 film *Bullitt*, which some say starred both Steve McQueen and the 1968 Ford Mustang, both symbols of urban rebellion, toughness and male power. In the 2000s the original footage was cleverly remixed for an advertisement for Ford, creating the illusion of McQueen driving the latest model of the Ford Puma. Thirty years on, the actor's iconic image still had the power to sell a car.

THE CAR – A SYMBOL OF THE INDUSTRIAL AGE

Himself an icon of the industrial age, Henry Ford used mass-production methods to make cars that would not be restricted to a wealthy elite. General Motors overtook the success of Ford when their cars became symbols of the "Roaring Twenties", and were designed and sold as representing the new-found liberation, sexual freedom and self-expression of the "Jazz Age".

During the 1930s depression in the United States, closed cars or sedans conveyed a sober and puritanical image. But this period was soon followed by an explosion of car sales and competition, with the post-war car being sold as a symbol of the "American dream". Advertising now portrayed cars as dream-mobiles, inviting potential owners to fulfil their desires for sex, speed, power, wealth and status.

To this day, cars occupy what Arnold Mindell might call the timespirit of progressiveness and success. Modern car designs and advertising are beginning to play with less gender-stereotyped symbolism, in which androgyny, and the blurring of sexual roles, are explored. Where previously advertising for cars was directed only at men, it is now aimed at both men and women.

CORPORATE IMAGE

A company or business image is considered of great importance in modern marketing. Corporate identity is often expressed symbolically through logos and corporate style, relating to the

"raison d'être" of the organization and to the impression it wishes to give to the outside world. Many apparently modern logos in fact have their roots in ancient symbolism. Tripartite symbols, for instance, which represent harmony and perfection, are used by companies such as Mitsubishi and Mercedes Benz. The ancient solar cross (an equal-armed cross within a circle) appears on the badges of Fiat and BMW. The golden arches of McDonald's can be interpreted as a giant M, but also match the ancient alchemical sign for fire.

Branding aims to identify the product with producers who can be trusted. Studies of corporate personality have shown the effectiveness of bright bands of colour when used as a part of the brand's image. One such colourful logo is that of Esso/Exxon, which also uses a tiger as a kind of company mascot – its famous slogan, "Put a Tiger In Your Tank", invited the consumer to identify with the power and beauty of the animal.

Company and brand names have significant impact on consumers faced with a market saturated with competing products. Each year the Chairman of the Board of Sony reinforces to staff the idea that the four letters S, O, N and Y are the company's most valuable asset, and that their actions must increase their value.

COUNTRY-SPECIFIC SYMBOLISM

Some widely used symbols and phrases have different meanings in different parts of the world, and the use of specific imagery or symbolism in many cultures can cause problems for global advertisers. In the West the colour green may mean "go" or can be associated with nature, whereas in other parts of the world it relates to danger and has a negative meaning. In China the colour red relates to happiness, good fortune and weddings, whereas in the West it is associated with danger, sexuality, or the command to "stop". One American company used the symbol of an owl to advertise a product in India, only to discover that the owl in India was a symbol of bad luck.

INTERNATIONAL ADVERTISING

The expansion of global markets has led to new challenges for international advertising, most of which relate to the meaning and values being communicated. One problem is the predominance of Western values and ideals depicted in adverts, which can both influence and offend other cultures. Countries with different moral or religious views often find the images of Western advertising sexually explicit, or disapprove of the roles played by women, and so the advertising may be experienced as subversive.

RIGHT The logo of McDonalds is an adaptation of the alchemical sign for fire, shown beneath.

BELOW In the 1920s car manufacturers presented their products as symbols of wealth, liberation and self-expression.

ABOVE Fiat's logo makes use of the ancient symbol of the sun cross.

TOP The tripartite Mitsubishi logo.

SYMBOLISM AND SCIENCE

THE CLOCK

Since it is closely related to modern concepts of control, productivity and autonomy, the clock is an important functional symbol of the machine age. In the 17th and 18th centuries clocks became sufficiently accurate to measure minutes and seconds, and during this period people shifted away from being guided by the symbolism and rhythms of nature, instead becoming ruled by the clock. The Jungian therapist Marie-Louise von Franz (1915–89) described the clock in post-Cartesian times as coming to symbolize a soulless universe.

BELOW The Copernican view of the universe.

Signs, symbols and symbolism play an important part in scientific research and the development of scientific theories. Scientific concepts are rooted in contemporary or emerging beliefs about nature, "symbolic models" or "paradigms" (patterns) that underlie and inform the development of understanding. Scientific dilemmas are often resolved through creative or irrational processes, even by the symbolism of dreams experienced by the scientific researcher. As science has evolved, so has its language – a shorthand of signs, symbols and formulae that enables scientists to formulate and communicate knowledge.

SCIENTIFIC PARADIGMS AND SYMBOLISM

New scientific eras come about through "paradigm shifts", characterized by a radical shift in the symbolic worldview that eventually shakes up and fundamentally reorganizes the technologies and social and economic structures of the day. When the pioneering chemist Antoine Laurent Lavoisier (1743–94) showed water to be a compound substance made up of different elements he was severely criticized, in particular by the pharmacist Antoine Baumé, for undermining scientific theories based upon the fundamental elements of fire, water, air and earth. Each change in scientific understanding is accompanied by doubts and resistance, and new paradigms inevitably involve radical shifts in the scientific foundations and belief systems of a civilization.

THE SCIENTIFIC REVOLUTION

In the medieval universe, Heaven and earth were seen as two separate realms. Heaven centred on God and was governed by eternal law, while earth and humanity were governed by natural law. Though Heaven was hierarchically superior, earth was considered to be the centre of the universe.

This worldview was overturned by the scientific revolution of the 16th century, which, challenged by the astronomy of Copernicus and observations made with Galileo's telescope, supported the view of a much larger universe centred on the sun, seriously challenging statements made in the Old Testament. The Catholic Church fought back but a new worldview emerged that symbolically removed both humanity and the earth from the centre of things.

THE MACHINE

The French philosopher René Descartes (1596–1650) was a key figure in the transition from medieval to modern scientific thought, proposing an analytic method of searching for scientific truth and accepting only things that are beyond doubt. In the Cartesian era, scientific enquiry favoured mechanistic values of quantity and function over the qualitative values of spirit, aesthetics, feelings, the senses and nature itself, and the machine became a central metaphor.

The steam engine, developed during the 17th and 18th centuries, paved the way for the invention of industrial processes, leading to mass production. The machine became a symbol of power, organization and human control over nature.

THE QUANTUM ERA

During the 20th century a radically new scientific perspective began to emerge, introducing a worldview of tendencies and interdependence: both observer and observed exist in a quantum entanglement, whereby the very act of observation affects the thing being observed. The physicist Werner Heisenberg (1901–76) stated that when we attempt to look objectively at nature and the universe we really encounter ourselves, suggesting that science has an inner and archetypal origin. To explore the relationship between archetypal symbolism and scientific concepts the scientist Wolfgang Pauli (1900–58) examined the deep

RIGHT Galileo's heliocentric universe challenged the symbolic importance of the earth, and he was forced to recant by the Vatican.

archetypal dreams he was experiencing, and he hypothesized a psychophysical unity, which Jung called the *unus mundus,* or "world soul".

DREAMS, SYMBOLISM AND SCIENTIFIC DISCOVERY

What is the connection between symbolism and scientific models? Science itself is not simply a rational process, as there are many examples of scientific discoveries being made through dreams and other irrational processes – such as the Newtonian legend that an apple falling upon Sir Isaac Newton's head led him to an understanding of the force of gravity. It seems that the unconscious can produce symbols that may inform the next step in scientific exploration.

The most famous example is the discovery of the benzene ring in 1865 by the German chemist Friedrich August Kekulé. The properties of benzene could not be explained in terms of linear molecular structures. One evening, dozing in front of the fire, Kekulé dreamed of long rows of atoms "winding and turning like serpents" until one of these serpents caught hold of its tail. On awakening he hypothesized the ring-like structure of benzene, leading to a prolific new period in the development of organic chemistry. At a convention in 1890 Kekulé advised his fellow scientists to "learn to dream" in order to seek the truth.

Also in the mid-19th century, a Russian chemist, Dmitri Mendeleev, dreamed the periodic table of the elements with remarkable accuracy, even predicting the existence of three previously "non-existent" elements, all of which were discovered within 15 years. In the early 20th century, the Danish physicist Niels Bohr, studying the structure of the atom, saw in a dream a nucleus with electrons spinning around it, and for his subsequent work received the Nobel Prize for Physics in 1922. Albert Einstein credited the source of his theory of relativity to a dream he had while at school, in which he rode upon a sled that accelerated to an incredible degree, transforming the stars around him into dazzling light as he approached the speed of light.

SCIENTIFIC SIGNS

In order to communicate, formulate and develop scientific knowledge, a shorthand language of scientific symbols and signs has evolved. The sciences of astronomy, botany, biology, chemistry, nuclear chemistry, physics, geology, mathematics and meteorology have each developed their own shorthand.

The earliest chemical symbols were used by the ancient Greeks, and adopted by Plato, to represent the properties of the four elements: earth, air, fire and water. The alchemists introduced a symbolic language – drawn from astronomy, astrology, cosmology and metallurgy – to depict various elements, including the seven metals. Copper was associated with the element earth. Gold, representing the perfection of matter, was symbolized by the sun. Mercury (or quicksilver), a liquid metal that transcended earth and Heaven, and life and death, was linked with the astrological planet of the same name, or the serpent. Silver was associated with the moon and tin with the planet Jupiter. Iron was represented by the symbol for the planet Mars and lead by that for the planet Saturn.

American astronomers use the symbol of a dashed circle to represent a group of galaxies, while a circle leaning to the right depicts a single galaxy.

MATHEMATICAL SIGNS

In mathematics two parallel lines together mean the same as or equal to (in the same dimension), while a group of three parallel lines shows an equivalence or similarity in identity where there is no real difference. Interestingly this same symbol in meteorology refers to mist, an atmospheric pattern in which everything looks milky-white and loses its identity.

The plus sign (which may have originated as an abbreviated form of the Latin word *et*, meaning "and") came into common use in the 16th century to denote addition. Signs for multiplication and division were introduced in the 17th century.

RIGHT, FROM TOP TO BOTTOM The alchemical signs for copper, gold, silver, mercury, tin, iron and lead.

PART TWO

SYMBOLS WE LIVE BY

From the words on this page to the starry constellations in the night sky, from the image of a god to a sense of the divine, from the winking of an eye to a colourful ritual mask, from the figures in our dreams to the traffic lights at a street junction, signs and symbols are integral to the world in which we live.

The following pages examine the use of symbols in many different aspects of human experience – from the mundane to the sacred, from the temporal to the eternal. There are chapters on symbols in society, in nature, in myth and sacred tradition, and in the human life cycle, as well as abstract symbols. Some of those symbols that have the most complex meanings – such as the cross, the serpent, the rainbow and the wheel – have been singled out and are discussed more fully. Although it is impossible to include here every different nuance, the aim is to give an overview of the range of meanings individual symbols can carry.

RIGHT The standing stone circle of Stonehenge, in England, has carried many different symbolic meanings over the centuries.

Everyday Living

THE SIGNS AND SYMBOLS THAT PERMEATE OUR CULTURE ARE OFTEN DEPENDENT ON OUR HISTORICAL AND SOCIAL CIRCUMSTANCES, BUT THERE ARE OTHERS THAT TRANSCEND CULTURE, AND ARE FAR MORE UNIVERSAL. THIS CHAPTER FOLLOWS THE COMMON THREADS THAT ARE FORMED BY THE SIGNS WE FIND IN OUR EVERYDAY LIVES.

Universal Themes

ABOVE The life-force and energy of nature permeates the "story" of life, in its rising and falling, birth and death.

ABOVE The swastika is an ancient nature symbol with multiple meanings, an example of how a symbol's meaning can shift and adapt. When it is facing anticlockwise it implies being against the currents of nature.

Over time, different cultures have evolved unique symbolic languages in an attempt to express their most powerful ideas, and emotional and spiritual responses to life. Symbolism displays cultural characteristics relating to the historical trends and geographical regions from which it emerges, and evolves in accordance with each culture's underlying core values and individual belief systems.

In spite of cultural differences, however, common themes also seem to underlie the world's rich diversity of symbolic expression. They may be thought of as a "living stream of dreaming" running like an invisible current through the everyday world.

ENERGETIC LIFE FORCE

Since the earliest times, people have described states and fields of energy that permeate and animate the universe. In many cultures, the universe, the Earth, and our bodies are thought to channel subtle energy, or "life force". In India this is called *prana*, in China and Japan it is *chi* or *ki*, in Polynesia it is *mana*, in the Western tradition it is etheric. In alchemy, the life force equates with the philosopher's stone, the *quinta essentia* ("fifth essence") or the "world soul".

Modern science understands that the material world, although it appears dense and solid, is fundamentally made up of energy, with atoms, protons, neutrons, electrons and particles vibrating together at different frequencies. The universe can be conceived of as held together by invisible energetic "glue". The psychologist Carl Gustav Jung saw this force in what he called the "collective unconscious", a giant reservoir of archetypal energy patterns that we tap into and express symbolically – whether in dreams, art, sacred tradition or science. This may help to explain our enduring fascination with symbols, why they appear in every conceivable form and why they have no single, correct definition.

MICROCOSM AND MACROCOSM

Attempts to explain the origins of life and the subsequent relationship between living creatures and the cosmos are two of humankind's most fundamental concerns. They lie at the root of philosophy, religion and science, and a great variety of belief systems and hypotheses have been formulated to provide explanations. A dominant theme is the idea that microcosm and macrocosm exist in parallel, so that the lives of individuals are intimately bound with the cosmos, "as above, so below". This concept existed in the ancient cultures of western Asia and has informed astrology, alchemy, divinatory systems, myth and sacred tradition throughout the world. In particular it dominated the mystical-symbolic thinking of medieval Europe, leading to ideas such as "cosmic man" – a human who embodied all the elements of the universe.

POLARITY AND WHOLENESS

Within a multitude of belief systems, another theme can be picked out: the symbolism of opposition. At almost every level, existence seems to be composed of binary pairs or opposites, such

as sky/earth, man/woman, day/night. In terms of the earth's magnetic energy field, this opposition is expressed as the polarity between positive and negative, attraction and repulsion or ebb and flow. Humans define abstract concepts in a similar fashion, seeing the world in terms of good or bad, success or failure, rich or poor, beautiful or ugly. Some traditions have created from this a moral universe in which one side of the polarity is favoured over the other, with far-reaching political and social implications. For instance, much of civilization has been built on patriarchal values with women's position seen as inferior.

Some traditions, however, while recognizing the pattern of opposites in nature, have seen the value of embracing the whole as an organic unity. This is the meaning of the Chinese yin/yang symbol or the alchemical figure of the androgyne, in which male and female were conjoined in a single body. A similar idea exists in different branches of psychology. In psychoanalytic theory, neurosis occurs when parts of the personality that are considered "bad" or unacceptable are "split off" and rejected. As a model for mental health, all aspects of the psyche need awareness, as they symbolize aspects of our fundamental wholeness.

Symbolism can be used to control and influence human lives, or to help us align ourselves with our deepest nature. Indigenous and aboriginal peoples recognize the importance of a sustainable relationship with nature, reflected in their symbolic world, which is also a living reality. They participate in the whole "web of life", honouring the Earth, sky, sun, moon, ancestors, nature spirits, fairies, animals and plants.

CHANGING SYMBOLISM

Although some symbols retain consistent meaning through cultures and ages, others rise and fall in significance, and their meaning evolves over time. An excellent example of this is how the symbolism of the goat has changed and developed through the centuries. In early Europe the male goat was a positive symbol of procreative power, the libido, fertility and the life force. The goat was particularly sacred to the Greek gods Dionysus and Pan. Pan, half man and half animal, with the horns of a goat, was the god of all things, in particular the procreative force.

In the Old Testament book of Leviticus, however, the goat became a "scapegoat" for the sins of humanity, and was sent into the wilderness, bearing this evil burden. From this point the animal increasingly came to symbolize sexual excess, with its rank smell associated with evil, until by the Middle Ages its characteristics had been attributed to the Devil. The personification of Pan, meanwhile, underwent a corresponding transformation into the goat-headed Satan. The goat has, however, maintained its positive associations around the Mediterranean, where it is viewed as a guardian, with the power to absorb malevolent influences.

DWELLINGS AS SYMBOLS

ABOVE The house is a symbol of the self, and the way we depict it can symbolize aspects of our personality or attitudes.

BELOW Squareness in architecture may symbolize the human desire to impose ourselves on nature.

The physical structures within which we work and live possess both functional and symbolic qualities, and are usually an interweaving of both. Our homes and other buildings are indicators of rank and privilege, archetypal patterns, connection to spirits and ancestors, and our relationship with both community and nature. Homes very often have cosmological significance, mirroring a relationship to the centre while at the same time having a more personal significance for the families or individuals who live in them. The rich symbolism of the home becomes especially important when we examine the part it plays in both psychology and dream interpretation.

THE FIRST HOMES

Caves, trees and earth were important means of shelter for early humans and have provided both the inspiration and the materials for later dwellings. The dwellings of many primitive peoples are suggestive of natural arbours, with walls made from tree trunks and branches, and leaves as roofs. The trunk of the tree provides the structure while the canopy and leaves provide shelter from the elements. When the forest in which they lived was destroyed, the members of an African pygmy tribe became hugely disoriented upon leaving their vertical and horizonless world of the trees to live on the plain, demonstrating how "at home" and psychologically rooted we become in the environment, shelters and structures with which we are familiar.

The hallways and rooms in modern buildings are reminiscent of the networks of chambers in caves. The cave or cavern-like dwelling is like a womb within Mother Earth, and thus is symbolic of birth, rebirth, nurture and creativity. The home as symbolic of "mother" is a universal concept.

As early as 15,000 BC the nomadic hunters of Europe discovered the usefulness of turf and earth for building and insulation. From primitive mud huts, complex designs for earth lodges have developed throughout the world. Building with earth led to the use of clay bricks. The children's story of the three little pigs and the big bad wolf demonstrates how bricks represent security for our domestic (or pig) nature from the force of nature (or the wolf). The third pig stays safe as the wolf huffs and puffs but just can't blow down his brick house. However, while bricks can symbolize permanence and security, they are can also be used as symbols of the repression of nature through human strength and rigidity.

SYMBOLIC PLACEMENT AND ALIGNMENT

How a building or community is sited on the land is considered very important in many cultures. Houses were often built on local sacred sites, and the foundation stone of a house was similar to the omphalos, or "navel stone", of a temple – the central holy object that allowed communication with the gods. An old building tradition in Ireland involved the lighting of the "needfire" by rubbing together two of the first construction timbers in the shape of Brigit's cross. The needfire was the hearth around which the rest of the house would be focused.

Hunters and gatherers traditionally aligned their houses and communities by visualizing their territory as representing a cosmic creator or original ancestor in anthropomorphic form. The mud houses and towns of the Dogon people, who live on the Niger river at Timbuktu, are arranged according to cosmological and anthropomorphic principles. Their villages are built in pairs, signifying the relationship between Heaven and Earth. The Dogon believe that when they die they go to a paradise that is identical to their homes in life.

In China, where the art of feng shui is practised, the "bagua" is a template for buildings, with eight "guas" surrounding the centre. Each of its zones corresponds to

an area of life: prosperity, fame and reputation, relationship, family, health, creativity and children, knowledge and skills, work, and helpers. The dwelling needs to be designed in a proper relationship to the four directions, in such a way that chi flows freely through the different zones for the wellbeing of the inhabitants.

In India, *vasta purusa* is the spirit of the house, described as a tightly coiled male body. To ensure good fortune, the house must be aligned with his body in such a way that his head, heart and limbs are not disturbed.

The Mongol yurt is a microcosmic representation of the macrocosm, with the sacred hearth on the square earth, the circular roof as the sky, and the smoke-hole in the roof as the eye of Heaven through which comes the light of the sun. The yurt is divided into living quadrants, each relating to the roles of the family or community.

The book *A Pattern Language*, by Christopher Alexander, Sara Ishikawa and Murray Silverstein (1977), describes patterns common to many buildings and towns throughout the world. The authors spent years attempting to formulate a language of patterns that when lived in, are conducive to the well-being of individuals, families and community. They feel that many of these patterns are archetypal in nature, connecting humanity with the essential nature of things. An example is

the alcove, or smaller space within a room, which enables a family to be together while at the same time being involved in different activities; this is an archetypal pattern as relevant to the yurt-dweller as to those who live in a castle.

THE SYMBOLIC VALUE OF THE HOME

Psychologists often view the house as symbolic of a person's inner being, so that when a client draws a house, or describes a dream about a part of it, they are describing their psychic structure. The outside of the house can be seen as representing their outer personality, with the windows and doors showing their relationship to others and the world.

Attics and basements are places where the light of consciousness does not shine. They can symbolize spiritual elevation and the unconscious. In his autobiography, C.G. Jung described going to the basement of a building where he discovered a primitive part of himself. The foundations of a house can symbolize our relationship to the collective unconscious, our ancient beginnings and the non-human realms.

The kitchen, where things are cooked, is a place of alchemical transformation where nurturing takes place, so it may have associations with good or poor parenting. In the hearth or fireplace, glowing embers or

flickering flames are the source of life and dreaming, and may also refer to the spark of imagination or genius. Almost every culture has valued the hearth as the heart of the home, though in modern times it seems to have been replaced by the television set, which also glows and flickers with symbolic stories.

The significance of bedrooms depends upon their occupants. A child's room may represent a place of play or fantasy, while adult bedrooms may point towards sexuality and a person's relationship to sex.

As with all psychological interpretations there is never really any fixed meaning to any of these symbols. What is most important in determining the significance of aspects of the home is the individual's associations with those areas. For example, two people may visualize the front doors of their houses closed. If the first person has always lived in houses where the front door stood open and people were always welcome, whereas the second has lived in houses where the back door was the place of relationship, and the front door was always closed, these similar images need to be interepreted differently. Similar differences in interpreting the same symbols will occur in dream analysis, where the meaning of each home-based image will depend on the person who has dreamed it.

ABOVE Mongolian yurts are circular dwellings constructed from wood and felt, serving both as nomadic homes and symbols of the cosmos.

ABOVE LEFT The Dogon village is an earth-bound representation of what the Dogon people believe paradise to look like.

ABOVE Tree-houses symbolize a relationship between humans and nature, and offer spaces in which children can free their imagination.

BELOW In modern times the television has replaced the hearth as a source of focus and symbolism for the family.

THE GATEWAY

RIGHT The entrance to this cave in Bali is a monster's mouth with guardian statues protecting the threshold.

There are many symbols of transition, but the gateway or door is an archetypal motif that represents an entrance to another world (a room, a city, a palace, a temple, a social institution) or another state of being that may be either heavenly or hellish, a paradise or a prison. To pass through a gateway is to cross a threshold, to move from the known to the unknown. Gateways may be open but are often closed and guarded, so that the traveller needs a key or password, or must undergo a test, in order to pass through. Hence gateways are also a symbol of initiation: typically there may be a series of gates or worlds to be negotiated, each one leading to greater wisdom, before the ultimate state of bliss is reached.

HEAVEN AND HELL

There are many examples in religion of Heaven and Hell being entered through a gateway or door. In Judaism, for instance, it is believed that there is one gate to the Garden of Eden (a symbol of paradise), but 40,000 to Hell, showing how much more difficult it is to find and enter Heaven. For Christians, Jesus is the entrance to salvation: "I am the door: by me if any man enter in, he shall be saved." (John 10:9). In Muslim tradition, different levels of paradise are reached through a series of gates, with 100 steps leading up to each level before the ultimate seventh heaven is attained. One teaching states that the key to these gates has three prongs: proclamation of Allah's oneness, obedience to Allah and abstinence from evildoing.

BIRTH AND DEATH

Doorways are often associated with death and also with rebirth. In ancient Egypt, the sun god Ra travelled through the underworld each night, passing through 12 gates representing the 12 hours of darkness before being reborn each morning. Ancient Egyptian coffins were sometimes painted with a small false door, symbolically allowing the *ha* (soul) to fly through. In ancient Rome the dead were often depicted in art as standing in front of half-open doors. The Hebrew word for "door" – *daleth* – also means "womb", the gateway of life.

GUARDIANS

Both good and evil influences can pass through a gateway, so guardians or protective deities may be assigned to oversee them. The gates of Chinese cities were set at the four compass points, watched over by fierce lions who attracted good but repelled evil influences, while the entrances to Babylonian and Assyrian palaces were guarded by gigantic winged lion-man sculptures called *lamassu*. In Asian temples, warrior figures called *dvarapala* performed the same function. Cerberus, the three-headed dog of Greek myth, guards the gates of Hades (the underworld of Greek legend), and his secondary function is to make sure that once admitted no one ever leaves.

In ancient Rome every section of a doorway was guarded by numina (minor deities); the god Forculus oversaw the door's panels, for instance, while the goddess Cardea looked after its hinges. The two-faced god Janus (see box) was the chief deity of

BELOW In myth and story, a small or hidden doorway can represent a secret entrance to a magical otherworld.

the gate. In China, it is the custom to paste images of the two Door Gods on the house door on New Year's eve, then lock it until midnight so that no evil spirits can enter, while in Japan *kadomatsu* – decorations made from the boughs of evergreen trees – are placed at the entrance to attract the gods and bring good luck. A similar tradition, linked to pagan customs, is practised in the West, where holly wreaths or bunches of mistletoe are put on front doors during the Christmas and New Year holiday: holly is associated with protection and good fortune, and mistletoe with magic and medicine – it was a symbol of immortality for the Celtic druids.

A cave mouth in Chalcatzingo, Mexico, has a monster's face carved around it, symbolizing the protection of the entrance as well as the transition from one world to another. In the Hindu tradition, a gateway also sometimes takes the form of a monster's mouth through which one must pass when travelling from life to death.

GATEWAYS OF VICTORY

Sometimes gateways are used as symbols of victory and power, both temporal and spiritual. For instance, the Ishtar Gate in ancient Babylonia (in modern Iraq) was built to glorify both the mother-goddess Ishtar and the great city of Babylon. It straddled the Processional Way, and provided an entrance to the city, which had walls so thick that two chariots could drive side by side along the top. In Beijing, the gates

RIGHT The Tori Gate is the largest Shinto *tori* in Japan. A tori is an open gateway symbolizing the transition from mundane to holy.

of the Forbidden City represented the Chinese emperor's might, while the triumphal arches of ancient Rome embodied national and political power. More recently, Napoleon (1769–1821), who emulated Roman imperialism when he became emperor of France, began the construction of the Arc de Triomphe in Paris, in anticipation of a victory that never happened. Subsequently the arch became a war memorial dedicated to the soldiers killed in World War I (1914–18).

HIDDEN DOORWAYS

Gateways do not always have to be large and ornate to be significant. Sometimes small or hidden doorways provide access to other, often magical worlds. The entrance to Wonderland in Lewis Carroll's Alice stories (1832 –98) is first down a rabbit hole and then through a tiny door, which Alice cannot get through until she shrinks. In *The Lion, the Witch and the Wardrobe* by C. S. Lewis (1899–1963) the gateway to the magic land is through a wardrobe. Many enchanted gardens of European folklore are reached through tiny gates that are often obscured; for instance, in the tale of Sleeping Beauty the

entrance to the palace where the princess sleeps is overgrown by briars, which the hero-prince must cut through to reach her.

OPEN OR CLOSED DOORS

In Japan open archways known as *tori* mark the entrance to Shinto shrines. They represent a divine state of perpetual openness, and symbolize the point at which a visitor passes from the everyday world to the sacred. In Chinese tradition, an open door is thought of as active, or yang, and a closed door as passive, or yin. The opening and closing of a door represents the cosmic dance between yin and yang, where first one and then the other holds sway. In Taoism, the opening and closing of the Gates of Heaven are related to human respiration, so that holding the breath equates with shutting the doors, and breathing with opening them.

KEYS

In Japan, the key is a symbol of happiness because it opens up the door to the rice pantry, symbolic of the source of life. In the Christian tradition St Peter is often depicted with the keys to Heaven. The Church adopted keys as symbols of authority: the papal coat of arms shows two keys, one silver, one gold, previously emblems of the Roman god Janus.

SEXUAL SYMBOLISM

The vulva can also be likened to a gateway, as it is both the passageway into life at birth, and the entrance to the vagina during coitus. In Eastern traditions such as Taoism and Tantra, sexual union is itself a gateway of transcendence, through which it is possible to achieve an altered state of consciousness and experience the "bliss body". The mythical Yellow Emperor, Huang-tsi, one of the Eight Taoist Immortals, ascended to Heaven on the back of a dragon partly because of his skill in the art of loving, while early Chinese "bedchamber books" refer to the penis as the jade stalk and the vagina as the jade gateway, jade being the stone of Heaven and a symbol of perfection and immortality.

TRAVELLING AND JOURNEYS

ABOVE A winding road symbolizes the twists and turns of the pathway through life.

ABOVE In myth and story, shoes can possess magical properties, enabling the traveller to cross great distances speedily and safely.

BELOW The chariot is a solar symbol and as such is used as the vehicle of gods, kings and warriors in many traditions.

Journeys symbolize quests for personal advancement, either material or spiritual, or both. To travel is to tread the (potentially hazardous) path through life in which the ultimate destination is not death but spiritual enlightenment, mythically embodied as a promised land (such as the Isles of the Immortals in Chinese tales or religious sites of pilgrimage) or a precious object with special powers (such as the Holy Grail or the Golden Fleece). Sometimes journeys are subterranean, symbolizing entry into the underworld, and sometimes through the air, suggesting spiritual aspiration.

THE TRAVELLER

Boots or shoes are a symbol of the traveller. The might of the Roman army was built on walking power, symbolized by the soldier's boot. Many stories of Western folklore involve "seven-league boots" that magically enable the traveller to cover great distances at great speed without becoming tired, while Hermes the Greek god of travel wore winged sandals. In

many cultures charms and talismans are carried on a journey for luck and protection, and the traveller is wished "good speed" (or "God speed").

THE HORSE

The animal that is the most archetypal symbol of travel is probably the horse. In Celtic culture, white horses were sacred and drew the chariots of priests and kings. They were associated with the goddess Epona, one of the few Celtic deities to be worshipped by the Romans. In the 16th century, Europeans introduced the horse to North America (though it may have existed there previously and died out), and its arrival had a profound effect on many native tribes. For them, horses became associated with thunder because of the sound of their running hooves, and the horse became a symbol of wealth and power.

Horses feature in many myths of otherworldly transport, often pulling the chariots of the gods, and are endowed with mythical characteristics. Slepnir, the mount of the Norse god Odin, has eight legs, while in Greek myth Pegasus has wings and pulls the chariot that brings Zeus his thunder and lightning. Mohammed is said to have ascended to Heaven riding on the hybrid creature Borak (whose name means "lightning"), a winged horse with a human head and a peacock's tail.

THE CHARIOT

Chariots, or "triumphal cars", are the carriers of rulers and gods – in Renaissance art they are shown

carrying deities such as Venus, Jupiter and Mars. Chariots symbolize the power to lead and vanquish and are often associated with warfare: the Celtic battle leader, Boudicca, is usually depicted in her chariot, while the Achaemenids, the rulers of ancient Persia, are described as going into battle accompanied by the chariot of the supreme god, Ahura Mazda, drawn by eight white horses. The chariots of Indian deities, sometimes lotus-shaped, are drawn by different animals, such as horses for Agni and Surya, and geese for Brahma. The English word "juggernaut" is derived from the massive chariot of the Hindu god Jagganath.

TRAVEL BY WATER

Sailing ships, boats and canoes are all used to symbolize the journey through life. In ancient Egypt, sails symbolized wind and breath, representing the fickle "winds of fate" that can blow a traveller off course. In Egypt, and later in Rome, a new ship was sacrificed each year to ensure fair winds and calm seas: inscribed with holy words, laden with perfumes and baskets of flowers, it was launched into the sea for the winds to take it.

Voyages across water are frequently associated with death and transformation, and symbolic ships of the dead are common to many civilizations. In Indonesia, the dead are exposed in canoes, and in ritual practice the shaman uses a boat to "travel through the air" in search of his patient's soul. In ancient Egypt, the sun god Ra travelled through the underworld

ABOVE Boats can symbolize death, and in ancient Egypt were believed to carry the souls of the dead.

and across the sky in the "boat of a million years", while in China and Japan, paper boats are used as conveyances for spirits. Hindus use miniature flame-carrying boats symbolically to carry solar energy or prayers.

There are also many accounts of heroic journeys in ships such as the Argos, in which Jason searched for the Golden Fleece, or the Pridwen, taken by King Arthur and his men on their journey to the underworld. The sea represents the perils of the unknown, and apart from the danger of shipwreck the journey may bring encounters with mythical beasts such as sea monsters or demons.

For island peoples, boats are particularly important. For instance, Maori war canoes are said to bestow mana (prestige) on all those who own or sail in them, an idea similar to one held by the Vikings. Sea vessels are also symbolic containers and emblems of security: in Judaeo-Christian belief it is Noah's ark that preserves humanity against disaster by saving a breeding pair of every living creature.

MODERN TRANSPORT

Cars, buses, trains and aircraft have symbolic associations that are usually seen in psychological terms. Driving a car can be seen as a metaphor for an individual travelling through life in conscious control of their direction; issues of safety and danger, of conformity or rebellion (obeying or ignoring the rules of the road), of having a sense of direction or of being lost can all be highlighted. Unlike the car, the bus is a public vehicle and can suggest a person's relationship to society, so that difficulties in boarding or wanting to get off can be significant.

Trains operate according to fixed rules. Being late, missing or only just catching a train, travelling without a ticket or in a lower or higher-class carriage can all be interpreted in terms of a person's relationship to the world. Many psychologists believe that the departure platform is a symbol of the unconscious, the starting point of literal and metaphorical journeys, and luggage a symbol of what is being "carried" by the psyche, so that heavy bags can signify psychological burdens, while light bags may indicate inner freedom.

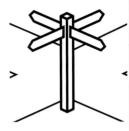

THE CROSSROADS

Traditionally a crossroads marks an important point of decision, and sacred monuments or shrines have been erected at such sites: for instance, votive stones left by travellers in the Peruvian Andes have built up into pyramids. The crossroads is a place of transition, a symbol of risk, opportunity, change, choice and transformation. Being the point where divergent pathways intersect, it is an important place of encounter, traditionally associated with otherworldly powers (both good and evil). In many places, crossroads are associated with ghosts, witches and troublesome spirits: in Europe, statues to Hecate, the Greek "dark" goddess, were erected at crossroad sites, while in Africa, the Bambara from Mali make offerings of tools, cotton and cloth to the Soba spirits who are thought to meddle in human affairs. Crossroads are also widely linked with divination: in Japan, people would go there at dusk, when the words of passers-by would reveal what fate might bring. This was linked to a belief that travellers might be deities bringing good fortune, and evolved into the custom of selling rice-crackers containing paper fortunes at crossroads.

The desire for flight is archetypal. Aircraft (and spacecraft) can symbolize spiritual aspiration, transcending human limitations by defying gravity, rising up to the purifying reaches of the sky and beyond. Aircraft can also be symbols of independence, freedom and speed. Running out of fuel, crashing or falling can suggest being brought "down to earth", a punishment perhaps for over-ambition, just as Icarus in Greek myth fell to his death after flying too close to the sun, which melted the wax of his wings.

ABOVE The horse is an archetypal motif. It symbolizes life-giving but dangerous forces, as well as power and strength.

BELOW A red car symbolizes male sexual potency and drive. It also suggests the thrill of speed and power.

THE GARDEN

ABOVE In the Hindu sacred tradition, as in many others, the garden is a symbol of paradise.

ABOVE Fountains are a symbol of life in many cultures, and are also an emblem of the feminine.

BELOW Pools and water features are often incorporated into gardens, with water used as a symbol of life in many cultures.

Almost universally, the garden is a symbol of earthly and heavenly paradise – the word "paradise" comes from *pairidaeza*, the old Persian word for a garden. Within the garden, the design and plants contribute to its symbolism. The first gardens were probably made in China around 4,000 years ago. From there they spread to the Mediterranean and Near East, and since then almost every culture that survives above a subsistence level has created gardens.

HEAVEN ON EARTH
Gardens are sacred symbols in many spiritual traditions. The Judaeo-Christian Garden of Eden is the ultimate Heaven on earth, created by God for man (Adam) and woman (Eve) to live in. Eden symbolizes the primordial state of divine innocence, when humans existed in harmony with God, nature and one another before they fell from grace after eating the forbidden fruit of the Tree of Life. The theme of Eden and the Fall is a favourite motif in

Western art and literature; representations include *The Garden of Earthly Delights* by the Dutch painter Hieronymus Bosch (c.1450–1516), and the epic poem *Paradise Lost* by John Milton (1608–74). In Islam, too, heavenly bliss is interpreted in the Qur'an as a garden, a home for the elect beyond the grave, and Allah is sometimes referred to as "the Gardener". In ancient Greece, the Elysian Fields, the place where the virtuous go after death, was also represented as a garden.

In China, the traditional lake-and-island garden was invented to attract the Eight Immortals – a group of Taoist saints alleged to live on the Mystic Isles – to Earth. The Emperor Wu Di's gardens of the 2nd century BC contained palaces and pavilions built on man-made mountains and connected by bridges to the islands that stood in the middle of a huge artificial lake.

PLEASURE GARDENS
In ancient Egypt, gardens were places of recreation. Pictures of gardens with pools and banks of flowers decorated tombs, suggesting the joys of the afterlife, as well as palace walls and floors. The Romans carried garden design to sophisticated heights, incorporating buildings, statues, stairways, colonnaded walkways, springs, grottoes, wells and fountains, and the garden became one of the symbols of civilization. This theme was developed during the European Renaissance, with the formal symmetrical designs of many gardens, such as the spectacular Italian gardens at Villa

Lante (Bagnaia) or Villa d'Este (Tivoli) symbolizing human power to tame nature.

In Mexico, the royal pleasure gardens of the Aztec emperor Montezuma combined the functions of a private garden with those of the botanical garden and zoo, preserving not only plants but also birds and animals, with some 600 keepers to tend them. Humans with unusual physical characteristics (such as dwarfs or albinos) were also housed there.

Gardens are widely associated with sensual pleasure, love and seduction. For instance, the classic Arabian erotic text on lovemaking is entitled *The Perfumed Garden*, while many of the great lovers of myth and legend (such as Rama and Sita in India) are frequently portrayed in a garden setting.

PARADISE GARDENS
In many cultures, the garden exists as a type of dream world, designed as an escape from the "real" world and intended to lift the senses from the mundane to the sublime. This is epitomized by the archetypal Persian garden, planted with fruit trees and sweetly scented plants and intersected by streams. In the hot desert land, both water (a symbol of life) and shade are important garden features.

The garden is enclosed and is usually entered by a magnificent gateway, a symbol of transition from one world to another. It is often designed around a large central pool, sometimes lined with blue tiles to create an impression of depth, with four

GARDENS OF THE ALHAMBRA

The gardens of the Alhambra Palace were created in the 14th century, following the quadripartite design of the Persian garden. Today four courtyards remain, including the Court of the Myrtles, with its still pool flanked by myrtle hedges, and the Court of the Lions, with sparkling fountains and slender columns directing the gaze heavenwards. Each courtyard is in full sunlight, but is approached by a dark, colonnaded passageway, symbolizing the road to paradise – the spiritual journey from darkness to light.

channels flowing from it; in large gardens, the grid pattern may be repeated, with fountains marking the intersections between the watercourses. As well as being cooling and refreshing, fountains symbolize the flow of life, while the intersections represent the connection between the everyday and the eternal. The geometric design is softened with vine fruits and flowers, particularly bunches of grapes and roses – in Persian, the words for flower and rose are the same.

In the Persian garden, moon-gazing was an important activity. Roses were planted to attract nightingales; the nocturnal habits of these birds linked them to the moon, while their song associated them with love and longing. Gazebos in the corners of the garden provided shelter for those viewing the night sky. The word "gazebo" is derived from a Persian word meaning "a platform for viewing the moon"; traditionally the structure would have a central hole in the roof through which the sky could be seen.

The gardens of Persia provided an oasis of inspiration for poetry, music and art. In his collection of poems and stories called the *Gulistan* ("The Rose Garden") the 13th-century poet Sa'di likened his thoughts to rose petals collected from the garden of his meditations. Persian garden

designs influenced some of the most famous gardens in the world, including the gardens of the Alhambra Palace in Spain, and the Mogul Taj Mahal in India.

THE ZEN GARDEN

In the East there is a saying that a sacred space is complete only when there is nothing more that can be taken away from it. The first Zen gardens in Japan were created by Buddhist monks as places of contemplation, designed to bring the mind to a point of stillness through simple but profound design. In a Zen garden nothing is left to chance and every element is significant. The aim is to create a harmony between the two cosmic forces of yin and yang, water and land. Traditionally, water is symbolized by gravel or sand, raked to form ripple patterns, while large stones

represent land. When plants are used, shrubs such as azaleas, cut-leaf maples, conifers and bamboos represent land, while moss represents water. Space is an integral part of the Zen garden, allowing the spirit of nature to move between yin and yang.

Unlike gardens in the West, which are designed to celebrate the changing seasons, Zen gardens are designed with permanence in mind, so they are more or less the same today as when they were first designed hundreds of years ago, and even the gravel is raked in the same patterns. This permanence symbolizes the transcendent spirit unbound by time or space.

BELOW In medieval times, the walled garden was a symbol of refuge. Here the Virgin Mary is shown surrounded by roses, symbols of her purity.

ABOVE The Court of the Lions at the Alhambra Palace in Granada is rich in symbolism, suggesting spiritual attainment and leadership.

WALLED GARDENS

In medieval Christian symbolism, the walled garden was the home of the soul and a place of refuge from the troubles of earthly life. Its enclosed, secret nature made it a symbol of the feminine principle and in particular of the Virgin Mary. The word "rosary", used to describe the string of beads used to count prayers to the Virgin, originally meant a garden of roses. Persian gardens were also surrounded by walls to separate them from the mundane world, and were filled with an abundance of perfumed flowers, upon which a range of symbolism is based; for instance, jasmine and rose are seen as the king and queen of flowers, while narcissus captures the scent of youth.

THE HOME

ABOVE The hearth has a central place in the home for all cultures: it is the source of warmth and light, but also a symbol of safety, comfort and a sense of belonging.

ABOVE The cauldron is an archetypal symbol of magic, mystery and transformation.

BELOW The broom is a symbol of removal, used to sweep away bad luck.

The traditional centre of domestic life is the hearth, an archetypal symbol, but many other common household objects enjoy a rich symbolic tradition: they include the broom and mirror, cooking pots, baskets and items of furniture. In the West some of these items – notably the hearth – are no longer in general use, but they retain their symbolic power.

THE HEARTH

As a source of light, heat and food, the hearth represents home and community, warmth, safety and family life. It has figured in the myths and religions of many civilizations. In Aztec tradition it was sacred to the androgynous Two-Lord Ometecuhtli, who was believed to live at the heart of the universe, while in both China and Japan the hearth gods attract abundance and good fortune to the household, with the Japanese god of the hearth residing in the hook on which the cooking pot is suspended over the fire.

THE BROOM

A humble piece of household equipment, the broom is also a symbol of sacred power and new beginnings. In some North African agricultural societies, the broom used to sweep the threshing floor is a cult object. In ancient Rome, houses were swept after funerals to clean away any bad spirits and symbolize a fresh start, and the Chinese observe a similar custom at the end of the year, sweeping the house to remove any bad luck in preparation for the next year.

THE CAULDRON

The freestanding cooking pot, or cauldron, is another powerful, cross-cultural and archetypal symbol. In Indo-European traditions, it is an instrument of mystical and magical power and transformation. In Celtic myth there are three types of cauldron: the Dagda's cauldron of plenty – an eternal source of food and knowledge; a cauldron of sacrificial death, in which the king of the old year was drowned while his palace was burned; and a cauldron of rebirth in which the dead could be revived.

In China, a three-legged cauldron had the power to bestow the ability of divination, the control of the seasonal cycle, and to grant immortality. The hero Yu the Great, founder of the Chinese Empire, cast nine sacred bronze cauldrons that were said to boil without fire and were filled by celestial powers. It was said that if the people of the Earth turned from virtue to vice, the cauldrons would disappear.

CONTAINING VESSELS

Aside from the cauldron, there are many other archetypal containers, including urns, vases, jars and bowls, as well as caskets, boxes, baskets and coffers, all of which have symbolic significance. In many cultures, rigid vessels are associated with death. The ancient Egyptians, when they mummified the dead, placed the heart and other internal organs in canopic jars – magical vessels that would protect the contents from evil influences. In Europe the dead are usually enclosed in a coffin before burial or cremation, and their ashes may be placed in an urn. In some South American countries, a broken vessel placed on a grave indicates the transition between life and death.

Urns and vases are also life symbols: the Mesopotamian goddess Ishtar is often depicted carrying an urn containing the waters of life. In the Kabbalah, the vase symbolizes spiritual treasure – a symbolism echoed in the Grail legends of medieval European literature, in which the Grail is the chalice or goblet said to contain the blood of Christ and with it the secret of immortality. In the Jewish Temple, golden bowls – a metaphor for vessels containing life – were used for ritual offerings.

Containers are also associated with the feminine principle. In the Americas, stories about baskets and basket-making are often related to women: for instance, in a Pawnee myth, Basket Woman is the mother of the moon and stars. The basket is a symbol of the womb and the attribute of many goddesses, including Diana of Ephesus, whose priestesses wore their hair dressed in a basket shape. Among the Shona of Zimbabwe, pottery bowls are sometimes shaped like a woman's body parts, and there is a saying that a husband must treat his wife with respect to prevent her from "turning the bowl upside down", or denying him access to her sexuality. Similarly, in the Japanese tea ceremony, the tea bowl represents the moon and yin, or the feminine essence.

MIRRORS

The Latin word for mirror is "speculum", and speculation – now an intellectual activity – originally meant using a mirror to scan the sky and stars. Mirrors – especially darkened mirrors – have also been used in divination, by gazing into them until visions were revealed: the Aztecs made polished black obsidian mirrors for this purpose, dedicated to the god Tezcatlipoca, or Smoking Mirror. In some Native American traditions, a blackened medicine bowl would be filled with water to create the same effect.

Sometimes mirrors are seen as reflecting the truth: in Greek myth, Medusa, whose gaze could turn others to stone, was turned to stone herself when presented with her reflection in Perseus' shield. The Chinese hang octagonal mirrors inscribed with the *Pa Gua* above the entry to a house, in the belief that by revealing the nature of evil influences the mirror will drive them away.

RIGHT The carpets of Arabia are associated with the home, and the colours and patterns used in their weaving are rich in symbolism. Every carpet has a mistake to illustrate the Islamic belief that only Allah can create perfection.

Mirrors are symbols of spiritual wisdom, knowledge and enlightenment: in Tibetan Buddhism, the Wisdom of the Great Mirror teaches that the world of shapes reflected in it is illusory, while for Taoists the mirror of the heart reflects Heaven and earth. Through its association with heavenly intelligence, the mirror is often a solar symbol: Japanese myth tells how the sun goddess Amaterasu was enticed from her cave by a sacred mirror to reflect her light upon the world. The mirror is also a female, lunar, symbol, and has associations with luck and superstition. In China, a mirror is a sign of harmony and happy marriage, with a broken mirror suggesting separation. In Western folklore, a broken mirror is said to bring seven years of bad luck to the person who broke it.

FURNITURE

In ancient Rome, emperors sat upon stools, while thrones were reserved for the gods. Today in parts of Africa stools are symbols of kingly office, while the golden stool of the Ashanti in Ghana is believed to enshrine the nation's soul. Because they elevate the sitter, chairs are associated with status and authority. In the Christian tradition, the Latin name for a bishop's chair was a "cathedrum" (from the Greek for chair, "kathedra"); churches presided over by bishops were therefore called cathedrals.

A table is a focal point, a meeting place where people

gather together to eat or talk. For Jewish people, the family dining table assumes the role of an altar when it is sanctified by ritual and prayer during the Sabbath meal. The Round Table of the Arthurian legends represented a select community, an idea echoed in business today when board meetings are held around a table.

Both carpets and curtains have sacred and secular associations. In the Middle East, carpets are associated with the home and with the mosque, and are used to beautify and delineate domestic and holy spaces. Together with screens and veils, curtains provide concealment and define space. In the Temple in Jerusalem, a curtain was drawn over the Holy of Holies, the innermost sanctum that only the Jewish high priest could enter, while in certain Muslim societies, curtains are central to the practice of purdah, which involves concealing women from public view. To perpetuate their holy authority, the emperors of China always kept a veil between themselves and their visitors so that they could see their guests without being seen.

ABOVE The mirror has many complex meanings, associated with both the sun and moon.

ABOVE Curtains symbolize separation between different realms, either opening them up or concealing them.

STATUS AND WEALTH

ABOVE Beaded jewellery is a mark of status among many African peoples.

ANOINTING WITH OIL

In many cultures oil is thought to bear special powers. Olive oil in particular is a symbol of both spiritual power and prosperity. In the Judaeo-Christian tradition, kings and priests were ritually anointed with oil as a sign of divine blessing and God-given authority, power and glory. The Greek word "christos" and the Hebrew "messiah" mean "the anointed". They are used for Jesus as symbols of his royal, prophetic and priestly authority.

Symbols can be used to communicate power and authority – both temporal and spiritual. Every culture has developed symbols of power and rank that accord with its social values, beliefs and customs. Many are associated with royalty and office or with wealth and possessions. Traditionally, valuable commodities have been used to signify wealth and rank. What the specific items are may depend on cultural values – the wealth of nomadic peoples, for instance, may be measured in terms of camels or sheep.

PRECIOUS COMMODITY

Some of humankind's most precious commodities – such as gold, silver and gemstones – are valued both for their beauty and their rarity. A symbol of purity and incorruptibility, gold is associated with divinity, royalty, the sun and the highest aspirations of the spirit. The golden apples of the Nordic heaven, Asgard, like those of the Hesperides in Greek mythology, prevent the gods from growing old, while images of the Buddha are often gilded as a sign of enlightenment and perfection. As a traditional symbol of wealth, gold features in the regalia of monarchy and high office, and it is also used to symbolize human achievement – as in a gold medal or, figuratively, in the notion of a "golden age".

Like gold, silver is also related to immortality; the ancient Egyptians, for instance, believed their gods had golden flesh and silver bones. Silver is associated

with the moon, the element of water, female energies and purity; it is also symbolic of wealth, used in currency and given in tribute.

In ancient Mesoamerica jade was valued more highly than gold or silver; it was a symbol of purity and life and the preserve of royalty. Animals and plants have also yielded precious substances – pearls and ivory, musk and ambergris, spices, resins and oils. Liquid chocolate was used by the Maya as currency, while pepper was such a valuable spice that, in the 5th century, Attila the Hun is reputed to have demanded 1350kg (3000lb) of peppercorns as ransom for the city of Rome.

ABOVE A lavish portrait of Russian Empress, Catherine the Great, is full of the symbols of kingship, including crown, sceptre and orb.

MONEY

As production of goods and services became more diverse and specialized, trade by simple barter ceased to be practical. Universally recognized tokens, which gradually developed into money, solved the problem: as long as everyone accepted the symbolic value of the tokens they could be exchanged for anything. Items such as shells and beads were used by some societies, but metal, when it was available, was more versatile and was most commonly used. Originally coins represented the intrinsic worth of the metal from which they were made, but the value of modern coinage, and of banknotes, is purely symbolic.

Designs impressed on the faces of coins usually signified the authority of the ruling body (typically the ruler's head). They also bore iconographic signs of the culture – such as horses, boars and trees on many Gaulish coins – a tradition that continues to this day. Chinese cash had a square hole in the centre symbolizing Earth surrounded by the circle of Heaven, with a superscription of the emperor, son of Heaven and Earth.

REGALIA OF OFFICE

One way of distinguishing rank is through ceremonial dress and accessories. The head is often seen as the "seat of the soul" and the noblest part of the body, and elaborate headdresses are almost universally used to indicate high status – the leader being the "head" of the group. They range from the elaborate feathered headdress of a Native American chief to the richly jewelled crown of a monarch. Many leaders carry a golden globe, or orb (a piece of regalia first used by Roman emperors to show their dominion over the world), and a sceptre similar to a staff. In Japan, one of the items of imperial regalia is a bronze mirror, associated with the goddess Amaterasu and passed down to the imperial family, who claim descent from her.

The principal item of clothing forming part of the regalia is typically a robe or cape. The

STATUS SYMBOLS OF THE MODERN WORLD

Many of the status symbols of modern Western culture are the products of state-of-the-art technology – electronic goods such as mobile phones, computers and hi-fi equipment, or expensive cars. Where people live, the way they decorate their homes, what they wear and even what they eat are all indicators of social position. Celebrities, perhaps the modern-day equivalent of mythical heroes, are used to advertise particular brands in an attempt to elevate the status of the products.

Chinese emperor's robe had a round collar with a square hem, identifying its wearer as the intermediary between Heaven and Earth. The robe of a shaman bears a wealth of symbolism: in ancient Uralo-Altaic cultures, for example, it was decorated with a three-branched emblem known as the mark of the bustard, which symbolized the communication between the worlds of death and rebirth. Today in the West, white ermine, symbolic of moral purity and justice, is still used to decorate the robes of state, judicial, ecclesiastical and academic dignitaries.

The trappings of power help to maintain the mystique of those who occupy a "seat of office" that sets them apart from the lowly rank and file. This "chair" takes many different guises: the chairperson is the head of an organization, while in academia, the holder of a chair in a particular subject is at the very top of that discipline. A throne is a special chair that symbolizes the authority of a god or sovereign. It is often positioned on a raised platform to signify the ruler's elevated status, and is usually richly embellished. In the Bible, King Solomon's throne is described as being of ivory, overlaid with gold, standing at the top of six steps, flanked by a pair of golden lions. The intricately decorated beadwork thrones of

the Bamum kingdom in Cameroon incorporate the figures of men and women to illustrate the monarch's wealth in people, while the beads themselves, the preserve of royalty, symbolize his material wealth.

SEALS

An ancient symbol of identity and authority is the seal, a small object carved with a unique design, which could be pressed into a soft clay tablet or into melted wax. It was used like a signature to guarantee the authenticity of a document such as a royal decree, and it could also ensure the security of a document in transit: when stamped into sealing wax securing folded or rolled paper, the seal could not be broken undetected. To this day seals are still used on legal documents, such as wills. Seals were sometimes worn in the form of rings, and inscribed with the names of deities or passages from holy texts, leading to their use as talismans.

ABOVE A sceptre or staff is a symbol of authority and rulership.

TOP A throne is the seat of power and authority in both the temporal and spiritual realm.

BELOW Traditionally, seals were symbols of authority and identity.

ALPHABETS AND WRITING

ABOVE The runic alphabet was used for a written, not spoken, language that was associated with magic, religion and prophecy.

ABOVE The Roman letter A stands for first grade or top class. It also symbolizes beginnings.

BELOW More than merely a writing system for the communication of information, Chinese script has been elevated into a poetic art form.

In almost every culture, alphabets and letters are laden with symbolic meaning. In ancient times, they were particularly associated with magic, divination and sacred knowledge. Knowing how to read and write was a mark of privilege and a source of power – something that still holds true today, when almost half the world's adult population cannot, or can only just, write. Written language also made possible the dissemination of knowledge and information, first through written documents and centuries later through printed books.

WRITING

Communication through writing relies on an agreed repertoire of formal signs or symbols that can be used in different combinations to reproduce the ideas the writer wants to express. It seems likely that the earliest writing systems – the cuneiform pictographs of ancient Mesopotamia, Egyptian hieroglyphs and Chinese ideograms – developed from the signs and paintings of pre-history.

When alphabets were developed (some time around 1000 BC) the number of different characters needed was drastically reduced: the Roman alphabet, which we still use today, contains 26 letters, while 1,000 basic signs are needed for writing Chinese.

ABOVE The pictorial cuneiform script could be used to infinite purpose. This inscription, dating back to the 13th century BC, is a contract for the sale of children.

ABOVE The first letter-based alphabet, reading from right to left, was probably the Phoenician one, from which Hebrew, Aramaic and Arabic scripts developed.

EARLY INSCRIPTIONS

The population of Mesopotamia consisted largely of shepherds and farmers, and one of the first uses of writing seems to have been for agricultural accounts: the earliest known Sumerian clay tablets list sacks of grain and herds of cattle. Cuneiform script was based on pictograms, so that, for instance, the outline of the head of a cow stood for the animal, but ideas as well as objects could be represented: a bird and an egg side by side meant "fertility".

The characters used by the ancient Egyptians are known as hieroglyphs, from two Greek words meaning "holy engravings". Hieroglyphs were created from stylized drawings – of human heads, birds, animals, plants and flowers, as well as some man-made objects – and were written in different directions, depending

on the text and where it was used. Like the Egyptians, the Chinese attributed a legendary origin to writing: according to one story the Emperor Huang-Tsi discovered it after studying the heavenly bodies and objects in nature, particularly bird and animal footprints. While hieroglyphs and cuneiform script were eventually supplanted by Arabic script, the system of writing invented by the Chinese remains essentially unchanged: the pictograms for words such as sun, tree, mountain, field and door have changed very little in 3,000 years.

ALPHABETS

The Phoenician alphabet is generally considered to have been the first, comprising 22 consonant characters and written from right to left. From

ILLITERACY AND THE SPOKEN WORD

In modern Western culture, illiteracy tends to be linked – erroneously – with ignorance. However, many great spiritual leaders, including Mohammed, the Zen master Hui Neng and the Indian sage Ramakrishna, were illiterate, indicating their direct and intuitive perception of divine reality, which does not rely on the written word. In some ways, writing can be seen as a debased form of speech, a symbol of loss of presence and the missing spoken word. The Buddha, Jesus and Socrates left no written works, while many of the world's great myths and cultures have their roots in oral rather than written traditions. Linguists have identified around 3,000 spoken languages in use in the world today, of which only about 100 are normally written down.

ABOVE In the ancient world, scribes formed an elite, high-status, social class, sometimes holding more state power and knowledge than the sovereign himself.

Phoenician, scripts such as Aramaic, Hebrew and Arabic developed, all of which are read from right to left, as well as some lesser-known writing systems, some of which have survived. These include Tifnagh, the script used by the Tuareg people of northern Africa, which is distinctive because of its highly geometric form. It is also very unusual as its use is confined to women, Tuareg society being matriarchal: a good example of the connection between literacy and social power. Other alphabets include Greek, Roman (which forms the basis of the English alphabet), Sanskrit and Cyrillic.

Individual letters of an alphabet may possess symbolic value. Scholars have noted that in many ancient alphabets most letters depicted an animal, a human gesture or a physical object, while some alphabets, for example Hebrew and runic, are a sequence of specific words rather than letters. The Hebrew alphabet begins, aleph (ox), beth (house), gimel (camel), and not A, B, G.

EUROPEAN TRADITIONS

Runes are the oldest scripted signs of the ancient Germans. The word *runa* means "secret" in Middle High German, and was borrowed by Finnish as *runo*, meaning "song". Allegedly created by the Norse god Odin, the 24 letters of the runic alphabet incorporate fertility symbols from prehistoric rock carvings and represent letters, words and symbolic concepts. For instance, the rune Ansuz (the equivalent of A) was concerned with messages and signals and was associated with the mouth as a source of divine speech, as well as the mouths of rivers, and the Norse trickster god Loki. The runic alphabet was linked to religious beliefs and magical practices, and was never used to represent a spoken language. Norse expeditions carried the runes to other places – Anglo-Saxon England, Iceland, Russia and possibly even North America.

Distantly related to the runes, the letters of the Celtic Irish or Ogham "tree" alphabet consist of 25 symbols, each made up of a series of horizontal or diagonal notches or lines. Originally cut into wood or stone, each glyph is named after a tree. One variation of the Ogham alphabet is named after its first three letters: beith (birch), luis (rowan) and nion (ash). The Ogham symbols were believed to come under the aegis of Ogma, the god of speech. Like runes, the Ogham alphabet was primarily a method of inscription and augury used by druids, seers and poets, rather than a system of ordinary writing.

ABOVE The letter Z comes at the end of the Roman alphabet and symbolizes endings.

BELOW A portrait of a scribe named Mery, head of the royal archives at Saqqarah, mid-4th dynasty (c.2575–2450 BC), on the door of his tomb. The fact that Mery had his own richly decorated tomb shows his high status in ancient Egyptian society. The relief shows Mery at work, making an inscription on a writing tablet, his stylus tucked behind his ear.

THE LETTER X

Many different symbolic associations are ascribed to the letter X. In countries where the Roman alphabet was used, illiterate people used it instead of their signature on legal documents such as birth certificates. After they had made their mark, it was customary to kiss it as a sign of their sincerity, which is why we use X to represent a kiss. In Roman numerals, X is the number 10, while in mathematics it denotes multiplication, or in algebra, a variable in a function. The latter, indicating an unknown quantity, has led to expressions such as "Mr X", where X expresses the idea of anonymity. The use of X to guarantee anonymity also occurs when voting. In contrast to a tick, indicating "correct", X is used to mark an error. On road and other signs it is a warning that something is forbidden or has been cancelled, and the use of crossed lines to pinpoint a position on a map has led to the expression "X marks the spot".

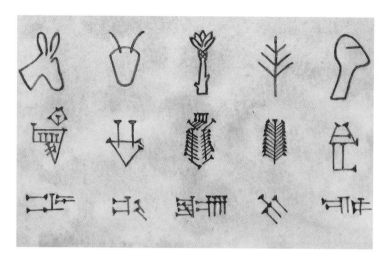

RIGHT These ancient Mesopotamian pictographs show the development of writing. The top row shows a simple drawing (donkey, ox, date palm, barley, head), while the next two rows show how the picture developed into cuneiform script.

BOOKS

The book is an important symbol in many traditions, variously linked with religion, wisdom, scholarship and divination. Judaism, Christianity and Islam are all "religions of the book", based on the holy texts or scriptures (meaning "writing") that have God-given status. Codes of conduct have evolved concerning the handling of holy texts: Moslems observe rituals of cleanliness before studying the Qur'an, and it is never put on the floor; in synagogues, books or scrolls that are too worn out to read, or pieces of paper bearing holy words, are not discarded but kept in a special box that is ceremonially buried when it is full.

In China, books were associated with Taoist sages and were symbols of great learning. In the ancient world, the Sibylline Books were believed to contain prophecies of Rome's destiny and were consulted by the Roman senate in times of emergency, while in medieval Europe books were thought to have divinatory powers, so that if a book was opened at random and a grain of wheat dropped on to a page, the text on which the grain landed would point to a future course of events or answer a question. Words from books have even been eaten as auspicious talismans, a way of ingesting the wisdom and power of the written word.

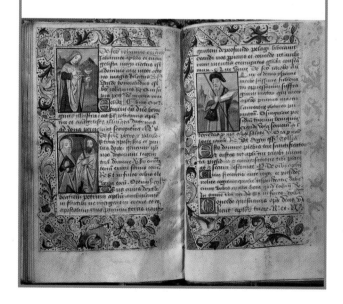

WRITING MATERIALS

Many different materials have been used for writing on, including papyrus (ancient Egypt), tablets of baked clay (Mesopotamia), marble (Greece), deerskin (Mexico), bamboo (Polynesia), silk (China) and wood (Scandinavia). Each material has called for the use of suitable writing implements, of which the most widely used are the pen and the brush.

In Islamic traditions, the pen (qalam) is highly symbolic. An agent of divine revelation, it was made of light and created by Allah to write upon the "book" or tablet. In Classical mythology, the stylus pen and tablet are attributes of Calliope, the Muse of Epic Poetry, and in Christian iconography the four Evangelists are sometimes associated with a quill pen.

In China, the writing brush, together with its accompanying ink and inkstone, are important symbols. With paper, they make up the "Four Treasures of the Study", symbols of the scholarly class that ruled China from the 2nd century BC, and they were used in calligraphy, in which writing was transformed into an art form practised by the elite. Calligraphy was also accorded high status in other Eastern countries, such as Japan, and in Islam, where inscriptions of texts from the Qur'an were used instead of religious imagery.

RELIGIOUS TRADITIONS

Almost universally, writing has been linked with sacred tradition. In ancient Egypt it was thought that writing was the gift of the god Thoth to humanity, while in India, Sarasvati, the goddess of speech, is also called the alphabet goddess; her consort Brahma, the creator god, is sometimes shown wearing a garland of 50 letters. According to the Biblical account, the Ten Commandments were presented to Moses inscribed on tablets of stone (which Moses symbolically broke when the precepts were not followed), together with the Torah, the primary document of Judaism.

For Kabbalists, the letters of the Hebrew alphabet are linked with numbers and thought to possess powers of creation, while in Islamic mystical traditions there is also a highly refined science of letters based upon their symbolic qualities. In Sufism, the letters of the Arabic alphabet can be classified according to the four elements (fire, air, earth and water), each of which, as a material representation of the divine word, bears a specific meaning. Some traditions have viewed vowels and consonants in terms of "spirit" and "matter" respectively. In antiquity, the seven Greek vowels were thought to symbolize the seven spheres of Heaven and the seven sets of stars moving within them.

SECRET CODES

Writing has always been linked with magic and the occult (meaning "hidden") and has been used in symbols purposefully created to conceal information from all but initiates or the learned, especially in esoteric traditions whose ideas go against mainstream thought. For instance, Hebrew letters, Latin words and Kabbalistic signs have sometimes been used in five-pointed magical seals called pentacles, impressed on virgin parchment or engraved on precious metals. These symbolize occult powers and have been used in spells and magic.

The Western occult or "hermetic" tradition traces its origins to the Hermetica, writings of the 1st–3rd centuries AD that allegedly contain the teachings of Hermes Trismegistus (the Greek name for the Egyptian deity Thoth, god of wisdom and

writing). They enshrine a number of concepts central to many esoteric and occult traditions – for instance, the duality of matter and spirit, and the idea that salvation can be achieved through self-knowledge rather than through faith or belief. During the Middle Ages, magical "recipe books" called "grimoires" set out a system in which self-knowledge could be attained using the power of symbols to invoke spirits that the magician then had to confront and overcome. Today psychologists might interpret these as facets of the magician's own personality. Many magical symbols (known as "sigils") were devised during the 15th and 16th centuries, such as those created by Dr John Dee, astrologer to the English court of Elizabeth I. Some of Dee's sigils bear a resemblance to letters, such as an inverted L or Y or a back-to-front Z.

ALPHA AND OMEGA

The first and last letters of the Greek alphabet symbolize that which is all-encompassing, the two poles of the universe between which is contained the totality of knowledge, being, time and space. In the Christian tradition, they are ascribed to Jesus Christ, who, in the Book of Revelation declares: "I am alpha and omega, the beginning and the ending... which is, and which was, and which is to come" (1:8). In modern parlance, the phrase "from A to Z" means "completely, thoroughly and in detail".

ABOVE Today runes are popular as a divination device, with each symbol inscribed on a stone and then "picked".

FAR LEFT This frontispiece to John Dee's *Little Book of Love* shows Venus with magic sigils on her scroll and trumpet.

LEFT The printing press revolutionized the production of books, making the written word more widely available.

BODY LANGUAGE

ABOVE This Indian gesture, known as namaste, symbolizes the reconciliation of the duality in nature. It is also used as a greeting in China.

ABOVE The CND sign was devised using the semaphore signals for the letters N and D.

RIGHT The V for victory sign, two fingers raised in a "V" shape, palms outwards, was first used by Winston Churchill, Britain's prime minister, during the First World War. It is now used as a sign for triumph over adversity all over the world.

The body is a channel of communication, whether the information it conveys is conscious or unconscious, intended or unintentional. Its language is organized both by culturally constructed meaning and symbolism and by the symbolism of the unconscious, or the realm of dreaming. The body is a great source of symbolic expression, communicating both to ourselves, in the form of "body wisdom", and to others. Expressions such as "You are a pain in the neck", "I will hold you in my heart", "I feel it in my bones" and many more, suggest that our bodies can be channels of meaningful and symbolic information.

GESTURE AND GESTICULATION

The intended language of the body appears in gesture and gesticulation. In early humans, the use of both tools and symbols became possible when moving on two limbs freed the hands so that humans were able to physically and mentally "grasp" or apprehend the world.

Gestures play a part in creating and communicating meaning. In India and China, placing the hands together in a praying position at chest height is the "namaste" gesture, which can be interpreted as "The god in me greets the god in you" and also symbolizes the reconciliation of the duality of nature. Some gestures – such as a deferential stoop or bow, smiling or shrugging – appear truly universal, yet even the commonest signs can have different meanings in different cultures. Though nodding the head signifies assent in most parts of the world, in India it is communicated by shaking the head from side to side.

Raising the thumb stands for "OK" in the USA, but is obscene or very impolite in Brazil, Russia and Greece. In Colombia, this sign placed over the nose implies that someone is a homosexual. Gestures implying a man finds a woman pretty vary widely: they include raising the eyebrows in America and Britain, grasping the beard in the Arab world, rotating a finger in the cheek in Italy and kissing the fingertips in France.

Sticking out ones tongue at someone can be seen as cheeky, provocative or insulting in many cultures. In Tibet, however, it is used as a polite greeting. In New Zealand, the Maori use it as a ceremonial warning. When visitors arrive a Maori warrior approaches them in a warlike manner, with bulging eyes and extended tongue, meaning, "We are willing to attack if you do not come in friendship." If the visitors react passively they are then welcomed warmly.

The v-sign, popularized by Britain's wartime leader Winston Churchill, is now used throughout the world as a sign for victory, or triumph over adversity. If the sign is reversed, with the palm facing inwards, however, it is seen as rude and offensive.

Gesticulations are bodily gestures that accompany and enhance verbal communication. They are used everywhere but are particularly prominent in Italy, where every conversation is seasoned with such a wide array of hand signals that it is possible to understand its thrust from the other side of a piazza. As an example, a hand drawn away from the chin as if growing a beard means, "You are boring."

SIGN LANGUAGE

Formal body language systems may involve gestures that depict objects and ideas iconically, or communicate by spelling out words. The Native Americans of the Plains used a complex, mainly

MUDRAS

The mudras are symbolic and meaningful hand gestures of the Buddha, portrayed in Buddhist statues since the 5th century AD. *Dhyana* mudra indicates balance and meditation. *Ksepana* mudra means the sprinkling of the nectar of immortality. *Varada* mudra signifies charity and the fulfilment of all wishes. *Uttarabodhi* mudra represents supreme enlightenment.

iconic, system of signing for communication between tribes without a common language. In 1755 the Abbé Charles Michel de l'Epée developed a system of signing for the deaf, which has been the foundation for many modern sign languages.

The semaphore signalling system, originally developed for maritime purposes, uses arm positions and flags to communicate letters of the alphabet. Semaphore is the source of the campaign for nuclear disarmament (CND) symbol, which combines the signals for the letters "N" and "D": two arms in a downwards facing "V" shape for "N", and one arm pointing straight up and the other straight down for "D".

RIGHT Charles Michel de l'Epée, the French educationalist who invented a system of signing for the deaf, teaches a group of students.

DOUBLE SIGNALS

When we communicate two or more different things at the same time, we are double-signalling. Body language may disturb the intended communication, as when we say to someone, "It's nice to meet you", but simultaneously turn away, so that our body conveys the message "I am not interested in meeting you", or "My focus is elsewhere."

NON-VERBAL COMMUNICATION

Communication theory understands communication as the exchange of discrete pieces of information through signals. We communicate linguistically through words and language, but also "non-verbally" through our tone of voice, posture, movement or positioning of our body, the direction of our gaze, and touch.

Our interpretations of other people's non-verbal signals may be very accurate, or they may fall wide of the mark due to our own preconceptions, projections or cultural variations. For example, the behaviour of the eyes can communicate relative social ranking, dominance, submission or respect. They can also signal aggression, love and sexual interest or disinterest. For black Americans, lack of eye contact shows respect, but this may be misinterpreted by white Americans, who expect a direct gaze. Maintaining eye contact in conversation is respectful or can indicate trustworthiness for Arabs, Latin Americans and southern Europeans, while for East Asians and Indians

"peripheral gaze" or no eye contact is more acceptable. In Greece, it is common for people to stare at others in public, and Greeks can feel invisible or ignored in a country such as Britain, where it is rude to stare.

PERSONAL SPACE

Customs, conventions and body language exist in order to define personal or community space. Each community has different symbolic rituals and methods of engaging with visitors and enemies at the edge of their defined territory. Every individual has different needs for personal space, and these change according to time and circumstance. For example, monarchs and political leaders commonly command a wide berth in public life, unless they are making significant gestures such as the symbolic embrace and handshakes of two leaders, or conferring an honour on one of their subjects. In a different situation, with friends or family, the same individual will reduce their personal space to allow greater intimacy.

ABOVE Eye contact is an important part of non-verbal communication.

BELOW The handshake is valuable both for guarding personal space and also for breaking through spatial barriers.

Body Art

ABOVE Painting the body with henna is an ancient art originating in Mesopotamia, and still practised in parts of India, as at this Hindu wedding, and the Middle East. It is the henna itself that symbolizes love, happiness and protection.

BELOW In this earliest known painting from South America, dated 1599, an Ecuadorian from Quito wears European dress but has the body piercings and jewellery of his own tribal tradition.

Though fashions and customs vary, people of all cultures use the body to express their identity and to mark rites of passage. They alter and adorn it in both permanent and temporary ways, from tattoos, decorative scarring and piercings, to jewellery, hairstyles, make-up and clothes. Body art is used to symbolize social and cultural allegiance and difference, to denote rank or power, to accentuate beauty, and to make a statement about gender and sexual availability. It also plays an important part in ritual and ceremony.

DRESS AND TABOO

Aside from their practical use as protection from the elements, clothes have a moral significance in many cultures. In Victorian Britain it was considered risqué for a woman to show her ankle, while one of the symbols of the "sexual revolution" of the 1960s was the mini-skirt. In cultures that do not view nakedness as something to hide, clothing signifies an embellishment of the human form.

Dress can show adherence to a specific body of belief or part of society. Teenagers in the West choose clothes that conform to a recognizable style to indicate their social allegiance. In many religious traditions, the robes of monks or nuns symbolize their non-attachment to the material world and a lack of concern with individual characteristics, focusing instead on their relationship with the divine.

BODY PAINTING

In many parts of the world women dye their skin with henna. In parts of India this practice, known as *mehndi*, has been a tradition for more than 5,000 years. The drawing of intricate patterns over the hands and forearms or feet forms part of the wedding ceremony, and it is thought that the deeper the colour on the skin, the longer the love will last between a couple. In Morocco, henna symbolically blesses the wearer and is said to protect from evil and promote fertility and good fortune. In Sudan, the wearing of henna is an expression of happiness and of a wife's love for her husband, while not wearing it is thought to represent grief or lack of love.

Make-up is used to accentuate desirable facial features but also as a disguise. Often it is a means of conforming to current fashions and ideas about what constitutes beauty, but today's Goths, for example, use white face make-up and black or purple lipstick as a way of challenging the dominant culture. In Japan, where white make-up represents a traditional ideal of beauty and is still the mask of the geisha, it was once customary for upper-class women to shave off their eyebrows and blacken their teeth as a sign that they had come of age.

BODY PIERCING

The piercing of the body as a symbolic act is common to many cultures. In South America, the Carafa Indians insert a thin cane into their lower lip to show that they are in the prime of life. Tongue piercing was practised in a ritual form by the Aztecs and Maya as well as by some Native American tribes such as the Tlingit and Kwakiutul. Among the Berber, Beja and Bedouin of the Middle East, nose rings are very common: the size of the ring denotes the wealth of the family, and when a man marries he gives his ring to his wife as a security if she is divorced or widowed. In India, it is common for women to wear nose studs on their left nostril; this is because in Ayurvedic medicine, the traditional healing system of India, it is believed to connect with the female reproductive organs via the body's subtle energy system, so the piercing is thought to ease menstrual pain and facilitate childbirth.

Body piercings are also governed by aesthetic standards. For instance, the women of the Makololo of Malawi wear plates called *pelele* in the upper lip to enhance their beauty. Body piercing is also associated with erotica: the Kama Sutra, the Indian text on the art of lovemaking, talks of *apadravya*, a vertical barbell inserted through the glans of the penis for increased arousal, while in 19th-century Europe the "bosom ring" was worn by women in high society to enlarge their nipples and keep them in a state of excitation. Today in the West, body piercing involving the lips, tongue, eyebrows, nose, navel, nipples and labia is enjoying a revival. Some people think this represents a need to connect to something more enduring than the ephemera of consumer society; it is also associated with asserting individual and group identity, rebellion against society's "norms" and sexual fetish.

SCARIFICATION

For many indigenous peoples the practice of scarification (deliberate scarring of the body) is highly symbolic. Among the Karo in Ethiopia a scarified line on a man's chest shows that he has killed an enemy from another tribe and is a mark of respect, while Karo women enhance their beauty and sensuality with deep cuts made into their chest and torso. In initiation ceremonies practised by the Barabaig of East Africa, pubescent boys' heads are shaved and their foreheads are cut with three incisions from ear to ear to mark their entry into manhood. In West Africa, young girls have scarification marks around the navel as a reminder of

their ancestral mother, while the Djuka people of Dutch Guiana in the West Indies mark faces, shoulders and arms with Kaffa designs handed down from their African ancestors.

TATTOOS

Mummified bodies found in many parts of the world, including Egypt, South America, Africa, Russia and Europe, suggest that tattooing is an ancient art linked to ritual and sacred ceremony. The body of a Bronze Age man preserved in ice in the Austrian Alps had a total of 57 tattoos, thought to be connected with healing. The Inuit and some Native Americans use them to protect against disease, and in the Sudan, Nubian girls have "welts" thought to strengthen their immune systems while pregnant.

The word tattoo is from the Samoan *ta tau*, which means "balanced" and "fitting". The *ta tau* is used as a sign of maturity, demonstrating a readiness for life. Male *ta tau* are applied in a particular order, starting at the small of the back, with the navel design (*pute*) always applied last. Female Samoans always have a diamond-shaped design (*malu*) on the backs of their knees. Any *ta tau* that remains unfinished is considered shameful as it indicates an uncompleted ceremony. In Maori culture, intricate tattoos known as *ta moko* signify achievements and social rank. Lines and spirals are worn on the face and buttocks of men, and on the chin, lips and shoulders of women. Those of high rank also have *ta moko* on

their faces, the left side relating to the father's line, and the right side to the mother's.

Tattoos may denote allegiance to tribes, clans or gangs. For instance, in America a winged skull tattoo is the emblem of the Hell's Angels motorcycle gang. A tattoo common among Hispanic gang members is the pachucho cross, placed on the hand between thumb and index finger; another consists of three dots in a pyramid shape, which means *mi vida loca* or my crazy life.

A tattoo establishes a symbolic link between its wearer and what it depicts, which acts as a totem. This means tattoos may have a protective function: Melanesian fisherman use a dolphin tattoo to avoid shark attack. Alternatively, tattoos can be symbols of aggression: in the West, designs include eagles with their talons drawn to attack, black panthers, scorpions, skulls, or images of death and demons. Tattoos can also symbolize love and allegiance, so another popular design in the West is a heart pierced by an arrow, inscribed with the beloved's name.

ABOVE The Kaffa designs on the shoulders of a young Djuka girl are made by cuts filled with ashes that are allowed to heal and then recut and refilled until the scars reach the right level.

BELOW Tattoos have become common in the youth culture of the West as an identity statement or to enhance eroticism and beauty.

PATTERNS AND GRAPHICS

SOME OF THE MOST COMPELLING SYMBOLS RELY ONLY ON PATTERN OR COLOUR, LINE OR GEOMETRIC SHAPE, AND IT IS OFTEN THESE MOST BASIC SYMBOLS THAT REPRESENT THE GRANDEST CONCEPTS, SUCH AS ETERNITY BEING REPRESENTED AS A SIMPLE DOT, OR THE SPIRAL CONVEYING THE VERY RHYTHM OF BREATHING AND LIFE ITSELF.

NUMBERS

ABOVE A six-pointed star is a symbol of balance and harmony. It is also an emblem of Judaism.

TOP Number one is the symbol of beginnings.

TOP RIGHT As a symbol of two twins represent doubled force, but also symbolize warring spirits.

The complex symbolism of numbers stretches back into antiquity. In many traditions, they are linked with cosmic principles that give order and structure to the universe, governing the movement of the moon and planets as well as plant, animal and human life. In ancient Greece, Pythagoras (c.569–475 BC) sometimes described as the first pure mathematician, is quoted as saying, "Numbers rule all things."

Numerology is one of the oldest sciences of symbols. Cultures all over the world have used individual numbers symbolically: here are some of the main associations for one to ten.

1 Number one represents beginnings and the primal cause. It is a symbol of creation and the

human species, and is depicted in the standing stone, the upright staff and the erect phallus. In monotheistic religions one is the number of God, while in Jungian psychology it is a unifying symbol. In the Native American Earth Count, one represents Grandfather Sun and fire, the spark of life. We use the expression "number one" to refer to our own importance as an individual. In Pythagorean theory one represents the male principle.

2 Chinese numerology is based on the number two, for in Taoist belief the universe is made up of polarity, expressed in the complementary forces yin and yang. Two represents pairs and duality, separating creator and created, spirit and matter, man and woman, light and dark. Many cultures regard sets of two, such

as twins, as especially lucky. In the Native American Earth Count, two represents Grandmother Earth, the body, Earth, death and introspection. For Pythagoreans it represents the female principle.

3 Number three expresses all aspects of creation, including birth, life and death; past, present and future; and mind, body and soul. To the Chinese it is a perfect number, expressing wholeness and fulfilment through the joining together of Heaven, Earth and humanity. In Pythagorean theory it represents perfect harmony, the union of unity (one) and diversity (two). In Islam the number three represents the soul, and for Native Americans it is linked with water and the emotions. Among the Dogon it symbolizes the male principle. The symbolism of three is linked with the triangle.

ZERO

The use of zero developed far later than our system for representing numbers, though Babylonion scribes sometimes left a blank space where it was intended to go. In ancient Egypt, there was no hieroglyph for nought. The Maya understood the concept of zero, and represented it as a spiral, suggesting the womb symbolism of the shell and foetal life. Zero represents the blank space of infinity, the void from which life arises and to which it returns. Zero is the symbol of complete potentiality.

1 2 3 4 5 6 7 8 9 0

4 The number four is related to the cardinal directions, the seasons, the elements and the phases of the moon. In Pythagorean theory, as the first square it represents perfection, and in the Native American Earth Count it symbolizes harmony. Its symbolism is connected with both the cross and the square, suggesting order, stability and solidity. In Islam it is related to matter, and in Christianity to the four Evangelists. It is a sacred number in the Hindu Vedas, which are themselves divided into four parts. The Japanese word for four, *shi*, sounds like the word for death, so it is replaced in conversation by *yo* or *yon*.

5 According to Pythagoras, five is the number of humanity, the human body with its four limbs and head fits inside a pentagram, or five-pointed star. In the Native American Earth Count, five denotes the human as a sacred being, bridging the gap between earth and sky, past and future and the material and spirit worlds. In China, it is the number of the harmonic union of yin (two) and yang (three), while in India and China it represents the elements – fire, air, earth, water and ether.

6 In China, six is the number of celestial power and longevity. In the Native American Earth Count it is associated with the ancestors. Expressed as a hexagon or six-pointed star, it signifies harmony and balance and is linked with the universal human, and in Pythagorean theory with justice. In Buddhism, there are several groupings of six, including the six realms of existence. Six is associated with sin in the New Testament Book of Revelation: as 666, it becomes the number of the beast of the Apocalypse.

7 Seven has widespread significance in magic and divine mystery. It is the number of the planets known in antiquity (Sun, Moon, Mercury, Venus, Mars, Jupiter and Saturn) and of the days of the week. There are seven branches to the shaman's cosmic tree, seven colours to a rainbow, and seven main chakras in the human body. In ancient Egypt, there were seven gods of light and seven of darkness, and seven was a symbol of eternal life. In Judaism the New Year begins in the seventh month of the Jewish calendar. Muslims believe there are seven heavens, seven hells and seven earths, while for Christians it is the number of heavenly virtues as well as deadly sins.

8 Almost universally, eight is the number of cosmic balance. For Native Americans it is the number of all natural laws. In Buddhism it relates to the dharmachakra, or eight-spoked wheel of life, and the eight petals of the lotus, representing the eight paths to spiritual perfection. Taoists revere the Eight Immortals and Eight Precious Things, while the Hindu god Vishnu has eight arms corresponding to the eight guardians of space. Eight is also an important number in African belief: among the Dogon there are eight hero-creators and eight primal ancestors, and eight is associated with water and semen.

9 The number nine relates to the symbolism of the triple power of three – the three trimesters (three-month periods) of pregnancy or the three triads of the nine orders of angels. In China it is highly auspicious because it is the number of the celestial spheres. Among the Aztecs, a nine-storey temple echoed the nine heavens or stages through which the soul must pass. In the Native American Earth Count, nine signifies the moon, change and movement.

10 In Pythagorean theory, ten represents divine power. In the Biblical tradition it is the number of God's commandments, and in Native American tradition it represents the intellect.

ABOVE Through its association with pregnancy, the number nine is associated with gestation and the fulfilment of creation.

TOP In antiquity, there were seven known planets, and the days of the week were named after them.

DOTS AND LINES

ABOVE In the Hindu tradition, the dot, or *bindu,* is a sacred symbol and is often worn in the position of the third eye.

BELOW A zigzag pattern is one of the oldest known geometric shapes, thought to represent snakes or water.

RIGHT The horizon is the line that appears to divide the earth from the sky, or, figuratively, the human and spiritual realms.

It may be hard to conceive that markings as basic as dots and lines could have any particular symbolic significance, yet these simple graphics are some of the earliest and possibly most profound symbols. As well as being important in their own right, they also form an integral part of many other symbol systems, including the visual arts, writing, mathematics, geometry and various forms of divination, as well as informing sacred traditions all over the world.

THE DOT

Like a star in the sky, the dot or point is the first emanation to appear from the infinite void, a pinprick of light from the world of spirit. It symbolizes the centre or source from which all life begins and to which it must one day return. It is emblematic of the bud or seed, symbolizing the start of a new life, of hope and promise for the future. It is the first sign of a presence and a source of power – the centre from which all else radiates and the essence that remains when all else is removed. It is the pupil at the centre of an eye and the navel in the middle of

the body – a visual reminder of the umbilical cord that connected the unborn child to life. As the full point at the end of a statement it can represent an ending, but also presupposes a new beginning with the start of the next sentence.

In Hindu teaching the dot is known as the *bindu* (from a Sanskrit word meaning "drop") and is a symbol of the absolute. It is represented in the yantra (a type of mandala) by the point at which the two triangles representing Shiva and Shakti (god and goddess of the universe) meet. The *bindu* is often seen painted or worn on the face at the "third eye" in the centre of the forehead. In Hindu and Buddhist traditions the *bindu* is the source of meditation and a symbol of spiritual integration or enlightenment; it is the centre at which all experience is compacted into total concentration before imploding back to its origin – the void or a transcendental state of consciousness. In Islamic mysticism it is a symbol of the creator and the eternal. Numerically it is related to the symbolism of zero.

HORIZONTAL AND VERTICAL LINES

As its name suggests, a horizontal line follows the direction of the horizon. It represents the division between earth and sky, the dividing line between human life and the realms of the gods, and

the base or ground we stand on. As an axis of direction, the horizontal line symbolizes movement on the earth plane: from left to right (west to east) or right to left (east to west), as well as movement in time. It is concerned with the temporal realm, with matter and substance, balance and stability. Traditionally it is linked with the female or receptive element, although in China it is a yang symbol, denoting active, masculine power. In mathematics, a short horizontal line is a minus sign.

If the horizontal line is associated with matter, then the vertical line embraces spirit and provides the link between the higher and lower worlds. It is associated with the male principle and describes the movement from above to below, from Heaven to Earth, from the nadir to the zenith and vice versa. Related symbols include the spine in the human body, the trunk of the World Tree, the staff, stave, sceptre or wand, and many different phallic symbols. It is also widely used in many alphabets: in the Roman alphabet it forms the letter "I", where it represents the authority of the self. In Greek it forms the letter "iota", which the ancient Greeks considered to be representative of destiny or fate. The vertical line is related numerically to the number one.

ZIGZAG LINES

One of the earliest carvings known is more than 300,000 years old. It appears on a bone fragment from Pech de l'Aze, in France, and shows a zigzag or meander pattern. A set of similar symbolic designs more than 40,000 years old was found in Bacho Kiro, in Bulgaria. It is thought that the zigzags represent either snakes or water: in ancient Egypt, the zigzag was the hieroglyph for water, while a horizontal parallel zigzag formation is used to represent the sign of Aquarius, the water carrier in Western astrology.

PARALLEL LINES

Running side by side and never meeting, parallel lines are symbolic of opposites as well as balance and equality. In early cuneiform script, parallel lines signified "friendship" while crossed lines meant "enmity".

Vertical parallel lines can be observed in pillars or columns, which in the architecture of the ancient and classical world were associated with both temporal and spiritual authority. Double pillars also appear in esoteric symbolism. For example, in the Tarot, the High Priestess is shown sitting between two columns, one black, one white, symbolizing the polarities of male and female, positive and negative, life and death, creation and destruction. This symbolism is echoed in esoteric Jewish lore with the two columns on the façade of Solomon's Temple in Jerusalem. The left-hand column, made of black stone, corresponded to the

moon, decay, the waning year and cursing and was called Jachin, meaning "it shall stand"; the right-hand column, made of white stone, was called Boaz, meaning "in strength" and corresponded to the sun, the waxing year and blessing.

ABOVE Buildings are constructed by combining horizontal and vertical lines or planes. The horizontal planes of floors and ceilings provide grounding and enclosure or protection, while the vertical planes represent stature, growth and aspiration.

DOTS AND LINES IN DIVINATION

The Chinese I Ching, one of the world's oldest divinatory texts, is based on a series of hexagrams composed of broken and unbroken horizontal lines. An unbroken line is yang and relates to the sun, daytime and the heavens, while a broken line is yin and relates to the moon, night and the earth. The patterns made by dots have also been used in divination, originally in the form of stones, nuts or seeds, which were thrown on to the earth and then interpreted. Dot patterns were later transferred to dice or dominoes, where they are used in gaming as well as prediction.

THE CROSS

ABOVE The ankh is the Egyptian version of the cross, and is one of its most ancient manifestations.

ABOVE The equilateral or Greek cross forms the ground plan of many early Greek churches, and is the motif of the Red Cross organization.

THE CROSS AND HEALING

Because of its various spiritual and esoteric associations, the cross is connected with healing and miraculous powers. At one time, the cross was considered to offer protection against disorders such as epileptic fits, or to have the power to ward off supernatural phenomena such as vampires and devils. It is now associated with medicine and nursing through the Red Cross charity, which provides care for victims of war and famine.

In Western culture, the cross has become almost inseparable from Christianity, yet it is actually one of the oldest and most all-encompassing symbols. Carved in stone or wood or worked in metal or bone, richly decorated or simply drawn, the cross has appeared all over the world. A stone disc with a carved cross, found in the Tata Cave, in Hungary, is estimated to be around 100,000 years old, while crosses carved on a mammoth statuette from Vogelherd, in Germany, date back more than 30,000 years. The cross is found in the ancient civilizations of China, Egypt and Central America, is a frequent motif in African art, and appears on Celtic pottery, jewels and coins. It is widely considered to be one of four basic symbols with the point, the circle and the square, to which it is also linked.

EMBRACING THE WHOLE

The cross creates a totality. Its intersection of two lines can be seen as the uniting of the male principle (the vertical) with the female (the horizontal). The two axes also stand for the dimensions of time and space, matter and spirit, body and soul, as well as the equinoxes and solstices.

Crossing horizontal and vertical lines are the basis of a "stick person", one of the most basic representations of the human figure, found in prehistoric rock art, and in children's drawings ever since. When aligned with the four cardinal points, the cross becomes a symbol of orientation to the terrestrial directions of north, south, east and west, which in turn informs the symbolism of the Native American Medicine Wheel. A cross within a circle also mediates between the square and the circle, emphasizing the connection between sky and earth. It has been suggested that the four arms of the cross represent the four phases of the moon, as well as the four elements, the four winds and the four seasons. Together with the square, the cross is closely linked to the symbolism of four, a number signifying wholeness and universality, although in China the number of the cross is five, the perfect number of the human being as microcosm. This is because the midpoint (where the two lines intersect) is also counted – emphasizing the centre or source to which everything is connected.

WORLD SYMBOL

In China the early symbolism of the cross was expressed in the ideogram meaning "Earth": an equilateral cross within a square. According to a traditional Chinese saying, God fashioned the Earth in the form of a cross. A similar view emerges in ancient Mexican mythic tradition, where the cross symbolizes the world in its

totality: The 1st-century Christian theologian, St Jerome, came to the same conclusion when he wrote, "What is it but the form of the world in its four directions?"

Although there are literally hundreds of different types of cross, several appear to be particularly significant.

THE GREEK OR EQUILATERIAL CROSS

The equal-armed cross is one of the simplest. When enclosed in a circle it becomes the solar cross or sun-disc, a symbol similar to that adopted by the Assyrians to represent the sun god Shamash. In this form the circle emphasizes the cyclical nature of the seasons, while the four-armed cross represents the shadows cast by the rising and setting sun at the two solstices. This may explain why the cross appears in many examples of megalithic rock art. The Neolithic structure at Loughcrew, in Ireland, was made in the shape of a cross, with the central passage aligned to the equinoctial sunrise.

Centuries later, the Celts combined the cross and circle in a distinctive pattern that originally had links with fertility – the cross symbolizing the male generative power, and the circle, the female. In time the Celtic cross was used as a Christian symbol to represent the union of Heaven and Earth.

THE SWASTIKA

The Sanskrit *svastika* means "well being", and in India the swastika is a symbol of fertility and good fortune. It appears extensively throughout Asia, in both secular

LEFT In Central Australia the Aborigines use the form of a cross to control the composition of many sacred works of art.

and religious contexts. It is an ancient and widely used form of solar cross. Some of the earliest European examples appear on Bronze Age pottery found in Anatolia, in central Turkey, dating from about 3000 BC. It also appears on bronze articles among the Ashanti in Africa and was used by the Maya and Navajo.

Essentially the swastika is a spinning cross, with the angles at the end of each arm suggesting streaming light as it turns, just as the sun's rays light up the earth. Spinning anticlockwise it is said to represent the female principle, and clockwise, the male. The anticlockwise swastika appears in Buddhism, Taoism and in Native American cultures. In the modern Western world, however, the symbol tends to be associated with anti-Semitism because of its adoption by the German Nazi party in the 20th century.

THE T-CROSS

The Tau, or T-cross, is another very ancient cross symbol. It may have developed from the axe, a widespread and ancient symbol of the sun god, and appears to be phallocentric, its shape denoting testicles and penis. It forms the basis of the Egyptian ankh, in which the upper arm is replaced by a loop. A symbol of immortality in ancient Egypt, the ankh was adopted by the Coptic Church as its unique form of the Christian cross. The handled cross also occurs in America, where it has been found engraved on monuments in the ruins of Palenque, in Mexico, as well as on pieces of pottery.

THE LATIN CROSS

There is disagreement about the type of cross that was used for the crucifixion of Christ. It was as late as the mid-2nd century that translators of the Gospels first used "crux" in descriptions of death by crucifixion. Many images show Christ hung either from a Y-shaped structure (*furca*) or a T-shaped cross, as well as the more familiar Latin cross, where the cross-bar is set approximately two-thirds of the way up. Over time, the Latin cross became the central symbol of Christianity. Some believe this coincided with the gradual tendency in the early Church to separate the spiritual and material realms in accordance with Christ's saying, "My kingdom is not of this world." This view has dominated ideas about spirituality in much of the Christian world, where earthly life (including nature), the world and the body have been seen as forces that have to be overcome, rather than parts of an organic whole.

For Christians, the crucifix is a seminal symbol, representing Christ's death, resurrection, the victory of spirit over matter and the redemption of humanity.

CROSS OF LORRAINE

A single vertical crossed by two horizontals (the upper shorter than the lower) is known as the double cross, or cross of Lorraine. When a third, smaller, horizontal bar is added, it becomes a triple cross, associated with the papacy. The cross of Lorraine is believed to represent the crucifixion, with the upper bar added for the inscription "INRI" (the Latin abbreviation for "Jesus of Nazareth, King of the Jews"), fixed above Christ by Pontius Pilate. The cross of Lorraine was the emblem of the medieval Dukes of Anjou, later the Dukes of Lorraine, and in World War II became the symbol of the Free French, in opposition to the swastika of the Nazis.

ABOVE The cross has become the most widely used version in depictions of the crucifixion of Christ, and as such has become perhaps the most widely recognised symbol of christianity.

T

ABOVE For the early Christians the three directions of the Tau cross linked it with the Holy Trinity.

SPIRALS AND CIRCLES

ABOVE Because of their circular shape, rings can symbolize eternity, hence their use as love tokens.

TOP Like the Earth, the circle is a primordial symbol of perfection.

TOP RIGHT This triple spiral at a Stone Age burial site at Newgrange, in Ireland, is believed to symbolize the Celtic triple goddess.

BELOW Megalithic monuments were often arranged in a circle pattern that aligned with the sun's movement through the sky.

Both the spiral and the circle occur in nature as well as in art, myth and sacred tradition. The earliest known use of these shapes was in the Paleolithic age, when they were carved into bone or stone or painted on cave walls. Antler bone batons found in a cave at Isturitz, in France, dating back to c.25,000–20,000 BC, bear a relief forming a complex pattern of concentric arcs and spirals. A disc from the same period, found in Brno, in the Czech Republic, has a vertical line incised from the edge to the centre and is thought to be an abstract representation of a vulva, suggesting a link with the goddess worship characteristic of this period.

THE NATURAL WORLD

The sun, moon and planets all appear circular in shape, while spiral galaxies form some of the most breathtaking patterns in space. In the plant and animal kingdoms, spirals and circles appear in many guises, such as the concentric pattern of tree-rings, the centre of a flower, the shape of a bird's nest, the spiral of a snail or conch-shell, a coiled serpent or a twining plant stem.

Weather and water patterns also form spirals and circles in tornadoes, whirlpools, ripples on a pond and ocean waves. Nature itself circles and cycles through the changing seasons and the endless rhythm of night and day.

THE SPIRAL

Beginning with a single dot, the spiral develops from the initial seed and moves forwards in a clockwise or anticlockwise direction; thus it is connected with movement, energy and growth. Since the earliest times it has been a favourite ornamental motif linked with the symbolism of the moon and with cyclic development, involution and evolution, resurrection and renewal. It has also been linked to the erotic symbolism of the vulva, female sexuality and fertility, while many cultures believe the spiral represents the soul's journey after death. The motif is widely used in Oceanic art, where it is carved into door handles or canoe prows or tattooed on the body. To the Maori the spiral represents creation, and in Polynesia it is thought to be the key to immortality.

DOUBLE SPIRALS

Spirals often appear conjoined in twos and threes. The double spiral is said to symbolize duality and balance. It is also moving simultaneously in two directions – towards involution and evolution, contraction and expansion, or birth and death. This motif is seen in the wreathing of the twin serpents around the caduceus (the rod of

Hermes), or the double helix around the Brahman's staff. In Aztec mythology, the S-shaped counter-rotating double spiral is a symbol of thunder and of the phases of the moon. Spiral oculi (double twists resembling eyes) appear on entrances to sacred sites throughout Europe and are thought to be associated with the equinoxes, when day and night are of equal length.

TRIPLE SPIRALS

The triple spiral is often referred to as the spiral of life and was used consistently in Celtic art for nearly 3,000 years. One of the most famous examples appears in the "womb" chamber of the megalithic structure at Newgrange, Ireland (c.3200 BC), where a shaft of sunlight falls upon it once a year, at the winter solstice. It represents the Triple Goddess – maiden, mother and crone – who in turn is associated with the phases of the moon (waxing, full and waning) as well as the birth-death-rebirth cycle. It has been suggested that triple spirals might also be connected with the three trimesters of human gestation.

SACRED DANCES

Initiation rites and sacred dances often follow a spiral pattern that represents death and rebirth. Spiral formation dances can be a way of acknowledging and celebrating life's pattern of change and evolution. For instance, at New Year the Zuni (Pueblo) Indians chant "spiral" songs and dance spiral dances. One of the best-known forms of sacred spiral dance is that practised by the *mevlevi,* or "whirling dervishes" in Turkey, who spin round and round like a top. Exactly like the centre of the spinning top, the trunk of the whirling dancer symbolizes the still point in the midst of dynamic movement, the eye at the centre of the storm. Circle dances also symbolize life's pattern of change and flow.

A STAIRWAY TO HEAVEN

In ancient times it was thought that the heavens were reached by climbing a spiral path that ascended to a wheeling circle of stars. Souls ascended to Heaven along this pathway in the skies, which was mirrored on Earth as a spiral path up a sacred mountain, or the spiral staircase around a structure such as a ziggurat.

THE CIRCLE

With no beginning and no end, the circle has been used to signify eternity and wholeness, the heavens, the cosmos, the absolute and perfection. In Islam, the circle is seen as the perfect shape, and poets praise the circle formed by the lips as one of its most beautiful representations. In many cultures the circle represents the continuing cycle of the seasons and the sun's endless progression through the skies. It is often used as a symbol for the sun (itself a symbol of perfection) as well as for the full moon.

THE POWER OF THE WORLD

In Native North American traditions, the circle is perhaps the most important shape, related to the Sacred Hoop or Medicine Wheel: the Lakota Sioux shaman Black Elk (1863–1950) asserted that the power of the world works in circles, and that the circle contains all things.

In social and political life the circle is the preferred shape for an assembly of equals: the campfire circle, the council circle, the Round Table of the Arthurian legend. It is the easiest geometric shape to draw accurately, with stick and string, and may also represent the idea of a home or dwelling place, which in early societies was often constructed on a circular ground plan. In Australian Aboriginal art from the Western Desert, concentric circles were often used to represent sanctuaries or camping places, while lines between them were the paths and tracks of people or mythological beings. Here, the circles suggest places where ancestral power can surface from the Earth and return again.

POWER AND PROTECTION

Being a closed circuit and all-embracing, the circle is associated with protection, providing safety for all who put themselves within

its boundary. The magic circle is used in occult traditions to guard against negative psychic forces, and the protective circle can also be worn – as a ring, necklace, bracelet, girdle or crown.

SPIRITUAL HIERARCHIES

Drawings of concentric circles have been used as a teaching device to symbolize different stages of spiritual development in Zen Buddhism, as well as in esoteric Christian schools such as Rosicrucianism. In Christian symbology, hierarchies of angels are sometimes shown arranged in circles around God and Christ, while in the Divine Comedy, the Italian poet Dante (1265–1321) describes Heaven, purgatory and Hell as being divided into different circles or levels.

ABOVE In ancient tradition the path to Heaven was seen as a spiral, reflecting nature's whirling patterns, an idea used by William Blake in his 18th-century painting of Jacob's ladder.

BELOW The spiral symbolizes movement, energy and connection with nature.

TRIANGLES AND SQUARES

ABOVE The triangle is often associated with sacred mountains.

PYTHAGOREAN TRIANGLE

The Pythagorean triangle was an important symbol to the Egyptians, who regarded the vertical and horizontal sides as the male and female forces respectively, and the hypotenuse as their "offspring". This triangle symbolizes construction and development.

BELOW The pyramids of Egypt were symbols of the creative power of the sun and the primal mound.

The triangle and the square are universally important motifs. They are connected to the symbolism of three and four and everything to which these numbers relate, and can only be separated from them in terms of their relationship with other geometrical figures. The triangle appears frequently in everyday life, for example on road signs or washing instructions, while, after the circle, the square is the most common geometric shape printed on textiles. Many buildings have a square plan and, in urban design, a central square is often a focus of activity, such as a town square.

THE TRIANGLE

An equilateral triangle has three sides of equal length. In Christianity it is a symbol of the Trinity, while in Islamic art it symbolizes human consciousness and the principle of harmony. The triangle features in many alphabets. It is the ancient Maya hieroglyph for the sunray, and in the Greek alphabet it represents the letter "delta", which for the ancient Greeks symbolized the four elements and hence was linked with completion and wholeness. Today the word "delta" is used in English to describe a triangular tract of land at the mouth of a river (such as the Nile Delta), which is often very fertile. The connection of the triangle with the four elements also appears in alchemy, where it is used in various formations to symbolize them.

UPWARD AND DOWNWARD TRIANGLES

The Maya likened the shape of the upward-pointing triangle to a shoot of maize as it breaks through the surface of the soil, linking it with fertility, and also the male principle (the erect phallus). For the ancient Hittites an upward-pointing triangle was a symbol of the king and of health. Among the Pueblo people of the south-western United States it represents a sacred mountain, while a downward-pointing triangle represents clouds.

The inverted triangle is also associated with female fertility, as it resembles an image of a woman's pubic region and her internal sex organs – the triangle formed by the two ovaries and the womb. The Sumerians used a downward-pointing triangle to represent woman, and it is also a feminine symbol in China. In ancient Greece, Rome and India triangles were often used as decorative motifs in friezes. In all instances they seem to signify the same: pointing upwards, they stand for fire and the male sexual organs; pointing down they represent water and the female sexual organs. In more general terms, an upward-pointing triangle can symbolize reaching for the sky and so may be associated with aspirations, the attainment of goals, and new possibilities. It is also associated with arrowheads and the theme of spiritual quest. A downward-pointing triangle, on the other hand, is associated with receptivity, movement inwards rather than outwards, and consequently is often used as a meditation symbol.

CONJOINED TRIANGLES

The tips of triangles touching, one pointing up and one pointing down, can be used to denote sexual union, while intersecting triangles represent synthesis. Positioned with their bases meeting, two triangles can also represent the waxing and waning phases of the moon.

The six-pointed star combines two overlapping equilateral triangles and so relates to the symbolism of the triangle. It is an alchemical symbol for conjunction, relating to the union of the four elements. As the Star of David, it is the pre-eminent symbol of Judaism, while as the Seal of Solomon in Judaic mysticism it stands for the sacred number seven, represented by the six points plus the space at the centre, the place of transformation. In India, a six-pointed star is known as the Star of Lakshmi (the goddess of prosperity and abundance) and is often drawn in powder on doorways or village thresholds to keep away hostile spirits.

THE SQUARE

The ancient Greek philosopher Plato thought that, together with the circle, the square embodied beauty and perfection, while in ancient Egypt it represented achievement. It is one of the most common abstract symbols, representing Earth, material existence and the created universe. The square's shape suggests structure, order and stability, but also limitations – echoed in the expression of feeling "boxed in" to describe being trapped and constrained. It is often seen in relation and in contrast to the circle of the heavens, or of the limited in contrast to the unlimited, of matter as opposed to spirit, of static versus dynamic.

A quadrangular form has often been used for areas set apart for sacred or other reasons, such as altars, temples, castles or military camps. City squares traditionally lie at the heart of urban life. The Forum in ancient Rome was the market square at the heart of the capital, through which the Sacred Way ran up to the Capitoline Hill and the temple of Jupiter; the ancient Greek equivalent was the Agora, the commercial centre of Athens, surrounded by temples and public buildings.

MYSTICAL SYMBOLISM

The symbolism of the square is connected with its four corners, which suggest the foundations and sum of life: the four elements, the four seasons, the four stages of life (childhood, adolescence, adulthood, old age) and the four cardinal directions.

In ancient China, space was measured by the four yang or square directions; the earth god was represented by a square mound, and the capital city and imperial palace were both square, with the emperor at the centre. In Hinduism the square is the anchor that assures the order of the universe, while in Islam the human heart is symbolized as a square, as it is thought to be open to four possible sources of influence: divine, angelic, human or devilish. In contrast, the heart of a prophet is triangular as it is immune to the devil's attacks.

RELATED SHAPES

It is the number of sides of a geometric shape that gives it its symbolic significance. Other important shapes include the pentagon (with five sides) and hexagon (six), as well as three-dimensional shapes such as the cube and pyramid. In the mystical Kabbalah, the pentagon relates to the fifth sephira on the tree of life, associated with justice, war and the planet Mars, while in Islamic mysticism, it is a symbol of the five elements (fire, water, earth, air and ether) and of the five senses. The hexagon is also associated with Islamic esoteric teachings, symbolizing the six directions of movement (up, down, forwards, backwards, left and right).

A cube is a six-sided solid figure representing the three-dimensional physical world. It also symbolizes the six directions of movement. In Islam it represents perfection: the Ka'ba in Mecca, said to be the centre of the world, is a black cube. In Freemasonry a cube of ashlar (smooth dressed stone) stands for the perfected human being.

With four triangular sides and a square base, the pyramid synthesizes the symbolism of both shapes, as well as the numbers three, four and five, connecting with the Pythagorean "tetrakis". The square base represents the earth plane, while the four upward-pointing triangles of the pyramid's sides meet to form a fifth point, suggesting the fifth element: ether. As the pyramid reaches up to the sky, its point represents the human soul striving to unite with the Cosmic One.

ABOVE Perhaps the most famous city square in history, Rome's vast Forum lay at the heart of the city's religious, commercial, ceremonial and public life.

ABOVE The cube's six sides make it a symbol of stability and truth.

THE TETRAKIS

The sum of the numbers 1+2+3+4=10. In Pythagorean theory, ten is a holy number representing divine power and the quintessence of perfection. It can be represented as a triangle of dots, four to each side and one in the centre, called the tetrakis.

COLOUR

ABOVE Red is the colour of sexual and romantic love, and symbolizes intense passion.

Together with shape, colour is one of the fundamental building blocks of visual symbols. It is also closely associated with mental and emotional states, and can affect them profoundly. The seven colours seen in the rainbow correspond with the mystical number seven and other groups of seven, such as the number of notes on a musical scale or the number of chakras in the body.

COLOUR SHORTHAND

Different colours are often used as a shorthand to describe emotional states, gender or social and political status. In the West colours are traditionally used to distinguish between the sexes – pink for a girl and blue for a boy – and colours are chosen to differentiate sports teams from each other.

Colloquial English expressions that describe states of feeling in colour terms include "in the pink", "green with envy", "in a black mood", "feeling blue",

"seeing red" or "off colour". During the 20th century red was linked to the Communist party, while the green movement aims to put environmental issues on the political agenda. Similarly, colour is used to denote race, so that "black" and "white" carry social and political meanings depending on their context.

RED

As the colour of blood and fire, red is widely associated with life and warmth. In Paleolithic times, red ochre was mined and ground into powder. It seems to have been endowed with life-giving powers, and its presence in Neolithic graves may have been to help the dead in the afterlife. Thousands of years later, in Anglo-Saxon times, red was believed to protect against evil and objects, trees and even animals were painted red, while warriors covered their axes and spears in red paint to endow them with magic powers – a custom also practised by some Australian Aboriginals.

Red is linked with love and fertility. In ancient Rome, brides were wrapped in a fiery reddish-orange veil (the *flammeum*), a custom still observed in parts of Greece, Albania and Armenia, while in China, the wedding gown and veil are red. Red eggs are offered to the couple when a child is born. Red has been used to suggest passion and erotica in Indian and western tradition, or to suggest high energy and speed.

Red is associated with danger (the most serious crisis is described as a "red alert"), anger

and aggression (it is linked with Mars, the Roman god of war), or wickedness or evil. In ancient Egypt red was an accursed colour. associated with the destructive god Set, and "making red" was synonymous with killing someone. Evil doings were referred to as "red affairs" and scribes used special red ink when writing words of ill omen.

YELLOW

Closely related to the symbolism of gold, yellow is associated with the sun and its life-giving generative powers. In the Aztec pantheon, Huitzilopochtli, the victorious warrior god of the midday sun, was depicted in blue and yellow, while in Mexican cosmology, the earth's "new skin" (before the rain comes and turns it green) was golden yellow.

In China, yellow was associated with the centre of the universe, and one creation myth describes how the first humans were made out of yellow clay. It was the sacred colour of the emperor. Australian Aboriginals use yellow ochre to symbolize death.

Sometimes a distinction is made between different shades of yellow: in Islam, golden yellow symbolizes wisdom, whereas pale yellow indicates treachery. In Egypt and medieval Europe, yellow was the colour of envy; it also signified disgrace, and is still associated with cowardice.

GREEN

The colour of plant life, green can stand for awakenings, new beginnings and growth: in China and Japan it relates to spring. The

Celtic Green Man is an important vegetation and fertility god, and there are many instances of green being linked with superhuman powers. In ancient Egypt, cats with green eyes were feared, and in medieval Europe green was associated with the Devil and wearing it was considered unlucky. The "green ray" is an extremely rare manifestation of light that can be observed occasionally at sunrise and sunset, and in alchemy, the secret fire, or the living spirit, was envisaged as a translucent green stone. In Islam, green is the most important colour: Mohammed's green cloak represented paradise, renewal and spiritual refreshment.

BLUE

Whether celestial or oceanic, blue evokes wide, open spaces and is linked with infinity and primordial emptiness. The blue of the sky has been associated with the male principle, distance and the gods. In ancient Egypt, gods and kings were often depicted with blue beards and wigs, and the Hindu divinity Krishna is portrayed as blue. Still, deep water, on the other hand, also associates blue with the female principle. As a symbol of peace and purity, it is the colour of the Virgin Mary. Blue is associated with dreamlike states, contemplation, introspection and yearning. In parts of the Arab

world blue is thought to offer protection against the evil eye, and the old English custom of brides wearing "something blue" is meant to ensure fidelity.

PURPLE

Historically, in the West, purple dye was the most expensive to produce as it was made from *Murex* or *Purpura* molluscs, which were rare and also costly to process. Only the rich could afford purple garments, hence the colour's symbolic association with royalty and the priesthood. It was the preferred colour of the Byzantine and Roman emperors.

In China, purple was the colour of the North Star, the centre of Heaven and the site of the "purple palace" of the heavenly emperor. To identify the temporal emperor as the Son of Heaven, his imperial palace compound at Beijing was called the Purple Forbidden City. Buddhists regard purple as a sacred colour, and in Thailand it is worn by mourning widows.

BLACK AND WHITE

In some parts of the Arab world, black animals are regarded as unlucky: black dogs bring death in the family, and black hens are used in witchcraft. White, the colour of light, is considered lucky. However, black is also a symbol of power and authority: it became an emblem of the Caliphate in the 1st century AD.

Death and mourning are symbolized in the West by black and in the East by white. In Africa, white is the colour of the dead, but is also believed to have the power to drive death away and so is associated with healing.

In ancient Egypt, black was the colour of resurrection and eternal life, perhaps because new life was seen as emerging from the darkness. It is associated with the mother goddess and fertility, when it is sometimes linked to red, the colour of blood. In China, black represents the feminine principle (yin), with its opposite being yellow.

In the West, white symbolizes spiritual purity and innocence, and is the colour traditionally worn for baptism robes and wedding dresses.

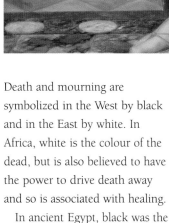

ABOVE Berenice (c.273–21 BC), Queen of Cyrene and Egypt, wears a purple toga as a symbol of her imperial status.

TOP LEFT Blue symbolizes divinity and peace.

TOP MIDDLE In the West, white symbolizes innocence and purity,

GREY

Traditionally, grey is associated with old age and with the planet Saturn. Saturn, or Cronos, was lord of time in the Greco-Roman pantheon, and wisdom was one of his attributes. On the Kabbalastic tree of life, grey is also linked with wisdom.

MYTH AND THE COSMOS

A WIDE ARRAY OF SYMBOLISM HAS BEEN USED TO DESCRIBE THE ORIGINS OF THE UNIVERSE. CREATION MYTHOLOGY USUALLY REFLECTS A SOCIETY'S GEOGRAPHY, CULTURE AND BELIEFS, AND SERVES TO ALIGN IT WITH NATURE AND THE PRECONDITIONS OF LIFE. A NUMBER OF ARCHETYPAL THEMES ARE INTERWOVEN WITH THE CREATION MYTHOLOGIES OF THE WORLD.

THE CREATIVE PROCESS

Creation may be described as one huge cosmic event, or a process in stages in which things become increasingly differentiated, sometimes leading to a natural hierarchy and at others to a sacred interrelationship between all aspects of nature. Whether the mythological creation of human beings coincides with the actual event of creation, or emerges slowly over time, the original man and the original woman are always seen as central symbols of primordial humanity.

BELOW This painting of God creating the world is rich with Christian symbolism, including the globe, symbol of power and totality, held by Adam, the Greek letters alpha and omega on the front of God's book, represent God's role as the beginning and the end, and the animals and plants, symbolizing the abundance and variety of God's created world.

THE CREATOR GODS

Creation is often actively brought about through the actions, dreams or reflections of divine beings. The Upanishads, Hindu scriptures of the 9th century BC, describe the Divine Self or Supreme Being who created the universe by reflecting upon nothingness and finding only itself. This fundamental act of self-consciousness led to the first word: "This am I." In Samoan mythology, the supreme god Tangaroa created the world from nothingness by thinking of it.

Australian Aboriginal stories more than 150,000 years old attribute creation to Ancestors living in the mythical space and time known as the "Dreaming". These beings lived much like their human counterparts, travelling, hunting, loving and fighting, and shaping the landscape through their "walkabouts". In sleep the ancestors dreamed the events of the next day, dreaming up all living beings, the sun, moon and stars. Australian Aboriginals believe that every being shares a fundamental connection with the source of creation, reflecting their deep respect for nature.

The book of Genesis describes God bringing about all of creation single-handedly. He completed his work on the sixth day with the creation of humans, who were to "have dominion" over all life. Thus the Judaeo-Christian cosmology gives humanity a special place under God in the hierarchy of nature.

CREATION FROM CHAOS OR THE VOID

The Greek term "chaos" refers to an initial dark, formless universe. From it sprang Eros, a fertility deity later associated with erotic love, but initially the creative urge behind life and nature. With Eros came Gaia, earth goddess, and Tartarus, god of the underworld. Gaia's son Uranus impregnated her, giving rise to the Titans and the Cyclops and then to the seas, land and other natural features.

Since oceans encircle the world, in many creation myths the universe arises from a chaotic body of water. The creation of the Egyptian world from water is fitting in a land that depended on the periodic flooding of the Nile: from Nu, the original water, a hill of dry land emerged, followed by the first sunrise on the new horizon, then the rest of creation.

The Japanese gods Izanagi and Izanami disturbed the primordial waters with a spear, and the drips from it coalesced to form the island of Onokoro. The Arunta people of central Australia tell of

LEFT The Egyptian sky goddess, Nut, whose body is arched over the earth, is separated from Geb, the Earth god.

a world covered with salt water that was gradually drawn back by the people in the north, revealing the first land. The myth of the Altaic shamans of Central Asia tells of a time before creation in which there was no earth, only endless water, over which flew a white gander, the god Kara-han.

CREATION FROM SEPARATION

The theme of separation explains the origins of life in terms of the splitting of a primordial state of unity. Usually this involves the rending apart of a male sky god and a female earth goddess, though in some cultures the male is associated with earth and the female with sky.

In Maori and other Polynesian myths the universe originally consisted of an eternal night or gloom. Eventually Rangi, the sky father, and Papa, the earth mother, coupled, creating the land and many divine offspring. They lived in darkness until it was decided to split the parents apart. Tu Matauenga, the god of war, hacked at the sinews joining his parents, which bled with the sacred colour of red ochre. But it was only Tane Mahuta, god of the forest, who was able to separate them, drawing them apart to allow light and air in between sky and earth. In a similar Egyptian myth, the sky goddess Nut and the earth god Geb were separated by their offspring.

CREATION THROUGH DISMEMBERMENT

A common theme is of creation emerging from the death and dismemberment of a primordial being. Such myths may help people to reconcile themselves with the violent preconditions of life and the need for death in order to sustain life.

According to Norse creation mythology, Odin, Vili and Ve killed the giant Ymir, from whose body the world emerged. His flesh formed the land, the sea and rivers flowed from his blood, his bones became mountains and trees grew from his hair. Ymir's huge skull became the heavens. Similarly, when the Chinese primordial being P'an-Ku died, his breath became the winds, his voice the thunder, his blood the water and his muscles the fertile land. His happy moods caused the sun to shine and his anger produced thunder and lightning. The Babylonian epic Enuma Elish, composed in the 12th century BC, tells of the god Marduk killing and cutting in two the body of Tiamat, the goddess of the ocean. The two halves became the sky and the earth.

Indonesian mythology tells of a time before creation in which there was no time, no birth or death, and no sex. Then a great cosmic dance occurred during which a single dancer was trampled and his body torn into pieces. Time began with this

murder and immediately brought about the separation of the sexes. From the buried body parts of the dancer grew plants and trees. And so the first death simultaneously produced the beginning of time, growth and procreation.

FIRST MAN AND WOMAN

The origin of humankind is symbolized worldwide in the images of the "first man" and the "first woman", representing the blueprint of humanity. But with humans comes the creation of evil or forces of torment with which they must contend.

In Sumerian mythology of the 3rd millennium BC, Enki, the fun-loving god of wisdom, with his mother/lover, the earth goddess Ninhursag, and twelve other goddesses, moulded the first humans out of clay from the bed of the river Euphrates. Having created perfect people, they had a contest to create people for whom the others could find no role, giving rise to human imperfection.

In the Biblical account, Adam (whose name means "made of clay") is created from the dust of the earth by Yahweh, the creator God, who breathes life into him. He is then given a female companion, Eve, who will be the mother of all humanity.

Although in both these myths the first humans are created from the substance of the earth, there are differences between them. Sumerian humans were created to be made slaves of the gods, Adam and Eve were created by one God and given dominion, and their task was to "subdue" nature.

FORBIDDEN FRUIT

The story of Adam and Eve living in the Garden of Eden represents them in a state of innocence in which there is no awareness of difference, sexuality, good or evil. By eating the fruit of the tree of the knowledge, the one thing God has forbidden, they gain a moral sense and are responsible for the corruption of human nature. It is often the apple that is portrayed as the forbidden fruit, but this probably dates from medieval rather than Biblical times, when artistic interpretations of The Fall were created. The pomegranate rather than the apple is often favoured by Hebrew scholars.

BELOW The idea of the first human beings, one man and one woman, is common throughout many world mythologies.

THE SUN

ABOVE Sunset symbolizes old age, endings and death in many cultures.

ABOVE The Eye of Horus was a symbol of royalty and immortality, and a talisman for protection.

MIDDLE The sun is an archetypal symbol, worshipped as a deity by many peoples.

TOP The lion is a solar symbol, a sign of power and leadership.

As our only source of light and heat the sun is crucial to life on earth and is one of the most important symbols in all world cultures. It is typically associated with power, manifesting both as a supreme deity and in emperors or kings. Its active energy is usually (though not always) regarded as male, and is associated with immediate, intuitive knowledge or cosmic intellect. The sun's counterpart in the heavens is the moon (often seen as female), and solar and lunar symbolism is contrasted by nearly all cultures. The solar principle is associated with animals, birds and plants (such as the lion, eagle and sunflower), with gold, and with colours such as yellow, orange and red. The sun is an important symbol in astrology, alchemy and psychology, where it represents the undivided self.

THE EYE OF THE WORLD

In many cultures the sun is likened to an all-seeing divine eye. It was the "eye" of the Greek god Zeus (and his Roman equivalent Jupiter), the Egyptian god Horus, the Hindu Varuna, the Norse Odin and the Islamic Allah. The Samoyed of the Arctic region regard the sun and moon as the two eyes of Num (the heavens), the sun being the good and the moon the evil eye. According to a myth of the Fulani of West Africa, when Gueno (the supreme deity) had finished the work of creation he took the sun out of his eye-socket and placed it in the heavens. He then became the one-eyed king, one eye being enough to see with, the other

providing light and heat. In many traditions the sun is poetically referred to as the "eye of the day".

SOLAR DEITIES

The link between the sun and divinity is archetypal, and many cultures have worshipped solar deities, including Shamash (Babylonian), Ra (Egyptian), Mithras (Persian) and Apollo (Greek and Roman). In Eastern traditions, the sun is the emblem of the Hindu god Vishnu and of the Buddha, whom some Chinese writers refer to as "Sun-Buddha" or "Golden Man". The Jewish High Priest wore a golden disc on his chest as a symbol of the divine sun, and Christ is sometimes compared to the spiritual sun at the heart of the world and called Sol Justitiae (Sun of Justice) or Sol Invictus (Invincible Sun), with the twelve disciples compared to the sun's rays.

Although the sun is usually regarded as male, in some cultures (African, Native American, Maori, Australian Aboriginal, Japanese and Germanic) the solar deity is female, because the female principle is seen as active through its life-giving powers. Japan's sun goddess, Amaterasu, retreats to a cave in protest at the neglect of his duties by her brother the storm god, and is enticed back out by other gods making much noise. In the cosmology of the Dogon of Mali, the sun is described as a white-hot earthenware pot (a symbol of the womb) surrounded by a spiral of red copper, representing the semen that will make it fertile.

TEMPORAL POWER

Many cultures and their rulers have claimed ancestry from the sun, including the Incas, the pharaohs of ancient Egypt, the Chinese and the Japanese. The Japanese imperial family are said to be direct descendants of the sun goddess Amaterasu, and the rising sun (represented by a red disc) is not only the Japanese national emblem but also the country's name (Nihon).

The rising sun is generally regarded as a symbol of hope and new beginnings, in contrast to a rayed sun, which signifies illumination. In China the sun was a symbol of the emperor who wore a sun design (a circle containing a three-legged crow) on his robes. Sun symbolism is a common motif on regalia. It appears on the thrones of the Kubu of southern Africa, while the Ashanti of West Africa use a gold sun disc to represent the king's soul. Modelling himself on the sun god Apollo, the French king Louis XIV (1638-1715) was known as the "Sun King", and court life revolved around him like planets around the sun, at his opulent palace at Versailles.

SUNRISE AND SUNSET

The disappearance of the sun each evening and its apparent rebirth the next morning make it a potent symbol of death, resurrection and immortality. This forms the basis of many myths and sacred rituals. In ancient Egypt the sun god Ra made a terrifying journey each night through the underworld, encountering his arch-enemy, the

monstrous snake Apophis, before rising again in the east; if Apophis were ever to defeat Ra, the sun would not rise and the earth would be plunged into darkness. In the Native American Cherokee tradition the sun is female, and when her daughter dies from a snake bite the sun covers her face in grief and the world becomes dark. To console her, the people dance and sing, whereupon she uncovers her face and the world becomes light. The Sun Dance of the Plains Indians is linked to this symbolism.

THE BLACK SUN

Some cultures refer to a black sun. The Aztecs showed it being carried on the back of the god of the underworld, while the Maya depicted it as a jaguar. As the antithesis of the midday sun at the height of its creative, life-affirming powers, the black sun is associated with death and destruction, foreshadowing the unleashing of disaster. Solar eclipses are therefore almost universally regarded as bad omens, heralding cataclysmic events that bring a cycle to an end: for instance, at the moment of Christ's crucifixion, the sun

ABOVE In many traditions, a solar eclipse was viewed with dismay and fear as a symbol of misfortune.

went dark. In alchemy, a black sun stands for unworked, primal matter yet to be refined; to the psychologist, it is an emblem of the elemental unconscious.

PSYCHOLOGICAL SYMBOLISM

The sun is often associated with the principle of authority, of which the father is the first embodiment. It is linked with individuality, will, ego and personality, at the highest level striving for psychic integration or enlightenment or at a lower level indulging in egomania, excessive pride and authoritarianism. The sun is also linked with creative energy, health and vitality, influencing both physical and psychological development. As the embodiment of male energy, it can be seen as a representation of the animus and may appear in dreams and myths as an emperor, king, god or hero figure.

SOLAR SYMBOLS

Symbols of the sun include a disc, a point within a circle (used in astronomy and astrology), a spoked wheel (a Celtic symbol) and a chariot – in many traditions (including Norse, ancient Egyptian and ancient Greek) the sun is viewed as a deity transported across the sky in a chariot. A rayed sun suggests illumination; a common graphic symbol is a circle with rays presented as alternating straight and wavy lines, suggesting the sun's power to generate light and heat. Traditionally there were seven rays, for the six directions of space and the seventh, cosmic, dimension. Sometimes the sun is depicted with a face – among the Native American Hopi, for instance, as well as in Western iconography. In Celtic myth, the sun was personified by Lug ("Light"), sometimes referred to as Grianainech ("Sun Face").

THE SUN AS DESTROYER

The sun's power causes drought. In ancient China, people would shoot arrows at it to hold it in check, while in Cambodia rain-making rituals involved the sacrifice of a "solar" animal.

ABOVE A halo of sunrays surrounds Amaterasu, sun goddess of Japan.

THE MOON

BELOW The stones of Stonehenge are believed to have served to astronomically measure the phases of the moon.

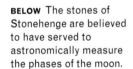

Being about 400,000 km/250,000 miles from the Earth, the moon exerts a powerful gravitational pull on both land and water. Its influence is most noticeable in the ocean tides, but many believe that plants and animals, including humans, are also affected. Next to the sun, the moon is the most obvious heavenly body, and its periodicity was of central importance in early concepts of time. The fact that its rhythms correspond almost exactly to the female menstrual cycle, and to the seasons and the annual cycle, led to obvious associations with the feminine and with earth or nature. The moon doesn't emit its own light, but reflects the light of the sun: the quality of this light has itself been a great source of religious and artistic inspiration.

THE MOON AND THE FEMININE

The symbolism attributed to the moon is predominantly (but not exclusively) associated with the feminine. The moon is connected to the imagination, intuition, psychic powers and dreaming, and is particularly associated with women, fertility and birth. Ancient civilizations performed fertility rituals and celebrated the moon at annual festivals dedicated to the goddess, to seek her help with conception. The time of ovulation for women was thought to occur during a full moon, and it was believed that during her time of menstruation a woman's powers of perception were heightened.

Moon goddesses are found in many ancient cultures. The moon is revered as a many-breasted mother of all, creator of all life on earth. The Greek goddess Artemis (the Roman Diana) is depicted with many breasts and with animals and plants springing from her head, limbs and chest. The Chinese moon goddess gave birth to all things after a flood; similarly, moon goddesses of Western Asia and Europe were the source of all living creatures. Inca beliefs about the moon changed over time: at first a goddess with no connection to the sun, she later became the sun's wife and the goddess of marriage. Her children were the stars. Finally she was thought to be her brother the sun's incestuous bride.

INNER WISDOM

The moon is a great reflector and embodies the qualities of receptiveness that are necessary for the intuitive process and to experience feelings. This receptiveness is another aspect of moon deities.

The moon is often associated with wisdom. The Greek and Egyptian goddess Sophia, or Lady Wisdom, is a moon goddess and the personification of divine knowledge. Shing Moo, a Chinese moon goddess, is called the goddess of perfect intelligence, and the Virgin Mary, sometimes called the Moon of the Church, is said to have perfect wisdom.

THE MOON AND THE MIND

As the moon pulls on the tides it can also be understood to pull on our emotions, which are often associated with water. Although the moon is sometimes linked with the acquisition of knowledge, it is more often associated with feeling, irrationality, and the unconscious or hidden. To be "under the influence of the moon" is to lose your reason, to be taken with moods and feelings, overwhelmed by the unconscious, which in its most extreme form manifests as madness or lunacy. (Despite all the folklore relating the two, there is very little reliable scientific evidence of a connection between the moon and madness.)

In early Japanese mythology the light from Tsukuyomi, Shinto god of the moon, could induce hallucinations and delusions. Hecate, the Greek goddess of the dark moon, bestowed visions but could also strike people down with madness. The same is true for most of the moon deities, with a thin line dividing inspiration and lunacy. There are stories of frenzied demons that are strongly influenced by the moon. The

CREATURES ON THE MOON

The craters and shadows on the moon have allowed people to project the images of all manner of creatures on to it. A common Western image is of the man in the moon. In China, it is a toad or a hare. The Altaic shamans see an old cannibal, imprisoned there to spare humankind. The Yakut of Siberia see a girl with a yoke upon her shoulders carrying buckets. In Peru they see a fox or a jaguar. The Incas saw a face into which they believed the jealous sun had thrown dust to make it shine less brightly.

ABOVE Since medieval times the Virgin Mary was associated with the crescent moon, in her role as reflector of the light of Christ.

Slavs tell of werewolves – people who are transformed into wolves by the light of the full moon. They are a great threat to people and are invulnerable to all weapons except for those made from silver, a moon metal.

PHASES OF THE MOON

The moon reflects the rhythms of life, undergoing an endless process of death and rebirth in its 28-day cycle; it therefore often represents transition and renewal and has come to symbolize cyclical time. The moon actually has 28 phases in its daily rising and setting, during which it passes through the entire zodiac. However it is more common to refer to four phases or quarters of the moon: waxing, full, waning, and the new or dark moon.

The waxing of the moon is associated with rising energy – mirroring pregnancy – and is often thought to be a good time to embark on new projects. The moon is at its strongest when it is full: it represents the fullness of female energy and echoes the symbolism of the circle, signifying wholeness. The waning moon is the time of decreasing, for letting go of things. The new moon is associated with restfulness and the beginning of the ascent from the underworld or death.

THE CRESCENT

As an emblem, the crescent moon is pre-eminently associated with female deities. The virgin goddess Artemis (or the Roman equivalent Diana) is usually depicted either holding a crescent or wearing one on her head. The upturned crescent is an attribute of the Egyptian goddess Isis, and in Christian iconography the Virgin Mary, inheriting some of the symbolism of Isis, is also sometimes shown on an upturned crescent. It is an attribute of the High Priestess of the Tarot, who is associated with mystery, intuition and the powers of the unconscious. In Hinduism the crescent moon is the emblem of Shiva, the god of transformation.

The crescent moon is a very important symbol in the Islamic world, symbolizing openness and concentration. Generally accompanied by a star, it is a symbol of paradise and of resurrection, frequently carved or painted on minarets and tombs. In the Arabic alphabet, the letter "n", shaped like a crescent with a dot above it, is the letter of resurrection, and prayers for the dead are written to rhyme with it; the letter is pronounced "nun", which is also the Arabic word for fish, and the fish is a symbol of eternal life in the Qu'ran.

LUNAR MYTHS

In Nordic myth, Mani the moon and Sol the sun were created by the gods and put in chariots to cross the sky. Mani's chariot often came close to the earth so that his light could have greater influence on those below. On one occasion he snatched two children who were fetching water, Hiuki and Bil, to be his companions, and they became the waxing and waning moon. Mani was often chased by the wolf Hati – when he caught him the atmosphere would become ghostly, and when he managed to drag him to the ground there was an eclipse.

TOP The new moon symbolizes the resting point of the cycle of life.

ABOVE A waning moon represents 'letting go' and 'decrease'.

MAN ON THE MOON

On 20 July 1969, Neil Armstrong symbolically made first physical contact with the moon, with the words: "One small step for man, one giant step for mankind."

THE STARS

ABOVE Stars are connected with spiritual illumination and divine presence.

RIGHT In the Christian tradition, it was a star that guided the Magi to the newborn baby Jesus, to whom they gave their gifts of gold, myrrh and frankincense.

ABOVE A five-pointed star was the emblem of the Assyrian goddess Ishtar (later Isis, Venus). It became a widespread symbol for spiritual and military ascendancy.

As pinpoints of light that illuminate the darkness, the stars have almost always been seen as heavenly symbols, signifiers of divine presence. They are archetypal symbols, appearing in sacred and secular traditions all over the world. According to the Yakut shamans of Siberia, stars were the windows of the universe. Their fleeting opening and closing gave or denied access to the upper world. In early societies, sky-watching was an important part of life, and astrology and astronomy were one. Celestial phenomena were of great practical significance, marking seasonal changes and providing a calendar for hunting and planting. As people noticed that certain occurrences in the heavens coincided with events on Earth, the parallels became fused into omens – a blood-red moon, for instance, was taken to indicate natural disaster or war.

STAR MYTHS

Many stories are told about the symbolism of stars. According to the Kalevala, the national epic of Finland, the stars were made from shell fragments flung out when the World Egg cracked. Among

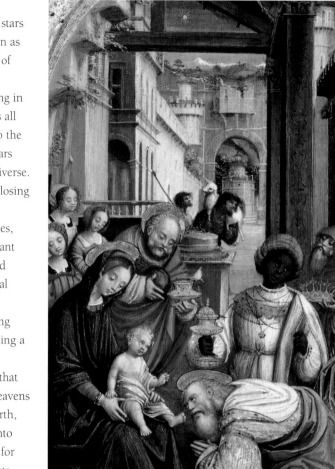

SHOOTING STARS
Generally regarded as a sign of divinity, shooting stars have been interpreted as sparks of heavenly fire or seeds of the godhead. They are said to perform a similar function to angels, acting as messengers between Heaven and earth and reminding human beings of their connection with spirit.

the Aztecs the Milky Way was called *mixcoatl* ("cloud-serpent"), and gave its name to Mixcoatl, the god of the Pole Star and of the hunt, who was thought to dwell in the stars. In the hieroglyphics of the Maya, stars are often depicted with rays of light shooting out from them. According to folk-belief in Guatemala and Peru, stars represent the souls of the righteous dead, while among the Inca the cosmic symbolism of stars extends to include not only humans but also animals and birds: they believed that in the heavens there was a double of every creature on Earth,

responsible for their birth and increase. In the Christian tradition, the birth of Christ was heralded by the appearance of the Star of Bethlehem. Today, stars are associated with dreams and wishes and the belief that if you make a wish when you see a shooting star it will come true.

THE MORNING STAR
Because the orbit of Venus lies within that of Earth it always appears fairly near the sun in the sky, and depending on its cycle it is seen near either the rising or the setting sun. It is therefore called both the Morning and the Evening Star. In Babylonian and

Assyrian mythology, Ishtar, the goddess of love associated with Venus, descended to the underworld in search of her lover then returned to life, just as the Evening Star disappeaed from view for a period, before reappearing as the Morning Star to herald the rising sun.

Among the Plains Indians the Morning Star is a symbol of the life principle – because it heralds the dawn and the rebirth of daylight – while the Cora Indians of the south-western United States give it equal importance with the sun and moon, with which it forms a heavenly trinity in their mythology. In the Mexican tradition, however, the Morning Star was thought to unleash disease, and doors and windows were closed at daybreak to protect against its dangerous light; in Mexican folk art it is often depicted with a bow and arrow and wearing a skull-mask. In the Christian tradition, one name for the devil is Lucifer, which means Morning Star.

THE POLE STAR

The Pole Star symbolizes the fixed and eternal point at the centre, around which the cosmos revolves. In many parts of Europe and Asia it is variously referred to as a pivot, hub, navel, life-centre or gate of Heaven. In the Turkic tradition it is described as the "tent-pole" of the heavens; the Mongols refer to it as a golden pillar, and the Saami of northern Scandinavia call it the Pillar of the World. In most northern Asiatic traditions it is placed over the summit of the World Mountain,

pinpointing the residence of the almighty god in the skies; consequently in these regions altars are usually set at the northern end of a temple.

The symbolism of the Pole Star as the apex of the heavens mirrors human hierarchies. In China, for example, the heavens, with the rest of the stars fixed according to their relationship with the Pole Star, are seen in terms of the structure of society, in which the emperor and ruling classes were the pivotal point around which everyone else revolved, each in their correct place. In India, the Pole Star is invoked in Vedic marriage ceremonies, representing the bridegroom as the pivotal point of the relationship.

STAR SYMBOLS

A five-pointed star is known as a pentagram and is an ancient magical sign. It is a shape that appears in art and classical architecture, as well as in nature (in starfish and certain flowers). The lines joining its five points divide each other in the ratio known as the Golden Mean or Divine Proportion, making it a symbol of wholeness and perfection. When drawn pointing upwards the pentagram is said to

be a symbol of the cosmic human, and in Christian tradition it is a symbol of Christ as "Alpha and Omega", beginning and end.

The followers of Pythagoras used the pentagram as an identifying sign, and it also appears frequently as an emblem in the regalia of Freemasonry, a society that traces its history back to the Pythagoreans.

In medieval Europe the pentagram was used as a talisman against evil to ward off demonic powers. When inverted, however, with two points uppermost, the pentagram was associated with the devil, the points being seen as signifying his horns.

ABOVE Two versions of the eight-pointed Star of Ishtar, used throughout the Near East for many centuries before the birth of Christ. The top star is a Babylonian version, the bottom is Phoenician.

THE PENTACLE

In the Western occult tradition upright five-pointed stars were engraved on discs of precious metals such as silver or gold to create a magic seal known as a pentacle. Hebrew letters, Latin words and Kabbalistic signs were sometimes inscribed within the star shape. The seal symbolized the power of the occult, and was believed to be able to cause earthquakes, inspire love, cause misfortune and cast spells, as well as offer protection against evil. The sign of the pentacle appears on the walls of ancient temples, carved into the stones of churches and as a pattern in stained-glass windows. When an apple is cut in half across the core, the shape of the pentacle is revealed: the European Roma call this the Star of Knowledge.

THE ZODIAC

ABOVE Aries resembles the head of a ram but also the fountain of life.

ABOVE Taurus resembles the head and the horns of an ox.

ABOVE Gemini symbolizes duality.

ABOVE Cancer suggests crab claws, and may represent a change in direction.

ABOVE Leo represents the lion's mane, or creative energy similar to the snake's.

ABOVE Virgo could be celestial wings, a woman holding a wheatsheaf or a snake.

Both a symbol in its own right and a collection of symbols, the zodiac is a belt of stars on either side of the "ecliptic", the apparent path across the sky of the sun, moon and planets. It is divided into 12 constellations or signs. "Zodiac" is derived from the Greek and means circle of living things. It is a concept that originated at a time when people thought that each heavenly body was inhabited by an astral spirit, and stems from a world-view that sees creation as a vast web of interconnected forces, reflecting or even influencing life and events on Earth. The constellations became associated with various life forms and objects, acquiring mystical significance in explaining human destiny and the complexities that make up human character. The signs are divided among the four elements, and each is given one of three "qualities": cardinal (creating or initiating), fixed (maintaining) and mutable (changing). Each sign is "ruled" by a celestial body.

ARIES, RAM
(21 MARCH–20 APRIL)
The astrological year begins at the spring equinox (in the Northern Hemisphere) when the sun enters Aries the ram. The ram is often shown running forwards but looking backwards. The sign is headstrong, enthusiastic, independent, ambitious and easily bored. Mars is the ruler of Aries; anatomically it relates to the head and face, its element is fire, its quality cardinal and its gemstone is the diamond.

TAURUS, BULL
(21 APRIL–21 MAY)
An ancient symbol of virility and fertility. Taureans are loyal, practical, calm, generous, understanding and patient. They enjoy sensuous pleasures, but can become stubborn and rigid. The ruler of Taurus is Venus; anatomically it relates to the throat and neck, its element is earth, its quality fixed and its gemstone emerald. A festival celebrating the Buddha's birth occurs on the first full moon after the sun enters Taurus.

GEMINI, TWINS
(22 MAY–21 JUNE)
As twins, Gemini signifies opposites and duality. Some traditions depict the sign as a man and woman, or as a pair of lovers. Gemini is associated with human contact, communication and the intellect. Its element is air, its quality mutable and its ruler Mercury. Anatomically it relates to the lungs, arms and shoulders, and its gemstone is agate. In India, the constellation is linked with Aditi, the Vedic mother-goddess.

CANCER, CRAB
(22 JUNE–23 JULY)
Cancerians are sensitive, moody, imaginative, romantic, protective and nurturing but can become possessive and overly emotional. Cancer is associated with the mother archetype; its ruler is the moon, its element water and its

RIGHT The zodiac circle is a symbol system representing cycles, stages of development, and aspects of the male and the female.

quality cardinal. Anatomically it relates to the chest and stomach and its gemstone is moonstone.

LEO, THE LION
(24 JULY–23 AUG)
When the sun enters Leo its power (in the Northern Hemisphere) is at its zenith and the sign is associated with warmth, generosity, creativity, courage and leadership, although it can also be egotistical, proud and autocratic. Its ruler is the sun, its element fire and its quality fixed. Anatomically Leo is related to the heart, and its gemstone is ruby.

VIRGO, VIRGIN
(24 AUG 23 SEPT)
Virgo, the virgin (in the sense of "independent woman"), comes at harvest. It has been associated with most major Western female goddesses, including Isis, Demeter and the Virgin Mary.

Virgoans are practical, discriminating, analytical and precise, but can be pedantic and critical. Ruled by Mercury, Virgo is related to the intestine, spleen and solar plexus. Its element is earth, its quality mutable and its gemstone carnelian.

LIBRA, SCALES
(24 SEPT–23 OCT)

When the sun enters Libra it is at the mid-point of the astronomical year when days and nights are of equal length. Librans are artistic, refined and good peacemakers, but can be indecisive. The ruling planet of Libra is Venus, its element is air, and its quality is cardinal; its gemstone is sapphire and anatomically it is related to the spine, kidneys and liver.

SCORPIO, SCORPION
(24 OCT–22 NOV)

The venomous scorpion is ruled by Mars and Pluto. It is associated in many cultures with decay and death. Scorpios are determined, forceful and inquisitive, with intense sexual energy and passion, although inclined to jealousy. Anatomically, Scorpio governs the kidneys and genitals, its gemstone is opal, its element water and its quality fixed. An eagle, phoenix or snake sometimes represents the sign.

SAGITTARIUS, ARCHER
(23 NOV–21 DEC)

The ninth sign, Sagittarius, represents the perfect human, a combination of animal and spiritual power and divine potential. It is usually shown as a centaur bearing a bow and arrow;

its glyph represents the latter, a symbol of humanity aiming for the stars. Sagittarius is a symbol of higher wisdom, the spiritual seeker, philosophy, learning and travel, but Sagittarians can also be unrealistic and unreliable. Its ruling planet is Jupiter, its element fire, its quality mutable and its gemstone topaz. Anatomically, Sagittarius governs the liver, thighs and pelvic region.

CAPRICORN, GOAT
(22 DEC–20 JAN)

Capricorn, the goat, is ruled by Saturn, and heralds the depth of winter. Its element is earth, its quality cardinal, its gemstone garnet; anatomically it rules the knees, teeth and bones. Capricorn represents order, structure and stability, as well as ambition and hard work. Its name is linked to Capricornus, the mythological goatfish, and its glyph reflects the shape of both fish and horns.

AQUARIUS, WATER CARRIER (21 JAN–19 FEBRUARY)

The water carrier's glyph represents water and communication. Saturn and Uranus govern Aquarius, which is

ABOVE The zodiac represents a perfect cycle, and its symbolism is therefore related to the wheel and to the circle.

usually linked with humanitarian ideals, freedom, eccentricity and original thinking. Anatomically it is related to the lower legs, and blood. Its element is air, its quality fixed and its gemstone is the amethyst.

PISCES, FISH
(20 FEB–20 MARCH)

The 12th sign is Pisces, symbolized by a pair of conjoined fish swimming in opposite directions, with its glyph representing this contradictory aspect. Pisceans often feel tugged in two directions and are typically dreamy, intuitive, artistic and impressionable, their psychic sensitivities making it difficult for them to live in the everyday world. Jupiter and Neptune, god of the sea, rule Pisces, its element is water and its quality mutable. Anatomically it governs the lymphatic system and feet and its gemstone is bloodstone. As the last sign of the zodiac, Pisces represents dissolution, the return to the watery abyss before the creative cycle begins afresh.

ABOVE Libra depicts a pair of scales and also a sunset.

ABOVE Scorpio is based on the Hebrew letter *mem*, and the arrow represents the sting in the scorpion's tail.

ABOVE Sagittarius signifies projection.

ABOVE Capricorn links the goat's horns with the fish's tail.

BELOW Aquarius's glyph represents water, and conveys the idea of passive dualism.

ABOVE Pices is two fish swimming away.

GODS AND GODDESSES

ABOVE Zeus sits in victorious judgement with the rest of the Olympians, and banishes the last of the Titans to Tarterus. As a supreme god, Zeus symbolized male power and authority for both divine and human worlds.

Every culture has created its own mythology, theology and sacred rituals in its quest to come to terms with the mysteries of the universe. Although these are rooted in and specific to the culture in which they arise, there

are nevertheless many striking similarities in the various deities of the world, making them powerful archetypal symbols that explore some of the most profound ideas of humankind.

SUPREME GODS

The idea of a supreme creator god is universal, symbolizing the primeval force from which all life begins. In many traditions, the deity is self-created and appears magically: for instance, in ancient Egypt, Atum (whose name means "the all") arose as a mound or hill from the chaos of the watery abyss, while the Zulu Unkulunkulu created himself from the vast swamp of coloured reeds that existed at the beginning of the world.

The supreme god frequently symbolizes male power and authority and is linked with the archetypes of father, king and warrior leader. He is seen as omnipotent and omnipresent, exercising authority over nature, animals and human beings. Odin, the warrior god of the Norse pantheon, was known as the "all-father". The Celtic Dagda, whose name means "all-powerful god", controlled the weather and the crops and offered his people protection and benediction. Both Odin and Dagda were renowned for their wisdom, another feature of supreme gods. At times the supreme god embodies righteous fury at human misdemeanours: the thunderbolt, which the god brandished when he was enraged, was an attribute of both Zeus, the ancient Greek ruler of Heaven and Earth, and the Inca creator

god Viracocha ("lord of the world"). Other examples of supreme gods include Quetzalcoatl (Aztec), Vishnu (India) and Tangaroa (Polynesia).

Not all supreme deities are male, however. The Chinese goddess Nu Gua, whose lower body was that of a snake or fish, made all living things as she transformed herself into a multitude of shapes, while in the Native American Navajo tradition, Spider Woman (or Changing Woman) brought creation into existence by weaving patterns of fate just as a spider spins its web. The Japanese creator deities, Izanagi and Izanami, were twins, a brother and sister who created the land by stirring the waters of the primeval ocean with a spear.

THE GREAT GODDESS

The concept of an all-powerful goddess is very ancient. Worshipped as the great goddess or the mother goddess, she is typically identified with nature or the earth. In South America, the fertile earth goddess was Pachamama (her cult was adapted to the Virgin Mary in the colonial period), and among the Maori was Papatuanuku (or Papa), the goddess of earth and rock and mother of the people.

The goddess is not only the creator whose limitless fertility and generous abundance generates, feeds and sustains life, but is also the destroyer, who demands tribute as part of nature's regenerative cycle of birth, growth, death and rebirth. She is often associated with the moon, reflecting her cyclical

QUETZALCOATL

One of the major deities of the Aztec pantheon, Quetzalcoatl created humans by sprinkling bones from the dead of the previous creation with his blood. He was also lord of knowledge, god of the wind and the zodiac, vegetation and the arts. He was a compassionate deity who taught peace and was a force for good. His emblems were a turquoise-encrusted snake and a cloak.

nature and her light and dark attributes. In some early societies she was represented by a cone or pillar of stone, sometimes white and sometimes black, corresponding to her bright and dark aspects. In Chaldea, in Babylonia (modern Iraq), the goddess was worshipped in the form of a sacred black stone, which some scholars believe is the same holy stone that has become central to the Islamic faith, the Ka'ba in Mecca.

Representations of the Great Goddess include Selene (Greco-Roman), Isis (ancient Egyptian) and Ishtar (Babylonian). In India the Great Goddess is known variously as Shakti – the ultimate creative force – Devi or Maha-Devi ("great Devi") and is regarded as a personification of the feminine principle and the mother of all things. In her dark aspect she takes on ferocious forms, including Durga, the warrior goddess, and Kali, the goddess of death. Durga is usually depicted riding a tiger and carrying weapons in each of her ten hands, with which she slays her enemies, while Kali is shown with a garland of skulls, brandishing a sword in one hand and a severed head in the other.

THE TRIPLE GODDESS
In many traditions the goddess is split into separate entities, typically three – maiden, mother and crone – corresponding to the waxing, full and waning phases of the moon. In the Greco-Roman pantheon, Artemis (Roman Diana), Demeter (Ceres) and Hecate represent the three aspects

of the Triple Goddess. Sister to Apollo, who is associated with the sun, the virgin hunter goddess Artemis is often shown carrying a silver bow and arrow, which she uses to protect but also to kill. Demeter is the goddess of the fruits of the earth, and her attributes are the wheatsheaf, sickle and cornucopia (horn of plenty). Hecate, goddess of night, darkness and death, is sometimes portrayed with three bodies or faces to symbolize her links with the moon. She is linked with places of transition as guardian of the gates of Hades, and goddess of the crossroads. Hecate is associated with magic and witchcraft in occult traditions.

LESSER DEITIES
There are gods and goddesses connected with practically every dimension of life – both in the natural world and in human society. Nature gods include deities of the skies, oceans and vegetation. For instance, Uranus (ancient Greek) and Rangi (Maori) are sky gods, Poseidon or Neptune (Greco-Roman) and Susanowo (Japanese) rule the oceans, while Tammuz (Sumerian) and the Green Man (Celtic) are fertility gods connected with nature and the renewal of life in the spring.

Although the Earth and the moon are typically associated with female deities, in some traditions they are male gods. Among the Inuit people, Igaluk, the spirit of the moon and a powerful and skilful hunter, is male, while in ancient Egypt the Earth was personified by Geb,

THE GODDESS ISIS
Isis was one of the most important deities of the ancient world. Her name means "seat" or "throne", and sometimes she is depicted wearing a throne on her headdress. She is also shown wearing a headdress of a pair of cow horns with a sun disc between them, linking her to Hathor, goddess of love and fertility. Isis was associated with magic motherhood, and nature. For the Greeks she offered protection to sailors, while in ancient Rome roses were her attribute.

who is usually depicted with a green body, to represent the earth's vegetation, and an erect phallus, showing his desire to reach Nut, goddess of the sky.

There are also deities of agriculture and fishing, mountains and forests, volcanoes and earthquakes, rivers and fish, the weather and wild beasts. Examples of these nature gods include the Hindu goddess Parvati, the consort of Shiva, whose name means "mountain daughter"; Pele, the Hawaiian god of volcanic fire; Chac, the Maya rain god; Thor, the Norse god of thunder; Sedna, the Inuit goddess of sea creatures; and the Native North American Selu, or Corn Woman, who brings the gift of knowledge of the cultivation of corn to her people.

In Africa, earth and water are invariably goddesses: among the Yoruba of West Africa, Ile is the mother goddess of the Earth and Yemoja is the goddess of water. Yemoja's messengers are the hippopotamus and crocodile, and her daughter is Aje, goddess of the river Niger.

BELOW The Hindu mother goddess Mahadevi is depicted here in her benign aspect, as Parvati (consort of Shiva), while the weapon-bearing arms symbolize Durga, the warrior goddess.

GODS AND HUMANITY

Many cultures honour deities connected with society and human values. There are gods of love and courtship such as the Greek Eros (Roman Cupid) and the Aztec Xochiquetzal, and goddesses of marriage and motherhood such as the Hindu Lakshmi and the Chinese Kuan-Yin, the goddess of mercy. The Domovoy of Russia and the Lares and Penates of ancient Rome are household spirits that safeguard the home and family. Deities of the arts and crafts include Benten, the Japanese goddess of music; Wen Chang, the Chinese god of literature; Tane-Mahuta, the Maori god of woodcrafts and carving; and Hephaestus/Vulcan, the Greco-Roman blacksmith god. Abstract concepts such as wisdom, justice, truth and knowledge are also deified by figures such as Athena/Minerva, the Greco-Roman goddess of wisdom and warfare; Maat, the ancient Egyptian goddess of truth and justice; and Brigid, the Celtic goddess of learning.

GODS OF LOVE

The need for love and relationship is fundamental to humankind. It is a force for integration and the resolution of conflict; through trust and surrender to the love partner, opposites may be synthesized, leading to union and wholeness for each individual. When depraved, however, it becomes a principle of division and death. Love can take many different forms – from sexual love and passion at one end of the scale to spiritual love at the other – and in its many guises is represented by a multitude of gods and goddesses. These include Kama, the Indian god of love; Aphrodite/Venus, the goddess of love in the Greco-Roman tradition, who was allegedly born from the foam of the sea; Iarilo, the Slavic god of love and regeneration; Freya, the Norse goddess of fertility, sensuality and erotic love; and Bastet, the ancient Egyptian goddess associated with pleasure and sexual love. Bastet loved music and dancing, and her sacred symbol was a sistrum or rattle. The spectacular annual festival held in her name attracted large crowds, and more wine was consumed then than during the whole of the rest of the year.

GODS OF WAR

Though war predominantly symbolizes aggression, destructive power and the triumph of brute force, warrior values such as courage and honour are upheld in many societies and sacred traditions. Even in Buddhism, a religion well known for its pacifism, the Buddha is referred to as a "warrior in shining armour". War can also be seen in symbolic terms as an internal struggle, a transitional stage in a move from darkness to light, bondage to freedom. Examples of gods and goddesses of war include the Ahayuta Achi, the powerful twin gods of war of the North American Zuni Pueblo people, and the Morrigan, the war goddess of the Celts.

The Ahayuta Achi were children of the sun and displayed great courage when they stole rain-making implements from a ferocious warrior group. They were brave fighters and fiercely protective of the Zuni people, slaying monsters and wrongdoers on their behalf. They were also responsible for providing tools and knowledge of hunting to the people. The Morrigan, sometimes referred to as the Queen of Demons, often appeared as a triple goddess, her three aspects representing war, slaughter and death. Skilful in magic and prophecy, she appeared on the battlefield as crows or ravens (her symbols), feasting on the dead. She used her shape-shifting abilities to seduce men to satisfy her sexual appetite and engaged in a spectacular sexual tryst with Dagda, the Celtic supreme god.

Sometimes war gods are also associated with peace. The

THE MIMI TRICKSTER DEITIES

According to an Aboriginal myth from Arnhem Land, in the Northern Territory of Australia, the Mimi are said to inhabit gaps and cracks in the region's escarpments. They are sometimes depicted in bark paintings as slender, ghostly figures, and it is said they can be heard at night when they sing and beat on the rocks. The Mimi have a dual nature: on the one hand they are generous and helpful, teaching humans how to hunt, yet if disturbed they can wreak havoc, bringing illness and misfortune. Consequently bush hunters call out to warn the Mimi of their presence and avoid harming any wallaby that seems to be tame, as it might be a pet of the Mimi, who will inflict death on anyone who injures it.

Japanese deity Hachiman, though primarily a Shinto deity, is also acknowledged in Buddhism, where he is called Daibosatsu ("great bodhisattva"). His attributes are a staff and a dove, the latter symbolizing the peace that follows his actions. His function is to protect warriors and the community at large. Another protective peace-keeping god is the Chinese Guan-Di, a god of war, loyalty and justice.

TRICKSTER GODS

The trickster god is a rebellious, amoral and anarchic figure, an anti-hero who enjoys disrupting and upsetting the status quo – whether this be among gods or mortals. He is often of mixed nature with animal, human and divine characteristics. His mischief-making is viewed with ambivalence – sometimes he appears as a malevolent saboteur,

and sometimes his actions help humankind. The Norse Loki, for instance, was both a friend of the gods and a thief who stole their treasures, while the Native North American Coyote is both a hero and villain. Among the Navajo, Coyote is a co-creator with First Man and First Woman and comes up from the underworld bearing plant seeds, which he distributes to the different tribes; yet the Apache hold him responsible for the arrival of the Europeans, and the Maidu of California for bringing sickness, sorrow and death to humankind. Other examples of trickster gods include Eshu, of the West African Yoruba; the Polynesian Maui, bringer of fire to humanity; and the Australian Aboriginal Mimi.

FREYA

Norse goddess of fertility, sensuality and erotic love, Freya protected not only women in marriage and childbirth but also warriors and kings. She was an expert in magic and had the ability to shape-shift, wearing a cloak of feathers and transforming into a falcon to fly through the underworld.

BELOW This ancient carving shows a curly haired Loki, the Norse trickster god.

THE GOD TANE-MAHUTA

In the Maori tradition, Tane-Mahuta was the son of Rangi, the sky god, and Papa, the earth goddess. He was responsible for creating the realm of light by pushing his parents apart with his feet, thus separating earth and sky. Because his parents were naked, he created trees and plants to cover his mother and spangled his father with stars. Tane became lord of the forest and all the creatures that lived in it (including humans) and of all things made from trees. Consequently, he became the god of all those that work with wood. Canoe builders rest their axes in his temple and pray to him the night before they chop down a tree to make a canoe.

HEAVEN AND HELL

NINE HELLS

In Aztec mythology there were nine hells through which the souls of the dead were conducted by a dog, which was sacrificed as part of the funerary ritual. Their souls were literally returning to the land from which they originated. After passing the eighth hell, the soul was plunged into the ninth, the eternal house of the dead.

The division of the above and the below is a common mythical theme, symbolizing a fundamental duality in the universe. Different values and meanings have been ascribed to the two polarities, with the above associated predominantly with the abode of the immortals, a place of bliss, while the below is the abode of devils and divinities, where the souls of the dead are tormented. By way of contrast, in animist or shamanic traditions the above and below are seen as interdependent; a perspective that honours both life and death, and values the natural cycles of life.

In different cultures, and different times, Heaven and Hell have been understood both as literal places and as metaphors of various kinds.

SUMERIA

The earliest description of the underworld is in Sumerian mythology of around 2700 BC, when the goddess Inanna descends to the underworld and undergoes a symbolic transformation. She leaves the "great above" for the "great below" to face her twin sister Ereshkigal, the ruling goddess of the underworld. As Inanna descends she can pass through the seven gates of invisibility only by stripping away her life and fertility in the form of her sparkling clothes and jewels, until she arrives naked before Ereshkigal. She becomes a corpse, but the trickster god Enki finds a way for her to return to earth if she can find a substitute soul. Discovering that her lover

Dumuzi has not mourned for her, Inanna banishes him to the underworld in her place, while she returns to life for six months of each year.

Inanna is the goddess of fertility, and this story symbolizes the seasonal fertility cycle, in which plant life grows, matures and dies, and then is renewed. The story also represents the psychological journey in which a person faces their whole self by sacrificing their ego.

ANCIENT EGYPT

The Pyramid Texts are long columns of hieroglyphs inscribed on the walls of burial chambers. It is thought that they were written to aid the ascension of the pharaoh to the heavens in order to live eternally by the side of his father, Ra, the supreme god.

The first ruler of the Egyptian underworld was Anubis, depicted as a man with the head of a jackal. As the god of putrefaction and embalming, Anubis oversaw the judgement of the dead and protected them in the afterlife. Eventually Osiris, originally a god of vegetation, took over the role of judge of the dead. To reach the underworld, he himself died and was embalmed by Anubis: his mummification symbolized for the Egyptians a new and longstanding belief in the afterlife.

GREECE AND ROME

The ancient Greek underworld was called after its ruler, the god Hades, whose name means "unseen one". The Romans knew him as Pluto, the "rich one", and depicted him holding a horn of plenty, reflecting his command of the earth's resources.

Greek heroes, wise men and initiates went to a light and happy place in the underworld called the Elysian Fields, which Homer described as located at the most western point of the earth. Centuries later, the Roman poet Virgil (70–19 BC) portrayed the Elysian Fields as a place of perpetual spring, with its own solar system. The deepest part of Hades was Tartarus, the prison of the Titans and those condemned to eternal punishment.

JUDAISM

In Judaism there is no clear concept of a hell. Gehenna, which is described as a challenging and unpleasant place, can be understood to be a place in which the soul is purified or spiritually transformed in order that it can finally ascend to Gan Eden, or Heaven. Gehenna was originally the name of a rubbish tip just outside of the walls of Jerusalem, where fires were continually kept alight by adding brimstone to burn up the refuse. The bodies of criminals who had been executed were dumped there.

CHRISTIANITY

In the Christian tradition Heaven is a place associated with light, while Hell is dark, lacking the light of God's presence due to the sins of humanity. The early Christians believed Heaven to be a physical place above the clouds, but this notion was challenged by new ideas about the nature of the universe. Modern Christians do not see it as a physical place, but

may still believe in its physical existence in another dimension.

The original biblical depiction of Hell is of an underground cavern to which the souls of the dead, both good and bad, went for eternity. Later books of the Bible describe it as a place of annihilation or eternal punishment, and a more modern Christian image of Hell is of a state of great suffering.

ISLAM

The Qur'an describes Heaven and Hell in vivid detail. Heaven is seen as a paradise and Hell as a place of fiery torment, though there are divergent beliefs among Muslims as to whether these descriptions are to be considered literally or metaphorically. In Islamic belief, each person is judged according to whether they have lived life to their best abilities in accordance with the truth. Infidels who reject the truth of Islam are given no mercy, and will fall down into Jahannam, or Hell, while the good will live in Heaven.

BUDDHISM

In Buddhism there are six realms of existence, representing states of mind, which people continually pass through in cyclical reincarnations, until they attain liberation from the physical state. The deva, or heavenly realm, is a place of pleasant things, but it is also an impermanent state. The realm of humans is a place that can be both happy and sad. The realm of the asuras (jealous gods or demons) is a place of fighting. The world of the hungry-ghosts is

a place of dissatisfaction and discontent, where there is always hunger. The animal realm is a place in which there is no faculty of reason. Finally, the realm of Hell is a place of great suffering and pain. Someone who has become free from attachment and has seen into their true nature ultimately achieves the state of Buddhahood.

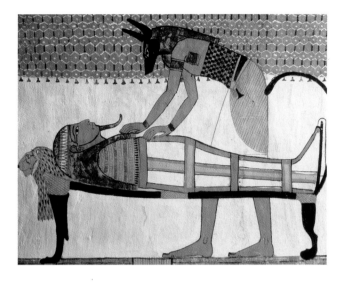

ABOVE The jackal-headed Anubis, first Egyptian ruler of the underworld, embalming a body on a lion-shaped couch.

BELOW Paradise (from the Old Persian word *pairidaeza*) is an enclosed or walled garden of pleasure where the righteous may live in the presence of God.

DEMONS AND ANGELS

THE IMP

A lesser or weaker demon associated with behaviour that is troublesome or mischievous rather than evil, imps are tiny, dark and shadowy creatures. They can shape-shift, becoming weasels or spiders, and are associated with minor misfortune.

BELOW RIGHT When illustrating John Milton's epic poem, *Paradise Lost*, William Blake said that, without realizing it, Milton had taken Satan's part and portrayed the Devil as having heroic status.

BELOW A more traditional image of the devil shows him as more beast than man.

Both angels and demons are beings with divine powers, existing somewhere between the gods and human beings. Angelic and demonic entities are predominantly characterized by qualities of light and shadow, and can also be associated with the light and shadow within the human unconscious. Jung noted that some religions split off the demonic aspect, focusing only upon the light, and pointed out that "divinity" is also symbolized within the realms of the shadow.

DEMONS

In Greek mythology, daimones were divine beings that carried out the will of the gods on human beings, in the forms of fate and destiny. A daimon was given to each person before birth, carrying their destiny as a set of images or patterns that must be lived out on earth. Destiny can be delayed and

avoided, but the daimon is irresistible and never goes away, demanding to be lived or else turning to possess the person, thus becoming their inner demon. With their ability to perceive someone's fate, daimones were thought to present flashes of intuition beyond rational thought, acting as inner guides.

The daimon is an individual's life calling, the equivalent of the Roman genius, the free-soul, animal-soul or breath-soul of the Inuit, the *nagual* of the Navajo, and the owl of the Kwakiutl of north-west Canada. In some cultures daimones are conceived of as particular animal species. They are often associated with fire, and a genius was described as a fiery nimbus or halo. For Jung, the term "daimonic" described a conscious relationship with the archetypal figures of the human psyche.

The origin of the concept of angels, and of angels and demons as embodiments of good and evil, lies in the interaction between Persian Zoroastrianism and Judaism. Zoroastrians describe the battle between two deities: Ahura Mazda, the "wise lord" and god of light, and Ahriman or Angra Mainyu, the "evil spirit" and god of darkness, in the midst of whose fiery battle the souls of humans are judged. Judaism, as a monotheistic religion, conceives of only one God. Thus the equivalent of the god of darkness, Satan, was symbolically cast out of Heaven.

Christianity inherited the idea of demons as angels who fell from Heaven when Satan rebelled

against God. Early Christians saw demons as vapour-like beings with no physical bodies, leading to great debate about whether or not they were divinities. In the 12th century, the Church conceded that demons, like angels, had spiritual bodies over which they were clothed with material bodies.

As pagan and polytheistic religions were increasingly taken over by monotheistic religions, daimones began to be portrayed as demons, and the hearing of inner voices came to suggest madness or the influence of the devil rather than divine guidance. The fallen angels, or demons, took on physical and mental deformities, and were portrayed with black hair, and human-like skin tinged with red, black or white. While angels had celestial wings and predominantly human characteristics, demons – in line

RIGHT A heavenly host of angels preparing for battle. Many religions tell of the battle between the angelic forces of good and the demonic forces of evil.

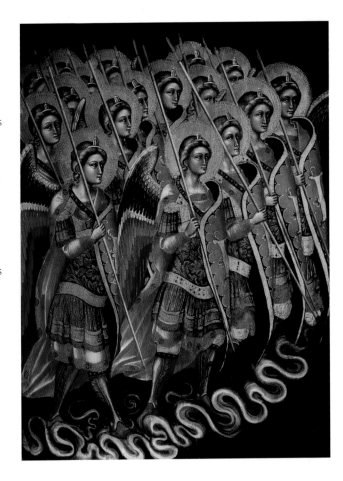

with the Judaeo-Christian attitude of superiority over animals and nature – embodied aberrant qualities of the animal kingdom, with bat wings, claws, horns and tails, associating their evil with pagan nature divinities.

THE DEVIL

Ahriman, the evil Zoroastrian deity, is himself a creator. In Christianity, however, the Devil is a being created by God. The name is derived from the Greek *diabolos*, meaning "slanderer", but the Devil is known by many other names, including Satan, Lucifer, Mephistopheles and Beelzebub, and titles such as The Antichrist or The Prince of Darkness. The name Satan comes from the Hebrew for "adversary" or "obstacle", as he is the adversary of God. Satan rebelled against God, and was exiled to Hell. In the Qur'an the Devil is known as Iblis or Shaitan.

During the early Middle Ages, Lucifer was seen as wicked but not frightening. As Christian imagery evolved, he was portrayed as a new, terror-provoking image of a beast with horns, cloven goats' hooves, wings and a spiked tail.

ANGELS

In one form or another, angels appear in most of the major religions as intermediaries between God and humans. They are invisible or semi-visible beings who act as guides to the soul, helping it to grow and evolve. They are also believed to organize the universe at its very foundations, keeping the planets on course, and controlling the growth of life on earth.

Early Christian images of angels were very similar to Greek and Mesopotamian deities. They had wings, reflecting their celestial quality. Angels are also central to Islam, and it is believed that the angel Gabriel dictated the Qur'an to the Prophet Mohammed.

ANGELIC HIERARCHY

Medieval theologians described a heavenly hierarchy of angels. In the first sphere are the heavenly counsellors: seraphim, cherubim and thrones. In the second sphere are the angels who work as heavenly governors: dominions, virtues and powers. And the lowest orders of angels, most familiar to humans, are the heavenly messengers, found in the third sphere: principalities, archangels and angels.

The seraphim, whose name means "to burn" in Hebrew, are angels who literally burn with passion for the creator, wrapping their wings around God and never revealing his presence. They continually sing his praises and regulate the heavens with the music of the spheres. The cherubim, whose name may come from an Assyrian word meaning "to be near", are the guardians of the light that shines down from the heavens and touches the lives of humans. After the Fall, God is said to have placed the cherubim east of the Garden of Eden, between it and the human realm, to protect the Tree of Life with flaming swords.

Called in ancient texts the "lords of the flame" because they are formed of pure light or energy, the archangels are the agents through which the creative will of God is executed. They bring loving guidance, protection and divine messages to humankind. The names of the archangels are Uriel, Tzadkiel, Khamel, Raphael, Haniel, Michael and Gabriel.

FAIRIES AND NATURE SPIRITS

ABOVE A Hamadryad, or wood nymph, reveals herself to a woodcutter as the guardian spirit of the tree.

BELOW Fairies are often described dancing in a ring of enchantment.

The idea of a parallel universe occupied by sentient beings is at odds with the contemporary Western view of nature, and thus fairies and nature spirits have become relegated to the realms of the storybook. In popular belief, fairies have been on the decline since the 17th century due to urbanization and the supremacy of science, but there are still people who believe that the natural world is imbued with spiritual consciousness. Depending upon our perspective, fairies and nature spirits may either symbolize human aspects projected on to nature or be seen as independent beings with their own qualities and consciousness, living within their own reality.

Belief in nature spirits or fairies is most common where spirit is believed to animate nature. In Ireland, where there is still a connection to Celtic roots, and in Iceland, which is surrounded by wild nature, respect for the fairy peoples still thrives.

The Old French word "faerie" or "feyerie" originally referred to a state of enchantment, glamour or influence. Essentially amoral by nature, fairies or nature spirits often represent forces of fate that influence the human world for either malevolent or benign purposes. The fairy kingdom is often described as mirroring the human hierarchical structure, with the king and queen at the top, and also provides a picture of the structure of nature itself.

CHILDREN AND FAIRIES

Fairies are often connected with children, who are said to be more able to see them, and sometimes resemble them. Fairies are sometimes called "little people". In South America winged nature spirits, known as *jimaninos* and *jimaninas*, resemble well-fed children; they are said to be visible on the Mexican Days of the Dead. The tiny *abatwa*, from Africa, are said to live in anthills and are visible only to pregnant women and children.

A Christianized Icelandic legend tells that fairies were originally children of Eve. She was washing them when God called her, and she hid those who were not clean. God punished her for her deception, saying that what was hidden from God should be hidden from humans, and made the children invisible. This connects the separation of the fairy realm to a patriarchal culture in which women, children and nature have been devalued.

FALLEN ANGELS

Another Christianized view of fairies, this time Celtic, is that they were angels driven out of Heaven with Lucifer. As they fell to earth they became nature spirits of the earth, air, water, fire and plants. The *sidhe* of Scotland and Ireland are such spirits, known for their beauty and musical abilities. They are as tall as humans and live in underground fairy palaces.

The Tuatha de Danaan of Ireland are the fairy people of the mother goddess Dana. Legend has it that they built the Irish megaliths as gateways to the fairy world, and were the original guardians of the treasures of the Holy Grail. Finvarra, the king of the fairies, was obsessed by mortal women and enticed them to fairyland with his enchanting music. When someone is entranced by the music of a *sidhe*, they enter a trance – possibly the origin of the phrase "away with the fairies".

TREE SPIRITS

In the classical world, hamadryads (wood nymphs) were female spirits who lived within trees as their guardians, and who died if a tree was cut down. "Dryad" is a more general name for tree fairies found in enchanted groves. Often depicted as wisps of light, dryads are playful creatures, who may help, hinder or tease

humans, and become particularly active during the full moon.

In Japanese folklore Uku-No-Chi is a deity who lives in the trunks of trees, and Hamori is the protector of leaves. The elder mothers are Scandinavian tree fairies who live within elder trees, which are believed to possess a most potent magical power. The beautiful Swedish wood nymph Skogsra is the guardian of the woods and wild animals. Ghillie Dhu is a solitary tree fairy who lives in birch trees in Scotland.

THE ELEMENTALS

Elementals are spirits of the four elements, earth, water, air and fire, which, along with the moon, stars and sun, were the sources of all creation in ancient Greek mythology. The Swiss alchemist and philosopher Paracelsus (1493–1541) named them as gnomes (earth), salamanders (fire), sylphs (air) and undines (water) who inhabit a kingdom situated between the spiritual and material planes. They are said to govern natural and magical energies that influence human thoughts and desires.

Gnomes are spirits of the earth, appearing in the mythology and folklore of northern Europe. Depicted as dwarf-like beings who live underground, these elementals are associated with earth magic, herbal healing, protection, fertility and prosperity.

The Green Man is the archetypal earth spirit of green nature, commonly depicted entirely covered with green oak leaves. He appears as a symbol across most of Europe, where he is associated with spring fertility festivals and the power to make rain. Stone and wood carvings of the Green Man were used to protect people against evil.

The elemental water spirits Paracelsus called undines inhabit caves beneath the ocean, lake shores, bogs, marshland and river banks. They possess the qualities of sunlit water, shimmering rhythmically. Nixies are water sprites of rivers, springs, lakes and marshes that often appear as beautiful maidens. They love music and dance and possess powers of prophecy. While they can bestow gifts upon humans, they can also be harmful, sometimes drowning people.

The water element is associated with the chalice, which symbolizes intuition and the emotions in the Western magical tradition, and with healing in such matters as love, sex, relationships and children. Water spirits can be consulted through "scrying", a form of divination that involves gazing into water in search of symbolic images.

The sylphs are ageless, winged elemental beings of the air, who live on mountaintops. They are commonly associated with logic, communication, learning and travel. Sylphs are invoked through the burning of incense or aromatic oils, and are connected to the ritual knife or sword, a magical tool of command.

Salamanders are elemental spirits of fire, originating from the fire lizard of the Middle Eastern deserts. Salamanders live in molten lakes, volcanoes and forest fires. They have flickering tongues and change shape like fire itself. They are commonly associated with power, light, inspiration, purification and creativity.

In the Islamic tradition fire spirits are called "djinn". They inhabit the mountains that encircle the world and are known for their immense powers and their ability to shape-shift, sometimes appearing as gigantic men. The djinni (or genie) of Aladdin's lamp is such a spirit.

BIRTH FAIRIES

Birth fairies are said to be present when a baby is born, and bestow gifts or talents that will send the person on a particular life path. In the fairytale *Sleeping Beauty*, the 13th fairy bestows a curse instead of a blessing.

EARTH LIGHTS

Will-o'-the-wisps or Jack-o'-Lanterns were earth lights that floated in groups, thought to be fairies guarding lost treasure, with the intention of leading travellers astray. The light was actually that of burning marsh gas.

FANTASTIC CREATURES

ABOVE Giants appear in the mythologies of many cultures and are often viewed with terror, but in some creation myths they are symbols of the formation of the world.

ABOVE The flame-breathing chimera of classical myth had a lion's head, a goat's body and the tail of a serpent.

It seems likely that in early cultures, imagination and reality were not separated in the way that is habitual to the modern mind. Instead they represented two equally valid dimensions of existence, an inner and an outer world, each with its own wisdom. Fantastic creatures are inventions of the human imagination and occur in many traditions. They are attempts to explain the inexplicable, to catch hold of a dimension of experience that resists objective analysis and to explore important human issues through their symbolism.

ELEMENTAL BEASTS

Fantastic creatures usually inhabit a dimension that spans both the everyday world and other, magical worlds, acting as helpful messengers or teachers, or else as monstrous obstacles that must be overcome to reach a goal. Often they are hybrids – part-animal, part-human, or a combination of different animals, bringing together the symbolic properties represented by each to create something new. They are generally endowed with supernatural powers and linked to one of the four elements – earth, air, fire and water – although some are associated with more than one element: for instance, a mermaid is a fish with a human torso, linking her with both water and earth. As creatures of light or darkness, they also symbolize the struggle between good and evil and the spiritual journey of the soul as fears are confronted and transformed.

GIANTS

Named after the ancient Greek *gigantes*, who fought the Olympian gods and lost, giants are humanoid beings of enormous size. They are relics of a former age, existing at the beginning of the world or even, in some traditions, creating it, and may embody forces of nature. In China, trees and rivers appeared from the body of the giant P'an-Ku, and in Japan, natural features such as mountains and lakes were created by giants called *kyojin*. In the Norse tradition, the world was created from the body of the frost-giant Ymir, who was killed by Odin and his brother gods. Ymir's bones became mountains, his skull the dome of the heavens and his blood the seas that drowned all the other frost-giants except Bergelmir and his wife, who later bore a race forever opposed to the Norse gods.

Giants are usually the cruel enemies of gods and humans, as is the one-eyed Cyclops of the Greco-Roman tradition, although humans may outwit them – as in the Old Testament contest between David and Goliath. Sometimes giants use their superhuman powers to help people: the Dehotgohsgayeh of the Native American Iroquois offers protection against evil.

THE WILD MAN

Many traditions have stories of a wild man who is closely allied to nature. The Tibetan Yeti is a

---

CHIRON THE CENTAUR

Some mythical beasts have a positive symbolism. In Greek myth, the centaur Chiron was exceptionally gentle and wise. He was taught by Apollo and Artemis, and in turn mentored several heroes, including Achilles. Wounded by Heracles, he gave up his immortality rather than continuing to live in agonizing pain. He is an example of the "wounded healer" – embodying the idea that suffering is part of the human condition and that experience of it can be used to help others.

fearsome, gigantic creature made of snow and ice and in the Native American tradition, Big Foot or Sasquatch (derived from a Salish word meaning "wild man of the woods") is respected as a supernatural spiritual being. In European folklore the wild man who lives in the forest is typically hairy, with large teeth and sometimes with horns. During the Middle Ages he was known as the "woodwose" and, like the Celtic Green Man, represents the forces of nature.

The wild man has links with the Greco-Roman satyr – a creature of the woods and mountains that had the upper body of a man and the horns and hindquarters of a goat. Libidinous and mischievous, but generally benign, satyrs represented the carnal instincts of men; the fertility god Pan was the chief satyr. Later, in the Christian tradition, the satyr was identified with Satan.

TAMING THE BEAST

Mythical creatures often symbolize the tension between instinct and reason, nature and civilization that is part of human life. It seems that the more civilized humans become, the more fearful and suspicious they grow of their "animal" nature, which is seen as an out-of-control beast that must be tamed. This is symbolized, in Greco-Roman mythology, by the conflict between the centaurs and the Lapiths of Thessaly. The lascivious centaur had a human head and torso on a horse's body, and represented the wild, lawless and

instinctive side of human nature. At the marriage feast of the Lapith king, the centaurs tried to abduct the bride, raped the female guests and attacked their hosts with tree trunks and stones. In the ensuring battle, the Lapiths defeated the centaurs, symbolizing the victory of intellect and reason over instinct and animal passion – which in this story led to barbarous chaos.

The dark, bestial side of humanity is also represented in Greco-Roman myth by the minotaur, a man with a bull's head and tail. Imprisoned by King Minos of Crete in the labyrinth below his palace, each year it devoured seven virgins and seven boys sent in tribute from Athens. Theseus, who was part of this tribute, killed the monster and used a thread given to him by Minos's daughter Adriadne (a symbol of divine guidance) to guide him out of the labyrinth.

Classical myth provides many examples of terrifying creatures that are eventually confronted and killed by a hero. The hydra was a swamp-creature with the body of a snake and anywhere between seven and 100 heads. If one of its heads was chopped off, two grew to replace it. Eventually the hero Heracles killed the hydra by cauterizing each neck stump as he severed its heads.

Another fearful monster was the chimera, a fire-breathing creature with a lion's head, a goat's body and the tail of a dragon or snake; it was sometimes depicted with a head coming from each part. It was the offspring of the monsters Typhon

and Echidna and was a symbol of elemental chaos and natural disasters (especially storms and volcanic eruptions). The Greek hero Bellerophon killed the monster, swooping down on it astride the winged horse Pegasus and thrusting a lump of lead between its jaws. The beast's breath melted the lead, and it choked to death.

ABOVE The beautiful white, winged horse Pegasus and the courageous hero Bellerophon symbolize the triumph of good over evil, as together they kill the monstrous chimera.

THE BASILISK

Also known as the cockatrice, the desert-dwelling basilisk has the wings, triple crest and claws of a cock on the body of a snake. A guardian of treasure, a basilisk's poisonous breath was deadly and its glance could kill – the only way to overcome it was to force it to look at its own reflection in a mirror. It was said to have emerged from a yolkless egg laid in dung by a cock, and hatched by a toad or serpent. In the Christian tradition, the basilisk became a symbol of the Antichrist and during the Middle Ages was associated with sins such as lust, treachery and disease (especially syphilis).

RIGHT The harpies or "snatchers" of Greek myth were terrifying hags with bird's wings and talons who were symbols of death.

LEVIATHAN

Possibly based on the crocodile, the Leviathan of Mesopotamian folklore is a primordial sea monster, referred to in the Old Testament as the "crooked serpent". In Judaism it was considered the counterpart of the Behemoth, the primordial land monster (associated with the hippo) by whom it will be eventually destroyed. Its eyes lit up the dark seas, and its foul breath caused the waters to boil. In Christianity, the Leviathan represents worldly power, while its gaping jaws symbolize the gateway to Hell.

THE GORGONS

In Greek myth, the gorgons were three terrifying sisters – Medusa, Euryale and Stheno – who had scaly skin, fangs and snakes instead of hair. Like the basilisk, their power was in their eyes: they could turn humans to stone by looking at them.

RIGHT Here the Hindu god Vishnu is shown flying Garuda, a giant bird of power and a solar symbol.

FEMALE HYBRIDS

There are many examples of female hybrids, all dangerous and destructive in some way. They represent male fears of the feminine principle, or anima, which is connected with instinct and irrationality. In classical myth, Scylla was a monstrous, six-headed creature with three rows of teeth in each mouth. She was named after the rock of Scylla where she lived, opposite the whirlpool Charybdis in the Medina Straits. She used her long necks to reach out and snatch sailors steering a course between the two obstacles.

The sirens were winged beasts with the heads and breasts of women and the bodies of snakes or birds. Similar to mermaids, they were known for the power of their singing, which they used to lure sailors to their death. Europeans once believed Amazonian manatees to be sirens.

In Greek legend the harpies were fierce and filthy flying hags, who could cause storms on land and whirlpools at sea; they were sent by the gods to inflict punishment on mortals. They symbolized sudden and early death and were also messengers of the underworld, to which they transported the souls of the dead. In common parlance, a "harpy" is a grasping or cruel woman.

MERPEOPLE

Mermaids and mermen appear in many mythologies. The Chaldean sea-god Ea was a man-goatfish, while the Philistine god Dagon, an ancient corn god, had a fish-like lower half. In Greek myth,

merpeople inhabit Poseidon's underwater kingdom. Poseidon's son Triton, half man and half dolphin, directed the waters by sounding a horn or conch shell (heard by humans as the roar of the ocean) and was a positive symbol of power and control.

In European folklore, mermaids represented elusive feminine beauty as well as fickleness and vanity (symbolized by the mirror). They had magical and prophetic powers and loved music, they were often depicted holding a comb, which they used to control storms at sea. Usually dangerous to humans (especially men), mermaids such as the German Lorelei could lure mortals to death by drowning.

DIVINE CREATURES

As well as dangerous monsters, many fantastic creatures represent higher consciousness and offer protection. Pegasus, the winged horse of Greek myth, symbolizes

the power for transforming evil into good. In China and Japan, lion-dogs are often placed outside temples and palaces to protect against evil forces and to signify the entrance to a holy or special place. In the Buddhist tradition, these creatures defend the Buddhist teachings, and male lion-dogs are sometimes depicted resting a paw on a globe, which signifies the *cintamani*, or Sacred Jewel, of Buddhism.

Popular among the Persians, Babylonians and Assyrians, the griffin has the head, wings and talons of an eagle (symbolizing vigilance and sharp-sightedness) and the body of a lion (symbol of strength). In ancient Greece it was sacred to Apollo (the sun god), Athene (the goddess of wisdom) and Nemesis (the goddess of vengeance). In medieval Europe the griffin represented strength, protection and solar power, and so became a symbol of Christ and the resurrection.

BIRDS OF POWER

Many traditions have examples of birds of power. In Hindu and Buddhist mythology, Garuda is the king of the birds and a symbol of spiritual power and victory. Half eagle and half man, Garuda is the emblem of the Hindu god Vishnu the preserver, who rides on his back. Garuda emerged fully formed from the cosmic egg and lives in the wish-fulfilling tree of life. He is the bitter enemy of the Naga – a legendary race of multi-headed serpents that inhabit the underworld and are symbols of water and fertility.

In the Native American tradition, the thunderbird is a powerful nature spirit. It is unimaginably vast (typically portrayed as an eagle) with lightning flashing from its eyes or beak and thunderclaps sounding when it beats its colossal wings. The Nootka of Vancouver Island believe it rules the heavenly realm, while tribes around the Great Lakes believe it is in continuous battle with the underwater panther, their battles causing storms that are dangerous to people in canoes.

THE PHOENIX

A mythical bird associated with fire and sun worship, the phoenix is one of the most important symbols of transformation, resurrection and immortality. It is often associated with the eagle and has fiery red or golden wings, suggesting the rising sun. In ancient Egypt it was known as the Bennu bird, and was said to return once every 1,400 years to

THE UNICORN

Usually white, with a single horn growing from its forehead, the unicorn is generally a symbol of purity. It has the body of a horse, the tail of a lion and the legs of an antelope, although it is sometimes depicted as a stag or goat. Unicorns were wild creatures that only virgins could capture, and so were associated with femininity and chastity. In Greek myth the unicorn was sacred to Artemis and Diana and was linked with the moon, while in Judaism the horn signifies unity of spirit. In the Christian tradition, the unicorn sometimes represented the Virgin Mary and also Christ – its horn was a symbol of the one gospel. In heraldry, its association with the moon makes it the counterpart of the sun-symbol lion. The unicorn also exists in China as the *qilin* (Japanese *kirin*), where it is depicted with a deer's body and white or yellow fur. This creature was so gentle that it would step on no living thing. Its appearance heralded times of peace and prosperity and it came to symbolize the wise rule of an emperor.

sit on the sacred *ben ben* stone at Heliopolis ("city of the sun"). In its most celebrated myth, the phoenix cremates itself on a wooden pyre set alight by the sun's rays, only to rise again from the ashes as a young bird. In Jewish tradition, the phoenix shrivels after 1,000 years, turning into an egg from which it re-emerges rejuvenated. In Persian mythology, it is called Simurg and is a symbol of divinity and of the mystical journey of the soul towards the light.

In China the phoenix is known as the Feng-huang; in its feng aspect it is a male, solar symbol, while as huang it is female and lunar, making it an embodiment of the union of yin and yang. It is depicted as a composite bird of colourful plumage, with the sun-like head of a cock and a swallow's back that suggests the crescent moon. Its wings signify the wind, its tails plant life and its feet the earth. Human qualities are also associated with the body parts of the phoenix, so that its breast signifies humanity and its head virtue. It is regarded as the emperor of birds and is one of the four sacred creatures (together

with the dragon, unicorn and tortoise) that bring peace and prosperity, its appearance heralding an auspicious emperor or prophet. Also known as the "scarlet bird", the phoenix is associated with summer, the south and red; it is also a Chinese bridal emblem, signifying unity through marriage.

In Japan the phoenix is called the Ho-O and is a popular symbol in Pure Land Buddhism, which emphasizes the reincarnation of the spirit. It is a popular motif on Shinto shrines (mikoshi) and, like the dragon, is a symbol of imperial authority.

ABOVE The phoenix is an archetypal symbol of transformation and immortality. As a solar symbol it is linked with death and rebirth in many cultures.

BELOW The griffin has the head, beak and wings of an eagle, the body of a lion and occasionally the tail of a serpent or scorpion. In Christian symbolism it is often used to personify Satan.

THE DRAGON

ABOVE The Eastern dragon is a benevolent sacred or magical being with a serpentine body a lion-like head, and bird-like talons.

BELOW The western dragon, fire-breathing and often green in colour, represents a force to be reckoned with. It has none of the benign and auspicious symbolism of the Eastern dragon.

Dragons appear throughout the world as symbols of great power, with central significance to the cultures in which their legends are told. Their name derives from the Greek *drakon*, meaning "serpent". Dragon myths frequently deal with themes of chaos and disaster, fertility, rebirth and the cycles of the cosmos. Many ancient cultures have dragons or serpents with cosmological significance, such as the Greek Ouroboros, a serpent swallowing its own tail, which represents the destruction and eternal renewal of the universe.

Eastern dragons are more commonly symbolic of positive qualities, such as wisdom and strength, whereas in the West the dragon often embodies negative forces, or obstacles to be overcome by a hero on a quest. As a composite beast, the dragon combines different strengths and qualities of the animal kingdom.

CREATIVE AND DESTRUCTIVE DRAGONS

The earliest surviving dragon legend is that of Zu (or Asag), the Sumerian dragon who stole from the great god Enlin the Tablets of Law that maintained the order of the universe. Zu was killed by Ninurta the sun god, who thus prevented the universe from descending into chaos.

The Babylonian creation myth tells of a great beginning in which nothing existed except the two elemental forces: Apsu, the male spirit of fresh water and the abyss, and Tiamat, the female spirit of salt water and chaos. Tiamat was a dragon, with the

head of a lion, a scaly body, feathery wings, the legs of an eagle and a forked tongue. When she was killed by the god Marduk, her severed body became the sky and the earth, and Marduk created humans from her blood.

In the Bible the dragon is interchangeable with the serpent as a symbol of political opposition to God and his people. Representing the issue of evil, the essence of the devil and mankind's enemy, the dragon does not exist in the natural world, but remains a metaphor for evil in its many forms. Similarly in Persian myth the *azhi*, or dragon, had no regard for humanity, was in opposition to good and despised by the gods. Scandinavian myths tell of a

dragon that lurks in the pit Hvergelmir, gnawing at the roots of Yggdrasil, the World Tree that supports the universe, in a continual attempt to destroy it.

THE WESTERN DRAGON

In Western legend, battles with dragons often represent the fight between good and evil. Western dragons also represent greed, as they often guard hoards of treasure. In psychological terms, a fight with a dragon may represent an inner battle with a covetous nature or a resistance to development. The dragon can represent a huge psychological barrier to gaining access to the riches of the self.

A common mythical theme is that of the hero who leaves his familiar surroundings and meets

RIGHT Two dragons on a wall in China reflect how Eastern dragons are thought to be able to resolve the conflict of the opposites.

RIGHT Two dragons on a wall in China reflect how Eastern dragons are thought to be able to resolve the conflict of the opposites.

the monster or dragon at the edge of the known world. He faces the power of the dark forces and by killing the dragon is able to reconnect to life and the personal powers he has gained. The legend of St George tells of his fight with a mighty dragon that was wreaking havoc in Cappodocia (modern Turkey). The people had offered up a virgin princess in an effort to rid the area of the monster. George charged the dragon, killing it with his lance, saved the princess and freed the people from their oppressor. His example of bravery in defence of the weak chimed strongly with Christian values, and in the 14th century he was adopted as patron saint of England.

The red dragon is the emblem of the Welsh. The Mabinogion, a 12th-century collection of Welsh legends, includes the tale of the struggle between this red dragon and a white dragon, symbolizing the invading forces of the Saxons. The dragons were buried in a coffin of stone, representing the harnessing of the two powers: their containment was believed to protect Britain against invasion, and the story symbolizes the fusion of the fates of the Celts and the Saxons.

THE EASTERN DRAGON

Everything to do with dragons in the Far East is blessed. The year of the dragon, which occurs each twelve years in the Chinese calendar, is very auspicious and those born in it are destined to enjoy a long, healthy life and great wealth. Chinese people call themselves Lung Tik Chuan Ren,

"Descendants of the Dragon". The Chinese dragon, Lung, is a divine generative creature, the symbol of the emperor and imperial law and a key influence in Chinese culture. Lung symbolizes greatness, power, goodness and great blessings, and will overcome any obstacle to achieve success. He is intelligent, bold, noble, persevering and full of energy. The Taoist Chuang Tzu (399–295 BC) taught of the mysterious powers of the dragon to resolve the conflicts of opposites, making him a symbol of unity.

Dragons in the East are angelic in quality, beautiful, benevolent and wise. Temples are built for them, usually near the sea or rivers, as dragons live in and rule the waters. They create heavy clouds full of fertilizing rain, and are also associated with lightning and thunder, uniting the rain of Heaven with the Earth.

The royal family of Japan trace their ancestry back 125 generations to the daughter of a dragon king of the sea known as Princess Fruitful Jewel, and the emperors were believed to have the ability to transform themselves into dragons. Whether through ancestral lineage, or though a present relationship with a dragon figure, the dragon's qualities of power and wisdom are made accessible to the people.

DRAGONS OF THE AMERICAS

There are many different mythical creatures in the legends of the indigenous Native Americans. Some dragons of the Americas are benevolent figures with great

skills and wisdom to teach the people, while others are forces of destruction.

The Piasa, or "bird that eats men", of the Illini Indians resembled a dragon, being a large winged animal that ate flesh and lived in a cave by a river. It was greatly feared and attacked victims who came too close. The Piasa was eventually tricked from its cave by a chief called Quatonga, who killed it with poisoned arrows. The Chippewa and the Quillayute tell of a great thunderbird who created thunderclaps and winds with his wings, and whose eyes sparked lightning. His favourite food was the whale, who was forced to escape many times, eventually retreating to the ocean depths.

THE AZTEC DRAGON

Quetzalcoatl was a benevolent dragon god of the Aztecs and Toltecs. Creator of humankind, he civilized the people by teaching them to write and introducing them to agriculture. He also introduced the calendar, music and dance. He was known to the Maya as Kulkulkan, and to the Quiché of Peru as Gucumatz.

BELOW Quetzalcoatl (left), god of learning battling Cuauhtli, the eagle-god of renewal.

CONNECTING WITH SPIRIT

EACH SOCIETY HAS DEVELOPED AN UNDERSTANDING ABOUT HUMAN LIFE AND ITS RELATIONSHIP WITH THE COSMOS AND HAS EVOLVED SOME SORT OF SPIRITUAL PRACTICE, MORAL CODE OR BELIEF SYSTEM TO MAKE A CONNECTION. SYMBOLS SUCH AS THE MAZE OR MANDALAS ARE SEEN AS PATHWAYS TO ENLIGHTENMENT, AND SACRED OBJECTS ACT AS CARRIERS OF THE SOUL.

SACRED OBJECTS

ABOVE Many sacred traditions use strings of beads as an aid to prayer or meditation.

BELOW A Buddhist prayer wheel is a rotating drum containing scriptures. Setting the wheel in motion is a symbolic act.

Every sacred tradition has its own ways of connecting with spirit and uses a variety of symbolic objects in its rituals and ceremonies. These are usually regarded as objects of power and are sometimes so sacred that they are unseen and untouchable.

PRAYER STRINGS

Common in many religions, the prayer string has beads or knots along its length and is a device to aid prayer or meditation. The number of beads usually has symbolic significance, and the string or chain is also symbolic: on one level it represents the connection between humans and the divine, but on another level a prayer string signifies the bondage of the human soul.

For Muslims, 99 beads symbolize the 99 names of Allah (the 100th being known only to Allah himself). Prayer strings are known as *misbaha* or *subha* and, as well as being used for the recitation of Allah's names and attributes, are a mnemonic device to aid the repetition of prayers. Hindus and Buddhists use a prayer string known as a *mala* when saying mantras, or sacred chants, in prayer and meditation. The 108 beads of a Buddhist string mirror the various stages of the world's development. A Catholic rosary usually has 165 beads, divided into 15 sets consisting of ten small beads and one large one. They are counted by saying prayers: each small bead represents an Ave Maria or Hail Mary and each large one the Lord's Prayer.

SACRED STICKS

Some cultures use sticks to connect with the divine. In the Native American tradition, special sticks for carrying prayers are made of painted wood and decorated with feathers, thread and other items. They are sometimes placed around the borders of a ceremonial site, or put into bundles and placed inside it. Maori priests use a god-stick to summon and hold the essence of a god or spirit. The stick, like a carved peg, is held by the priest or thrust into the earth. When people want to make a request, sacred strings are attached to the god-stick and pulled to grab the attention of the spirit residing in it.

PRAYER WHEELS, FLAGS AND STONES

Widely used in Tibetan Buddhism, the prayer wheel, or *khorlo*, is a rotating drum that is inscribed with and usually contains prayers, a passage from a holy book or a complete paper scroll. As the vehicle for a sacred force, setting the wheel in motion establishes contact between the person at prayer and the heavenly beings. It is rotated clockwise as prayers are recited. Large prayer wheels placed outside Buddhist shrines are rotated by pilgrims as they walk around the holy site.

Stones and flags are also used to carry prayers, and inscribed stones are a common sight along the pilgrimage routes of Tibet. Prayer flags originated in China and India, but have become a

RIGHT A *mani* stone tablet, in Tibet, inscribed with "All hail the jewel in the lotus", referring to the pristine consciousness.

colourful feature of the Tibetan landscape. People write their troubles on pieces of cloth and pin them to trees or suspend them on lines for the wind to blow the worries away.

As part of the natural landscape, stones are widely regarded as sacred objects and are often connected with myth and folklore: in China and Japan beautiful river stones were thought to hatch into dragons, and special stones were used to invoke rain and to bring a woman sons. In Nepal and Tibet *mani* stones, with prayers carved on to them, are put in temples and houses and alongside trails and passes, and probably number in their thousands.

In West Africa, the priests of the Yoruba god of thunder carry sacred stones that are thought to have been created by lightning. In the Celtic tradition, round stones with a central hole (known as "holey", or holy, stones) were used for healing and fertility rituals – it was thought that the hole would trap bad spirits.

MEDICINE BUNDLE

Native Americans use a special pouch to contain sacred objects such as stones, herbs and amulets. Known as a medicine bundle, it may be for personal use, or used by a shaman. Sometimes the bundle is a collective representation of the spiritual power and cohesiveness of the tribe. During the ceremonies of the Crow tribe the medicine bundle would be opened and the women would dance with the weasel skins to

obtain supernatural powers that ensured the fertility of the sacred tobacco, and so the growth of the Crow tribe as a whole.

CANDELABRA

Candlesticks and candelabra are sacred objects in many traditions. They illuminated Greek and Roman temples, appearing in classical art to represent piety and sacred ritual, and are used on Christian altars and in Buddhist ritual. In Mexico, "tree of life" candelabra combine pre-Christian symbolism with images of Adam and Eve and the serpent of knowledge, while death may appear as a skeleton in the "branches". The menorah is a seven-branched candelabrum that symbolizes the Jewish faith.

AMULETS AND TALISMANS

An amulet is a small object or piece of jewellery that is believed to possess magical or divine power; an object inscribed with a charm is known as a talisman. Both are thought to connect humans with the otherworldly powers they represent.

In ancient Egypt, mummies were covered in amulets made of gold, bronze or stone to ensure the immortality of the dead; the scarab beetle, the eye of Horus, the girdle of Isis and the ankh (the symbol of life) all featured on amulets used for protection or to gain qualities such as vitality or knowledge. A popular Hindu amulet is the *vishnupada*, the image of Vishnu's footprint. In the Native American tradition, animal amulets such as bears' claws are

thought to embody the spirit of the animal. In China, talismans are sometimes written in invisible ink or "ghost script", so that only the spirits can see them. In Japan, talismans known as *gofu*, designed to bring good fortune, are sold or given away at Shinto shrines: they are usually pieces of paper bearing the name of the deity. In the Islamic tradition, a common talisman is the *tawiz*, a stone or metal plaque bearing an inscription from the Qur'an.

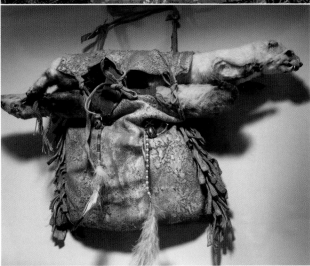

ABOVE A Native American medicine bundle is a pouch containing sacred objects of power. This bundle contains tobacco.

THE MENORAH

The seven-branched menorah dates back to the Exodus of the Jews from Egypt. According to tradition it created itself from gold cast into the fire by Moses. Its seven branches symbolize the planets, the days of the week and the seven levels of Heaven.

ALTARS AND SACRED PLACES

ABOVE Salt can be used as an offering as a symbol of the earth, and also as a symbol of its life-preserving qualities.

TOP Burning incense is an ancient ritual act of consecration, the smoke often symbolizing the soul's journey heavenwards.

The word "altar" comes from the Latin *altus*, meaning "high", and describes a raised area that forms the focus of sacred ritual and worship. It is usually erected within a building or area dedicated to a deity, although some altars are not fixed but set up for particular ceremonies and then dismantled. Shrines also provide a focus for sacred activity, and vary from a small niche containing some kind of holy object (such as a statue) to a place of pilgrimage. All sacred sites, whether natural or constructed, symbolize ways of connecting with spirit and are places of meaning and power.

ALTAR SYMBOLISM

The altar reproduces on a small scale the entire sacred tradition it represents, and can even be seen as a microcosm of the universe. It has sometimes been thought of as the spiritual centre of the world, so its symbolic meaning is related to the world tree or the cosmic mountain. An altar may also symbolize the time and place where a person became holy or performed a holy act. Like the hearth at the centre of the home, the altar is the focal point of sacred activity: in the Christian tradition, transitional ceremonies

or celebrations such as weddings and funerals take place before it.

Traditionally altars were a place of sacrifice. The earliest altars were open to the sky, so that the smoke of burnt offerings rose up towards the gods; it was only later that they were enclosed in purpose-built temples in honour of specific deities, but the association with fire remains. In the Philippines, palm leaf prayer books are used as offerings, burnt on stone altars (*batong buhay*), while candles and incense are placed on altars in many traditions, symbols of the illuminating and otherworldly qualities of fire and smoke. Native Americans often use tobacco (which they believe to be a sacred herb), and sometimes salt, as an altar offering.

SHRINES

In many cultures shrines are an everyday part of life, appearing at the roadside, in the home, in shops and offices, as well as in holy buildings. In many Christian countries it is common to see roadside shrines dedicated to the Virgin Mary or to specific saints, while in India, China and Japan household shrines are dedicated to various deities to gain their blessings for the home. In a similar way, the lares and penates, the household gods of ancient Rome, were honoured with daily prayers and offerings.

A shrine may commemorate the dead: in China, ancestor deities appear on household shrines. A Christian grave, with its tombstone and offerings of flowers, is also a type of shrine.

THE SACRED IN NATURE

In traditional societies in which people are closely connected with nature, holy sites tend to be places in the landscape. Practically every feature of the natural landscape has been associated with some kind of sacred tradition. There are holy mountains, rivers and lakes, caves, canyons and craters, as well as trees and forests. Mount Fuji, a dormant volcano and Japan's largest mountain, is revered by both Buddhists and Shintoists and is the site of many temples and shrines – even at the bottom of its crater. The Nile was sacred in ancient Egypt and remains so today among traditional African peoples, while Lake Titicaca, the largest freshwater lake in South America, was sacred to the Incas, who believed the god Viracocha rose from it to create the sun, moon and stars.

SACRED MOUNTAINS
Mountains are significant in Taoism as a medium through which people can communicate with the immortals and earth's primeval powers. Taoism has five holy mountains: Taishan, Hengshan, Huashan, Hengshan and Songshan.

For Australian Aboriginals, Uluru – possibly the world's most famous monolith – is the sacred site of the Dreamtime. The gigantic Serpent Mound of Ohio is a sacred effigy built by Native Americans; it is in the shape of a snake and is possibly connected with worship of the earth as a divine mother.

In Europe, the site of Chartres Cathedral was once a sacred forest, as was the site of the Temple of Apollo, at Delphi, in Greece, and groves of oak trees were sacred to the Druids. The Ajanta Caves, in India, are rock temples carved into almost vertical cliffs above a wooded ravine with cascading waterfalls; the caves contain five Buddhist temples and 24 monasteries. A meteor crater near Flagstaff, Arizona, which is deep enough to hold a 50-storey building, is regarded as a sacred site by the Navajo, who believe it was made by a flaming serpent god. Chaco Canyon in New Mexico was the dwelling place of the Anasazi, or "ancient ones", ancestors of the Hopi and Zuni peoples. It contains circular chambers known as *kivas*.

SACRED BUILDINGS

As societies became more complex, people began to construct sacred buildings and towns and cities grew up around them. Varanasi, on the banks of the holy river Ganges, is India's most holy city, with 6km/4 miles of riverside temples and palaces. In the central highlands of Java, Borobudur (which means "temple of the countless Buddhas") is the largest Buddhist shrine in the world. The way up to the summit was designed as a clockwise path of pilgrimage, with each tier representing a progressively higher level of spiritual experience.

There are many examples of the sacred sites of one culture being adopted by another. Ephesus in Turkey was once renowned as a centre of magic and the occult arts, and its temple to Artemis, the moon goddess, was alleged to be the greatest of the seven wonders of the ancient world. After Christians destroyed the temple the site became associated with the Virgin Mary; it has been a shrine for many centuries.

The great golden-roofed Potala Palace in Lhasa is the holy residence of the (currently exiled) Dalai Lama, and is a place of pilgrimage for Tibetan Buddhists. Its name, meaning "Pure Land", comes from the mythical Mount Potala, in India, a place roughly equivalent to paradise and the home of the Bodhisattva Avalokiteshvara, of whom the Dalai Lama is the incarnation. The palace houses the tombs of earlier Dalai Lamas, one of the most splendid of which has a massive golden stupa and a beautiful mandala encrusted with more than 20,000 pearls.

ABOVE The magnificent Potala Palace in Lhasa, Tibet, is a place of pilgrimage for Tibetan Buddhists and stands at one of the highest points of the world.

ABOVE LEFT This gigantic meteor crater at Flagstaff (Arizona) is a sacred site for the Navajo.

ROCK-CUT CHURCHES
One of Africa's most important Christian pilgrimage sites is at Lalibela, in Ethiopia. Dating back to the 12th century BC, 11 rock-cut churches burrow deep into the rock face, and connecting passageways and tunnels wind back into the hills, leading to secret crypts and grottoes. This network of sacred places is the eighth wonder of the world.

ALCHEMICAL TRANSMUTATION

ABOVE Alchemists at work, in a 14th-century manuscript. The transformation processes they used in their scientific practices (here, distillation) have since become symbols of psychological and spiritual progress.

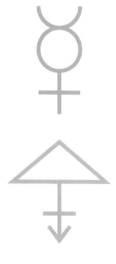

ABOVE The alchemy symbols for Mercury (top) and Sulphur (above).

Alchemy is a philosophy and practice that spans both science and mysticism. It has influenced the development of modern chemistry and even modern depth psychology. The alchemist sees direct relationships between matter and spirit and between organic and inorganic nature.

First conceived as a process similar to fermentation, in which common metals might be transmuted into gold or silver, the alchemical process became an analogy for psychological and spiritual transformation. The earliest references to alchemy are to be found in the records of ancient Egypt. The art was developed in ancient Greece and the Arab world, returning to Christian Europe via Moorish Spain during the 12th century. But alchemy – particularly the theoretical connection between

gold and longevity – was also known in ancient China and India. The process is described using a wealth of symbolism derived from astrology, astronomy, mythology and early science.

HERMETIC WISDOM

The philosophy behind alchemy is directly linked with the teachings of Hermes Trismegistus ("Hermes the Thrice-greatest"), who was described as a great teacher and imparter of wisdom. He appears to be a syncretization of the Greek god Hermes, who conducted souls to the underworld and carried the messages of the gods, with the Egyptian deity Thoth, patron of learning and magic. Hermes was represented wearing a winged cap and sandals and carrying the caduceus, a winged staff entwined with two snakes. His attributes symbolized the linking of the underworld with material reality and the transpersonal experience of "winged flight": he was essentially a mediator or guide between the worlds. Hermes Trismegistus was said to be the author of thousands of texts on science, philosophy, the occult and many other subjects that encapsulated all the wisdom of the ancient world.

Hermetic philosophy centres on the interrelationship of the microcosmic and macrocosmic worlds, contained within the idea "as above, so below", and that all things come from "the One". Applied to alchemy, this means that the human microcosm, where body, soul and spirit meet, is directly related to the elements,

the stars, planets, moon and sun, all of which are understood to be mirrored within each person as the "cosmic soul".

THE SYMBOLIC MAP

C.G. Jung considered alchemy to be a useful symbolic map for inner experiences. He related the different phases of the alchemical process to the stages a person goes through when receiving analytical therapy. Jung commonly used the term *unus mundus*, which he borrowed from the medieval alchemists. It is a description of a "one world" experience, in which the individual's body, soul and spirit are consciously reunited with the cosmic soul.

ALCHEMICAL TRANSFORMATION

The alchemical process, also known as the opus magnum or "great work", is essentially a process of change or transmutation, which may be physical, psychological or spiritual. The goal of alchemy is the transformation of a basic substance into a higher substance. This can be understood as changing base metals into gold, or as transforming the most basic of human awareness and experience into deep insight.

The result of the alchemist's dedication to the process was expressed as the *lapis philosophorum* or "philosopher's stone", an "inner treasure" or state of perfect harmony symbolized by the correct mixing of sulphur and mercury (which the alchemists believed were the principal materials of all metals). Alchemy is also associated with the process of prolonging life and striving for immortality by creating an "elixir of life" or "drinkable gold".

STAGES OF THE WORK

The *prima materia* is the raw material of the alchemical process, the prime matter that precedes the division into the four elements – water, air, earth and fire. In this raw state all the oppositions of life are present. The *prima materia* corresponds with the psychological state of minimum awareness.

The basic raw material is contained in an athanor, or oven, consisting of an egg-shaped glass vessel heated over a fire. The oven symbolizes the human, in which body, soul and cosmos are linked. It can also represent a ritualized space in which any transformative process is contained. The fire represents the generative force behind the process of transformation. Air from the alchemist's bellows is required to kindle the flames and amplify the process. The warmth within the vessel corresponds to a natural vital energy that is said to be within all things.

The *nigredo,* or "blackening", phase is the stage in which the raw material melts into a black liquid. This symbolizes the early awakening of awareness, and is also associated with the archetype of the wounded healer and the beginning of healing power. The *nigredo* can represent depression, through which a person begins to examine their life and face feelings of guilt, worthlessness

and powerlessness. As the elixir continues to be heated the next phase is the *albedo,* or "whitening", during which the molten metals begin to recombine in a purer form. In psychological terms this represents something like daybreak, during which depression shifts and life begins to return. The final phase of the great work is called the *rubedo,* or "reddening", and is analogous to sunrise. This is a point of great intensity in the work, in which the opposites begin to unite in the *coniunctio oppositorum,* or "sacred marriage", resulting in the the philosopher's stone.

SACRED MARRIAGE

The main symbol of alchemy is the uniting of the king and queen within the fire of love. The union is symbolized by the marriage of sulphur (masculine) and mercury (feminine) or of the sun (spirit) and moon (soul). Alchemy presupposes that humans are in a state of chaos and discord, having lost their connection with "Eden", the primordial state of contentedness. The image of the sacred marriage refers to the renewal of this integral nature through the coming together of the central forces within us.

The marriage of the king and queen also corresponds with a surrendering to our androgynous nature, represented by the half-male, half-female figure of the hermaphrodite. A hermaphrodite symbolizes the attainment of intuitive insight, as opposed to the one-sided power of rational knowledge and discourse. The term hermaphrodite is a

RIGHT Every tool, ingredient and scientific process in alchemy has its own sign or symbol.

combination of the names of two gods; Hermes, the god of the intellect and communication and Aphrodite, the goddess of sensuality and love. This androgynous unity represents a primordial state of humanity, before the fall into the world of opposites. It is embodied in the philosopher's stone, a kind of spiritual solidity.

BELOW The science of alchemy has a wealth of symbolism of its own, with every element and process given its own graphic sign, but it also has great thematic symbolism, rooted in the way the alchemists looked at the world and explored its possibilities for change.

LABYRINTHS AND MAZES

ABOVE The classic shape of the maze.

ABOVE The labrys, an axe whose double curved blades link it with the moon, and with the root of the word "labyrinth".

BELOW RIGHT This modern picture portrays modern cosmopolitan life as a maze (looking also like computer chip circuitry).

BELOW This classical Italian maze design is an example of a unicursal (one-path) maze.

The labyrinth is a symbol for life that has been interpreted in different ways to represent the central spiritual and psychological concerns of each culture that makes use of it. As a "walk-through" symbol, it is a creative or ritual space that reflects our sense of unknowingness and disorientation as we move through the challenges and obstacles of life. The labyrinth charts the connection between everyday life and the underworld, our conscious self and the unconscious or collective unconscious, and our waking consciousness and the dreaming process. This ancient symbol represents both the womb and the tomb, and the thread that helps us find a way through it represents the awareness needed to get through life.

The ancient root of "labyrinth" is "la", meaning "stone", referring to something firm and on the ground. The labrys is a double-headed axe from Crete, whose two curved blades symbolize the waxing and waning moon, in the centre of each blade is an image of the four-pointed cross. It is often shown held by a goddess who is guarding the entrance to the labyrinth or the underworld. The word "maze" is derived from the Old English *amasian* meaning "to confuse".

LABYRINTH FORMS

A labyrinth is "unicursal": it has only one path that twists and turns but eventually leads to the centre. A "multicursal" maze can have many pathways, and therefore dead ends. The first will disorientate, but the second can both disorientate and render you completely lost.

The simplest form of labyrinth is the "three-circuit" design, but the archetypal pattern is the classical, "Cretan" or "seven-circuit", labyrinth. It has only one entrance and one route to the centre. It may be either square or circular, and is found in Europe, North Africa, India, Indonesia, and North and South America. Almost every ancient labyrinth follows this design. Classical labyrinths with 11 or 15 circuits have been found, such as the 11-circuit labyrinth made from boulders at Visby, Sweden.

MEDIEVAL DESIGNS

The Romans elaborated the genre with meandering, spiralling and serpentine patterns, working them as mosaics on walls and floors. It was later adopted by the Church: the oldest known example dates from the 4th century and is in the pavement of the Basilica of Reparatus at Orleansville, Algeria. Church labyrinths became more common in the 9th century, and designs large enough to be walked as pilgrimage or penance were laid out in the naves of French cathedrals: the most famous was constructed at Chartres around 1230. A six-petalled flower at its centre represents the flowering and healing union of the masculine (Christ) and feminine (Mary) energies.

In the late Middle Ages a new form developed in the gardens and palaces of Europe. These mazes, constructed in topiary, included many wrong turns and dead-ends. The "simply connected" maze, although complex, has one continuous wall and it is possible to navigate by keeping one hand on the wall at all times. By the 19th century "multiple connected" mazes were formed with islands in them, which could not be solved by the "hand on the wall" method.

THE SACRED JOURNEY TO THE UNDERWORLD

Early labyrinths were maps to aid the passage of the soul to the underworld after death. Ancient labyrinth dances and rituals depicted the movement between life and death, through the

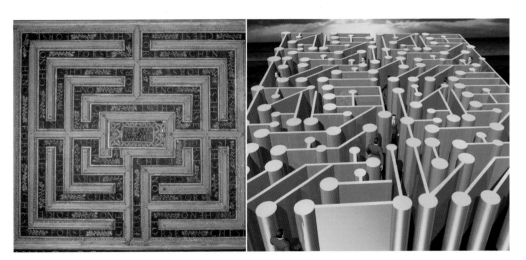

gateway of the tomb and into mother earth. The earliest recorded labyrinth was described by Herodotus in the 5th century BC, built by twelve Egyptian kings as their memorial beside a vast man-made lake. A pyramid rose from one wall of the labyrinth, which had an upper and an underground level. It enshrined the bodies of the twelve kings, and tombs of sacred crocodiles.

THE HEROIC JOURNEY

The most famous labyrinth is that of King Minos at Knossos in Crete, which is associated with the myth of Theseus and the bull-headed monster called the Minotaur. Theseus, King Aegeus of Athen's son, vowed to kill the creature to bring an end to Athen's enforced tribute to King Minos. Minos's daughter Ariadne fell in love with Theseus and gave him a ball of golden thread, the end of which she held as he descended into the labyrinth. Theseus met the Minotaur at the centre of the maze, killed him and returned to Ariadne by following the thread.

This myth has several important symbolic features: the "penetration" of the labyrinth, the experience of disorientation, the meeting and killing of an inner monster, and the resolution of the maze symbolized by the thread, which represents the cord of life joining the two worlds, upper and lower, with awareness. The relationship between male and female principles is another theme. The myth of Theseus and Ariadne describes a golden thread between man and woman. At the

Rad labyrinth in Hanover, Germany, and at the 300-year-old turf labyrinth at Saffron Waldon, in England, a ritual was enacted in which a girl stood in the centre and two young men raced to claim her.

PATHS TO SALVATION

The adoption of the labyrinth by Christians led to a change in symbolic meaning. The centre no longer meant an encounter with death or a monster but represented salvation, with the labyrinth as the path through the entanglements of sinful human nature. A symbolic pilgrimage or penitential journey through the labyrinth might be prescribed for sinners too frail to undertake a longer pilgrimage, and medieval monks might walk church labyrinths in contemplation.

FERTILIZATION AND BIRTH

The entrance to the labyrinth may represent the vulva, and the centre the ovum or the womb, suggesting a fertilizing journey of new hope, life and the potential for rebirth. This theme is connected to the journey into the earth mother and the underworld, thus linking the themes of life, death, fertility and birth.

A fivefold labyrinth with nine circuits is used as a motif on baskets woven by the Pima people of Arizona and also forms the great seal of the Piman tribal council. This design unusually features an entrance at the top, and is thought to depict a heroic journey into the womb.

The Chakravyuha labyrinth is an evolution of the classical form, and is found in India. It is based upon a threefold centre rather than the usual cross, displaying a spiral at its centre, and is thought to symbolize birth, mapping the way for the unborn child through the labyrinthine uterus. In the Indian epic the Mahabharatha, the Chakravyuha is an inescapable circular formation of standing warriors devised by the magician Drona.

Hopi labyrinths from the 12th century found in Arizona come in two forms. The Tapu'at form suggests a baby curled in the womb, or newly born nestling in its mother's arms; the entrance and exit paths suggest the umbilical cord and the birth canal. The second form is more rounded and symbolizes the sun father, who gives life. It represents the journey through life, and may also depict the boundaries of the Hopi territories.

ABOVE Theseus holds the thread, by which he maintained his link with the everyday world, given to him by Ariadne. This myth depicts Theseus as the symbolic hero-saviour, who overcomes the brutish aspects of his own nature as well as that of the Minotaur. The labyrinth, therefore, becomes a symbol of initiation and rebirth.

MULTIPLE DIMENSIONS

Adding a third dimension brings new levels of complexity to maze design, making it possible to move between levels by bridges or stairways. It is theoretically possible to keep adding dimensions to mazes, but this moves them out of the realm of the everyday world. Computer game designers use multi-dimensional mazes and labyrinths to create a "hero's journey" in the player's own home.

MANDALAS AND YANTRAS

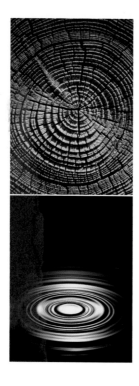

ABOVE The ripples created when a stone is dropped in water form a type of mandala

TOP Mandala patterns occur in nature, as the concentric circles on this tree trunk show.

BELOW Mandalas are meditation devices in spiritual traditions such as Buddhism. This one from Tibet is used in the Vajrayana Diamond or Thunderbolt vehicle.

The Sanskrit words "mandala" and "yantra" mean "circle" and "instrument" respectively, and describe schematic images designed to both represent and assist spiritual experience. Although rooted in the sacred traditions of the East, many aspects of their symbolism seem to be archetypal, and they appear in different guises all over the world. Mandala-like patterns occur in nature as well as in traditions as diverse as those of the Maya, Native Americans, Celts and Christians. They also feature in dreams and in spontaneous doodles and drawings, leading Jung to suggest that they are an attempt to preserve psychic order and a symbol of the individuation process.

THE TEACHINGS OF THE MANDALA

Just as a rainbow is created only when water droplets, light and the observer's sight come together, so the visual effects of a mandala are such that nothing exists except as an encounter between various fields and patterns of energy. The order of the cosmos is depicted through the balanced arrangement of geometric shapes (predominantly the circle, square and triangle), colour, and symbols such as deities or spiritual beings. Within an outer circle or square, concentric elements of the design radiate from and to the sacred space at the centre, symbolizing the divine presence. In Hinduism, this space is the *shunya* ("absolute void") and the *bindu* ("cosmic seed"), the creativity and spiritual fulfilment that emerge from

nothingness, the space from which all things are born and to which everything returns. Although the symbols used on the mandala are culture-specific, its overriding purpose is to bring the mind to a place of stillness and emptiness, disentangling it from the illusions of permanence in the everyday world in order to experience transcendence.

The traditional Hindu mandala is a square subdivided into smaller squares. As well as an image for contemplation, it is also a template for the ground plan of Hindu temples: the central square is the Place of Brahma and contains the womb-chamber, the holy area of the temple where the altar is situated.

Tibetan Buddhists create mandalas on rolled cloths called *thang-ka*. These are usually rectangular paintings showing the teachings of the Buddha, the wheel of life, the cosmic tree, saints and other spiritual guides in richly coloured images. Circular mandalas called *kyil-khor* are also used for meditation. Each symbol is considered in turn, moving from the edge inwards. Meditating Buddhas, protective and destructive creatures, clouds, mountains, flames and thunderbolts are all common icons on Tibetan mandalas, symbolizing the obstacles that must be faced before the centre can be reached.

MANDALAS IN NATURE

Many mandala-like patterns occur in nature, such as the concentric circles of a tree trunk, ripples on the surface of a pond, a spider's

web, a snowflake or a sunflower. Even natural formations in the landscape have been compared with mandalas. Mount Kailas, one of the tallest peaks in the Himalayas, has four distinct facades facing north, south, east and west, and is compared to an enormous diamond. Buddhists regard it as a mandala, a sacred circle from which four holy rivers (the Indus, Sutlej, Bramaputra and Ganges) flow like the spokes of an eternal wheel.

At the levels of both the macrocosm and microcosm, mandalas seem to be a universal pattern of life: the earth rotates around the Milky Way, while in the cells of every living creature electrons spin around a central nucleus. Even the human eye is a type of mandala.

SAND MANDALAS

Mandalas are not always painted. In Tibetan Buddhism, the *kalachakra*, or "wheel of time", a flat representation of all the cycles of the universe, is created in coloured sand as a symbolic ritual. It begins with a ceremony to call on the goddess of creation and consecrate the site. The mandala is then created from the centre outwards, symbolizing the growth of life from a single egg into the universe. One monk works at each of the four directions, pouring sand from a metal rod called a *chak-pur*. Once the mandala is finished, its role is complete, and a final ceremony is performed to release its healing powers into the world. The sands are swept up from the outside to the centre of the circle and placed

in an urn. This is carried in a ceremonial procession to a nearby river where it is emptied, carrying the healing sands out into the ocean to bring peace and harmony to the whole planet.

The Navajo also use sand paintings in healing rituals. The medicine man or woman performs a ceremony centred on a mandala sand painting called the *iikaah* ("the place where the spirits come and go") – a doorway through which helpful spirits will pass as they are called upon in the ritual. The ceremony begins at dawn and takes place in the hogan, a sacred lodge that has been blessed for the ceremony. The mandala is created using string and other markers, as the positions of the spirit figures must be precise to create a place of harmony. The base of the painting is built from sand, corn and pollen or crushed petals, then charcoal and ground stone are carefully poured to create outlines. The figures are solid shapes, with the image of their bodies, both back and front, poured into place to bring their complete presence into the circle.

At dusk, the person in need of healing comes to the hogan and sits in the centre of the mandala, with the images of the spirits in direct contact with his body to draw away the illness so that it falls into the mandala. The sand is then ritually disposed of.

YANTRAS
A variation of the mandala, the yantra is used in both Hinduism and Buddhism. It is a complex geometric figure that visually expresses a mantra or prayer. Sometimes the mantra is written to "fix" it, but predominantly geometric symbols are used in a mystical representation of creation and the interaction of cosmic forces. The powers inherent in the yantra are brought to life through ritual acts, such as smearing it with perfume and chanting the mantra over it.

The *shri-yantra*, considered one of the most potent yantra designs, is used in Hindu tantric ritual. It consists of a square, concentric circles and nine intersecting triangles. The external square functions like a city wall, with gateways to the four points of the

compass. It represents the physical world and protects and encloses the interior. The concentric circles represent spiritual expansion and cosmic unity, while the triangles represent the joining of the linga (phallus), represented by the upward-pointing triangle) with the yoni (womb), represented by the downward-pointing triangle, or the sexual play of the divine couple, Shiva and Shakti.

The *shri-yantra* can be engraved only on eight surfaces: gold, silver, copper, crystal, birch, bone, hide (including paper) and a special "Vishnu" stone named after the preserver deity. Only these materials, in combination with the correct colours – red, to symbolize the female, or white, symbolizing the male – will create the necessary balance and harmony of energies.

BELOW Yantras use abstract geometric shapes in their design, typically triangles, squares and circles.

ORACLES AND DIVINATION

ABOVE Tarot cards and a crystal ball are two methods of divination still used today.

RIGHT In a medieval illuminated manuscript classical Greek astronomers inspect the stars from Mount Athos. They believed that reading these patterns would help them predict likely future events.

URIM AND THUMMIN

Traditionally, the high priest of the ancient Hebrews wore a jewelled breastplate containing the Urim ("shining") and Thummin ("perfect"), two stones that were used to cast lots and divine God's wish.

Speaking in a symbolic language, oracles and divination are a way of communing with the unseen influences beyond the reach of the everyday world. From a psychological perspective, they can be seen as a way of tapping into the deeper layers of the unconscious mind.

Above the entrance of perhaps the most enduringly famous oracle in the ancient world, the Greek oracle at Delphi, was carved the inscription, "Know thyself." Divination is not a method of predicting the future – this would imply that life is a fixed programme – but is best understood as something fluid, a process that involves an ongoing dialogue with the spiritual or mythical dimension. Through this relationship it is possible to read certain signs that would otherwise remain hidden, thereby increasing self-awareness.

ORACULAR DEVICES

Divination uses chance to create a doorway for the spirit to express itself through symbolic patterning. This can be anything from random patterns in tea-leaves, bones or sticks, cloud formations, weather patterns, the formations of the stars and the communications of plants and animals to sophisticated symbol systems such as the Tarot or the I Ching. To read these patterns and elicit meaning involves an intuitive leap of faith, as oracles will not be understood by the rational mind, which tends to reject or overlook the significance of information that comes through by chance.

THE I CHING

Paradoxically, the only certainty in life is change. In all change, however, there are patterns, and it is this predictability that the shamans of ancient China referred to when they were called upon to give advice on forthcoming events. Originally, the answer to a question was divined from the patterns on animal bones or tortoise shells. This developed into the I Ching, or "book of changes", which became much more than an oracular device: for the ancients it symbolized the workings of the whole universe.

The basis of the I Ching is the trigram, an arrangement of three lines that are either solid or broken. The solid line represents yang energy, and the broken line yin energy, yin and yang being the two opposing principles that

underlie the whole of creation. Eight arrangements are possible, and the trigrams symbolize eight stages in the cycle of growth and decline, or ebb and flow, observable in all areas of life. Each has a name taken from nature: Heaven, earth, thunder, water, mountain, wind/wood, fire and lake. Trigrams once decorated the clothing of temporal and spiritual leaders and can be used as amulets. Combined in pairs, the trigrams make up the 64 hexagrams of the I Ching, with names such as "the creative", "decrease", "the receptive", "family", from which interpretations of human situations are made. These are further amplified by "changing lines", which increase the possible number of permutations to more than 10,000.

THE TAROT

The exact origins and purpose of the Tarot are unknown, but it was in use for gaming and divination in Italy, France and Germany by the late 14th century, though medieval churchmen denounced it as "the Devil's picture book". The Tarot is a card-deck illustrated with highly symbolic imagery. It may have been a way of disguising spiritual teachings that ran counter to the prevailing doctrines of the Church, but also seems likely to have formed part of a memory system. During the Renaissance, *ars memorativa* (pictorial memory systems) became linked with magical talismans or amulets for invoking a particular power.

The Tarot divides into two parts: the 22 cards of the Major Arcana and the 56 cards of the Minor Arcana. "Arcane" means mysterious or secret, and the Tarot is sometimes known as the Book of Secrets. The Major Arcana deals with archetypal themes that reflect turning points in life, symbolized by cards such as the Fool, the High Priestess, the Lovers, the Hanged Man and the World. The Minor Arcana is sub-divided into four suits, which are related to the four elements as well as everyday concerns: wands (fire and ambition), swords (air and ideas), cups (water and emotions) and pentacles (earth and material resources).

AUGURY

Today the term "augury" refers to all forms of divination. Originally, however, it meant interpreting oracular messages from birds,

often viewed as messengers to humans. Augury is one of the oldest forms of divination. Accounts from China, India, Persia and many other regions show that people paid careful attention to birds for divinatory purposes – their songs, movement, flight patterns, behaviour, even their eggs, as well as the particular species. For example, the Kakajarita, a 9th-century Tibetan text, gives detailed instructions for divining the meaning of crow cries.

Augury does not, however, require an organized system of signs. Originally it must have depended on an intimate rapport between birds and humans, with people entering into a mystical experience of bird-consciousness. The Roman state always referred to the augur before making an important decision, while by tradition, the site of the Aztec city Tenochtitlan was chosen when an eagle was seen on a cactus with a snake in its mouth, seen as an auspicious sign from the gods. The Bununs of Taiwan rely upon the chirping and the flight patterns of birds as hunting omens: a chirp on the left side is seen as a bad omen, and they invariably return home .

THE CLEDON TRADITION

Oracles can work in many different ways. In the classical world, words heard at random or out of context that struck a chord with the listener were regarded as oracular messages. Known as *cledon*, these symbolic fragments of speech that seemed to answer a

RIGHT An audience listens intently to the oracle, since the correct interpretation of a message was as important as the words themselves.

question or give advice were usually uttered unwittingly by strangers, children or passers-by. As with any other oracle, the success of the method depends as much upon the recipient's openness to the message and ability to comprehend it as on the oracle itself, divining being an interactive process.

THE DODONA OAK

One of the most revered oracles of antiquity was a great oak tree growing at Dodona, in north-west Greece. For centuries, pilgrims travelled to seek the tree's guidance. In the earliest stories about Dodona, oracles were delivered by the oak itself, but by the time of Homer, around 800 BC, a group of interpreters called the *selloi* – who, according to the Iliad, were "of unwashed feet and slept on the ground" – had established themselves at the site. Pieces of wood taken from the tree were said to have the same oracular power.

THE RAVEN

Often presaging death, the raven is usually seen as a bird of ill omen, but it may also augur well. In Genesis it was sent off by Noah to determine the extent of the flood, but never returned. The raven also appears in the flood stories of the Algonquin Indians. In Scandanavia ravens are thought to be the ghosts of murdered people, while according to a Chinese tradition, the soul of the sun takes the form of a crow or raven.

THE CYCLE OF LIFE

How humans see their bodies, their physical position in the world, and their own lifespan, gives rise to the rich symbolism that surrounds birth and death, love and relationships, ritual and creativity. Iconic symbols such as the heart and the wheel are central, but so are thematic symbols such as marriage and sunrise.

THE HUMAN BODY

ABOVE The human body is a rich source of symbolic meaning. The female form can represent different aspects of woman, such as fertility and female sexuality.

ABOVE The head is associated with humans' thinking capacity. It can also be used to describe a person in charge.

Many ancient traditions saw the human body as a microcosm (literally a "little world"), containing in miniature all of the various stages of creation. The Chinese regarded the body as both yin and yang, and thus a symbol of perfect balance and wholeness. In some traditions the body is regarded as a "temple of the soul", which mediates between Heaven and earth, assisting each person to realize their divine purpose and unique potential. Other traditions have viewed it as an enemy that has to be overcome, the repository of the base instincts and passions that threaten to lower humanity to the level of the animal world. In addition to the symbolism of the body as a whole, practically every individual part has its own symbolic associations.

THE HEAD

Almost universally, the head is considered to be the seat of learning, the instrument of reason and of the spiritual and social capacities that raise humans above animals. Symbols of authority such as crowns are worn on the head, while bowing the head denotes submission to a higher being. In many African tribal cultures an elongated head is a sign of good character, wisdom and leadership, and elaborate hairstyles and headdresses are designed to accentuate this quality.

The head is sacred in Maori tradition, and the Celtic cult of the sacred head is illustrated by numerous myths. In many traditions, beheading an enemy is thought to humiliate the individual. The Hindu goddess Durga is often shown holding her own decapitated head, while Christian iconography has many instances of saints carrying their own heads, signifying the power of the spirit to conquer death.

THE HAIR

The hair often represents virility and strength, as in the Old Testament story of Samson, who lost his strength when Delilah cut his hair. The Khalsa community of Sikhs let their hair and beards grow because they believe it is a symbol of God's love. In China a shaved scalp was on a par with emasculation and could debar a person from public office. A shaved head can also indicate sacrifice or submission: monks and nuns in both Buddhist and Christian traditions may cut off their hair as they enter religious life. For the Gauls and other Celtic peoples' long hair was a symbol of royal power, or of liberty and independence.

Long loose hair in women once indicated youth and virginity, while braided or bound hair could symbolize either a married woman or, conversely, a courtesan. In Christian art the redeemed and sanctified St Mary of Magdelene is often shown with very long, loose hair as a symbol of her chastity, love and humility.

Haircuts and hairstyles are frequently signifiers of social or religious difference, as with Rastafarian dreadlocks or the long ringlets of Hassidic Jews. In Hindu and Buddhist traditions, the topknot is believed to cover the area where the divine spirit enters the body at birth and leaves at death; it is associated with holy people. Body hair is associated with virility or animal tendencies: in Christian art it is used as a symbol of the devil.

THE EYES

As may be expected, the symbolism of the eye is connected with perception and vision, the ability to see beyond the purely physical to the realms of soul and spirit; consequently blindness is often used as a metaphor for the inability to see spiritual and moral truth. However, blindness can also be associated with wisdom and spiritual gifts.

In some traditions, including Hindu, Taoist and Shinto, the eyes are identified with the sun and moon, with the right eye corresponding to the active and the future (the sun) and the left to the passive and the past (the moon). To unify perception, some cultures believe in the existence of an invisible "third eye" in the middle of the forehead. Both the Hindu god Shiva and the Buddha are depicted with a third eye, the vehicle of perception that is directed inwards in meditation.

In ancient Greece the eye symbol had magical powers, and eyes painted on the prows of warships had the power to guide them. In ancient Egypt the wadjet, or eye of Horus, had a healing and protective function. One of the symbols of Freemasonry is a single, unlidded eye (a symbol of divine knowledge) enclosed within a triangle – an image that appears on the back of the US dollar bill. The phrase "eyes wide open" signifies a state of awareness.

THE MOUTH

As the organ of speech and breath, the mouth embodies the power of spirit and the inspiration of the soul, an elevated state of consciousness and the ability to reason and communicate. Through its association with eating the mouth is also linked with destruction, as with the mouth of a monster: in Christian iconography the entrance to hell is a fanged demon's mouth. Medieval artists depicted small demons flying from a person's mouth to signify evil words or lies.

The tongue and teeth have their own symbolism. In African sculptures, teeth can indicate a creature's terrifying power to consume, although they can also be associated with strength and growing wisdom. In Persian and European love poetry, teeth are frequently compared to pearls. The tongue is sometimes compared with flames and in the Christian tradition tongues of fire symbolize the Holy Spirit. It symbolizes speech but is also associated with ferocity: rolling tongues were depicted on ancient Chinese tombs to frighten away evil spirits. In Tibet, sticking out the tongue is seen as a friendly greeting, while in Maori culture it is a defiant, provocative (and also protective) gesture.

THE HEART

In the West the heart has been linked with romantic love since the Middle Ages. In the ancient world, however, it was a symbol of the centre and was often thought of as the site of the soul. In China the heart was also thought to be where the *shen*, or spirit, resides, and was considered the source of intelligence. The heart is also associated with moral courage and truth.

ABOVE The heart is not a symbol only for love but also for truth.

BELOW Mary of Magdelene is often portrayed with long, loose hair as a symbol of her chastity, and an allusion to the time she washed the feet of Jesus.

LEFT In the act of washing the feet of his disciple Peter, Jesus demonstrated his humility and indicated that he was a servant of humankind rather than its king.

as their servant, a gesture that was later imitated by English kings who washed the feet of the poor to show their humility. In the Fon Republic of Benin, the god of war is usually shown with large feet, symbolizing his ability to stamp out his enemies.

BREATH AND BLOOD

Both breath and blood are associated with the life force and divine power. Native Americans use the breath to pass power between people, and it had magical properties for the Celts: the Druid Mog Ruith was able to turn his enemies to stone by breathing on them.

Many cultures consider blood to be sacred because it embodies the soul: in West African voodoo, sacred statues are smeared with chicken's blood to bring them to life, and a similar practice was performed by the Norse, who smeared their sacred runes with ox blood to activate them. Blood has been used to seal oaths, and 14th-century Japanese warriors stamped their fingerprints in blood to assure a contract. Christians ritually ingest the blood of Christ, in the form of wine, at the Eucharist ceremony.

However, in some traditions blood also has the power to contaminate. In the Shinto religion, the word for blood (chi) is taboo, while neither Jews nor Muslims are permitted to eat meat that contains any residue of blood. Jews regard menstrual blood as unclean, though it has also been linked with fertility, as in ancient Egypt.

THE NAVEL

As well as being a visual reminder of the body's connection to life through the umbilical cord, the navel is often used as a symbol of the centre of the world from which creation emanated. Muslims describe Mohammed's birthplace as the "navel of the world", and in ancient Greece Delphi was the site of the sacred *omphalos,* or "navel stone", a cylindrical stone with a rounded top that symbolized the connection between the three worlds (Heaven, earth and the underworld).

The pole star is sometimes referred to as the navel star, around which the heavens seem to rotate. In West Africa, the navel is viewed as an ancestral matriarchal symbol that relates to fertility; scarification marks are ritually made around a girl's navel at puberty.

HANDS AND FEET

Traditionally the hand is a symbol of active divine power. Handprints frequently appear in Australian Aboriginal cave art, representing the artist's spiritual imprint and signature. In Hinduism and Buddhism, the hand is a guardian and fragment of the universal soul, and in India handprints on walls, doors or other objects signify protection. In Christian iconography, a hand represents God's blessing and intervention, and the "laying on of hands" is used in churches in healing and ordination rituals.

The foot is the part of the body that most closely relates to the earth. It is associated with both stability and movement. Bare feet traditionally indicate humility, and have also been a sign of mourning. When Christ washed the feet of his disciples, he was using the act to symbolize his role

BELOW The symbolism of the navel is connected with the centre of the world, life and creation.

SEXUAL ORGANS

The sexual and reproductive organs of both men and women carry a profound symbolism. As well as being linked with fertility, the womb is associated with protection and mysterious hidden powers. Vessels of transformation, such as the crucible and cauldron, are linked with womb symbolism, as are natural features in the landscape, such as caves. The womb is often linked with the mother goddess: Delphi in ancient Greece, the site of the oracle and sacred to the great mother of earth, sea and sky, was named from the Greek word *delphos*, meaning "womb".

The vulva is also usually associated with mother goddesses. In Hinduism it is symbolized by the yoni, represented as a vulva-shaped shallow basin and the graphic symbol of the triangle. The Bambara of Mali refer to it as "lovely big mother" and regard it as a gateway to hidden treasure and knowledge. The vulva symbolizes the dark, devouring aspect of the goddess, the jealous, possessive, over-protective mother who won't let go of her children, or the woman her lover. The concept of the vagina dentata ("toothed vagina") may be associated with this aspect and may also represent a man's castration anxieties – that once he enters a woman's body he will be unable to escape – and the fear of surrender to his instincts.

The phallus is a symbol of the masculine, active principle, the power of procreation and a channel for the life force. It is worshipped in many cultures as the source of life. In Hinduism it is associated with the god Shiva and is symbolized by the linga, an upright stone that typically appears conjoined with the yoni, symbolizing the union of spirit and matter, of the male and female principles. Phallic objects were worshipped in ancient China, and the Japanese god of marriage is portrayed in a phallic shape. Fertility gods such as the Roman Priapus are often depicted with an erect phallus, and satyrs were shown with gigantic erections as symbols of their libidinous nature. In Kabbalistic thought, the phallus was responsible for maintaining equilibrium; through its hardening or softening in the presence or absence of energy it is a balancing agent whose role is to sustain the world.

THE ENERGY BODY

Many traditions believe in an animating force that runs through every living thing, including the human body. Known by various names (such as chi in China and prana in India), the life force runs along a web of energy pathways known as meridians (China) or *nadis* (India). Esoteric and healing systems, such as yoga, reflexology and accupuncture, are based on this system, associating physical and emotional distress with imbalances in the body's energy field. In Hindu and Buddhist thought, subtle energy enters and leaves the body through chakras, or energy centres, which are gateways between the physical and the immaterial realm. The principal chakras are arranged along a central meridian running from the base of the spine to the crown of the head.

BELOW Hindu linga stones are shown nestling in round-shaped yoni carvings. The linga and yoni symbolize the male and female reproductive organs and the masculine and feminine principles.

BIRTH AND DEATH

Both birth and death are feared and welcomed in every culture, each representing both beginning and ending. Birth is the beginning of life, but may also be considered the ending of a previous life or soul journey, and the end of gestation. Death is an ending, but for some it is also the beginning of a significant new journey to the underworld, Heaven, or the next incarnation. Both are events of mysterious beauty, awe and terror, sources of inspiration and superstition for a huge body of symbolism informing religion, culture and science.

BIRTH AND DEATH FORETOLD

A great deal of symbolism surrounds the foretelling of birth or death, perhaps because these events are so mysterious, unpredictable and life-shaking. Astrology predicts likely times for births and deaths, and unusual heavenly signs have often been interpreted as pointing to the comings and goings of important people. In ancient times the sighting of a new star was the sign of a newborn king; thus the birth of Christ was predicted on this basis, possibly when Jupiter (known to the Jews as the "king's star") aligned with Saturn,

creating the "star of David".

Many signs and symbols in nature are taken as omens of birth or death. Perhaps because it is a symbol of transformation, the butterfly is variously taken to portend either. In the Orkney Islands a rainbow presages a birth, and an old English folk rhyme associates the sighting of magpies with birth: three for a girl and four for a boy. In Europe the death's head sphinx moth was commonly taken to predict death because of the outline of a skull on its back. The Samoans believed that if they captured a butterfly they would be struck down dead. The Celts believed that seeing a butterfly flying at night signified death, and in Christian art a chrysalis is a symbol of death.

The ancient Romans hated owls as they saw them as portents of death. Many carrion-eating birds, particularly ravens, are thought to be able to smell death before it occurs, and they are therefore a bad omen, but in African and Native American cultures the raven is also a helpful guide to the dead on their journey. The howling of a dog or the sighting of a ghostly black dog may both warn of death. Dogs also appear in shamanic lore as guardians and guides to the underworld.

BIRTH SYMBOLISM

Many cultures consider giving birth a powerful and natural initiation, and give great importance to the various stages for both mother and child. The birth process mirrors the process of initiation. Traditionally the

mother is removed from society – leaving her usual roles behind – to a sacred place for birth, and undergoes rites of purification and cleansing. Labour has strong associations with the "threshold" phase of initiation, in which there is often great pain and mystery, and in many cultures post-partum blood is considered powerful and unclean, possibly because it represents a strong link with the world of the spirits. During childbirth the gods and spirits are often deemed to have great influence. The Anglo-Saxons prayed to the goddess Freya during birth. Celtic cultures sometimes hid the birth from supernatural creatures that might otherwise have created mischief.

THE PLACENTA

The placenta is revered in many parts of the world, symbolizing life, spirit and individuality. It is often buried in the ancestral territory to provide a sacred link between the child and the land: the Maoris call the placenta *whenua*, which also means "land". The Aymara and Quecha people of Bolivia consider the placenta to have a spirit. It is washed and buried secretly by the husband, otherwise, they believe, the mother or baby may become ill. The Ibo of Nigeria and Ghana give the placenta a proper burial as they believe it to be the dead twin of the newborn, and the Hmong of South-east Asia consider it to be a "jacket" – the first clothing of the child. They bury it in the belief that after death the soul will travel back to find its clothing.

THE MIDWIFE

Traditionally, midwives had a similar status to shamans or priests. In modern society the midwife may no longer have such high status, but midwives protect and support the mother and child. In British Columbia, the word for midwife among the Nuu-chah-nulth people means "she can do everything" and for the Coast Salish people it means "to watch, to care". The Greek goddess Hecate was the divine midwife.

SECOND BIRTH

Water has always been symbolically important for birth rites. Christian baptism, which may involve total immersion of the child or adult in blessed water, symbolizes a "second birth", representing the death and rebirth of Christ, and the cleansing of sin. The ritual is thought to have originated in India, where priests still practise a similar rite today. An ancient Irish tradition was the immersion of the child in milk, based on the belief that its spirit was formed through being breastfed. The Catholic Church banned the practice in 1172.

DEATH SYMBOLISM

Death has many emblems, most of them alarming, although the symbolism of hope and that of fear sometimes appear simultaneously. In art the most familiar depiction of death is the Grim Reaper, a skeleton robed in black and carrying a scythe, trident, sword or bow and arrows, and sometimes the hour glass that

he uses to measure a life's span. Other symbols of death include the skull, or a tomb or gravestone and the plants poppy, asphodel and cypress. Death ships or barges symbolize a journey to the afterworld, particularly for the ancient Egyptians.

BURIAL AND CREMATION RITES

Funerary rites vary tremendously according to cultural attitudes and beliefs, and the combination of fear and celebration with which people approach death. The practice of burial is known to date back as far as 80,000 years, and is common in societies where doctrines of bodily resurrection are popular. At sites such as the Shanidar Cave in Iraq, Teshiq-Tash in Iran and the Grotte des Enfants in France, bodies have been found buried with tools and jewellery, and often decorated with red ochre, to symbolize the blood of the earth.

Australian Aboriginal death rites are complex and vary by clan and region. Essentially death

is understood as a transformative event involving the parting of dual aspects of soul from the body. The spiritual being is thought to reintegrate with the ancestors in the Dreaming, in a sense returning home. After death the community sing songs containing symbols of death, such as a worm-eaten mangrove tree representing the dead body, or the tide marks of a "king tide", referring to a cleansing process and removal of the physical being. The coffin is a talisman painted to ask the spirits to help the deceased on his journey.

To ancient Indo-Iranian peoples and across Europe, from the Bronze Age onwards, cremation symbolized purification, sublimation and ascension. The fire itself signified the freeing of the soul, while the smoke symbolized its ascension. Roman funerals involved a procession to the tomb or pyre, with important relatives wearing masks of the deceased ancestor. Nine days later a feast was given, and the ashes were placed in a tomb.

ABOVE The black skeletal image of Death was a common medieval image.

ABOVE LEFT The first baptism, of Christ by John the Baptist. is used to symbolize divine grace and rebirth.

BELOW The gravestone, the Grim Reaper, and the hourglass symbolize the negative view of death.

SEX AND FERTILITY

ABOVE Water is a prime symbol of fertility, especially when in the form of rain.

TOP Sex and fertility have many symbolic associations, from the everyday to the sacred.

TOP RIGHT In this depiction of Love fighting Chastity, the symbols of chastity – her girdle and the arrow-deflecting shield – are in evidence.

ABOVE Grain is a symbol of the earth's fertility and is also used to symbolize human fertility.

Human beings are first and foremost sexual creatures, and to ensure the continuation of the species nature has ensured that sex is a pleasurable, health-promoting activity. Many traditions recognize a connection between sex and spirit, seeing sex as a vehicle for both bliss and transcendence.

FERTILITY RITES

In many traditions there is a connection between the fertility of the land and sexual symbolism. The Mongols and early Chinese saw rain as "seeds" sent from the sky to fertilize the earth; similar beliefs persist in parts of Africa and Australia, where women may lie down in the rain to help them get pregnant. In the myths of hunting societies, knowledge and power, and even human life itself, come from animals, and it is not uncommon for these gifts to have been obtained by sexual means. For instance, the survival of the Mandan of the North American plains depended on the bison. Human society was thought to descend from a sexual transfer of power between a bison and a woman, and the people's sacred buffalo dance mirrors this primordial act. In a ritual dance of the Blackfoot, a man decks himself with feathers and imitates the mating display of a prairie cock to ensure a good harvest.

Fertility and the attraction between male and female have been regarded as gifts of the goddess, associated with the Earth's seasonal cycles. In ancient Babylon, the king and the high priestess would perform ritual

intercourse as a fertility rite, symbolizing the mystical marriage of Tammuz, son and lover of the goddess Ishtar. The myth of Tammuz and Ishtar concerns the goddess's journey to the underworld to seek the release of her dead lover. While she is away, the earth is barren, but on her return, fertility returns to the land. This archetypal myth is echoed in the ancient Egyptian account of Isis and Osiris, or the ancient Greek story of Demeter and Persephone.

FERTILITY SYMBOLS

The bow, as a symbol of stored energy, is associated with dynamic sexual tension, and is an attribute of the god Apollo, a symbol of the sun's fertilizing power. Paintings of gods of love with bows often symbolize the tension of desire.

As the sacred tree of life, the fig tree also has sexual symbolism. For the Greeks the fig was an attribute of Priapus and Dionysus. In Egypt and in India it is linked

with procreative power, in particular that of Shiva and Vishnu. Graphic links between the fig leaf and the male genitals may have begun because of the milky juice that can be extracted from larger varieties. It was fig leaves that Adam and Eve used to hide themselves behind when they had eaten fruit from the tree of knowledge. The fruit of the fig is linked with female genitalia, but the fruit most commonly linked with sex and fertility is the apple, which appears almost everywhere in Europe as an emblem of love, marriage and fertility. The fish is a phallic symbol of sexual happiness and fecundity, linked with their prolific spawn, the fertility symbolism of water and analogies of the fish with the penis.

Corn dollies are traditional pagan fertility talismans made at harvest time. Sometimes they are decked with red ribbons, symbolizing blood and vitality, and set over the hearth until spring. The advent of spring is celebrated by a ritual dance around the maypole. The pole, decorated with ribbons, is both a phallic symbol and a representation of the world axis, or cosmic tree.

INFERTILITY

Just as crops are signs of the earth's abundance, so children are the "fruits" of a couple's sexual union. Traditionally the inability to have children was attributed to a woman's "barrenness", and divine assistance was often invoked. This involved petitioning fertility goddesses such as the Sumerian Inanna or the Greek Artemis, or ithyphallic (perpetually aroused) gods such as Legba, a deity of the Fon of West Africa. Phallic emblems are also common fertility charms.

ABSTINENCE, RESTRAINT, CHASTITY

While some cultures believe that expending sexual energy can inspire similar activity in nature, others think it may interfere with the earth's fertility: the Akan of Ghana believe that if a couple have sex outside they will be struck by madness and the earth goddess will make the ground where they lie infertile. Another belief is that by abstaining from sexual activity, a store of energy will be built up that will help the earth replenish its resources.

Chastity is often personified as the foe of erotic love, often a woman carrying a shield as a defence against the arrows of love or desire. Another common personification of chastity is the

unicorn, while other symbols include the colours blue and white, bees, chestnuts, doves, girdles, hawthorns, irises and lilies. Ermine was associated with chastity because its white winter coat linked it to purity.

TANTRA

Sometimes referred to as "the technique of ecstasy", tantra is a Sanskrit word meaning "web" or "weaving". Although the philosophy has many different schools, a common theme is that the everyday world (samsara) contains seeds of that which is eternal and unchanging (nirvana or enlightenment); similarly, the body-mind is a mirror of the universe. Hence enlightenment may be achieved through conscious participation in everyday life rather than through denial, and the body is a vehicle for transcendence.

A common tantric theme is the idea of cosmic sexuality. Through the desire and interplay of the primal couple, Shiva and Shakti, an all-encompassing creation arises; the couple are sometimes depicted in Hindu iconography as the hermaphrodite Ardhanarishvara. Through ritualized sexual intercourse, the divine fusion of the male and female principle is re-enacted, with each partner aiming to activate the energy of the opposite sex to achieve energetic and psychic wholeness. Sexual energy is symbolized by a coiled serpent (or kundalini), which lies dormant at the first chakra, at the base of the spine. Through sexual practice it is awakened and

refined into increasingly subtle levels until it finally merges with cosmic energy and a state of blissful euphoria occurs.

Tantrikas (followers of tantra) were often found living in graveyards, a symbolic reminder of the impermanence of the world and the desire for sublimation that transcends death. The teachings of tantra were often considered shocking and a threat to the social order, as its practice was specifically designed to break caste barriers and taboos.

CORNUCOPIA

The cornucopia or horn of plenty, is a classical symbol of inexhaustible fecundity. Perpetually filled with abundant flowers and fruit, its phallic, hollow shape represents the fertile union of male and female. Zeus/Jupiter was said to have created the cornucopia from the broken horn of Amalthea, the nanny goat who had suckled him, so that it represented divine and unasked-for bounty. Over time, it came to mean generosity, prosperity and good fortune, as well as the harvest season.

BELOW Ardhanarishvara, the Hindu hermaphrodite figure of Shiva and Parvati conjoined, symbolizes the reconciliation of opposites, and the achivement of union.

LOVE AND KINSHIP

The bonds that draw us together may be sexual attraction, a sense of common purpose or meaning, a marriage commitment or family and community. Since love does not always accommodate itself to social forms and conventions, the symbolic systems and rituals of love and kinship are diverse and changeable, as are the meanings associated with them.

Eros, who originated as a primeval creative force, became the Greek god of love and the son of Aphrodite, goddess of love. His Roman counterpart was Cupid (or Amor), the son of Venus, a cherubic winged boy shooting arrows of desire from his bow. His equivalent in Hindu mythology is Kama, who shoots sweet but painful arrows of desire into people and gods, suggesting the pain involved in love – his five arrows of flowers can make the heart glad, lead to great attraction, cause infatuation, weaken, or kill in a pleasurable way. In psychology the term "eros" refers to the libido and the urge for life, but to the Greeks it was a passionate and impersonal kind of love. Plato understood eros as desire that seeks a deep quality of beauty, an ideal of which the person before us is a reminder, hence the term "platonic love".

The Greek term "agape" refers to a kind of spiritual or selfless love, the love of God for humanity and of humanity for God, which also includes a love for fellow humans. Agape was not passionate but compassionate love. Agape feasts were rituals in which early Christians celebrated the Eucharist and the Jews celebrated Passover. Another Greek term, "philia", refers to a fondness and appreciation for the other, and is closer to what we understand as platonic love, meaning friendship and loyalty.

"Amor", derived from a name for the Roman god of love, described a new approach to love as a high spiritual experience: the courtly love celebrated by the troubadours, the poet-musicians of medieval Europe.

ROMANTIC LOVE

Courtly love was a personal and romantic form that involved two people falling in love with one another's virtues, rather than with an ideal. A knight was expected to show deep respect to the lady with whom he was in love, and had to be willing to suffer for his love. Much Renaissance literature refers to common motifs of love as a "torment" or "disease", with lovers becoming sick or unable to sleep and eat. Women took on an almost divine symbolism: their eyes became centrally important as channels of emotion, while their feet, ideally white and narrow, with a high arch, became a powerful sexual symbol.

LOVE SYMBOLS

Flowers frequently symbolize love. For Hindus it is the white flowering jasmine, in China the peony; to the Romans red roses were the flower of Venus, and have remained a strong love symbol in the West. In Iran wild olives and apples both symbolize love. A pair of mandarin ducks represents enduring and committed love to the Chinese, and doves and pigeons commonly represent lovers, either because they mate for life or because they coo while looking into each other's eyes. Lovebirds, colourful small parrots from Africa, also represent lovers because they sit close together in pairs.

ADINKRA LOVE SYMBOL

The people of Ghana weave symbolic designs into brocade called adinkra. The love symbol is called *osram ne nsoroma*, and it features a star "woman", above a moon "man"; it is used to symbolize a faithful, harmonious and fond love.

ABOVE Red roses are a well-used modern symbol of love, courtship and romance.

ABOVE The indestructable quality of the diamond makes it a symbol of enduring love.

ABOVE Heart-shaped items are used endlessly, and across cultures, as a symbol of romance.

ABOVE Rings symbolize eternity and are perhaps the ultimate love symbol.

Precious stones are significant emblems of love, first because they are "precious", and second because of their individual qualities. The diamond, because it is indestructible, represents enduring love. The red ruby symbolizes passion, sexual desire and power. Lace became a symbol of romance because a woman might drop her lace handkerchief so that the right man could pick it up for her. But the most enduring and cross-cultural of love symbols is the human heart: whole, bleeding, or pierced by arrows of love, the heart feels the passions and pain of love. It also represents warmth and openness to the "other".

Each culture uses its own symbol system to designate relationship status. Traditional Mennonites paint their door green if their daughter is eligible for marriage, and the Zulus of South Africa use beads of seven colours to depict a person's status: for example, a white bead (representing purity and spiritual love) next to a blue bead (representing faithfulness) is commonly used to show

engagement, while blue, white and black beads show marriage.

The wedding ring dates back to Egyptian times, when brides were given circles of hemp or rush. The Anglo-Saxons used a ring as a token of the promise of love, and the gold wedding ring has become a symbol of eternal love and unity. The Egyptians and Romans believed that the vein in the third finger (*vena amoris*) was connected with the heart; so wearing a wedding ring on that finger symbolizes the linking of the couples' hearts. Christian priests would count the Holy Trinity from the thumb, and end up at the ring finger, using powerful unifying symbolism. The Irish wedding ring is the *claddagh*, with two hands holding a heart and crown to symbolize love, loyalty and friendship.

MARRIAGE AND KINSHIP
Kinship is a "family-like" relationship that is essential to the effective functioning of societies. Its structure and rules vary from culture to culture, but kinship systems are often built on the institution of marriage. Though

this is usually the formalized bond between a man and a woman, other successful forms also exist, such as same sex marriage, polygamy and marriages of convenience. Marriage serves as a foundation for living, working and surviving together, for reproduction and sustaining a family.

For most traditional cultures, the predominant form is the arranged marriage, in which the parents or elders determine who will marry whom. In the Western world after the Middle Ages it became increasingly acceptable to marry as a consequence of falling in love. Marriage itself is a symbolic act in which the partners become two halves of a symbolic whole or "we". It is depicted in the symbolism of rings, "tying the knot", and the sharing of property and dowry.

LEFT One of the Hindu symbols of love is white flowering jasmine, given by lovers to each other as a sign of their commitment.

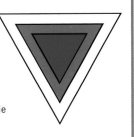

RITES OF PASSAGE

ABOVE A Muslim woman hands out sceptres to three boys in white costumes preparing for their circumcisions at an Istanbul mosque. On the day of their circumcision, Muslim boys become a prince for the day.

THE BIRTHDAY

Much symbolism associated with birthdays has ancient origins. The birthday cake may have originated in moon-shaped cakes given as temple offerings to Artemis. The candles may suggest the glowing of the moon, while in Germany a large central candle represents the "light of life".

Formalized rituals symbolically mark the passage of an individual or group through major life transitions, such as birth, puberty, marriage and death. Others mark important societal transitions and the celebration of nature. All are powerful symbolic processes.

INITIATION RITUALS

Many cultures value initiation ceremonies as part of the movement through life transitions. They all involve recognizing the role or status a person is moving into, and throwing off the old one. Most initiation ceremonies are grounded in cultural stories and symbolism. The French anthropologist Arnold van Gennep (1873–1957) saw the rite of passage as an essential process in cultural rejuvenation and described the phases of initiation as separation, transition and incorporation.

Separation involves removing a person (or sacred object) from a previous situation or status. It may involve the removal of identity, such as the removal or changing of clothes, hair or teeth, or scarification and tattooing. Another important factor is the preparation of ritual space, by drawing a circle, erecting a building or travelling to a different location such as a cave or mountain. The church, the mosque, and the medicine wheel are all examples of ritual spaces that allow people to separate from their everyday reality to connect with the divine. The registry office, where people are legally married, is an example of a legal ritual space.

Transition, the "threshold" or "liminal phase", involves undergoing certain trials, tests, ordeals or ritual actions, which essentially involve a metaphorical death and rebirth. The previous identity is broken down, making the way for a new identity to come forth. Taking an oath is an example of this phase, as when a person becoming a citizen of the United States pledges allegiance to the national symbols of the American flag.

Incorporation means returning to the "body" of the community, or else reconstituting the person, with new roles, awareness and responsibilities. The ringing of bells after the coronation of a monarch symbolically celebrates their new role. After a major sports tournament, such as the Olympic Games or the World Cup, the successful teams often return to their homeland and parade the streets victoriously. Eating and feasting is common symbolism for the incorporation phase. The Christian holy sacrament involves symbolically incorporating or swallowing the body and blood of Christ in the form of bread and wine.

PUBERTY

The time of puberty marks the transition from childhood to adulthood, involving dramatic physical and emotional changes, as well as changes in roles and responsibilities. Ritual initiation at puberty varies from culture to culture, but fundamentally honours and marks this major life transition In the Muslim tradition, boys of 10 to 12 who undergo circumcision are paraded as princes for the day, sometimes on a horse, and often showered with gifts. The Luiseño people of southern California proudly celebrate the onset of menstruation in their daughters, who are partially buried in warm sand, possibly to symbolize their strong connection with the earth.

A Jewish boy becomes bar mitzvah ("a son of the commandment") at the age of 13. On the first Saturday following his birthday he reads from the Torah in the synagogue and may lead part of the service. In preparation he must study Jewish history, ancient Hebrew and his spiritual roots, discussing his learning with the rabbi and his family in relation to his own life and oncoming adulthood.

BAPTISM

The Jewish and Christian practice of initiating people into the faith by dipping them in water represents the purification and cleansing of the spirit. Early

Christian writings describe a meal of milk and honey accompanying baptism, representing the entry of the Israelites into the promised land of Canaan. Roman Catholic baptism also involves the exorcism of the devil and anointing with olive oil, a symbol of the gifts of the Holy Spirit.

MARRIAGE

The meaning and symbolism of marriage reflects the underlying beliefs of the culture, but most are redolent with the ancient symbolism of a couple attaining a semi-divine state of wholeness necessary to create and protect new life. This idea of the union of the human and divine is echoed in the Christian tradition of calling its nuns "brides of Christ".

One of the most significant symbols of marriage still in use is the ring, a circular symbol of eternity, union and completeness. This is echoed in the Christian ceremony when the couple's hands are joined together by the priest, and in the Hindu ceremony when the bridegroom ties a ribbon around the neck of his bride. Other symbols of

marriage include bells, as a means of proclaiming good news, and peach blossom, which is believed by the Chinese to be linked with immortality, longevity, spring, youth and marriage and is also an emblem of virginity.

Symbols of fertility were once central to wedding ceremonies, and are echoed in modern times by the rice (or confetti made of rice paper) thrown over the couple. The wedding cake was once a symbol of fertility, food being a sexual symbol and its formal sharing during the feast a symbol of the two families coming together. Bridesmaids are symbols of sympathetic fertility magic, while the flowers they carry are further symbols of femininity and fruitfulness.

DEATH RITES

A person's death represents a considerable transition, for both the individual and the family and community around them. The deceased is ritually prepared to move on, possibly as part of a journey into another reality, and the mourning process employs a great deal of symbolic ritual to

RIGHT Weddings are a significant rite of passage in most cultures. However they are celebrated, the central theme is transition.

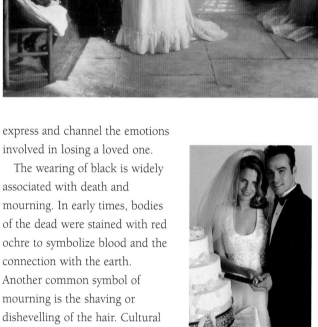

express and channel the emotions involved in losing a loved one.

The wearing of black is widely associated with death and mourning. In early times, bodies of the dead were stained with red ochre to symbolize blood and the connection with the earth. Another common symbol of mourning is the shaving or dishevelling of the hair. Cultural values are clearly mirrored in funeral rites. Even the expressing of emotion reflects cultural attitudes: in some cultures, such as Sikh, wailing is discouraged, whereas in others it is expected.

The deceased are often treated as if they are undergoing a journey: they are dressed in special clothes and accompanied by personal and religious objects or talismans. Burying the body may symbolize the person's return to Mother Earth or to the dead ancestors. Cremation represents the liberation of spirit and release from Earth. For the Hindus, the flames symbolize Brahma.

LEFT In a Hindu funeral the colour of mourning is white, and coffin, deceased and mourners are all dressed in it.

ABOVE A bell is one of the symbols of a wedding, and is often used as a motif on the invitations, orders or service and menus, and silver bell-shaped ornaments might be carried by the bride and bridesmaids.

TOP The Romans would break the cake over the bride's head, but in modern ceremonies the cutting of the cake symbolizes the first task in the couple's life.

CHILDHOOD AND GAMES

ABOVE Painting allows the child to mix the worlds of symbolism with the everyday world.

TOP Children use building blocks to explore creation and destruction.

BELOW Children love dressing-up as adults. Here a group of boys dress up as musicians at the Indian spring festival of Bahag Bihu.

In cultures dominated by logic, intellect and linear thinking, life becomes a problem to be solved rather than a mystery to be enjoyed. Yet creativity and play are essential to human development, and are natural activities that children engage in spontaneously. Through creativity and play we journey into archetypal or mythical realms, experiment with roles, relationships and social structures, and engage in a symbolic dialogue with the trends and movements of history.

CREATIVE SYMBOLISM

The word creativity comes from the Latin *creare*, meaning "to bring forth, produce, and cause to grow". It is the generative force at the root of symbolism. Jung described it as a process that connects us with archetypal themes, expressed in a language relevant to the present day. For instance, an archetypal theme such as the battle between good and evil is given creative expression in modern society in the form of computer games. Jung believed that the creative impulse can compensate for the one-sidedness of the present, so that part of the artist's role is to comment on or challenge the prevailing norms. Both the artist and the child are inspired by a creative impulse, and then create a language or metaphor to express what has moved them.

THE CHILD

In many cultures, the child is a symbol of innocence and spontaneity. In the Hindu tradition, childhood is a heavenly state of innocence prior to any knowledge of good or evil.

In the Christian tradition, Jesus said that unless adults become like children they will not enter into the kingdom of Heaven, which also reflects the relationship between the child and paradise. In Taoist literature the child embodies the qualities of the holy sage – innocence and open-heartedness.

Though he was writing at the end of the 19th century, when children were largely undervalued and to be "seen and not heard", J.M. Barrie created Peter Pan as an archetypal pattern for the child within us. Peter teaches the other children to believe in their imaginations, their ability to fly and to travel to Neverland. Peter is an example of the eternal child, the childlike imagination, which lives in us all.

PLAY

In modern society, we tend to associate play with childhood and regard it as something that people stop doing once they have "grown up". However, in other parts of the world, play continues to be highly valued in adult life, often in the form of ritual enactments. In Burkina Faso and Mali, masquerades entirely created by children, independent of the adults, are considered highly important to the wellbeing of the whole community. Eastern coastal fishing villages in Korea enact communal shamanic rituals known as *kut* – a mixture of prayer, laughter and play thought to bring the gods down to the level of human beings, helping them to deal with the powerful emotions surrounding major crises and death. The kut are healing rituals that involve a playful and symbolic participation in theatrical representations of the pain, beauty and mystery of life.

In Hopi society "sacred clowns" help to balance society by mocking and making fun of excessive behaviour, so setting and balancing moral standards.

Play and playfulness involve a loosening of, or detachment from, our everyday identities, and an interest in entering into and experimenting with other roles and possibilities.

In their early years, children engage in "embodiment play", exploring with their senses, making sounds, rhythms, marks and movements, beginning to imitate and relate to toys and objects around them and creating stories. At this point they are developing the skill of interacting symbolically and beginning to understand and experiment with different roles and relationships, and objects can have meaning and significance attached to them. It is not uncommon for young children to become attached to a certain toy or blanket, a symbol of security, love or friendship.

FANTASY

For children the everyday world is interlaced with the world of fantasy and the imagination. Children love to role-play through dressing up as their favourite characters and creating dramatic stories around them. Through the medium of play, the child learns, grows and develops.

Many archetypal or mythical figures emerge in children's play. The ancient Chinese believed that the playful songs that children sang spontaneously were intimately linked with the divine, and even listened to them to guide them in matters of state. Through fantasy and play, children explore the great underlying themes and spirit of the times, stories of good and evil, love, magic and power. They explore the "evil" in terms of monsters, giants and witches, and play with the forces of good, magic and transformation through the roles of fairies, white witches and wizards. They experiment with rank and power by playing kings and queens, famous leaders and the rich and famous, and they explore heroic themes as superheroes, with action figures and toy soldiers.

TOYS AND GAMES

Games are models for archetypal forms of relationship and interaction, involving different combinations of chance, skill and creativity. In the game of chess, the movement of the kings, queens and pawns may be understood as metaphors for the shifts of power in war or conflict at various levels in the universe. Many games reflect the creative impulses of the universe, as in the throwing of dice and other games of chance, which probably originated from ancient divinatory practices in Mesopotamia, India and East Asia. Pick-up sticks, also known as "spillikins", which involves dropping a set of sticks in a heap and then trying to pick them up one at a time without disturbing the others, may have its origin in the Buddhist divinatory practice called Chien Tung, in which a person's fortune is foretold by shaking a box of sticks until one emerges.

The origin of the spinning top, or dreidel, is completely unknown, but it has been used as a toy or for gambling throughout the world. The dreidel is itself the symbol of the Jewish festival of Hanukkah, when rabbis allowed games of chance to be played and the four-sided dreidel came out for gambling. Its four sides represent "take nothing", "take everything", "take half" and "put in". Another symbolic quality of the spinning top relates not to how it falls down by chance, but rather to how it stays up as it spins, a beautiful symbol of life and the universe.

The universal game of tag, or chase, involves passing a symbolic quality from one person to another. One child is chosen to be "it", and chases the other children with the purpose of transferring the "it-ness" to another. The child who is tagged is then "it" and so the game goes on. The symbolic quality may represent authority, infectiousness, or any other differential. The appeal of the game lies in the challenge of the chase, and the excitement and tension engendered by coming near or in contact with the person who is "it".

ABOVE The Dreidel, a four-sided top, played with by Jewish children, is seen as a symbol of life and the universe.

BELOW The game of chase has many variations and is played endlessly by children all over the world.

THE WHEEL

ABOVE The traditionally shaped wheel, as in this representation of the Buddhist eight-spoked wheel, holds the symbolism of the sun and the cosmos. The wheel is also an enduring symbol of human endeavour and advancement.

The symbolism of the wheel relates to the passage of time, the world, and the unity that exists at the heart of diversity. It is associated with the zodiac and with life's ups and downs (as the wheel of fortune); as the Native American medicine wheel it provides a blueprint for living. As an archetypal motif, the wheel's significance relates to its shape – a circle containing spokes radiating from a central hub – and its mobility. It combines the symbolism of the circle with movement, representing the cosmos as an eternal round of creation and dissolution. In many cultures it appears as a sun symbol, with countless beliefs associating it with solar myths, although some have argued that it was pre-eminently a lunar symbol, signifying the continuous cycle of the moon.

SOLAR AND LUNAR SYMBOLISM

The wheel has both solar and lunar associations. The simplest form has four spokes, which may reflect the four directions and four seasons (as in the medicine wheel), as well as the four-stage lunar cycle: waxing, full, waning and dark. Arianrhod, the Welsh goddess of weaving and spinning, was connected with the moon; her name means "silver wheel".

Wheels with 12 spokes appear frequently in Indian literature and art, suggesting the movement of the sun through the zodiac, while the traditional Chinese wheel has 30 spokes, signifying the lunar cycle. In classical antiquity, the wheel was linked with the god Apollo (and so with the sun), as well as to thunderbolts and the lighting of fires.

The wheel as a solar symbol persists in European folklore. It was traditional to carry blazing wheels by torchlit procession to a hilltop at the summer solstice and roll the wheel down the hillside at the winter solstice.

SACRED TRADITION

The wheel, or chakra, is an important symbol in both Hindu and Buddhist traditions. In Hinduism, the wheel represents the unity of time and space and is a symbol of completion: a six-spoked wheel is one of the symbols of the preserver deity, Vishnu. In Buddhism, the eight-spoked dharmachakra is the wheel of the law or truth (dharma). It often appears on carvings representing the footprints of the Buddha and symbolizes the power of his teachings to roll over and stamp out lies. Like human fate, once the wheel is set in motion there is no power that can stop it or reverse its direction. The eight spokes represent the eightfold path of Buddhism, the hub the moral anchor of the Buddha's teachings, while at the motionless centre stands the *chakravarti* ("he who makes the wheel revolve"), the Buddha himself. His Celtic equivalent is Mag Ruith, the mythic druid who was an incarnation of the supreme god, the Dagda. Mag Ruith was the *magus rotarum*, or "wizard of the wheels", and it was with the help of wheels that he spoke his druidic oracles.

In the Old Testament, Ezekiel compares the throne of God to a chariot with four wheels, each wheel representing one of the Four Living Creatures and the seasons, while in Daniel's vision flaming wheels appear around God's head. On early Christian gravestones, the wheel is sometimes found as a symbol of God and of eternity.

THE CATHERINE WHEEL

As the emblem of St Catherine of Alexandria, the wheel is associated with torment. She was said to have been a Christian convert of the early 4th century, who was mystically married to Christ in a vision. The Roman emperor Maxentius desired to marry her, and when she refused him he ordered her to be tortured on a spiked wheel. The wheel miraculously broke when she touched it, but she was eventually martyred with a sword. She is usually depicted with the wheel, which subsequently gave its name to a spinning firework.

THE WHEEL OF LIFE

In Hindu philosophy, the symbolism of the wheel is used to refer to samsara, the continuous cycle of life, death and rebirth. In Chinese symbolism, the hub relates to Heaven and the rim to Earth, with humankind represented by the spokes that link the two. The Chinese noria (waterwheel), and the Taoist sage Chuang Tzu's potter's wheel both represent the ceaseless whirlpool of creation and the never-ending life–death cycle. The point of liberation is at the hub, pointing to the spiritual journey as a movement from the periphery to the centre, from activity to stillness, which is the purpose of meditation. In the Celtic tradition, the year is seen as a wheel, with the summer and winter solstices and the spring and autumn equinoxes marking four points of transition as the sun's power rises and decreases with the changing seasons.

WHEEL OF FORTUNE

Its turning nature means that the wheel has often been associated with chance and fortune, both fickle and fortuitous. It frequently appears as a motif in medieval European art and was an attribute of Fortuna, the Roman goddess of fate (Tyche was the Greek equivalent). Fortuna represents each moment's potential for luck or ill, with the turning of her wheel bringing happiness and success to some, and ruin and

RIGHT A blindfolded Fortuna, goddess of fate, rolls her wheel at random and without mercy over crowned kings.

misery to others, in a seemingly random way. She is often depicted as blind or blindfolded, because fate is morally blind. Her wheel teaches that what goes up must come down and vice versa – so that success and failure follow on each other's heels, just as life and death cycle and circle. In the Tarot, the Wheel of Fortune is the tenth card of the Major Arcana and represents an important turning point.

THE MEDICINE WHEEL

In many traditions, the wheel is a symbol of the world. This forms the basis of the Native American medicine wheel – a cross within a circle emanating from a central hub. The wheel is drawn on the ground, and the four spokes represent the four seasons, the four elements and the four directions. The seasons symbolize time, and the compass points, space. The fifth and sixth directions (above and below the wheel) represent father sky and mother earth. Each place on the wheel is associated with a particular colour, an animal totem and a quality, and the whole wheel represents the journey through life.

RIGHT The Native American symbol of the medicine wheel, a circle segmented by a cross, is reproduced here in stone.

FLORA AND FAUNA

THE SYMBOLISM OF TREES, PLANTS, FLOWERS AND ANIMALS HAVE BEEN CENTRAL TO SYMBOLIC CONCEPTUALISATION SINCE PREHISTORIC DAYS. ANIMALS HAVE BEEN PARTICULARLY IMPORTANT, WORSHIPPED AS GODS OR PROTECTIVE SPIRITS, AND, LIKE FRUIT AND VEGETABLES, VITAL FOR LIFE IN THE FOOD THEY PROVIDE.

TREES

LEFT In ancient times sacred groves of trees were places of sanctuary and worship.

ABOVE The banyan tree is sacred to the Hindu gods: watering its roots and placing offerings is thought to bring happiness and fertility.

ABOVE The European oak is a symbol of strength, stability, firmness and an enduring nature.

The tree is a central and archetypal symbol in most parts of the world. In the West, trees are deeply associated with time and historical continuity. Elsewhere they tend to have stronger associations with life, health and potency. Ancient peoples worshipped in sacred groves, with their trunks and canopies of branches, which were later echoed in the design of churches. The words "truth" and "trust" are derived from the Old English word for "tree".

THE WORLD TREE
The cosmic tree, symbolizing the ultimate reservoir for the forces of life continually regenerating the world, is central to many creation myths. It frequently represents the axis of the universe, connecting a number of realms: its branches hold up the heavens, its trunk stands in the earthly realm and its roots descend into the underworld. Other commonly associated symbols are reptiles crawling in the roots and birds in the branches symbolizing shamanic flight.

The world tree is usually represented by a species that is particularly important in a geographical region. Norse mythology tells of the ash tree Yggdrasil, which grew between Asgard, the realm of the gods, Midgard, the realm of humanity, and Hel, the underworld. The ancient Egyptians believed a holy sycamore grew at the threshold between life and death; in Mesopotamia the world axis passed through a palm tree. Hindus hold the banyan tree as sacred, while the Maya believed in Yaxche, the sacred tree whose branches supported the heavens. The Chinese sacred tree was thought to grow from the centre of the world, emitting no echo and casting no shadow. The sakaki tree is venerated as the "heaven-tree" of Japanese mythology, and a branch is stuck in the ground as a sacred centre around which a wooden Shinto shrine is built.

THE MAYPOLE
In Europe, on 1 May, the spring fertility ritual of the maypole dance symbolizes the marriage of the vegetation god to the May queen. The pole, representing the spirit of the tree (and with obvious phallic symbolism), was erected and decorated, and danced around with abandon.

RIGHT The tree is seen as a link between this world and the otherworld in many spiritual and mythological belief systems.

Trees are also powerful symbols of the interconnectedness and ecology of life. The Native American elder Black Elk saw in a vision the "sacred hoop" of his people combining with many others to create a larger hoop, within which grew a mighty and holy tree of protection. The world tree of the Amazon region is the ceiba, or yuchan: the Huaorani creation myth tells of the giant ceiba tree Bobehuè, which contains all forms of life. It thus represents an entire ecosystem central to life on earth, which may be not far from the truth.

TREES AND THE ORIGINS OF HUMANITY

The world tree is commonly associated with the origins of humankind. The Yakut of Siberia believe in a tree with eight branches, which stands within the golden navel of the earth, growing into a primordial paradise where the first man was born and suckled on the milk of the woman, who was herself part of the tree. The first man in ancient Indian mythology, Yama, drank with the gods beside a magnificent tree.

A common Indo-European mythical theme describes an apocalypse during which tempests, fire or floods devastate the earth, leaving as the only survivors the ancestors of humanity, who are made of wood.

TREES OF LIFE AND IMMORTALITY

In one of its aspects, the world tree is the tree of life or immortality. It is often associated with a nourishing and protective universe from which the elixir or bounties of life may be received – a state of grace from which humans may fall. The Egyptian sky goddess Nut was depicted emerging from a sycamore fig to offer the bread and water of eternity to the dead.

Seraphim wielding swords of fire guard the biblical tree of life. In Taoist tradition it is the divine peach that confers the gift of immortality, while the apples of the goddess Idun are the source of the powers of the Norse gods.

The Qur'an describes the prophet Mohammed coming across the tree of Tuba standing in the heart of paradise, glowing with emeralds, rubies and sapphires; milk, honey and wine sprang from its roots.

THE INVERTED TREE

The symbol of the inverted tree is found in the Jewish Kabbalah and in the Hindu yogic Bhagavad Gita. This tree of life has its roots in the heavens and its branches below, representing God in Heaven as the origin of all things. The inverted tree image can be related to the human nervous or chakral system, underlining the connection between the human microcosm and the macrocosm.

TREE DRESSING

The practice of tree dressing is found throughout the world. The Karan is a Hindu ritual in which a tree in the centre of a village is covered with butter, and decorated with vermillion, turmeric and garlands, after which women dance with marigolds in their hair. In Africa trees are revered as the centre of life and fertility, and are dressed as a way of connecting with the ancestral spirits. Evergreens are dressed at Christmas in Christian cultures as a symbol of life.

TREES OF DEATH

Evergreen trees are ancient symbols of death and the potential for eternal life, but the cypress tree symbolizes the finality of death because, once cut, it will never again sprout from its stump. Images of tree stumps or trunks are found in heraldic emblems representing death and rebirth.

In Britain, the yew tree is most closely associated with death. It was considered immortal by the Druids, and is commonly found in graveyards and at ancient sacred sites. Its roots were believed to soak up the spirits of the dead, releasing them to the winds from its branches.

THE MULBERRY

In China the mulberry tree represents the cycles of life. Its berries start white, representing youth, then turn red for the middle years, and finally ripen to black, suggesting wisdom, old age and death.

CHRISTMAS TREE

The modern variation of decorated trees at Christmas originated in 16th-century Germany, where fir trees were dressed with apples and coloured paper. The tradition has become a Christian ritual, perhaps refering to the tree of paradise, but its roots are older, an emblem of rebirth dating back to at least Roman times when the celebrants at the feast of Saturnalia used evergreens to celebrate the birth of the new year.

PLANTS, HERBS AND SPICES

ABOVE In European folklore, the mandrake was associated with death, insanity, witchcraft and magic. When picked it was said to utter a piercing human-like scream.

ABOVE Saffron, the stamen of a type of crocus, is a sacred herb in Buddhism. In Europe it is associated with royalty.

The symbolism of plants is closely related to their perceived magical properties and power to influence humans on many different levels – physical, mental, emotional and spiritual. In symbolic terms, they are associated with ideas of balance and cosmological order, which have often been reflected in sophisticated theories of the nature of health and disease.

THE DOCTRINE OF SIGNATURES
According to the "doctrine of signatures", everything in nature is marked with a pattern or sign that indicates its potential properties. The name evolved from the Signatura Rerum (The

Signature of All Things) by Jakob Böhme (1575–1624), a German shoemaker whose philosophy was informed by a mystical vision in which he saw the relationship between God and humans. The doctrine was applied to the powers of plants for medical application. For example, the heart-shaped leaves of the purple foxglove were used as a heart medicine (digitalis), while the purple veins and yellow fleck of the eyebright flower, which suggest an unhealthy-looking eye, designated the plant as a remedy for eye ailments.

Because of its resemblance to the human form, the mandrake was credited with human and superhuman powers in European folklore. It was said to thrive around the gallows, fed by the faeces and urine falling from those hanged, and to scream when it was pulled up or disturbed: the sound led to deafness and insanity in those unfortunate enough to hear it. The mandrake was associated with witchcraft and used in love magic, and a mandrake root doll was said to have the power to

BELOW In European plant lore, rosemary is a symbol of remembrance, love and fidelity.

make its owner invisible. Medicinally, it was also used to treat arthritis, ulcers and inflammation, to induce menstruation, ease delivery in childbirth and aid conception. In the Jewish tradition the mandrake is associated with fertility and love – its Hebrew name means "love plant".

HERBS
A great variety of symbolic meanings are attached to common herbs. In ancient Greece, students wore sprigs of rosemary to improve memory and concentration, and the plant came to symbolize remembrance. It was also associated with love and fidelity and became a symbol of immortality in funeral rites. Sage was also associated with immortality and was thought by the ancient Greeks to promote wisdom. It takes its name from the Latin *salvare,* meaning "to save" and in European herbal medicine was thought of as a cure-all. Native Americans consider sage a healing and cleansing herb, especially the variety known as white sage; its

BELOW Sage is a sacred herb in Native American traditions, used for cleansing and purifying.

dry leaves are often formed into smudge bundles for burning, the smoke being ritually smudged, or wafted, to purify the atmosphere. In ancient Rome, peppermint was associated with clear thoughts and inspiration and was used as a brain tonic, while in the Arab world it was widely believed to stimulate virility and has been drunk as a refreshing tea for centuries, offered to guests as a symbol of hospitality.

In India, *tulsi*, or sweet basil, is sacred to Vishnu, and the funeral custom of laying a basil leaf on the chest of the dead was thought to open the gates of Heaven for the departed; in Tudor England departing guests were given a miniature pot of basil to help them on their journey. In the central Congo, basil leaves protect against evil spirits and bad luck, while in ancient Greece they were an antidote to the deadly venom of the basilisk, a fabulous creature whose glance was fatal. The plant takes its name from the Greek *basilikon*, meaning "royal".

SPICES

Many spices are similarly rich in symbolism. Black pepper, one of the earliest known spices, was widely regarded as an aphrodisiac in antiquity. Saffron is a species of crocus (*Crocus sativus*) whose stamens yield a deep yellow dye. Traditionally it was used to dye the robes of Buddhist monks, and the colour became associated with the Buddhist paradise and with wisdom. In Europe, saffron was linked with royalty and gold because of its costliness as well as its colour. In ancient China,

coriander seeds were believed to contain the power of immortality, and cardamom pods share a similar symbolism in India and the Middle East. In China and Japan, cloves represent sweetness and health, and in Japanese art they were one of the objects associated with the Seven Deities of Good Fortune.

TOBACCO

The tobacco plant is indigenous to North America, and the Native Americans are said to have been the first people to use it. They regard it as sacred, and it has widespread ritual and ceremonial use. The Machiguenga of Peru use the term *seripegari*, meaning "he who uses tobacco", to describe a shaman; roasted tobacco leaves (*seri*) are used in shamanic rituals. To many Pueblo people, tobacco was the gift of the hummingbird, who brought smoke to the shamans so that they could purify the Earth.

In Europe, smoking tobacco was originally associated with dissolute young men and soldiers, so that when women first began to smoke in public in the late 19th century it was regarded as shocking. Today the symbolic associations surrounding tobacco are ambiguous. On the one hand it has become synonymous with deadly illnesses such as cancer and heart disease, yet on the other it retains an element of sophistication and rebellion.

MISTLETOE

The Celts associated mistletoe (*Viscum album*) with magic and medicine. To the Druids it was a

CANNABIS

Rastafarians, who know it as ganja, regard cannabis as a holy herb mentioned in the Bible, where it performs a sacramental function, producing an altered state of consciousness through which it is possible to attain a glimpse of the divine. The cannabis leaf became a symbol of Rastafarianism, as well as representing a protest against the dominant social order, which had deemed its use illegal. In the Western world today, many teenagers see the cannabis leaf as a symbol of rebellion against adult authority and mainstream society.

GARLIC

An ancient Egyptian medical papyrus includes more than 200 prescriptions for garlic. It was used to treat headaches, physical debility and infections, and raw garlic was included in the diet of Egyptian workers to keep them strong. In ancient Greece and Rome garlic was a symbol of strength, and athletes chewed it to maximize their chances of winning races. In many traditions, garlic is believed to offer not only physical but also metaphysical protection, hence the popular belief in European folklore that garlic cloves can keep werewolves and vampires at bay, or in ancient China that it could ward off the evil eye.

symbol of immortality and the soul of their sacred tree, the oak, on which it grew. The Celts believed that mistletoe was created when a lightning bolt struck an oak tree, giving it magical properties, and ritual demanded that a white-robed Druid cut mistletoe after the winter solstice using a golden sickle (both a solar and a lunar symbol). The plant had to be caught in a white cloth, as it was believed that it should never touch the ground. Mistletoe was used to treat many different health conditions and was also a fertility symbol. The custom of kissing under the mistletoe at Christmas has its roots in the plant's ancient associations.

BELOW Mistletoe is a symbol of immortality and was associated with magic and medicine for the Celts.

FLOWERS

While the aesthetic beauty of flowers has inspired poets and artists through the ages, they also have a long tradition of use in healing and ritual – more than 100,000 years ago, the Neanderthals made flower offerings to their dead. To this day, flowers are given as tokens of love or thanks, to acknowledge achievement, honour the dead and to mark transitions of all kinds. They have become symbols of a wide range of human experiences and are woven into myth and sacred tradition.

In general, flowers represent the culmination of a growth cycle and a crowning achievement. Growing from the earth and receptive to the sun and rain, they are related to the power of the passive, feminine principle, manifesting beauty literally and physically as well as spiritually and metaphorically. In Hindu ritual, the flower corresponds to the element ether (or spirit); in the Taoist text The Secret of the Golden Flower it represents the attainment of a spiritual state.

SAY IT WITH FLOWERS

Many different cultures, including those of China, Egypt and India, have evolved their own "language of flowers". Contemporary audiences of the plays of William Shakespeare (1564–1616) would have been familiar with the hidden meanings contained in his floral references: for instance, thyme symbolized sweetness, oxslips meant comeliness, the violet meant "love in idleness", eglantine or honeysuckle meant "united in love", and pansies stood for thoughts. The Victorians developed this language into a popular art, instilling meaning in the colour, arrangement and presentation of flowers as well as the species.

IKEBANA

Practitioners of ikebana, the Japanese art of flower arranging, have developed a complex symbolism to reflect the precepts of Zen Buddhism. The Zen ideal of *wabi* (deliberate understatement), for instance, is reflected in the minimalist form of the arrangement. Traditional ikebana arrangements follow a ternary plan, with the upper spray representing Heaven, the central one humanity, and the lower one earth – a symbolic pattern of all that lives, with humans as the intermediaries between Heaven and earth. In the "flowing" style, the sprays hang down, suggesting the decline and flow into the abyss, while the "standing", or *rikka,* style reaches up, symbolizing loyalty – between husband and wife, to the emperor and to the divine. Rikka arrangements are asymmetrical and are intended to suggest an aspect of nature, such as the interplay of light and shade.

LOTUS

In the East, the lotus is the flower most commonly associated with the elevation of the spirit. Brahma, the Hindu creator god, was born from a golden lotus sprouting from Vishnu's navel (a symbol of the centre of the world). A thousand-petalled lotus is a symbol of spiritual enlightenment. The Sanskrit names for lotus are *padma* or *kamala,* which also describe the vagina, and lotus blossom also represents the vagina in China.

LILLIES

In the Christian tradition, the lily is associated with repentance: it is said to have grown from the tears of Eve as she left the Garden of Eden. It is the flower of the Virgin Mary: the white Madonna lily symbolizes purity and chastity; it also represents purity in alchemy. In Australia, the Gymea lily is linked with courage and

steadfastness: in an Aboriginal dreaming story the young man Kai'mia rescued members of his tribe even though he was wounded, and lilies grew where his blood fell. In China and Japan, the day lily (*Hemerocallis*) was believed to have the power to dispel grief, and women wore them in their belts to forget the sorrow of a lost love.

ROSES

In classical antiquity it was said that the first rose was created by Chloris, the goddess of flowers (whose Roman equivalent is Flora), from the body of a beautiful nymph. It was sacred to Aphrodite/Venus, the goddess of love. In the Arab tradition, the first rose was brought to life by the rays of the rising sun in the Great Garden of Persia, spreading its seeds to all other lands, and was a symbol of fertility, beauty and purity. A nightingale sang when the first white roses bloomed, but was so overcome by their perfume that it dropped to Earth, its blood staining their petals red.

In Islam, the rose is sacred to Mohammed; for the mystic Sufi sect, the rose is associated with pleasure, but because of its thorns, it is also linked with pain.

In Christianity, red roses symbolize the blood of martyrs and life after death, while white roses are associated with the Virgin Mary. The Rosicrucian Brotherhood, a Christian sect founded in Europe in the 15th century, combined the symbol of a rose with the cross to form the emblem of their society.

TULIPS

In ancient Persia, the tulip was a symbol of perfect love, exalted in poetry as one of the blooms found in the gardens of paradise. During the Ottoman period, the Turkish word for tulip was spelled using the same letters that form the word "Allah", so the flower came to symbolize divinity, and the tulip became the emblem of the Ottoman rulers. Tulips were exported from Turkey to Europe in the mid-16th century, and were hybridized to produce rare and distinctive flowers. Their value rose to fantastic heights in The Netherlands during the 1630s, when they became symbols of wealth and beauty. The tulip is the symbol of The Netherlands.

CHRYSANTHEMUMS

In China and Japan, the chrysanthemum is linked with autumn and is a symbol of long life, good luck, happiness and wealth. Its radiating petals make it a sun symbol, leading to its use as the emblem of the Japanese imperial family and Japan's national flower. With the plum, orchid and bamboo, the chrysanthemum is one of a group called the Four Gentlemen, believed to represent the virtues of a Confucian in their simplicity, uprightness and hardiness. In the West the chrysanthemum is associated with autumn and is used in art to represent decadence and death.

POPPIES

Because it produces the narcotic opium, the poppy was associated with sleep and death in ancient Greece, where it was dedicated to Hypnos and Morpheus, the gods of sleep and dreaming. It was also linked to the myth of Demeter and Persephone – the latter was picking poppies when Hades abducted her – in which it came to represent the annual death of nature. Since World War I, red poppies have commemorated fallen soldiers: the flowers grew on the battlefields of Flanders. In Britain red poppies mark Remembrance Sunday, the day when the sacrifice of soldiers in all wars is remembered.

SUNFLOWERS

The sunflower arrived in Europe from the Americas, where the Spanish called it *girasol*, or "turn to the sun" because of the way it turned to face the sun. In China the sunflower was linked with immortality, and eating its seeds was said to promote longevity.

BELOW In Japan, the art of ikebana has developed its own symbolic language and ritual and reflects the simplicity of Zen Buddhism.

FRUIT

ABOVE In this allegory of the Earth, the artist uses an abundance of fruit to symbolize wealth and prosperity, the cornucopia suggests plenty, and the beautiful, curvaceous young woman reinforces the symbolism of fertility.

ABOVE In addition to its role as the "fruit of knowledge", the apple has also been used as a symbol of love, marriage, youth, fertility and longevity.

Most of the symbolism of fruit appeals directly and powerfully to the senses. The eating of fruit easily conjures up associations with eroticism and sensuality, and this imagery has been much used in art. Fruit also suggests abundance and fertility: it spills out of the cornucopia in classical mythology, representing the generosity of the gods and a good harvest. The fruit of the tree of life is food for the immortals, and contains seeds for reproduction and growth.

APPLES

The apple is identified as the "fruit of knowledge", whether of good and evil, as in the Garden of Eden, or of life, wisdom and immortality, as in the Greek myth of the golden apples of the

Hesperides. The Celts saw the apple tree as the "otherworld" tree, the doorway to the fairy world. Celtic kings and heroes such as King Arthur took refuge on the legendary Isle of Avalon, the "apple orchard".

In China, apple blossom symbolizes feminine beauty, and apples are symbols of peace. But as the Chinese word for "apple" is very similar to the word for "illness" it is thought inauspicious to give an apple to an invalid.

New symbolism evolved around the apple in the early 19th century, when Johnny Appleseed pursued his dream of a land of blossoming trees where no one went hungry, by planting apple seeds throughout America. The great metropolis New York City is known as the "Big Apple".

FIGS

The fig tree and its many-seeded fruit are symbols of plenty and fertility often associated with feminine qualities. The Ruminal fig in the Palatine temple in Rome was said to be the tree beneath which Romulus and Remus were suckled by a wolf. Romans considered figs lucky or unlucky according to whether they were light or dark.

In the Book of Genesis, Adam and Eve used fig leaves to cover themselves when they became shamefully aware of their nakedness, and the forbidden fruit they ate may have been a fig rather than an apple. In Africa, the Kotoko people of Chad connect the fig with childbearing, and its milky sap is thought to increase lactation.

BANANAS

The banana plant's botanical name, *Musa sapientum*, means "fruit of the wise men" and was given by Linnaeus, a Swedish botanist, who had heard that Alexander the Great encountered sages in India who lived entirely on bananas. According to the Qur'an and in Islamic stories, the banana was the forbidden fruit in paradise. For the Buddha, the banana tree symbolized the transient nature and weakness of matter and mental constructions. In the Hindu tradition it is a symbol of fertility and prosperity, due to its tendency to fruit regularly, and thus bananas may be left in front of houses where a wedding is taking place.

CHERRIES

A cherry colour in the lips of a Chinese woman is considered a quality of great beauty, and the phrase "eating cherries" is a euphemism for sexual intercourse. In the West the cherry is associated with the hymen, and the phrase "losing one's cherry" refers to the loss of virginity. Cherry blossom is the national flower of Japan. Samurai warriors would meditate upon life and death beneath a cherry tree, as at the height of its flowering the blossom would gracefully fall to the ground and die, paralleling the Samurai's willingness to face death in his prime.

PLUMS

In the Far East the plum tree is a common symbol for the spring, and also for the end of winter: as it blossoms at the threshold

between the two seasons, it represents the renewal of youthfulness. It was also thought that the immortals fed from plum blossoms, so the tree was connected with immortality. In both the Japanese and Christian traditions it is a symbol of fidelity.

PEACHES

The peach tree originated in China, where it was considered the holy tree of life, producing an elixir of immortality. The Taoists associated peach blossom with virginity and with the female genitalia. ("Tao" is the Chinese word for "peach".) In early Europe the peach was called the "fruit of Venus" and was sacred to Hymen, the Roman god of marriage. In Christian imagery a peach in the hand of the infant Christ symbolizes salvation.

APRICOTS

In China the apricot is associated with a woman's beauty and sexuality. Red apricots symbolize a married woman who has taken a lover, and the eyes of a beautiful woman are often compared to the stones of apricots. It has also been used to symbolize female genitals.

POMEGRANATES

Growing in Mediterranean climates, by the end of the summer pomegranates swell to become red-orange spheres glistening inside with juicy red, jewel-like seeds. Their name means "apple of many seeds". It was one of the gifts of Allah in the Qur'an, and for the Israelites it represented the charm of their land and the wisdom of its

people. The pomegranate has often been associated with fertility – symbolizing the womb – but also with death. Pomegranates were left as food in Egyptian tombs to accompany the dead on their journey. In Greece, at weddings and on New Year, a pomegranate is broken on the ground as a symbol of fertility and abundance.

DATES

The date palm originated near the Persian Gulf, and has always grown prolifically in Iraq. To the Egyptians the fruit was a fertility symbol. The date palm is referred to as the "king of the oasis" and a "tree of life" by the Arabs, who state that the tree is at its best when its feet are in water and its head is in the fires of the heavens.

LICHEES AND MANGOES

The lichee is a small fruit from southern China with a rough reddish brown skin and a large shiny brown stone. Placing lichees under the bed of a married couple expresses the hope that they will be blessed with children.

Mangoes, with their succulent orange flesh, are native to eastern India, and Burma. In India they are considered sacred, representing fertility and good fortune. Legend has it that the Buddha was given a mango grove in which he could seek repose.

ORANGES

The orange tree's Latin name, *Fructus aurantia*, refers to the golden colour of the orange, whereas *naranja*, the Spanish

word for the fruit, comes from the Persian *narang*, meaning "interior perfume". The orange suggests both virginity and fruitfulness, as the flowers and fruit appear simultaneously. Orange blossom featured in ancient marriage ceremonies because of its association with fertility, a tradition that has continued to the present day. In Christian imagery, an orange in the hand of the infant Christ represents fertility and good fortune; for the witches of Europe, the fruit represented the heart. In China the orange is still eaten as a symbol of good fortune on the second day of the New Year.

GRAPES

Vines and grapes often appear in Roman art, suggesting wealth and pleasure, and are associated with Bacchus, the Roman equivalent of the Greek Dionysus, god of the vine, sexuality, fertility, and the liberation of passion and expression. Grapes from the Promised Land represented the possibility of new life for the Israelites. For Christians, wine is a symbol of the blood of Christ.

ANIMALS

ABOVE Cats were sacred to the ancient Egyptians and appeared throughout the culture in sculpture and in paintings.

ABOVE The wolf is at times associated with courage and victory, and at others with cruelty, cunning and greed.

TOP In China, the tiger (and also the leopard) is king of beasts and guards the gates of Heaven.

Throughout history, animals have played an important part in the symbolic language of many different cultures. They have been worshipped as gods and seen as sources of wisdom and power, as harbingers of good or bad fortune, as protective spirits and guides to other worlds, as well as symbolic representations of human characteristics. Animals have been used in ritual sacrifice and hunted to provide food, medicine, clothing and cosmetics, as well as to satisfy human vanity. Symbolically, they touch on all levels of the universe – Heaven, Earth and the underworld.

DOGS AND WOLVES

The dog is probably humankind's oldest domesticated animal, and signifies loyalty, protection and companionship. Dogs are widely connected with death and the spirit world: the Ainu people of Japan believed their dogs had the psychic power to detect ghosts; for the Incas, the howling of a dog could signal the death of a relative; and in Greek myth, Cerberus the watchdog guarded the underworld. The Maya buried dogs with their masters so that they could guide them through the afterlife.

Along the north-west coast of America the wolf is a powerful spirit animal that can endow the shaman with supernatural abilities, and many shamanistic cultures speak of sorcerers obtaining their powers from a woman disguised as a wolf. In Christian tradition, the wolf is usually contrasted with the lamb, the latter symbolizing the faithful and the wolf the powers that threaten to destroy them. The colloquial expression "a wolf in sheep's clothing" refers to feigned innocence, while the American Plains tribes regard the prairie wolf, or coyote, as a trickster and figure of deceit. This idea also appears in European folklore in the story of Little Red Riding Hood, in which the wolf symbolizes a predatory male.

THE BIG CATS

Because of its mane, golden coat and regal bearing, the lion is an ancient solar symbol and the embodiment of earthly power. In ancient Egypt, the pharaoh was often depicted as a lion, and African kings used images of lions as personal symbols. In alchemy, the lion represented sexual passion, while a green lion was linked with the wild forces of nature. The lion was also associated with the mother goddess – it was one of the symbols of the Babylonian goddess Ishtar. In the classical world, it was a guardian of the underworld and a symbol of divine protection. Both the Buddha and Christ have been associated with the lion, making it a symbol of spiritual zeal and enlightenment.

For the Chinese, the tiger, rather than the lion, is the king of beasts. A guardian spirit, initially of hunting and later of farming, it is the third sign of the Chinese zodiac. The white tiger is associated with the moon and, because it can see in the dark, it symbolizes illumination. In Hinduism, the tiger represents unbridled passion and loss of control – the deities Shiva and Durga ride tigers when destroying demons, demonstrating their ferocity and fearlessness.

Among the pre-Columbian civilizations of Central and South America, the jaguar was king of the jungle and was said to have given humans the gift of fire and hunting. The Maya considered it a creature of the underworld that knows the mysteries of the earth; by gazing into its eyes it was thought possible to see the future. Today, many Amazonian tribes continue to revere the jaguar as a *nagual* (spirit guardian) and a source of healing, associating it with fertility, water and rainfall; the Matses people believe that jaguars eat the souls of the dead.

DOMESTIC CATS

The ancient Egyptians venerated and mummified cats, and it was a capital offence to kill or injure one. Conversely, in Buddhism, cats and snakes were cursed because they did not weep when

the Buddha died – although from a different perspective this may be perceived as a sign of spiritual wisdom. The early Jews reviled cats as unclean, while medieval Christians associated black cats with witchcraft.

RABBITS AND HARES

Both the rabbit and the hare have lunar associations and are fertility symbols in many cultures. Eostre, the hare-headed Saxon goddess of spring, brought dawn and new life. In China the hare represents reproductive power and longevity. The hare and rabbit both appear as trickster figures, most notably in the Brer Rabbit stories, traditional African stories taken to American plantations by slaves.

ELEPHANTS

Both Africa and India are often symbolized by the elephant. It is a symbol of strength, longevity, wisdom and good luck; ridden by rulers, it also represents power and authority. In the mythology of India and Tibet, the elephant holds up the world and symbolizes unchanging stability. Ganesh, the Hindu elephant-headed god, is the remover of obstacles. In Buddhism, the white elephant is sacred: the Buddha's mother dreamt of one at his conception. In Thailand, Laos and Cambodia it is said to grant rainfall and bounteous harvests.

BULLS AND COWS

Traditionally the bull is a symbol of virility, the cow of motherhood and fertility. Because its curved horns resemble the crescent moon, the cow is a celestial symbol of mother goddesses (such as the ancient Egyptian deities Isis and Hathor). In Norse mythology, the primordial cow – the Nourisher – licked the ice to create the first human. For the Hindus, the cow is a sacred animal and may not be killed; the animals wander the streets of India freely.

Unlike the cow, which has rarely been sacrificed, the bull's use as a ritual animal is widespread. In ancient Rome, a bull was sacrificed annually as its blood was believed to fertilize the earth and confer virility; echoes of such beliefs survive today in Spanish bullfighting. Because of its roar, the bull was the animal of thunder gods such as the Norse Thor. The Apis bull in ancient Egypt was a symbol of creation and was often shown carrying the sun disc of Ra between its horns, yet it was also sacred to Osiris, god of the underworld.

BISONS AND BUFFALO

Evidence from cave art (such as in Lascaux, France) reveals the central role played by bison in the physical and spiritual life of early hunter societies. Related to and at times synonymous with the bison, buffalo were also revered.

The Zulus believe the buffalo is able to possess the soul of a human, while the Dakota Sioux see it instead as a manifestation of the supreme creator, and it plays a central role in vision-quest ceremonies.

BEARS

In many shamanic traditions, the bear is associated with medicine, healing and magical wisdom. In northern Europe, the bear is king of the animals and is associated with warriors: the feared Norse "berserkers" went into battle dressed only in bearskins. In Christian symbolism, the bear was regarded as cruel and vicious and a devilish image of carnality.

ABOVE A Mughal emperor is shown riding a white elephant, a symbol of royalty, power and wisdom in India.

MONKEYS

The baboon god Thoth of Egypt was credited with the invention of numbers and writing. The Maya believed that the monkey created art, numbers and writing.

THE HORSE

An ancient animal symbol, the horse is linked to sun and sky gods. It represents the elemental power of wind, storm, fire, waves and running water. Death is shown riding a black horse, while the white horse is a symbol of light, life and spiritual illumination. The Buddha is said to have left his earthly life on a white horse. Horses drew the sun chariot in classical, Iranian, Indian, Nordic and Babylonian myths.

BIRDS

ABOVE The Seal of the President of the United States of America, changed by President Truman in 1945 from the original 1880 version; the turning of the eagle's head from right to left (towards the olive branch, symbol of peace) was thought at the time to signify a move from war to peace.

BELOW In Greek myth the markings on a peacock's tail feathers were said to be the eyes of the slain giant Argos.

BELOW RIGHT In Western folklore, the stork is said to bring babies to their mothers, while in many parts of the world it is the bearer of good news.

Because they can fly, birds are often seen as mediators between Heaven and Earth, acting as messengers of higher or otherworldly powers. They are also widely regarded as embodiments of the spirit or soul, because flight symbolizes freedom from the physical restrictions of the earthbound world and is frequently used as a metaphor for mystical experience.

BIRDS OF PREY

Warriors and nobles have been associated with birds of prey, especially the eagle, hawk and falcon. Falcons, used for hunting by the aristocracy of China, Japan and Europe, have come to symbolize nobility; in China, the banners of high-ranking lords bore falcon-headed images. In ancient Egypt, the falcon was the king of birds, and the hieroglyph for falcon meant "god"; it was also the symbol for the sky god Horus. Native American tribes regard the hawk as a messenger of the ancestors, while in Polynesia the bird is connected with the powers of healing and prophecy. In China, the hawk denotes war, as well as being a solar symbol. For the early Christian Church, the hawk signified evil, but a tamed

hawk represented a converted pagan and a hooded hawk hope for illumination.

The eagle is widely associated with power and leadership and has been adopted in various guises by ambitious, expansionist civilizations (including ancient Rome and the USA) as a symbol of national identity and sovereignty. In China, the eagle symbolizes strength, while in Celtic folklore it is a symbol of longevity and rejuvenation. For Christians the eagle symbolizes the omnipotence and omniscience of God, as well as Christ and St John the apostle. In many Christian churches, the Bible is placed on an eagle-shaped lectern, symbolizing the power and inspiration of God's word.

RAVENS AND CROWS

Many cultures do not distinguish between the raven and the crow, and the birds share a similar symbolism. Both are widely seen as birds of ill omen, war, death and the supernatural. In the Judaeo-Christian tradition, the raven is the dark counterpart of

> ### THE DOUBLE-HEADED EAGLE
>
> An ancient solar symbol, the double-headed eagle appeared in Mesopotamia more than 4,000 years ago. Its symbolism is thought to link the twin gods of power and omniscience, or earthly rule with deities. Centuries later, the symbol was adopted by the Holy Roman, Prussian and pre-revolutionary Russian empires.

the dove; it was also believed to be the spirit familiar of witches. In the Greco-Roman tradition, crows were sacred to Athene/Minerva, goddess of war, but they were prevented from landing on the roofs of her temples as this foretold a death. The name of the ancient Welsh king Bran means "raven"; his head is said to be buried beneath the Tower of London, and ravens are kept there in line with the popular myth that if they should ever depart the English would fall.

Some Native American tribes believed that the raven brought light and fire to the world. The Inuit of Siberia and Alaska share a similar belief – that the bird came from the primeval darkness and stayed to teach the first humans how to survive. Consequently the raven represented the creator god, and it was said that killing one would bring misfortune and bad weather. The crow is a bird of prophecy in China.

DOVES

Today the dove is widely used as an emblem for world peace. In the Old Testament, it was the bird that returned to Noah's ark bearing an olive leaf, indicating reconciliation between God and humankind, while in Japan a dove bearing a sword announced the end of war. The dove is also a symbol of purity and the soul; in the Christian tradition, it represents the Holy Spirit; in Arthurian legend it is associated with the Grail. For Romans, the dove was sacred to Venus, and in China it was associated with fertility and longevity.

BIRD FEATHERS

The indigenous people of North, Central and South America use feathers as decoration in spectacular head-dresses. The Aztecs used green quetzal tail feathers for their rulers (a symbol of their supreme god, Quetzalcoatl), while for Native Americans, the feathers contain the power or "medicine" of the bird they come from, with eagle feathers being most prized.

PEACOCKS

Because of its grandeur, the peacock represents divinity, royalty, love and beauty. In Persia, it dwelt in the gardens of paradise, and the court revolved around the "peacock throne". In Hindu tradition, the bird is the cosmic mount of Kama, the god of love, and sacred to Sarasvati, goddess of wisdom and the arts. The peacock's distinctive tail markings have long been identified with eyes, and likened to the stars, as well as to solar symbols. In Buddhism it denotes compassionate watchfulness.

STORKS

In many cultures, the stork is the herald of good news. As a migratory bird, it is the emblem of the traveller, and in the land to which it migrates it represents the arrival of spring and hence new life. In ancient Greece the bird was sacred to Hera, goddess of marriage and protector of childbirth. The Western saying that the stork brings babies relates to the idea that the souls of unborn children live in marshes

and ponds – the stork's natural habitat – and are discovered by the stork as it searches for fish.

SWANS AND GEESE

Both the goose and the swan are large, web-footed water birds that have otherworldly associations in many cultures. In Siberia, the swan symbolizes the shaman's immersion in the underworld, and according to the Tungu it was the guiding spirit of the first shaman. The migrating goose is also regarded as a spirit-helper, carrying the shaman on celestial adventures.

In Hinduism, the two birds are mythically interchangeable, so that the Hamsa – one bird made of two – can appear as either a goose or swan, and symbolizes perfect union and balance. Because swans often mate for life, they are associated with fidelity in Western traditions.

OWLS

With its night excursions, haunting call and intense eyes, the owl is widely associated with supernatural powers. It was the

bird of death in ancient Egypt, India, China and Japan: in China, its hooting was thought to sound like the word for "dig dig", predicting that someone was about to die and a grave should be prepared. The owl's superb night vision may account for its traditional link with prophecy. Among the American Plains tribes owl feathers are worn as magic talismans, while for the Pawnee tribes of Nebraska, the owl is a nocturnal protector. In ancient Athens, the bird was sacred to Athene, goddess of wisdom; similarly, in alchemy, the owl is considered to be the wisest of the birds and also a symbol of the true alchemist.

MAGPIES

In Australian Aboriginal lore, magpies are associated with happiness and enthusiasm, while in China the bird's name means "bird of joy". When shown carrying a Chinese coin, they represent the desire for world peace. However, in European folklore, magpies are regarded as thieves and birds of ill omen.

ABOVE LEFT In the Greco-Roman tradition, the swan was sacred to Aphrodite/Venus; it also appears in the myth of Leda, who is seduced by Zeus when he takes the shape of a swan.

ABOVE In many traditions, the owl is associated with magic, the otherworld, wisdom and prophecy.

CRANES

In China and Japan, cranes are traditional symbols of longevity, wisdom and fidelity. In Western art they personify vigilance.

AQUATIC CREATURES

ABOVE The ancient Greeks revered dolphins as symbols of wisdom and prophecy.

BELOW Ancient Egypt's crocodile-headed god, Sobek, linked with evil, is a symbol of destruction.

The symbolism of aquatic creatures relates partly to their habitat, partly to their appearance and behaviour and partly to the significance they have for human society. Water creatures have been variously revered as deities, feared as monsters and hunted for their flesh, oils, eggs, skin and bones. They play a significant role in myth, folklore and religion.

FISH

Many traditions use the fish as a symbol of spiritual wisdom. In Christianity it is a symbol of Christ, and in Hinduism, Vishnu appeared as the fish Matsya to save humankind from the flood and reveal the Vedas, or holy scriptures. Because of the vast number of eggs they lay, fish are also widely linked with life and fertility. In China they are symbols of good luck.

Particular species have been singled out for their symbolic properties. For example, in Japan, the carp symbolizes love, courage, dignity and good fortune, while the Celts associated the salmon with wisdom, prophecy and inspiration.

WHALES, SHARKS AND DOLPHINS

In Japan, the whale was one of the Seven Deities of Good Fortune and was worshipped as a god of fishing and food. In Maori tradition, it symbolizes plenty and abundance; the *pakake* figure – a stylized whale with large spirals for its jaws – is a popular motif.

In the Judaeo-Christian tradition, the Old Testament account of Jonah and the whale associated it with death and rebirth. It is sometimes claimed that the story relates to a man-eating shark rather than a whale, and the Hindu god Vishnu is at times portrayed as emerging from the mouth of a shark. They are symbols of the dangers of nature.

In ancient Greece dolphins were linked with Apollo and his gifts of wisdom and prophecy, and with the water-born goddess of love, Aphrodite, signifying a union of the masculine, solar world and the feminine, watery realm; the dolphin's Greek name, *delphis*, is related to *delphys*, "womb", after which the sacred site of Delphi is named. In many Native American cultures, the dolphin is both a divine messenger and a form of the Great Spirit, while the seafaring Nabataean Arabs believed that dolphins accompanied the souls of the dead to the underworld.

CROCODILES AND ALLIGATORS

Crocodilians inhabit two worlds – land and water – making them symbols of fundamental contradictions. Some African tribes revere crocodiles as intermediaries between the everyday and the spirit world and as oracles for water deities. In many parts of West Africa the crocodile's liver and entrails are credited with powerful magic and are sometimes used by shamans to cast destructive spells.

In ancient Egypt, crocodiles were sacred and were sometimes mummified. A cult centre existed at Crocodilopolis, where tame crocodiles were adorned with golden earrings and ritually fed in order to honour the crocodile god, Sobek. Sobek was linked both to the evil and destructive powers of Set, god of the underworld, who took crocodile form after the murder of his brother, Osiris, and also to Ra, the benevolent solar deity.

For the Aborigines of Australia's Northern Territory, large crocodiles embody the spirits of important people and are associated with wisdom, while the Madarrpa peoples of north-east Arnhem Land believe that Crocodile Man created fire. In China, the alligator or crocodile was the inventor of singing and the drum, and plays a part in the rhythm of the world. In early Christian belief, being eaten by a crocodile indicated that a person had gone to Hell.

FROGS AND TOADS

Traditionally both frogs and toads were lunar animals, and their radical growth stages were linked with the changing phases of the moon. Both creatures are also linked with fertility, the watery processes of birth and rainfall and with transformation and

ABOVE In the fairy story, the frog is changed into a prince when kissed by the princess, symbolizing transformation.

ABOVE The turtle is a sacred animal in many traditions. In Native American traditions it is a symbol of the earth.

SHELLS

Because it is a structure that shelters life, the symbolism of the shell is often connected with the womb, birth and creation. In Greco-Roman myth, Aphrodite/Venus emerged from a huge scallop shell, and in Hinduism, the conch shell symbolizes the origin of existence, its shape forming a multiple spiral evolving from one central point. Conch shells have been used as ceremonial horns by the Maya and Aztecs and are also one of the emblems of Buddhism. In Benin, cowrie shells were once used as currency and are associated with wealth, royalty and prestige. In Christian iconography, the Virgin Mary is sometimes compared to an oyster shell, and Christ to the pearl.

immortality – hence the theme of frogs changing into princes in Western folklore. To the Celts, the frog was lord of the earth and the curative powers of water, and for the Maya and Aztecs it was a water deity whose croaking predicted and made rain. In ancient Egypt, Heket the frog goddess was associated with magic and childbirth, and in China and Japan both frogs and toads were associated with magic. In Japan, the toad was associated with lunar eclipses and in China with wealth and longevity. Both frogs and toads were linked with magic and witchcraft in medieval Europe. In the Bible, frogs were one of the ten plagues of Egypt.

TURTLES

Because of the sturdiness and shape of its shell, the turtle (or tortoise) is a symbol of the world in many cultures. It is the oldest Native American symbol for the Earth or earth mother – while earthquakes and thunder are the cosmic turtle shaking its earthly shell. The Maya also envisaged the Earth as a huge turtle, as did the Chinese, who regarded the marks on the turtle's shell as a map of the constellations and used them in divination. Of

China's four sacred creatures, the turtle was the only real animal (the others being the dragon, the phoenix and the unicorn), and it was a symbol of longevity.

In Hindu myth, the turtle Chukwa is one of the ten incarnations of Vishnu. It is a symbol of meditation and spiritual wisdom. In Australian Aboriginal myth, the turtle was said to arise from the creative waters that were melted from the primeval mountain of ice by the sun goddess, while in Polynesia, the turtle embodies the power of the ocean deities. Among African tribes, turtles are often sacred to water gods.

SEALS AND WALRUSES

In some Inuit stories, these creatures figure as primordial ancestors, capable of assuming human form and teaching people to swim and hunt fish; they are also messengers, moving between the world of spirit (water) and matter (land). Inuit custom dictates that, when the animals are killed in a hunt, their bladders are thrown back into the sea, as it is believed they will then be reborn as living seals or walruses. The walrus is also known as the sea elephant.

CRABS

Because its movement is governed by the lunar tides (hunting as the tide comes in, retreating as the tide goes out), the crab is often associated with the moon. In Inca tradition, it was an aspect of the great mother, who devoured both time and the waning moon.

OCTOPUSES

In classical antiquity, the octopus was seen as a monster that would attack shipwrecked sailors by pulling them apart. Like the crab, it was associated with the moon and the summer solstice. The octopus was much used in the art of the Minoan and Mycenean civilizations in the Mediterranean, where it sometimes occurs in conjunction with the spiral or swastika. Its tentacles associate it with the unfolding of creation from the centre.

CORAL

According to an ancient Chinese belief, coral came from a tree growing at the bottom of the sea. In alchemy it was known as the tree of life, filled with a blood-like substance (because of its colour). In Buddhism, coral trees are said to grow in paradise.

BELOW Seals play a prominent role in the myth and custom of the Inuit, where they are often seen as primordial ancestral figures.

INSECTS

ABOVE This portrait of Napoleon makes use of the motif of the bee, embroidered not only on the emperor's robes but also on the podium on which he stands. It is a symbol of equals under one leader.

BELOW RIGHT The butterfly is a symbol of spiritual growth and transformation. In Latin America it is also used to describe a prostitute, flitting from one man to the next.

From a perspective that sees the universe as an interconnected web of being, every part of nature is significant, no matter how small or ordinary. Consequently even the tiniest insects are rich in symbolic associations, frequently associated with the gods, spirits and the otherworld. For instance, in the mythology of Central America, small flying insects were regarded as the souls of the dead revisiting earth, and a similar belief endures in Guatemala, where they are linked with the stars. As with other animals, the symbolic associations of insects are based on their behaviour and physical characteristics and are rooted in culture and time.

FLIES

The name of Beelzebub, the chief devil mentioned in the Bible, comes from a Hebrew word meaning "lord of the flies", pointing to the fairly common belief that flies are harbingers of disease and devilish misfortune; they were the third of the ten plagues of Egypt. However, in the ancient Egyptian New Kingdom (1550–1100 BC), flies were noted for their persistence and bravery and were adopted as warrior symbols: magic wands decorated with fly amulets have been discovered from this period. Among the Navajo, Dontso ("big fly") is a spiritual messenger associated with healing.

BEES

Because of their diligence, social organization and collaborative labour, bees are often used as models of human society. The beehive became a metaphor for the ordered and charitable life of Christian monastic communities. Bees have also long been valued for their honeycombs, a source not only of sugar but also of wax, used in the making of candles. Thus they are associated with both sweetness and light. In ancient Egypt they were a solar symbol, born from the tears of the sun god Ra.

As the hive is organized around the queen bee, the bee was a regal symbol: it was adopted by the medieval kings of France and revived by Napoleon as an emblem of equals under a single leader. In Chinese art, a bee or butterfly hovering around a flower (symbolizing a woman) suggested buzzing desire. In ancient Greece, honey was

---

DRAGONFLIES

In some Native American cultures, dragonflies symbolize dreams, change and enlightenment and are associated with shamanistic powers. To the Chinese, the dragonfly represents summer, and, because of its darting, unpredictable movement, is also a symbol of unreliability.

THE ANTHILL

In the cosmologies of many African peoples (notably the Dogon and Bambara of Mali) the anthill plays a significant role. It is linked with language and the art of weaving, the female sexual organs and creation: it is a traditional fertility custom for a woman to sit on an anthill. The traditional pattern of Dogon huts is based on the anthill design, and the belief that ants know the location of underground streams means that wells are often sunk near an anthill. In Tibetan Buddhism, the anthill is a symbol of an industrious life.

associated with eloquence, while in the Celtic world, mead (a fermented drink made from honey and water) was regarded as the drink of the gods.

BUTTERFLIES

Because of its metamorphic life cycle, the butterfly is an archetypal symbol of transformation, mystical rebirth and the transcendent soul. Some Australian Aboriginals regard butterflies as the returning spirits of the dead, while in Greek myth, Psyche (the soul) is often represented as a butterfly. The creature's grace and beauty make it an emblem of woman in Japan, where two butterflies dancing together symbolize marital happiness, and in China it is associated with the pleasures of life and high spirits. Someone who flits from one thing to another and is never satisfied may be described as a butterfly, while in Latin America, the Spanish word for butterfly (*mariposa*) can refer to a prostitute, moving from one man to the next. The Aztecs associated the butterfly with women who had died in childbirth, while for the Mexicans it was a symbol of the "black sun" passing through the underworld during its nightly journey.

SPIDERS

In Australian Aboriginal cultures the great spider is a solar hero, but in other traditions it is a female force, a personification of the Great Mother in both her creative and devouring aspects. Among the Amazonian Tukano people, for instance, the spider's web is likened to the placenta, while Ixchel, the Mayan goddess of midwifery, appears as a spider. In Japan, spider-women are thought to ensnare travellers, while in the West predatory women are sometimes likened to spiders, using their feminine wiles to lure men into their web. Among the Ashanti of West Africa spiders are associated with Anansi, the trickster god, who taught humans the art of weaving. In some Native American myths the spider is said to have taught humans the alphabet, tracing the shapes of the letters in its web.

Because of the web's strength and near invisibility, Native American warriors decorated themselves with web designs. For the Celts, the web is the invisible structure that holds the pattern of life in a grand design. For Hindus and Buddhists, the web stands for the illusions of the world, while in Christianity it represents Satan's snare. In European folklore, however, it is unlucky to kill a spider, which is linked with money and good fortune.

SCORPIONS

Because of its poisonous sting, permanently unsheathed and ready to strike, the scorpion is associated with death and destruction: in Africa, many people use a euphemism for the creature since even uttering its name would release evil into the world. The scorpion has many links with the underworld: the zodiac sign of Scorpio is ruled by Pluto, lord of the underworld, while the ancient Egyptian scorpion goddess Selket (a sorcerer-healer) was one of four goddesses who protected the dead Osiris. Through its association with the desert, the scorpion can represent drought and desolation. Some Amazonian peoples believe it was sent by a jealous god to punish men for having sex with women whom he himself desired. In one version of the Greco-Roman myth of Orion the hunter, he died when he was stung in the heel by a scorpion, and both were turned into constellations, placed on opposite sides of the sky.

WORMS

The symbolism of the worm links new life with corruption and death. According to Chinese myth, the human race has its origins in the worms that fed on the corpse of the primordial being, and a similar belief exists in Icelandic tradition, where the worms feeding on the frost giant Ymir (from whose body the earth was created) assume human form. The legendary Irish Celtic hero Cúchulainn was said to have been born from a worm. In psychological terms, worms may be associated with destructive processes that erode personality.

ABOVE The scorpion is widely linked with death and destruction. In parts of Africa, many people refuse to say its name in the belief that this would bring evil into the world.

THE SNAKE OR SERPENT

ABOVE The goddess of the snakes is a Cretan Earth Mother, shown here holding the snakes of death and rebirth.

Of all animal symbols, the snake is probably the most significant and complex. From very early times, snakes seem to have been linked with eternity, as creators and destroyers of the universe, and associated with both healing and wisdom; they have also been demonized and aligned with temptation, immorality and Satan.

SNAKES AND THE FEMININE

The snake was often associated with deities, particularly mother goddesses and Mother Earth. The ancient Phoenician fertility goddess Tanith, who is linked with Eve and Lilith, was associated with snakes. In Egyptian mythology Buto was a snake goddess, often depicted as a cobra. Her image on the Pharaoh's forehead protected him from his enemies. The matriarchal cult at Delphi was symbolically dissolved when the god Apollo killed the female serpent Python, and the Iliad tells of Calcas interpreting an eagle carrying a wounded snake in its talons as a sign that the patriarchal Greeks would overcome the matriarchal traditions of Asia.

FROM PRIMARY GOD TO EVIL SERPENT

In many parts of the world snakes, with other reptiles and fish, have been used to represent nature in its most primordial or fundamental aspects. Because the snake sheds its skin and then starts life anew, it embodies the cycle of death and resurrection. The serpent was a primary god, existing at the roots of life, and has a strong chthonic or underworld connection, arising from the depths of Mother Earth, and psychologically from the collective unconscious. He was the lord of the tree of life, where time and eternity meet. Sumerian seals from 3500 BC show the serpent with the tree and the goddess giving the fruit of life to a visiting male figure.

The Canaanite deity was a mother goddess who was strongly associated with the serpent and represented the mysteries of life. When the Hebrews introduced a male god into Canaan, the female deity and the snake were

NAGAS AND WISDOM

In Indian mythology, nagas (from the Sanskrit word for "snake") are divine water-serpents, benevolent and wise, portrayed with a human face and the hood of the cobra. Indian alchemy, *nagayuna*, aims to unify the body's energies in a journey of self-realization to preserve the elixir of life.

relegated and associated with evil. The snake in the story of the Garden of Eden has Satanic characteristics, tempting Eve into the sin of disobedience against God, whereas the Nassene Gnostics (*nass* means "snake") honoured the serpent in the form of the Sumerian god Enki, a liberating influence who helped to make Adam and Eve fully human by introducing them to the tree of knowledge.

For Jung, snakes symbolized that which is totally unconscious and instinctual, nevertheless possessing an almost supernatural and unique wisdom, which can come into conflict with conscious

LEFT Eve pictured with the devil-serpent, and the forbidden fruit that it uses to tempts her to sin.

attitudes. The snake can therefore symbolize both evil and wisdom, easily overriding human morality. To dream of a snake suggests that there is a large gulf between the conscious and unconscious, and that the unconscious is making itself known in a compulsive and reflexive way. A snake in our dreams might also suggest that we have strayed from the serpentine path of our individuation.

THE SNAKE AS CREATOR AND DESTROYER

Serpents appear as the source of life in many creation myths, though they can also be figures of destruction. The Sumerians and Akkadians of Mesopotamia described the mingling of the waters of Apsu and Tiamat, from which emerged Lakhmu and Lakhamu, two monstrous serpents who gave birth to Heaven and Earth. The Rainbow Serpent appears in Aboriginal rock art in Arnhem Land from between 6,000 and 8,000 years ago. This Dreamtime ancestor is a life-giving creature associated with fertility, abundance and rainfall, as well as often being the creator of human beings. Its destructive side involves punishing those who go against the natural law by swallowing them in great floods and regurgitating their bones.

Ancient Germanic mythology associates the serpent with death and the continual undermining of the roots of the world tree. Norse tradition foretold a deluge that would destroy the world when Jormangand, the Midgard serpent, was awoken.

HEALING AND DEATH

Serpents have long been associated with healing and mediation between life and death. In Greek mythology, Asklepios, the son of Apollo and the mortal Coronis, was able to metamorphose into a snake and could bring the dead back to life, thus angering Hades, god of the underworld. One tale tells that he became a serpent to end a plague in Rome, and the Romans came to worship him as the god of medicine and healing. The Asklepian healing process, called incubation, involved the patient spending the night in a sacred place. They would be visited by the god in a dream, and its message was interpreted by a priest, resulting in a remedy.

The Asklepian symbol of a tree snake wrapped around a staff represents healing and is today used as a medical symbol. It is often confused with the caduceus, or "winged staff", of Mercury, on which two snakes were twined. These snakes were involved in a fight in which Mercury intervened, revealing his nature as a psychopomp, or conductor of souls between worlds.

The serpent's association with healing, life and death is found in the pagan-Christian Slavonic story of Bogatyr Potok, who when his young bride died, had himself buried with her, fully armed and on horseback, in a deep tomb. At midnight many monstrous reptiles appeared, including a great fire-breathing serpent. Potok cut of its head and brought his wife back to life by anointing her body with it. The homeopathic

principle that "like cures like" is essential to the poisonous/healing nature of the snake.

THE TUKANO ANACONDA

The Tukano people of the Amazon ascribe a complex and contextual symbolism to the anaconda. They believe that monstrous anacondas live in forest lagoons and deep pools beneath waterfalls. They also compare the motion of the Milky Way to the intertwining of two copulating anacondas, reflecting seasonal periods of insemination, germination and fertility. The anaconda is the path that twists through the forest like the river, and when travelling upstream it represents a journey of initiation.

ABOVE Two snakes entwined upon Mercury's "winged staff" represent the transformative power to change male to female and vice versa. The Asclepian staff with its single snake was the original medical symbol; however, possibly mistakenly, this caduceus is also used for this purpose.

BELOW The art of the Australian Aboriginals often depicts the snake, and its association with fertility and abundance.

THE LIVING PLANET

INEVITABLY, MUCH CULTURAL SYMBOLISM STEMS FROM THE EARTH AND HOW WE LIVE OUT OUR LIVES ON OUR PLANET. SEASONS AND CYCLES, TIME, DISTANCE, THE ELEMENTS AND THE LAND ITSELF HAVE ALL GIVEN RISE TO HUMANITY'S MOST ANCIENT SIGNS AND SYMBOLS, WHICH REMAIN CONSTANT DESPITE THE WAY SCIENCE HAS INCREASED OUR KNOWLEDGE OF THE PLANET WE LIVE ON.

SEASONS AND TIME

RIGHT The 22,000-year-old stone carving known as the Venus of Laussel. The horn she holds is thought to be marked with a year of thirteen lunar cycles.

Humankind has always used symbolism and ritual to relate to the rhythms and cycles of life. Nature punctuates existence with life events – the moments of conception, birth and death – and life goes on in interdependent cycles. The phases of life have always preoccupied us, and have been given their own universal symbolic language.

PLEIADES

The constellation of the Pleiades has many symbolic associations. The stars represented the mother goddess Net in ancient Egypt, and in China they were the blossom or flower stars. The Khoikhoi tribe of South Africa call them Khuseti, the rain-bearing stars. In Hindu tradition they are the flames of Agni, the god of fire.

CALENDARS AND TIME
Early calendars were based on the phases of the moon. Cave paintings at Lascaux, in France, show that they were counted around 17,000 years ago, and the carving of the Venus of Laussel, which is about 22,000 years old, shows her holding a horn with thirteen markings, representing a year of lunar cycles. The lunar calendar is associated with the menstrual cycle, and predominates in civilizations that

worship The Goddess. Britain's Stonehenge is a symbolic monument aligned with the movements of both sun and moon. Lunisolar and solar calendars emerged with the shift from female to male values.

To this day Jews and Muslims continue to use lunar calendars. The Chinese calendar, another example of a lunisolar calendar, is still used to establish the timing of holidays and festivals, and is important to Chinese farmers who still plant by the moon.

Whereas time was originally associated with rhythm, rebirth and renewal in nature,

symbolized by the circle and the yoni, the influence of Judaeo-Christianity led to the foundation of linear time. In the 14th century, Europeans conceived the universe in terms of clockwork, and in the 17th century, Isaac Newton characterized time as being absolute and uniform.

Technological advances have enabled us to ignore or colonize "nature's time", growing crops out of season and literally extending daytime into the night. It is only in recent years, since Einstein's theories of relativity, that time, along with space, has again been thought to bend.

THE TYRANNICAL CLOCK
In Charles Dickens's 1848 novel *Dombey and Son* the clock is a tyrannical figure that makes itself heard and felt everywhere. Mr Dombey, an emotionless character, does everything by the clock. It is used as a symbol of a mechanistic way of life, showing how time had come to dominate the consciousness of industrial society.

THE CELTIC WHEEL OF THE YEAR

In the Celtic tradition, a symbolic circle of time represents transitional points during the year: Samhain, winter solstice; Imbolc, spring equinox; Beltane, summer solstice; Lughnasada, autumn equinox. The wheel of the year describes the cycles of death, birth, youth, maturity and renewal of life, and each point is marked by seasonal celebrations.

Samhain (31 October–1 November) is also the Festival of the Dead, when the veil between the living and the dead is thought to be at its thinnest. The year begins in the dying and decaying part of the wheel, reflecting the Celtic understanding of the importance of ageing and death in order for life to thrive. This time is symbolized by the figure of the old woman, who is also an elder. Youth, beauty, growth and productivity are symbolized later in the Celtic year by the maiden and the mother, the other two aspects of the triple goddess.

SEASONAL SYMBOLISM

Early measurements of time were based on the appearances and disappearances, and the changing paths of the sun and the moon. The main phases of the day had their own symbolism that still has resonance today. Dawn was a universal symbol of hope, joy and youth, while noon was the hour of revelation in Jewish and Islamic tradition. Twilight was often linked with the shadowy and uncertain time of decline and therefore with death.

Again inspired by the cycles of the moon, and the rising and setting of the sun, the four seasons were universal symbols of birth, growth, death and rebirth. In Western art, spring is depicted as a young woman, at times a child, sometimes linked with blossom, the lamb or kid and with the Greek goddess Aphrodite. Summer is again a woman, this time in the full beauty of maturity, crowned with ears of corn and sometimes carrying a sickle. Autumn is associated with Dionysus and with harvest, and also with the hare. Winter is at times depicted as an old man or woman; the blacksmith god Hephaestus is associated with this season, as is the salamander and the duck.

HARVEST FESTIVALS

Festivals of thanksgiving at harvest time are common to all agrarian cultures. They are times to appreciate the forces of nature and the ancestors, bringing the community together to share ideas and experiences, tell stories and strengthen social bonds.

The harvest moon festival in Korea, called Chusok, takes place on the 15th day of the eighth lunar month. The same day in China and Vietnam is Chung Ch'ui, considered the birthday of the moon and celebrated with a feast and special "moon cakes", symbols of togetherness.

Pongal is the southern Indian Hindu harvest festival, which starts on 14 January. Its name means "boiling over" – a reference both to the bounties of nature and to a sweet rice dish. The festival lasts three days, and offerings are made to the rain and sun gods, who watered and ripened the rice, and to the cattle, which are essential to a prosperous community.

The Sikh festival of Baisakhi is a northern Indian harvest festival celebrated on 13 April, the first day of the Sikh solar year, in which dancers and drummers re-enact scenes of the sowing, harvesting, winnowing and gathering of crops.

BELOW A procession of Sikhs at the festival of Baisakhi, which celebrates the beginning of the corn harvest, and takes place on the first day of the solar year.

GOD OF TIME

The Greeks conceived of two types of time: Chronos (shown above, the snake around him symbolizing eternity), was the god of absolute, linear and quantifiable time, whereas Kairos was the god of timing, opportunity and chance.

THE EARTH

RIGHT The view of the planet Earth from space changed the way we view our world, and symbolizes the wholeness and inter-connectedness of life.

What the Earth means to us has changed markedly over time. Its symbolism is strongly linked to our collective state of mind or consciousness, and reflects changes in human values and our relationship with nature.

THE FLAT EARTH

Most early societies conceived of the Earth as flat, as a huge wheel or disc. The ancient Chinese described the Earth as a flat square on top of a truncated, four-sided pyramid, below the circular heavens. In India, the Rig Veda described the Earth and sky as two wheels at either end of an axle. Classical, Hindu, Buddhist

BELOW The Psalter Map, with Jerusalem in the middle, is the earliest surviving map symbolizing Christ's role as overseer of the world.

and Jain texts agreed that the Earth was in fact a flat disc, though some Indian myths saw it as spherical.

The ancient Hebrews, Egyptians and Babylonians all had flat Earth cosmologies. According to the Hebrew book of Enoch, the angel Uriel guided Enoch to the ends of the Earth, where he saw huge beasts and birds, and beyond which he saw Heaven resting on the edge of the Earth. The Egyptians envisaged a rectangular Earth, with the sky goddess Nut stretching her body like an enclosing dome over the land. The Babylonians imagined a flat land surrounded by ocean, with the vault of the sky resting either on the ocean or on pillars. In the West, the earliest description of the Earth is in the Iliad, where Homer described the sky as a bowl-like hemisphere, covering a flat, circular Earth.

THE ROUND EARTH

Although most early people thought the Earth was flat, there were exceptions. Japan's indigenous people, the Ainu, thought of it as a ball floating in the ocean, but their word for Earth means "floating land", suggesting that this was the localized perception of an island people. In 375 BC Plato described the Earth as a globe, in the context of an Earth-centred universe, and Aristotle (384–322 BC) suggested it was a sphere based upon his observations of circular shadows cast on the moon during a lunar eclipse. In 200 BC, the Egyptian Eratosthenes calculated the Earth's diameter

using trigonometry, by measuring the length of the shadow of a vertical tower in Alexandria, when the sun was directly above Aswan, 800km/500 miles away.

However, the paradigmatic shift from a flat to a round Earth took place over many hundreds of years. In 1492 Christopher Columbus, by sailing partly around the world, proved by experience what, until then, had been surmised through calculation: that the Earth was indeed a sphere. It seems likely that Galileo and Copernicus were greatly encouraged by Columbus's experience, and dramatic new theories concerning a universe centred on the sun, around which the spherical Earth and moon orbited, rapidly followed.

EARTH AS A DEITY

The Earth was worshipped in ancient times as the supreme mother goddess and was believed to be both alive and divine. Mother Earth was a figure of great compassion and the source of all life and fertility. Paleolithic images of the mother goddess, dating from around 22,000-18,000 BC, include the Venus of Laussel, a rock carving from the Dordogne in France, and the statuettes

known as the Goddess of Lespugue, found in Haute-Garonne, France, and the Goddess of Willendorf, found in Austria. Each depicts a female form with pendulous breasts and a full, rounded womb.

In the West, the last Earth Goddess was Gaia, no longer the supreme mother but nevertheless a conscious and living deity. In Greek her name means "land" or "earth". She was a triple goddess, differentiated as the maiden, or Persephone, the mother, or Demeter, and the crone or Hecate. During the Classical period there was a shift in emphasis from Gaia to her great-grandson Zeus, reflecting the replacement of the image of the divine mother with a far more remote male god, which swept across Europe, the Middle East, North Africa and India, gaining particular prominence in the Judaeo-Christian God.

In Christian times Mary, the mother of Christ, embodies or echoes some of the qualities of the ancient mother goddesses, and acts as an intermediary between Heaven and Earth. Meanwhile, the male God exists in Heaven, outside the earthly sphere, symbolizing a separation between Earth and deity.

THE HIERARCHY OF HEAVEN AND EARTH

The Judaeo-Christian worldview stresses a hierarchical relationship between Heaven and Earth, placing humanity closer to God than other living creatures, with the responsibility to assume dominion over the Earth and nature. This has been interpreted by many to justify an image of the Earth as a resource for human use. With the divine no longer synonymous with nature, the Earth could easily become an object of interest and exploitation. Francis Bacon (1561–1626) spoke of nature in feminine terms, and advocated its domination for human benefit. He suggested that nature should be "bound into service", "moulded" by the machine and made into a "slave" – simultaneously representing prevailing attitudes towards both women and nature.

THE LIVING EARTH

When in 1969 the scientist James Lovelock conceived his Gaia hypothesis, he described feeling like an astronaut looking at the Earth while standing on the moon, and that at times he has felt that the whole planet is partaking in something like a "sacred ceremony". His vision of the Earth as a complex and self-regulating closed system, which operates as if it were a living being – a pragmatic and scientific view – has aroused a great deal of speculation concerning its potential as a modern religious symbol. Using the name of the Greek Earth goddess Gaia may well have furthered the power of this scientific model and symbolic imagery. For many, Gaia has come to represent the idea of the "living Earth", despite the theory's stress that the Earth acts only "like" a living system. For Lovelock, Gaia is something that humans can reconnect to by maintaining a sense of wonder for nature.

To the Kono people of Sierra Leone, the Earth is indeed a living being: she is God's wife and is hugely productive and fertile. The emphasis of the Kono lifestyle, like that of many indigenous peoples, lies in maintaining the harmony of nature, through human relationships and community, and relationships with the land and unseen forces.

NEW SYMBOLISM

The image of Earth as seen from space offers a meaningful symbolism for contemporary humans. It is Earth as seen from the "heavens", and this changed view shows us that the separations we perceive between different cultures, and between us and nature, are immaterial when viewed from a distance. Earth seen from space offers the symbol of a renewed relationship between humankind and nature.

THE HOLLOW EARTH

Since the scientific revolution, scientists have hypothesized that the earth may be hollow. John Cleves Symmes (1779–1829) believed it consisted of four hollow concentric spheres, with spaces between each, which were possibly habitable on their inner and outer surfaces. He believed there were two enormous holes at the North and South poles and proposed an expedition to the inner spheres. "Symmes' hole" became a phrase of ridicule in the 1820s.

MAPS AND DIRECTION

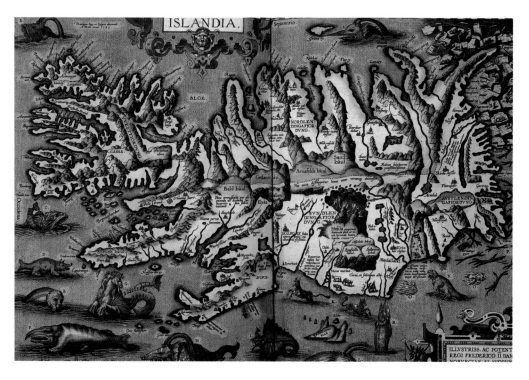

CHARTING BY SONGLINE AND STORY

Australian Aboriginals believe that the topography of their land was created by the journeys, or "songlines", of the Ancestors. These songlines criss-cross Australia, and are sung by Aboriginals as they follow the sacred pathways.

In a hunting culture such as the Alaskan Nunamiut, a young man must learn the details of the hunting terrain before he can join the hunt. He builds up a symbolic map of the local topography by listening to the myths of spirits and heroes who populate the hunting grounds.

ABOVE A map of Islandia (Iceland), charted by Abraham Ortelius in the late 16th century, displays a wide array of sea monsters, polar bears, icebergs and the erupting volcano Mount Hekla.

BELOW A stone disk containing an Australian Aboriginal songline design. The Aborginals believe that the songlines draw together diverse groups into one common dreaming relationship with the land.

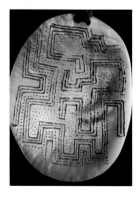

The symbolism of orientation and direction focuses on how people move through life and the world, what it means to be in a certain place at a certain time, and the relationship with places beyond our everyday experience.

MAPPING THE WORLD

How a map is drawn depends upon the worldview and beliefs of the cartographer, and what is considered central or peripheral, what is known, mysterious or threatening to the culture. The early *mappa mundi*, or world map, was a symbolic representation of the known world infused with the *imago mundi*, or the image of the world as an ordered cosmos. Early maps were as much cosmological and mythical as they were tools for practical orientation. The Beatus map, drawn by a Benedictine monk in AD 787, charts the world in a rectangle encircled by a world

sea. This form, called a "T-map" was common until the late Middle Ages. T-maps divide the world into three, the number of the Holy Trinity: Jerusalem usually lies at the intersection, with Eden either at the top or to the east, and the rest of the world divided into Asia, Africa and Europe. As the medieval worldview receded during the Renaissance, Jerusalem and Eden were no longer charted as central features and the edges of maps began to display unexplored regions, with strange hybrid creatures at the edges of the known world. The Carta Marina, by the Swedish Archbishop Olaus Magnus, first printed in Venice in 1539, showed the North Sea around Scandinavia filled with threatening sea creatures. It was the first map to chart the Nordic regions, which had previously been considered terra incognita (unknown lands).

THE COMPASS

For some people the compass is a neutral symbol that unifies the people of the Earth, since we all share the directions north, south, east and west. However, it is also a symbol of exploration, orientation, expansion and even the conquering of nature. The phrase "moral compass" is now commonly used in the United States to refer to morally "straight" actions.

Practitioners of the geomantic art of feng shui (which means "wind and water") use a special circular magnetic compass known as the *luo pan* to locate houses and tombs where the energies are in harmonious balance for good fortune. Dragon lines, or dragon currents, which are thought to run through the land, consist of a negative yin current, symbolized by a white tiger, and a positive yang current, symbolized by the blue dragon. A yin countryside will have gently undulating feminine features, and a yang landscape will have sharp or mountainous male features.

ORIENTATION

Travellers and explorers on land and sea have, since ancient times, orientated themselves according to the positions of the stars in the night sky. Orientation is necessary both in everyday reality, to know where we are and where we are going, and for our personal and cultural sense of meaning and identity. Many cultures consider a place sacred to them to be the centre of the world, this might be represented by a holy mountain, world tree or sacred site; the people will "centre" themselves in relation to it in an act of renewal or balancing of nature and spirit.

Places of worship such as mosques, temples and churches, and graves and burial grounds, often align with the east-west axis, the directions of the rising and setting sun. Wherever they are in the world, Moslems face their sacred centre, Mecca, in daily prayer. Native Americans offer prayers to the four cosmic directions, often beginning with the east, where the sun rises.

THE HORIZON

An important orientation symbol, the horizon represents the furthest point the eye can see on the earthly plane. It is the place of vision, exploration and new discoveries. The sun on the horizon signals the dawn of a new day, world or era, and points to the potential for new beginnings and bright futures.

SACRED JOURNEYS

Myths and legend are filled with stories of journeys. Tales of migration, exploration, conquest, heroic quests and pilgrimage serve to focus or renew a people's identity, commune with the gods and spirits, and justify or honour their relationship with the land.

The Hebrew story of the Exodus describes how Moses led the Israelites out of servitude to a land promised to them by God. The Aztec migration of the 12th century was a journey of cultural renewal, in which the Mexica people were guided by the god Huitzilopochtli in their travels from the island of Aztlan to Tenochtitlan, their future capital.

A pilgrimage is a symbolic journey – representing spiritual reorientation, religious devotion, healing and renewal – through a sacred or meaningful landscape. A physical pilgrimage is a liminal act, meaning that at some point the pilgrim crosses a threshold, leaving their everyday life behind them and travelling towards a sacred destination.

In Islam the hajj is a pilgrimage to the holy city of Mecca. The ancient Greeks would travel to receive guidance from the oracle at Delphi, or healing from the shrine of Asklepios at Epidaurus. In 9th-century Europe many pilgrims journeyed to Santiago de Compostela in north-west Spain, at the outer edge of the known world, to visit the miracle-making relics of St James.

Hindus make a pilgrimage to Mount Kailas, the physical manifestation of the mystical Mount Meru, the centre of the world. The journey to Mount Sinai, where Moses received the tablets of the law, like many pilgrimages, reflects the spiritual, as well as physical, journey of Moses himself.

ABOVE The luo pan, or feng shui compass, was used as a source of guidance by ancient Chinese emperors and sages. The encircling symbols, such as 24 mountain stars, 64 hexagrams, 60 stems and branches and 12 mountain dragons, were used in helping to site and orient buildings, and for divination.

LEFT A Muslim prayer involves standing and then bowing or prostrating in the direction of Mecca.

BELOW The horizon often symbolizes our earthly limits, the end and the beginning of new possibilities and exploration.

THE LAND

Whether we think we own the land, or whether we borrow it or share it with the gods, it features prominently in world symbolism. From a perspective of ownership, the claiming of land is a symbolic act of power, wealth, nationhood or individual identity. The "discovery", conquest and colonization of other lands is often symbolized by setting foot on the soil, planting a national flag, or writing legal deeds conferring ownership.

For many indigenous peoples land is not owned by individuals but is understood as a living entity or divine gift, which warrants respect and relationship. The indigenous peoples of the Philippines, for example, consider the land as God's gift, and its ownership is assigned to their ancestors and the nature spirits. The land is held by them in trust and guardianship.

EARTHQUAKES

Understandably, the shock and turmoil of earthquakes have often been associated with the anger of the gods in reaction to the degeneracy of the people. The Japanese considered seismic activity to come from the storm god Susano-O, and the Greeks believed that the storm god Poseidon, also known as Enosicthon ("earth shaker"), was the cause of earthquakes. According to Plato, earthquakes and floods consumed the legendary civilization of Atlantis in a single day.

Earthquakes may be taken as omens predicting a huge change in religion or politics: the New Testament describes the quaking of the Earth at the time of Christ's death. Like other natural disasters, earthquakes frequently symbolize the vulnerable qualities of humanity in relation to the natural forces of the Earth.

THE SOIL

Fundamental to food production, soil is seen as "black gold" by agrarian societies. The Burmese consider it to be as valuable as metals such as gold, silver, iron, copper, lead and tin. Many creation myths tell of humans

LEFT In antiquity, earthquakes were seen as a sign of a deity's wrath, and early Christianity was no exception: here it is angelic trumpets that shake the Earth.

being shaped from clay, and we all share a dependence on the life-sustaining fertility of the soil.

Soil from a particular field or region may possess special qualities or essences. The Finno-Ugric people known as the Chuvash practise a ritual in which they "steal" a clod of earth from a productive field nearby to improve the fertility of their own land. Modern biodynamic growers make special preparations such as burying herbs in a cow horn during an astrologically significant time, then homoeopathically potentizing the mixture by stirring it in water and spreading it on the land. This is said to concentrate cosmic forces in the soil, so raising the vitality of the plants and those who eat them.

The fertility ritual of performing sexual intercourse in a field is common in pagan traditions. It is also found in a Greek myth about Demeter, goddess of the soil. She and the Cretan youth Iasion had sex in a thrice-ploughed field, as a result of which she bore a son, Ploutos ("wealth").

MOUNTAINS

A natural symbolic significance of mountains is that they are the part of Earth closest to the heavens, where humans may communicate with the gods. A high peak is frequently held sacred by the local culture as it is considered to be the world axis, linking Earth with Heaven. Moses climbed to the peak of Mount Sinai to receive the Ten Commandments, and Jesus made his ascent to Heaven from the

Mount of Olives. For Hindus, Jains and Tibetan Buddhists, the mythical Mount Meru is the centre of the universe, with its roots in the underworld and its peaks in the heavens. Its earthly manifestation is Mount Kailash in the Himalayas.

Sometimes mountains are literally thought to be the bodies of divinities. In Shinto tradition, Japan's Mount Fuji is a physical manifestation of the gods. The Navaho of North America believe particular mountains embody important male and female nature spirits. A male spirit stretches across the Chuska and Carrizo chains, with his head lying at Chuska Peak, while the female spirit spans the valley with her head on Navaho Mountain.

STONE AND ROCK

Rocks are symbols of eternity and immovability, and are often associated with divinity – many are thought to be inhabited by particular gods and spirits. Rocks store heat, cold and water, and crystals reflect and refract light – all qualities that lend themselves to symbolism – and astrology associates many precious stones with planetary influences.

The Sami of north-eastern Russia believe that certain stones are inhabited by the spirits that control the surrounding animal life, and rituals are performed at these rocks to ensure good hunting. The Tungu people believe that the forest master, a fearsome woodland spirit, may take on the form of a rock, and thus they avoid rocks that have an animal or human shape. In Vietnam, stone is endowed with living qualities, and is thought to bleed when it is struck.

Unlike the symbol of the tree, which embodies the cycles of life, stone signifies the eternal and unchanging. The Greek omphalos, or navel stone, represented the birthplace of the cosmos. Ancient standing stones in northern France and the British Isles are thought to have been used by early agrarian societies to pin and harness the powerful energies of the earth, and were commonly aligned with cyclical movements of the cosmos. Stonehenge became the main ritual centre in the south of England in around 2,100 BC and was probably used for sun worship. The phallic stones of Brittany have been associated with orgiastic rituals and were approached by women wishing to conceive a child, who would rub their bellies with dust and water from the stones' surface. Rocks with holes through them are also believed to have fertilizing qualities, and to pass through the hole can symbolize regeneration through the feminine principle. In parts of Africa, large stones are thought to hold ancestral souls.

ABOVE Tibetan Buddhist pilgrims circle the base of Mount Kailash, sacred mountain to both Buddhists and Hindus, and believed to be the home of the gods.

TOP LEFT Stonehenge is the most famous of England's stone circles, thought to have been built to link in with the movement of the planets.

THE DESERT

Symbolically, the desert may be understood in two different ways. It represents the primordial state before the emergence of life, but may also depict the superficiality of life, beneath which reality lies. The desert is barren and sterile, yet in Christian thought it may also symbolize the most divine grace when infused with the presence of God, and it was the chosen home of the earliest Christian monks, the "desert fathers".

WATER

ABOVE Waves in the ocean symbolize the movement of life from its most gentle to its most stormy aspects.

EL DORADO

The idea of a spring or fountain that can confer eternal youth occurs in various legends and myths. When the Spaniards landed in what is now Florida they were seeking a city called El Dorado (the gilded one) with a fountain from which flowed the elixir of life.

Like the other fundamental elements of life, water plays an important part in world symbolism and creation myth. It often represents the source of life, but also inevitably leads to death or the underworld. Water moves downward from above, always taking the easiest course, and for this reason it is a powerful shape-shifting symbol. Water is both dynamic and chaotic, moving in waves and spirals and never taking a straight path. Water's sacred powers are universal; as a psychological symbol it is linked with the unconscious, the soul, feelings and the flow of life.

POSEIDON

The Greek god Poseidon was the ruler of waters and earthquakes. He was a raging and stormy god who provoked intense fear and possessed powers to stir up life, using his trident to create surges of thunder, rolling waves and lightning. Poseidon had affairs with both goddesses and mortal women, who gave birth to monsters, heroes, and even the legendary ram with the golden fleece. His sacred animals were the horse, a symbol of gushing springs, and the bull, representing Poseidon's fertilizing power.

THE OCEAN

The vastness of the oceans of the world explains how a limitless body of water was often the precondition for creation in many mythologies. As bearers of all life, oceans have been endowed with maternal and life-giving qualities, nourishing those who live from her fruits. But seas are also unpredictable, representing sudden danger, lurking monsters, storms and the underworld.

For early Jewish writers the sea was a creation symbol. Conversely, the Dead Sea, which is saturated with salt, is lifeless and is described in Hebrew symbolism as a spiritual wilderness. The iniquitous cities of Sodom and Gomorrah are thought to have been on the southern shore of the Dead Sea.

RIVERS

A flowing river commonly represents time, history or the span of a human life. Its source can represent conception and birth, while its outlet into the sea often symbolizes death and the afterlife. Islamic, Jewish, Christian, Hindu and Buddhist traditions tell of four rivers of life that flow from paradise towards the four directions, symbolically dividing the earth into quarters. They are associated with enlightenment, spiritual power, nourishment and death.

The life-giving nature of rivers probably relates to the fertility of their banks, which led early civilizations to grow up around the Nile in Egypt, the Indus in India, and the Tigris and Euphrates in Mesopotamia. Rivers are also natural boundaries, and mythical rivers often separate the dead from the living, such as the sacred Styx that bounded Hades, and the Japanese Sanzunokawa.

The Yoruba of West Africa believe that the goddess Yemoja transformed into the river Ogun. In Russia, the Votjak throw offerings into the river to appease the water spirit after the festivities of Twelfth Night. The river Ganges is also revered as the goddess Ganga. Pilgrims take water from her *shakti*, or female

LEFT A painting that depicts Poseidon, or Neptune, creating the horse, one of his sacred animals, and a symbol of natural springs.

source, in the Himalayas and pour it over a lingam (phallus) at a village called Ramesvaram, 3,200km/2,000 miles away, uniting the river goddess with Shiva, the male god of fertility.

SPRINGS, WELLS AND WATERFALLS

Water emerging from the ground has a special connection with the underworld and the source of life. Wells and springs are commonly associated with the womb of the earth and were thought to have powers to fulfil wishes, foretell the future and confer healing. In Europe, holy wells sprang up in sacred places where saints had been martyred, dragons had been defeated or the Virgin Mary had appeared. Those known as "granny wells" were believed to aid fertility and childbirth, and a closed well symbolized virginity.

Prophecies were often read in wells or pools by observing movements in the water surface, patterns made by floating leaves, or fish and eels swimming in their depths. At Glastonbury, in Somerset, England, the waters of the Chalice Well were said to be tinged red by the blood of Christ, which was carried to England in the Holy Grail.

Springs and wells commonly symbolize the source of life. The Zuñi people of New Mexico believe that the first humans emerged via springs from the underworld, and also tell of a plumed serpent living in the waters of their sacred springs. The Zuñi therefore avoid killing snakes to protect their water supply.

WHIRLPOOLS

The interaction of opposing currents in large bodies of water leads to vortices, which at their most powerful can suck a boat into the depths. In the Odyssey, the whirlpool that tries to suck Odysseus' boat into the sea is personified as the monster Charybdis, offspring of the gods Gaia and Poseidon. Odysseus survives only by clinging to the branch of an overhanging tree. In his poem The Wasteland, which explores the theme of loss, T.S. Eliot uses a whirlpool to symbolize death and annihilation.

FLOODS

All flood stories can be understood as symbolizing the chaos that arises when humanity is out of alignment with the spiritual laws of nature. The biblical stories of the flood that wiped out the human race probably originated in southern Mesopotamia (now Iraq), where the Tigris and Euphrates meet – a fertile area prone to severe floods, which may also have been the origin of the Garden of Eden. The biblical story of Noah describes

the Flood as God's punishment of human sinfulness. Noah, the virtuous man, builds an ark and survives the flood, eventually repopulating the world. In the Babylonian epic of Gilgamesh, Utnapishtim tells Gilgamesh of a seven-day flood, which he survived by building a ship for his family, servants and animals; it finally came to rest upon a mountaintop, whereupon the gods granted Utnapishtim and his wife immortality.

Flood stories are told in many other cultures. The Kimberley people of Western Australia have a place called Wullunggnari, where three stones represent a Dreamtime flood that devastated all, except for a boy and a girl, who grabbed the tail of a kangaroo that took them to higher ground. The two became the ancestors of all human beings.

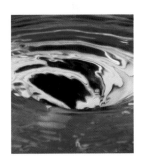

WATER AND ISLAM

In the Islamic tradition water features centrally as the source and sustenance of life and for purification. Rain, rivers and fountains are symbolic of the benevolence and mercy of Allah, who is said to love those who purify themselves with water.

AIR AND SKY

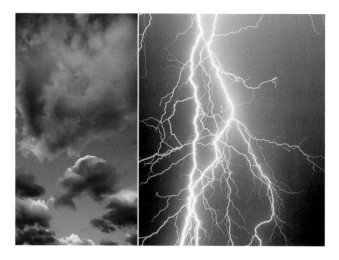

ABOVE In mystical Islam, clouds are a symbol of the primordial, unknowable state of Allah before creation.

ABOVE RIGHT In many cultures, thunder and lightning are symbols of divine power.

The skies are the dwelling place of the gods, who control the elemental forces that impact on human life on earth, inspiring both fear and wonder. Hence clouds, wind and storm, thunder and lightning have all been seen as divine manifestations and imbued with symbolic associations. Air fills the space between earth and sky and in symbolic terms is linked with the wind, the breath and spirit. It is an invisible, animating force that links the individual with the cosmos, and very often is the medium by which the gods communicate with humankind. Air is usually related to the masculine archetype.

WEATHER VANE

The wind is a symbol of change – a new wind direction signals changing weather conditions. On churches, the traditional design for a weathervane is a cockerel perched on top of a cross indicating the four directions. The bird symbolizes watchfulness against evil, which could be "blown in" by the wind.

THE WIND

Typically, the wind is associated with the four compass directions. Each is represented by different deities or qualities, and is the harbinger of different weather conditions according to the local climate. Along the north-west coast of America, the native Tsimshian believe that the four great winds were the great chiefs of the four corners of the world; after deliberating how their powers should be balanced, the four seasons were established. For the ancient Greeks, the four winds were viewed as boisterous and rebellious gods imprisoned in the caverns of Aeolus, chief god of the winds; their names were Boreas (the north wind), Auster (the south wind), Eureus (the east and morning wind) and Zephyr (the west and evening wind).

Knowledge of air currents and their effects is central to the Chinese art of feng shui. The Chinese identify eight rather than four winds, corresponding to the eight trigrams that form the basis of the I Ching. According to one legend, the wind was the creation of the White Tiger of the West, while in another story the winds were let out of a sack. The Japanese god Fujin was also said to keep the wind in a sack. The Celts used their knowledge of the winds to predict the weather, while the supernatural "Druid's wind", created at will by the exhalations of a Druid, signified power over the elements and allied the breath with the wind as a vehicle for magic.

Among the Native American Apache, the whorls on the fingertips are said to show the path of the wind entering the body at the time of creation, while the whorls on the soles of the feet show how the wind (or soul) will leave the body at death. The wind is widely thought to communicate with humans: among the Navajo, Wind's Child whispers to the heroes of their stories. Alternatively, the wind may "speak" through an instrument: examples include the bull roarer used by Australian Aboriginals and Native American shamans, and the Aeolian harp of the ancient Greeks. The wind's many "moods" are described in vocal terms such as "roaring", "sighing" or "whispering".

CLOUDS

Because of their cloaking character and their connection with the heavens, clouds are associated with the mysteries of the divine in many traditions. In the Judaeo-Christian tradition, clouds sometimes indicate the presence of God: in the Old Testament he appeared as a pillar of cloud to lead his people through the desert during the Exodus, and in Christian iconography he is sometimes represented as a hand emerging from a cloud, while Christ is said to have ascended to Heaven on a cloud. The Taoist immortals rose up to Heaven on clouds and, in Norse mythology, the Valkyries (female spirits and servants of Odin) rode on clouds.

As bringers of rain, clouds are connected with fertility and nature's abundance. In China, the word for cloud is a homonym for

RIGHT The Norse god of thunder, Thor, wields his mighty hammer, Mjölnir, in a fight against giants.

WIND OF THE SOUL

In some traditions, it is thought that the vital energy of the cosmos is carried in the air, so that when people breathe, they are breathing in life force, known to the Chinese as chi and to Hindus as prana. The Inuit have a similar concept, known as sila, an all-pervasive, life-giving spirit that connects every living being with the rhythms of the universe. When a person is out of touch with sila, they are disconnected from their spirit.

"fortune", associating clouds with good luck. It is also said that wispy dawn clouds brought the five Chinese elements (fire, water, air, earth and metal) down from the five sacred mountaintops, and that clouds were formed from the union of yin and yang. In Taoism, they are symbols of the state that humans must pass through before reaching enlightenment – the mental fog that exists before clarity is attained. The colloquial expression "head in the clouds" suggests someone who is lost in fanciful ideas and out of touch with reality, while "living under a cloud" suggests a burden or disgrace. The Maori name for New Zealand – Aotearoa – means "Land of the Long White Cloud".

STORMS

Violent winds such as hurricanes, whirlwinds and tornadoes are symbols of elemental and divine power. Storm deities are figures of awesome power who embody the forces of disorder and turmoil; they include the Japanese Susano-O, the ancient Greek Poseidon

and the Maya storm god, Huracán, from whom we get the word "hurricane". As bringers of rain, they may also be associated with fertility, as with Baal, the ancient Canaanite storm god. The Maori say that blustery winds and storms are created by the wind god Tawiri-Matea to punish his disobedient brother Tane-Mahuta (god of mankind and the forests), who separated their parents, the earth and sky, to create light. In the West, storms have been seen as the work of the devil. In some Native American traditions, moths are associated with whirlwinds because of the swirly pattern of their cocoons and the whirring noise of their wings.

Storms are often associated with warrior gods and supreme male deities: Indra, the Hindu warrior god, was known as Vajiri ("wielder of thunderbolts") as thunder and lightning were his chief weapons, and a thunderbolt was the main weapon of the supreme Greek god, Zeus.

In the Bible, thunder is the voice of an angry God. The Celts interpreted it as a cosmic disturbance, a punishment from the gods who were invoking the wrath of the elements. In Africa, thunder and lightning are also associated with earthly rulers. The Yoruba of West Africa believe that Shango, the great god of thunder, was the greatest of their warrior-monarchs, while in Benin, thunderbolts are symbols of kingship, sometimes shown as brass pythons zigzagging down from the turrets of high buildings.

In Hinduism and Buddhism, a diamond-shaped thunderbolt

(*vajra*) symbolizes destructive and creative powers – destroying illusions and wrongdoing so that clarity and good can prevail. In Native American myth, the spirit of thunder and lightning is symbolized by the thunderbird, a fierce beast but also a protector of humanity; thunderstorms are believed to be the sound of its battles against underworld beings.

THUNDER HAMMERS

In many cultures the hammer or axe is a symbol of thunder and lightning. The symbol of Shango, the thunder god of the Yoruba, is a double-headed axe, representing the thunderbolts of stone that the god unleashes from the heavens. In Norse mythology, Mjölnir was the hammer of the thunder god Thor. Mjölnir created lightning when struck against stone and could turn into a thunderbolt when it was thrown. It was also a symbol of Thor's beneficence and was used in ceremonies to bless infants and brides.

BELOW This relief of the Canaanite god Baal shows his status as the god of storms by depicting him holding a thunderbolt, but Baal was also associated with fertility because of his rain-bringing qualities.

FIRE

The symbolism of fire is wide-ranging, though it repeatedly arises as a central motif for the life force. It can be an intimate and personal force of love, passion and warmth, or aggressively pent up in the form of hatefulness and revenge. But fire is also a universal symbol of divine power, wrath or truth, and also of the uncontrolled forces of nature wreaking destruction and bringing about renewal. In many world cosmologies fire is associated with both creation and apocalypse, shining in paradise and burning in Hell.

Fire has been harnessed by humans for protection, light and warmth, and as a focus for stories, trance and dreaming. It is an essential element of transformation in cooking, initiation and funerary rites, and in driving the physical and spiritual processes of alchemy and science. The Chinese associate fire, rising upwards, with yang, or male, qualities. It is an active element associated with creativity and upward striving, and never rests until it has consumed that which fuels it.

Fire is often associated with strong emotions, conflict and war. Conflict can be the source of great emotional energy, and, like a fire, can lead to warmth, heat, motivation and light, but can also burn, damage and destroy. In the alchemical sense, the fire of conflict can truly lead to transformation, as long as it is neither given too much air, nor deprived of air or consciousness.

FIRE THEFT

The theft of fire is a symbolic theme pointing to its origins and its value to humanity. The act separates humans from animals in harnessing a force unavailable to them. Australian Aboriginal myths tell of the secret of fire being stolen from the birds or animals. In Greek mythology, the cunning Prometheus stole fire for humankind from the supreme god Zeus. In revenge, Zeus ordered the creation of the first woman, Pandora, and presented her to Prometheus' brother. She brought with her a box containing great afflictions, which spread over the earth.

VOLCANOES

Every volcano in the world has a particular character or personality, from dormant giants erupting violently after long periods of time, to volatile fuming mountains that never quite simmer down. Whatever their character, volcanoes command both respect and fear. Psychologically they symbolize power, volatility and simmering or pent-up anger, followed by outbursts of violent aggression.

Vulcano was the name of a small island off Sicily, and also the chimney for the forge of Vulcan, the Roman blacksmith god. In his forge Vulcan beat out

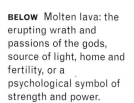

THE PHOENIX

A mythical bird of Arabia, the phoenix was the size of an eagle with magnificent scarlet and gold feathers. At the end of its life it made a fire from its own nest and was consumed in flames, then reborn from the ashes. The ancient Egyptians viewed the phoenix as a symbol of immortality, while Christians related the myth to the resurrection and for Romans it represented Rome's undying nature. The Chinese saw the phoenix as a gentle creature, feeding on dewdrops and, through the union of the energies of yin and yang, embodying the qualities of virtue, grace, wealth and power.

FIREWORKS

It is thought that gunpowder was invented either in China or in India. The first firecrackers were made in the Chinese Han Dynasty (206 BC-AD 220) and was originally used to frighten away evil spirits. Later it was associated with prayers for happiness and prosperity. In America the early settlers celebrated holidays by firing black gunpowder. Nowadays, when many rites of passage have been lost, fireworks are used in dramatic displays marking important events such as New Year and American Independence Day.

MAYA FIRE CEREMONIES

The Maya believed that by creating a vortex of energy they could open a portal to the spirit worlds of the ancestors, through which they could pay respect and receive healing. They formed a sacred fire by drawing a circle of sugar on the ground, then placing on it resin, cedar, sage, rosemary, tobacco, lavender, flowers, and finally chocolate and honey, representing life's sweetness. The circle was set alight, with the belief that the offerings would be answered with blessings.

thunderbolts for Jupiter and weaponry for Mars, the god of war. Vesuvius in Italy is well known for entirely burying in ash the Roman towns of Pompeii and Stabiae in AD 79. The Roman poet Virgil (70 BC-AD 19) described its craters as seeping with the blood of giants, and wrote that a giant called Alyconeus lay beneath it. At the time of the eruptions, stories emerged of giants leaping through the smoke and ripping the mountainside to pieces.

In Hawaii, the islands have been formed by continuous volcanic activity, and legends tell of Pele, a most beautiful goddess of volcanoes, who is prone to periodic outbursts of anger. She caused earthquakes through the irate stamping of her feet and made volcanoes erupt by digging in the earth with her magic stick, the Pa'oa. Kilauea is the most active volcano on earth and is considered to be Pele's home.

Volcanoes are often associated with the wrath of the gods, but are also sources of light, power, and the tremendous fertility of volcanic ash. In British Columbia, the Tsimshian people believe that

the trickster Raven brought light to humanity from a volcano.

The Aztec goddess of the hearth, home and fertility was also the goddess of the volcano. She was a symbol of both pleasure and pain, and was the ruler of wealth and precious stones. The Taal volcano in the Philippines, which enchantingly floats in the Taal Lake, is one of the smallest volcanoes and yet is considered to be deadly. It is said to symbolize the fearless strength of the people of the Batangas province, which is hidden beneath their apparent calmness.

FIRE IN RELIGION

In many religious traditions, fire is associated with the truths and illusions organizing spiritual experience. Zoroastrians consider fire to be the source of all creation, and each household has a sacred fire, the lighting of which is associated with a blessing. Zoroastrian fire temples are places of community worship, attended by priests who feed the sacred fires with incense. These fires symbolize interaction with Ahura Mazda, the lord of wisdom.

Judaism considers fire to be a fundamental element that should accompany all offerings made to God, and perpetual fires were kept burning at the altar of the Temple. The image of the angel of the Lord appearing to Moses through a burning bush illustrates the Hebrew belief that fire signifies true communication from God. In Christianity, candles are a reminder of the presence of God, and also represent hope and life. Fire is a powerful symbol of renewal and baptism, burning away sinfulness to leave only God's truth.

Buddhism often uses fire to symbolize forces that remove a person from enlightenment, such as desire, greed, hatred and ignorance, and therefore the extinguishing of these fires symbolizes nirvana. But Buddhism also uses an inner flame to represent enlightenment.

THE GOMA

Japanese Yamabushi monks, adherents of Tendai Buddhism, have performed Goma fire ceremonies for 12 centuries, to appease the wrath of Fudo Myo-o, the lord of calamities such as war, earthquakes and destructive fire. The heart sutra is chanted to the beat of a drum, followed by the blowing of conch shell horns. The priest feeds a fire with oils, seeds and cedar to create the smoke that carries prayers to Fudo Myo-o.

BELOW Jews believed that God's appearance in fire marked it as a true divine communication.

THE RAINBOW

ABOVE The rainbow has variously been associated with healing and good fortune, dreams and imaginary worlds, fertility and childbirth, and even with transsexual experience.

Elusive, ethereal and transient, the rainbow appears symbolically in myth and folklore, sacred tradition, art and science, as well as in contemporary Western culture, with a range of meanings as diverse as its colours. In different traditions the rainbow has been venerated as god and goddess, feared as demon and pestilence, seen as a symbol of optimism and hope, of divine covenant and peace and as an omen of war and retribution. Its arching shape links it symbolically with the circle, the bridge and the bow, while in some traditions it is also associated with the serpent.

THE RAINBOW BRIDGE

The bridge is an archetypal symbol of transition, and in this guise the rainbow is the pathway between Heaven and Earth, or a link between different worlds. In the Japanese creation myth, the twin deities Izanagi and Izanami stand on the Floating Bridge of Heaven to create the land, and a belief of southern Gabon states that human ancestors arrived on Earth by walking down a rainbow. In Norse myth, Bifrost was the rainbow bridge that connected Asgard, the land of the gods, to Midgard, the earthly realm. Bifrost was said to be very strong and built with more skill than any other structure in the world. Heimdall, the guardian of Asgard, lived beside it to alert the gods to enemy invaders.

The Navajo believe that the rainbow is a bridge between the human and spirit worlds, while shamanic traditions across North America believe that supernatural journeys to the land of the dead involve crossing a rainbow bridge. Shamans of the Buryat, in Siberia ascend to the spirit world via the rainbow, which they symbolize with a pair of red and blue ribbons tied to a ceremonial birch tree. Some rainbow bridges are manmade structures: the name was given to Chinese bridges of woven construction, spanning streams that were too wide or swift for conventional pier bridges – one built in the 13th century still bears traffic today. There are also rainbow bridges over the Niagara River and in Tokyo Bay.

DIVINE PRESENCE

The rainbow is often interpreted as a divine attribute and a sign of divine presence. Ishtar, the Babylonian goddess of love and war, wore an iridescent necklace, and the Inca believed that rainbows were the feather crown of Illapa, the god of thunder and rain. The bow – the archer's weapon – can betoken the god's wrath. Indra, the Hindu god of war, shot his thunderbolt from a

RIGHT The gods of the Vikings descend from Heaven to Earth using the rainbow bridge that the Norse legends named Bifrost.

rainbow, and in Cambodia and parts of India the rainbow is known as "Indra's Bow". Tiermes, the thunder god of the Lapps of Scandinavia, used the rainbow to fire arrows at evil spirits.

In contrast, in the Judaeo-Christian tradition the rainbow is a sign of peace and compassion, a symbol of God's promise after the Flood not to destroy humankind. Christ is sometimes shown enthroned on a rainbow at the Last Judgement, demonstrating

RIGHT There is no consensus on the colours of the rainbow. According to the Dogon, there are four: black, red, yellow and green. In Buddhist iconography there are five: blue, white, green, red and yellow. Western science usually admits seven: red, orange, yellow, green, blue, indigo and violet.

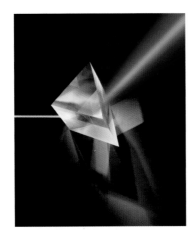

his heavenly power and his mercy. In Tibet, where rainbows occur at transitional times of the year and indicate changing weather, they are associated with blessings from the bodhisattvas of Tibetan Buddhism.

There is a widespread belief among Central African Pygmies that the rainbow is an instrument of divine communication, and in some cultures it marks the location of a divinity or person of high birth: in Hawaiian folklore the noblewoman Hoamakeikekula was tracked by following a rainbow. The rainbow was associated with Iris, the golden-winged messenger of the Greek gods, who is often depicted holding a caduceus, the messenger's snake-entwined staff. The Maya made offerings of gold and silver to the patron deity of women, Ixchel, goddess of medicine, fertility and the rainbow, who controlled the rain.

RAINBOW LEGENDS

There are many legends and customs surrounding rainbows. The Sioux say that the rainbow is where all the bright flowers are stored before and after their brief blooming period on earth. In Irish folklore, the leprechaun is a mischievous sprite who keeps a pot of gold at the end of the rainbow; in Celtic tradition, rainbow coins were to be found there, buried in the earth but revealed after heavy storms.

However, rainbows are not always associated with beauty and

good fortune. Ancient Peruvians claimed that if a rainbow were to enter a person's body, it would cause illness; a cure was to unravel a ball of rainbow-coloured threads to undo the rainbow's ill effects. Ideas of rainbow-borne disease also appear throughout Africa, Asia and Australia: for the Senoi of Malaysia, walking underneath a rainbow causes fatal fever, and Australian Aboriginals associate it with leprosy. Pointing at rainbows is considered foolhardy in many parts of the world: Hungarian folk belief insists the pointing finger will wither, while the Sumu of

Honduras and Nicaragua hide their children in huts to stop them pointing or even looking at a rainbow. Getting jaundice, losing an eye, being struck by lightning or even disappearing are some of the dangers associated with rainbows.

ABOVE When Christ is pictured with a rainbow in Christian art it is usually a symbol of the merciful aspects of his heavenly powers.

THE RAINBOW BODY

Related to the chakra system, the rainbow body may be thought of as fields of energy surrounding the human body, each associated with different qualities.

Level	Colour	Body	Qualities
1st outermost circle or layer	red	physical (temporal)	the foundation upon which all other levels are constructed
2nd	orange	etheric (temporal)	early emotional environment and formative influences; the body's energy pattern
3rd	yellow	astral (transitional)	influences of culture and society, such as religious and educational institutions, and how these shape thought and action
4th	green	mental (transitional)	achieves purpose in life through relationship with others; interface between the temporal and eternal
5th	blue	causal (transpersonal)	attuned to soul; repository of the soul's memories, empowers its journey
6th	indigo	diamond (bliss body) (transpersonal)	thinking superseded by intuitively received knowing
7th innermost layer or core	violet	celestial (eternal)	enlightenment; the individual soul merges into the cosmos, union with the divine

PART THREE

DIRECTORY OF SIGNS

From early cave drawings to contemporary logos, graphic symbols have been used to carry ideas, concepts and meaning. The following pages contain over 1000 ideograms, graphic motifs, symbols and line drawings. Each sign or symbol has a brief explanation of its meaning or use. Some of the most primitive symbols have multiple meanings, or meanings that have now been lost or superceded, others, like the spiral, have a universal consistent meaning. Many of the signs in these pages are talked about in more depth in other sections of the book. Signs such as the cross or alchemical symbols such as mercury, have an astonishing number of variations, and many of these are included to show the fascinating diversity of the symbols human society uses to convey both the tangible and the abstract.

RIGHT Cave paintings of the human hand have been found in South Africa, South America and Australia. Did the hands have the same poignancy to those who painted them, were they meant as signatures? We will never know, but it is universal signs like this that weave a continuous fabric of communication throughout our cultures.

A The first letter of the alphabet, used to signify the best, first.

ACTIVE INTELLECT Unknown origin, also one of the signs for water.

ADINKRAHENE Most important of the Ghanaian adinkra symbols, signifying the importance of playing a leading role.

ADONI Hebrew word meaning a lord who is not God.

AEROPLANE Spiritual aspiration, and the transcendence of human limitations.

AIR The element. Kabbalistic sign.

AIR The element. Old chemistry symbol.

AKOBEN Ghanaian adinkra symbol meaning vigilance and wariness. The akoben is a horn used to sound a battle cry.

AKOKONAN "Leg of the hen", Ghanaian adinkra symbol meaning mercy, nurturing. Inspired by the hen's habit of treading on her chicks without hurting them, being a protective but also corrective parent.

AKOMA NTOSO Ghanaian adinkra symbol meaning understanding and agreement.

ALCHEMY, the art of. The sun sign is at the centre, surrounded by the four elemental triangles, crowned with the Christian cross, and then placed in a circle representing the eternal or spiritual dimension.

ALCHEMY, the art of, variation. Used in the 17th century, this sign was created under the influence of Pythagorean geometry mysticism.

ALCHEMY, the art of, variation. This symbol is also engraved on rock faces dating from 1000 BC in Uxmal,

Central America. The symbol was adopted by Rudolf Steiner and is associated with Steiner's anthroposophy.

ALCOHOL Alchemistic sign.

ALCOHOL Early chemical sign.

ALEMBIC Alchemistic sign for distillation flask or still. Also used in early chemistry.

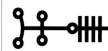

ALGOL The fixed star, used in some Kabbalistic mysticist contexts on magical amulet seals.

ALGORAB The fixed star, used in Kabbalistic magical amulet seals.

ALINEA Typographical sign used in printed texts, meaning the beginning of a new train of thought.

ALL IS WELL Ground to air emergency code.

ALMOND An important symbol with pagan and Christian roots associated with purity and virgin birth. Its juice was associated with semen in the ancient world. Biblical tradition says that Aaron's priestly status was shown by his rod blossoming and producing almonds. Western art often shows Mary and Jesus enclosed in an almond-shaped aureole.

ALPHA The first letter of the Greek alphabet, associated with beginnings. Linked with God, who is said to be the alpha and omega – the beginning and the end. Also once a secret sign of the Christian faith.

ALPHECCA The fixed star, used as a Kabbalistic magical amulet seal.

ALUM Alchemistic sign.

AMALGAM Alchemistic sign.

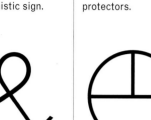

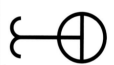

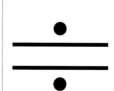
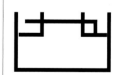

207

AMALGAMATION Alchemistic sign.

AMPERSAND Typographical sign meaning "and".

ANARCHISM Synonym for the political movement.

ANCHOR In early Christianity, a secret sign for the cross; hope, salvation. Also a symbol of the sea; of steadfastness and safety; and of the self.

ANGEL Symbol of divine will in several traditions, heavenly creatures in Jewish, Christian and Islamic traditions, thought to be evolved from Semitic and Egyptian winged deities. Seen as messengers, warriors, guardians or protectors.

ANIMALIA The animal kingdom, 18th century.

ANKH A cross topped with a loop; ancient Egyptian symbol of immortal life. Later adopted as a Christian symbol by the Egyptian Coptic Church.

ANSUR Rune for A

ANT Hard work, organized community. The anthill is a symbol of industrious life in Tibetan Buddhism; in parts of Africa it is associated with fertility and creativity.

ANTARES The fixed star, Kabbalistic magical amulet seal.

ANTELOPE In Africa associated with the moon and fecundity; for the Bambara (Mali) the animal was sent by the creator god to teach humans agriculture.

ANTI NUCLEAR CAMPAIGN The emblem of the Campaign for Nuclear Disarmament, made up of the semaphore signs for the letters "N" and "D".

ANTI-CLOCKWISE SPIRAL Dynamic symbol of life force, cosmic and earthly.

ANTIMONY Alchemistic, also used in medicine.

ANVIL In Polynesia and parts of Africa, associated with the female principle and fertility; in Scottish folklore, linked with magical powers of the blacksmith.

APE Respected in ancient Egypt, Africa, India and China, but distrusted in the Christian tradition, where it is a symbol of vice and lust.

APHRODITE Sign of the goddess.

APOLLO This symbol of the god is based on the shape of the lyre, which was Apollo's instrument.

APPLE Symbol of bliss, especially sexual; emblem of love, marriage, spring, youth, fertility and immortality. Linked with the forbidden fruit of the Garden of Eden and so a Christian symbol of temptation and original sin.

APPROXIMATELY EQUAL TO Mathematical sign.

APRICOT In China, the apricot is a symbol for a beautiful woman; the Japanese plum (*ume*) is sometimes called an apricot.

AQUA REGIA Alchemistic sign for "king's water".

AQUA REGIA Alchemistic sign for king's water, variation.

AQUARIUS Zodiac sign.

ARATHRON Planet, mystical Kabbalistic sign for the first Olympic spirit.

ARCH Triumph and victory; grand human achievements.

ARCTURUS The fixed star, Kabbalistic magic amulet seal.

ARES Sign of the god.

ARES Sign of the god, variation.

ARES Sign of the god, variation.

ARIES Zodiac sign.

ARK OF THE COVENANT One of the symbols of the Jewish faith, a chest that was God's pledge of divine protection. The ark was kept in another symbol of Judaism, the Tabernacle.

ARK OR BOAT A symbol of salvation and preservation found in the mythology of peoples all around the world. In Christianity the ark stands for the Church, for Mary or for Christ; in secular symbolism it is a symbol of the Earth adrift in space.

ARM Symbol of power and strength; the many arms given to

Hindu gods symbolize their complexity and power. An upraised arm can suggest either a threat or a blessing. The arm also has protective connotations.

ARMOUR In medieval Europe, armour symbolized the knightly virtues of courage, protection, honour and strength; symbol of warrior class in China and Japan.

ARROW As directional sign.

ARROW/ARROW HEAD Penetration – by light, death, love or perception. Linked to sun symbols and the piercing darts of love.

ARROW, CURVED Ancient sign found in prehistoric cave art in Western Europe.

ARROW, WAVY Sea currents.

ARROW, WEAPON In Islam stands for the wrath of Allah, in Christianity for martyrdom and death. Bundled or broken in Native American symbolism, arrows stand for peace.

ARSENIC Alchemistic sign.

ARSENIC Alchemistic sign, variation.

ARSENIC Alchemistic sign, variation.

ARSENIC Alchemistic sign, variation.

ASS The god, later oss, rune for rapids or waterfall.

ASS See Donkey

ASTERISK Typographical sign for footnote.

ATOM Also uranium, nuclear reactor (on maps), nuclear research, nuclear physics.

ATOM, less common variation than above.

AUDI Corporate emblem of the car manufacturers, symbol of unity and togetherness.

AUROCH The rune Ur, sign for auroch.

AUTUMN Old Germanic time sign.

AUTUMN Old Germanic time sign, variation.

AXE Almost universal symbol of decisive power and authority. Associated with the creative force of the thunderbolt. Linked with ancient sun and storm gods. Used to invoke thunder and rain in West Africa; symbol of the union of families in Chinese marriage.

BADGER Linked with playfulness in China; in Celtic tradition with slyness, deceit.

BALL Symbol of childhood games; in China, associated with the sun and the yin/yang symbol.

BAMBOO Chinese symbol of resilience, longevity, happiness

and spiritual truth; Japanese symbol of truth and devotion.

BANANA Freudian phallic symbol.

BASILISK A medieval symbol of lust and disease.

BASKET Womb symbol; in the Americas, stories about baskets and basket-making are related to women.

BASS CLEF Music notation.

BAT Associated with death, symbol of fear and superstition, linked with witchcraft and the occult in Western folklore. In Africa and ancient Greece it was a symbol of perspicuity. Can signify madness. Underworld divinity in Central American and Brazilian mythology.

BATH Associated with bathing and thus with purification, both spiritual and physical.

BEANS Symbol of fecundity, used as love charms in India and to ward off evil spirits in Japan.

BEAR Emblem of masculine courage and primeval force; while she-bears symbolize care and warmth – although Jung linked them with dangerous aspects of the unconscious. In Christian and Islamic traditions the bear is cruel and lustful.

BEARD Important aspect of male symbolism, representing dignity, sovereignty, virility and wisdom. Sign of a king; in ancient Egypt beardless rulers, including women, were depicted with false beards to proclaim their status.

BEE/BEEHIVE Society, industry and working together; honeybees are also linked with romantic love in European, Chinese and Hindu traditions. Bees are linked with death and the otherworld in European folklore.

BELL The voice that proclaims the truth, especially in Buddhist, Hindu, Islamic and Christian traditions. In China it symbolizes obedience and cosmic harmony. Small tinkling bells can represent happiness and sexual pleasure. Worn on Hebrew dresses as a sign of virginity. Linked with the

feminine principle, also protective. Marks the passing of time and proclaims good news, warns of danger and tolls for death.

BELT OR GIRDLE Female chastity, marital fidelity or seductiveness. Magic girdles appear in myth as emblems of strength and became a symbol of honour in England. The rope girdles of monks allude to the scourging of Christ. The Hindu girdle is an emblem of the cycles of time.

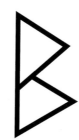

BEORC Rune for B.

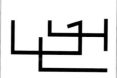

BETHOR The planet; mystical Kabbalistic sign for the second Olympic spirit.

BIOHAZARD Warning, USA.

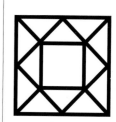

BIRCH Beneficial, protective, sacred to Germanic gods. Cosmic tree of Central Asia. In shamanic rites it symbolized human ascent to the spirit world.

BIRDS Symbol of the human soul, representing goodness and joy, standing for wisdom, intelligence and the swift power of thought. Aboriginal stories suggest they bear information. In Western art birds can symbolize air and touch.

BIRTH CHART Elizabethan England, 17th century.

209

210

BISON/BUFFALO High-status animal in India and South-east Asia. In China the domestic buffalo is associated with the contemplative life. For North American Indians it symbolizes strength, prosperity, plenty and supernatural power.

BJARKAN Rune associated with new life and growth.

BLESSED SIGN One of the blessed signs that appears, among other places, in the early symbolism of the Buddha's footprints in India. In the West this symbol stands for the hexachord, and for harmonics in general.

BLESSING/HARMLESS A variation of the pope's cross.

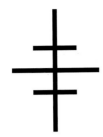

BLINDFOLD/BLIND Spiritual blindness; in Masonic ritual, removing the blindfold symbolizes spiritual illumination. In classical antiquity, Fortuna (goddess of fortune) is blindfolded to show that she favours none above any other.

BMW Corporate emblem of the car manufacturer, a variation of the sun cross, the ancient structure for the sun's energy.

BOAR Primordial symbol of strength, aggression and resolute courage

across the northern and the Celtic worlds. Sacred as a sun symbol in Iran, and a moon symbol in Japan. It became a Christian symbol for tyranny and lust.

BOAT Symbol of womb-like protection, also linked to the salvation and regeneration symbolism of the ark.

BOIL/ABCESS Alchemical sign.

BOIL (verb). Old Germanic.

BOIL (verb). Alchemistic sign.

BONES Symbol of possible reincarnation or bodily resurrection for ancient societies. Ancient beliefs held that the essence of a person was contained in the bones, a connection that is echoed in the phrase "felt in the bones".

BOOK Symbol of knowledge and wisdom in many sacred traditions (Judaic, Christian, Islam); in ancient Egypt, the Book of the Dead was a collection of sacred charms buried with the dead to assist them in the afterlife.

BORAX Alchemistic sign.

BORAX/TINKAL Alchemistic sign.

BOW Symbol of stored energy, willpower, aspiration, love, divine power and tension. Emblem of war and hunting. In Oriental thought it also represented spiritual discipline.

BOWL/VESSEL Alchemistic.

BOX Symbol of womb and female unconscious, associated with secrets and hiding. In classical myth, Pandora's box is a symbol of what must not be opened.

BRACELET As jewellery can denote rank. May also be used as identity tags.

BRASS Alchemistic.

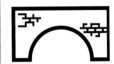

BREAD A staple of life, associated with hope in the Hebrew tradition, unleavened bread symbolizes purification and sacrifice. Christian metaphor for the food of the spirit, and the body of Christ.

BRIDGE Spans two distinct realms (Heaven and Earth, matter and spirit, the visible and the invisible); transition symbol, the crossing of one state to another.

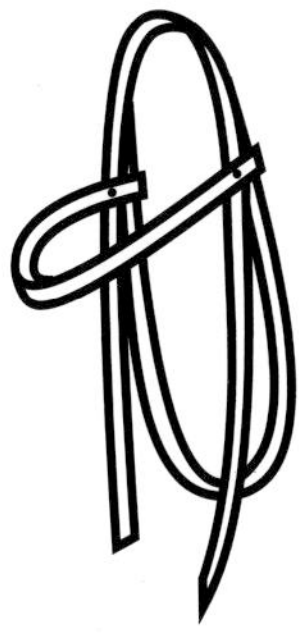

Bridle In classical antiquity, said to have been invented by Athena, goddess of peace and war; associated with temperance and restraint, as in "bridling" or the reining in of passions.

Broom Associated with magical powers from ancient times. A symbol of removal. Western folklore links brooms with witches due to the belief that evil spirits could bewitch the implement used to drive them out.

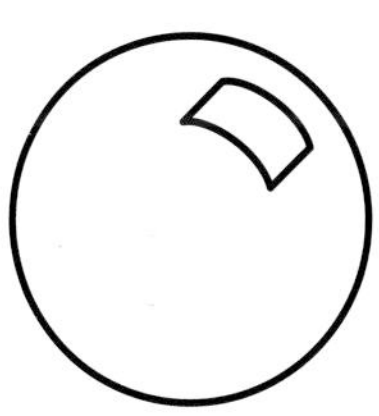

Bubble Symbol of illusion (Buddhism, Taoism); the transient and ephemeral.

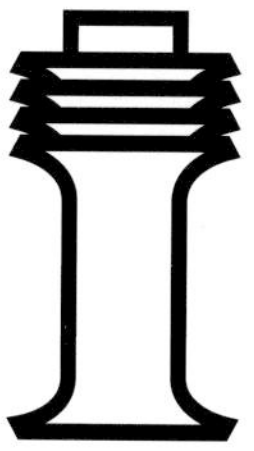

Buckle of Isis Ancient Egyptian protection sign.

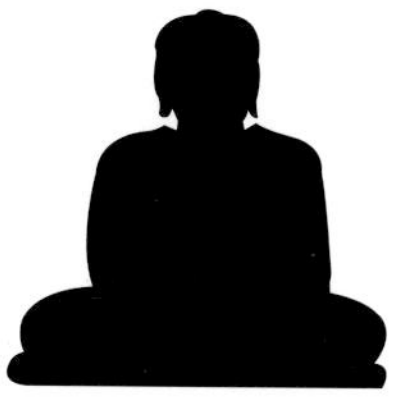

Buddha The seated Buddha is a symbol of enlightenment.

Buffalo See Bison

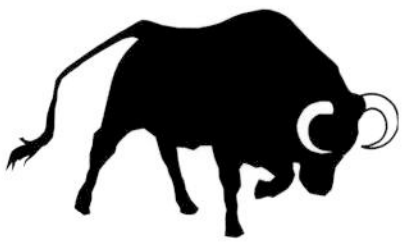

Bull Hugely symbolic animal representing moon, sun, earth, sky, rain, heat, feminine procreation, male ardour, matriarch and patriarch, death, regeneration. In cave art the bull is a symbol of vital energy. The bull's bellowing stamping energy is linked with thunder and earthquakes, especially in Crete.

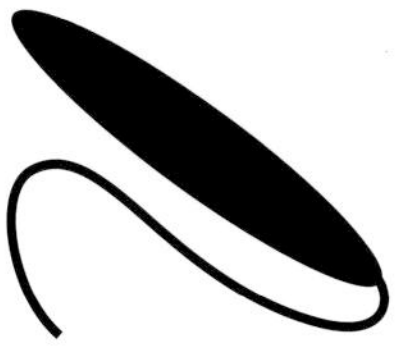

Bull roarer Musical instrument and cult object common to indigenous peoples (Americas, Australia); when whirled in the air, it makes an otherworldly roaring sound, similar to the sound of thunder. Used in shamanic ritual and initiation ceremonies to communicate with the spirit world and with the ancestors.

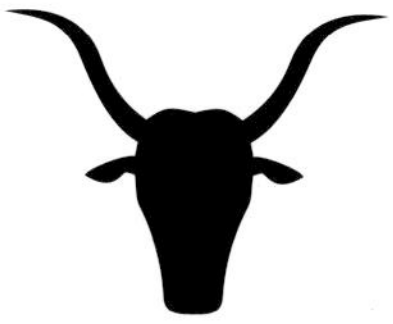

Bull's Horns Linked with the crescent moon.

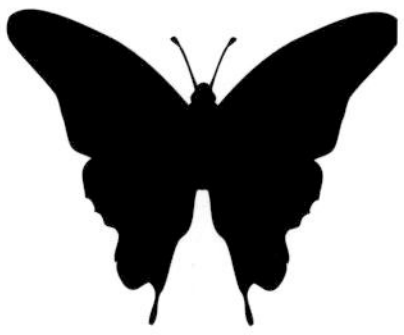

Butterfly Symbol of the soul and resurrection as far apart as Congo, Mexico and Polynesia. Also a symbol of life and its cycle; in Western art Christ is sometimes depicted as holding a butterfly.

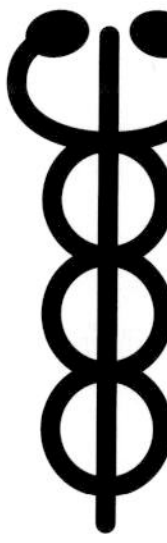

Caduceus The staff of the snake, the attribute of the Greek god Hermes, and the Roman equivalent Mercury, symbolizes the mediation between opposing forces and has been interpreted as an emblem of homeopathic medicine. The caduceus is also a symbol of commerce.

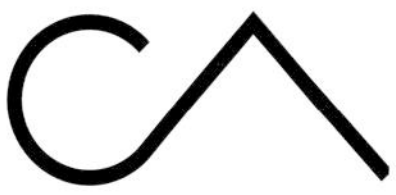

Calcinations Alchemistic sign.

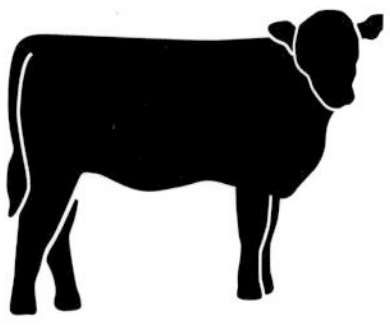

Calf Associated with feasting, hospitality and celebration (as in "the fatted calf") and also with sacrifice (Judaism).

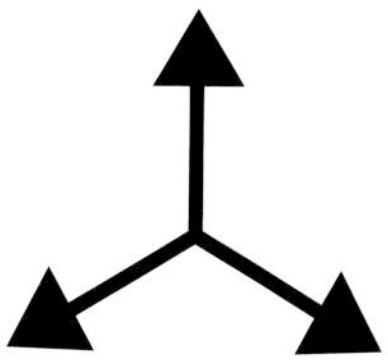

Caltrap Heraldic device, originally spiked objects used in battle to bring down cavalry horses.

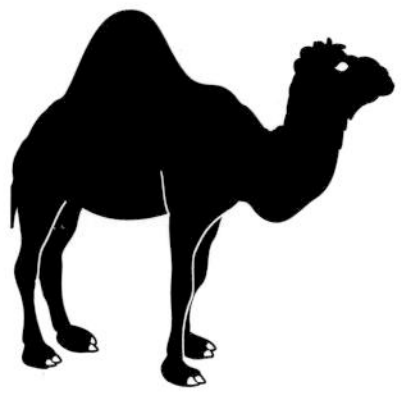

Camel Traditional symbol of wealth and status in the Middle East; in medieval Europe a symbol of temperance; in Christianity the camel is associated with humility and obedience.

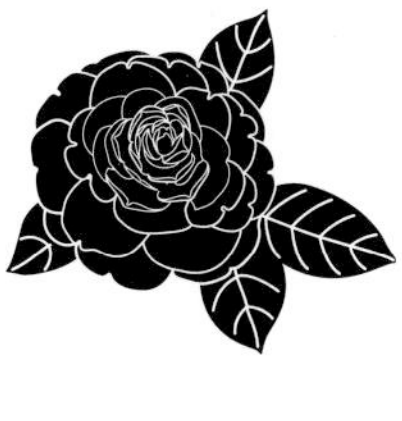

Camellia A Chinese symbol of health and fortitude. Associated in Japan with sudden death.

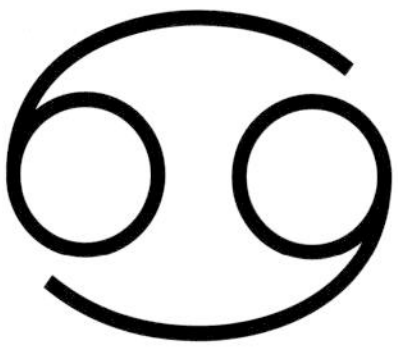

Cancer Zodiac sign.

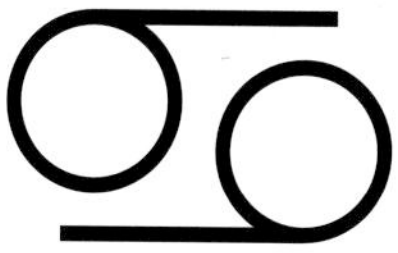

Cancer Zodiac sign, variation.

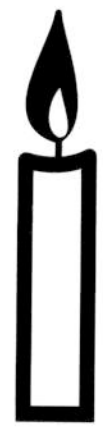

Candle A symbol of spiritual illumination, witness and joy. Its short-lived flame is a metaphor for the solitary, aspiring human soul.

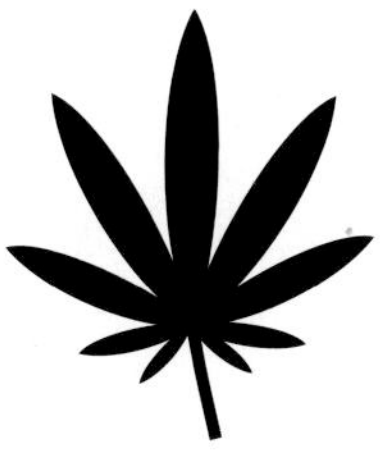

Cannabis leaf Symbol of Rastafarianism, whose followers believe it is a "holy herb" whose use is grounded in scripture; a symbol of protest against white mainstream society; also a symbol of youth culture in Western society.

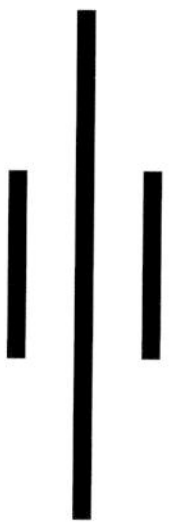

Cannon/gun Also iron in early chemistry.

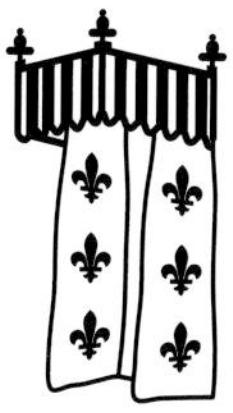

Canopy Shade and protection, also associated with royal power, symbol of heavenly protection.

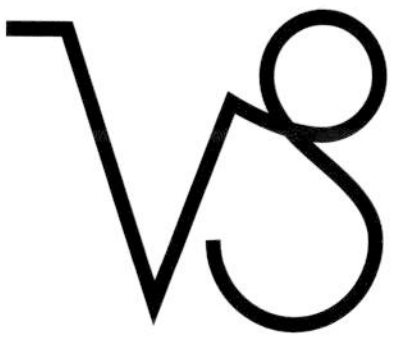

Capricorn Zodiac sign.

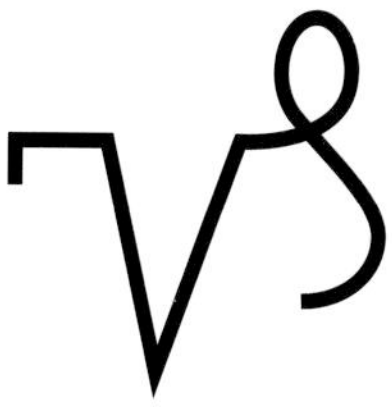

Capricorn Zodiac sign, variation.

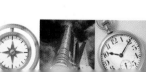

CAPRICORN Zodiac sign, variation.

CAPRICORN Zodiac sign, variation.

CARDS, PLAYING Associated with gaming, gambling and fortune-telling in Europe and Asia. The cards themselves contain symbolic imagery (the court cards, joker, the four suits) and numbers.

CARP In China an emblem of longevity, virility and scholarly success. Images of carp were used on ship's masts or roofs to ward off fire.

CARPET/RUG Sacred and secular use in the Middle East; used to mark and beautify holy and domestic spaces. In Europe, carpets have symbolized status, with a red carpet having ritual use in public ceremonies involving high-ranking dignitaries, royalty and celebrities.

CASTLE/FORTRESS Archetypal symbol of protection and a place of refuge (spiritual and temporal); a place that is set apart and hard to enter, containing the heart's desire.

CAT Symbol of transformation, clairvoyance, agility, watchfulness, sensual beauty, mystery and female malice. In Rome seen as emblem of liberty. Their nocturnal habits and powers of transformation were distrusted.

CAT, BLACK Linked with evil cunning in the Celtic world, with harmful djins in Islam and with bad luck in Japan. Associated irrevocably with witchcraft and the Devil in the west.

CATERPILLAR In India, a symbol of the transmigration of souls; for the ancient Romans, it was an emblem of greed and ugliness.

CAULDRON Linked with magic, symbol of transformation, germination, plenty, and the possibility of rebirth or rejuvenation. Also linked with torture, trial or punishment.

CAVE Most primal symbol of shelter, linked with the womb, birth, rebirth, origin and the centre. Darker meanings include the entrance to Hell or the unconscious.

CAVE Very old ideogram for cave, farm, village or fortress, also used on modern maps for cave.

CEDAR Symbol of power and immortality.

CELTIC HARP Symbol of the bardic tradition, but also has links with the underworld. Used as a symbol for Ireland.

CELTIC KNOT Symbol of the universe, because it was drawn in a continuous line, and therefore used as a protective sign.

CENTAUR A mythical hybrid creature, half man and half horse, became a symbol of duality, of man trapped by his physical or sensual impulses, especially lust and violence.

CERBERUS Guardian of the entrance to the Greek underworld, symbol of the fearful uncertainties of death.

CERES Asteroid.

CHAI The Hebrew word for "life", commonly used on necklaces and other ornaments.

CHAIN A symbol of attachment and connection, the relationship between two things. Gold chains signify honour and status. A modern symbol of slavery and captivity. Broken chains symbolize the fight for freedom, and the achievement of liberty from oppression.

CHAIR Universal symbol of authority and superior rank, linked to the throne. Among the Swahili (Zanzibar) the "chair of power" is for visitors and the most important members of the family.

CHALICE/CUP A vessel of plenty and also of immortality; in Christianity, the chalice is a ritual cup used at Eucharist; in Medieval Europe, this cup was associated with the Holy Grail. In Japan, exchanging cups is a symbol of faithfulness and forms part of the marriage ceremony.

CHARIOT A dynamic symbol of rulership in ancient iconography; a symbol of spiritual authority and the mastery of gods and heroes. Hindu mysticism associates charioteering as a symbol of the Self, and in moral allegory it is an image of the triumphant journey of the spirit.

CHER Rune for harvest. Also known as Jara.

CHERRY A Samurai emblem in Japan, the fruit is a symbol of virginity in China, and its blossom is highly auspicious. In Christian iconography the cherry is an alternative to the apple as the fruit of paradise.

CHERUB A type of angelic being in Islamic, Judaic and Christian traditions; in Christian art cherubim are shown as winged children representing innocence, with blue wings that symbolize the sky.

CHEVRON A symbol of rank in military and heraldic contexts.

CHEVRON A heraldic variation.

CHICKEN In parts of South America (Makumba cult), the Caribbean (Voodoo) and Africa, a cult animal; a guide of souls in initiation rites, sacrificial animal. Tenth sign of the Chinese zodiac.

CHILDBIRTH Child is born, genealogy.

CHIMERA A mythological snake-lion-goat hybrid creature, symbol of the victory of spirit over matter.

CHIMNEY A phallic symbol in Freudian psychology.

CHINA Used from the earliest Chinese writings as a symbol of how they viewed their civilization, as the "empire of the Middle", set between Heaven and Earth, and in the centre of an otherwise uncivilized world.

CHRIST A monogram formed by the initials of Christ in their Greek form, PX. In this variation the X is turned 45 degrees to form a cross.

CHRIST Monogram, variation.

CHRIST Monogram, variation.

CHRIST Monogram, variation.

CHRIST Monogram, variation.

CHRIST Another monogram symbolizing Christ, this one is built up by

CHRIST Monogram, variation, combined with the Greek letters alpha and (lower case) omega, the first and last letters of the Greek alphabet to symbolize Christ as first and last.

CHRIST Monogram, variation, the triangle at the base is a symbol of divinity meaning that Christ is the centre of the Holy Trinity.

CHRIST Monogram, variation.

a cross above the letters alpha and omega, signifying that Christ is the first and the last.

CHRONOS God.

CHRONOS God, variation.

CHRONOS God, variation.

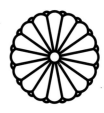

CHRYSANTHEMUM A solar and imperial symbol in Japan, linked with longevity and joy; a Chinese Taoist symbol; and in Western art it is used as a symbol of autumn.

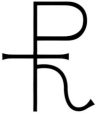

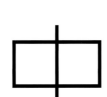

CHRYSLER Corporate emblem of the car manufacturer, a variation of the pentagon combined with the pentagram.

CHURCH In Christianity an image of the world; also associated with the Bride of Christ and the Mother of Christians, and therefore with motherhood.

CINNABAR Alchemistic sign.

CIRCLE Intersected with diagonal cross, modern sign for zero position on machines.

CIRCLE Intersected with diagonal line, Greek letter phi, commonly used in computer programs for zero. In other contexts it signifies diameter or average number.

CIRCLE Intersected with horizontal line, another of humankind's earliest ideograms, found on rock paintings in the inner Sahara and many early systems of writing. Used in modern contexts to mean open. On ships it is the main part of the plimsoll mark.

CIRCLE Intersected with upright cross, a rare sign sometimes used in alchemy for oil or wax. In musical notation it signifies "to be repeated".

CIRCLE AND ARROW One of the most common ideograms in Western culture. Sign for the planet Mars. Also for iron and zinc, and morning.

CIRCLE On horizontal line, ancient ideogram perhaps signifying greatness and power.

CIRCLE On several decreasing horizontal lines, meaning unknown; appears in several prehistoric European caves.

CIRCLE On vertical line, ancient ideogram; in ancient Greece it was a sign for Aphrodite; in alchemy a sign for night.

CIRCLE With vertical line continuing downwards, one of the oldest ideograms, it also appeared in the runic alphabet where for a while it stood for the m-sound.

CIRCLE Divided by horizontal line, often found on rock carvings. In early Chinese calligraphy it denoted the sun; in the Greek alphabet it is the letter theta.

CIRCLE Divided by vertical line, an ancient sign in early alphabets from the Near East. Alchemistic sign for nitrogen.

CIRCLE Empty, one of the oldest ideograms. Sometimes represents the sun or the moon, and also openings such as eyes or the mouth. Used in ideographic writing for up to 5000 years.

CIRCLE Filled, perhaps the most common of the ancient ideograms found in many ancient cultures.

CIRCLE Semi, on vertical line, iconic sign for rising sun, used for dew in meteorology.

CIRCLE Another very early ideogram, associated with the divine or powerful. In Buddhist and Christian art it is used to denote charisma or halo.

CIRCLES Small, connected by straight lines, very old structure found in ancient China and in Nordic rock carvings. In Kabbalistic mystical contexts, similar signs are used for stars and sounds.

CIRCLES Three, filled, known as bowl hollows, these have been found in Nordic rock carvings; also used in modern maps to indicate ruins or sights worth seeing. Used in meteorology for rain. In mathematics and geometry it means therefore. Used upside down, the sign means because.

CITROËN Corporate emblem of the car manufacturer, inspired by the V symbol for victory and military superiority.

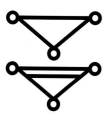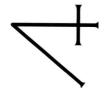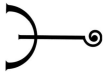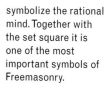

CLAY Alchemistic sign.

CLOAK Its symbolism of metamorphosis and concealment is due to the instant change it makes to the wearer's appearance. In Teutonic and Celtic legends, magic cloaks are associated with invisibility and forgetfulness. The cloak also symbolizes intrigue, and the world of espionage.

CLOCK Symbol of time and of the transience of life; a stopped clock can symbolize death, and in South America they are placed on graves to symbolize the transition between life and death.

CLOUD Symbol of fecundity and revelation; in China pink clouds are signs of happiness. Cloud nine is mystical bliss. Modern associations are with gloom, obscurity or depression.

CLOVES Represent health and sweetness in Japan and China; in Japanese art, they were one of the Myriad Treasures carried by the Seven Deities of Good Fortune.

CLUB Has a dual role representing either primitive brutality or heroism in art.

CLUBS Suit of playing cards.

COAGULATE/FIX Alchemistic sign.

COBRA. In India cobra divinities, (nagas) were guardian symbols, generally benevolent. The Hindu cobra has a jewel in its hood and symbolizes spiritual treasure. The erect, hooded cobra is the protective serpent emblem of royal power, used by the pharaohs as an emblem to strike down enemies. There is a general link between snakes and wisdom or prophecy.

COBRA On ancient Egyptian headdresses the cobra was a protective sign and a symbol of royal power.

COCK Generally positive symbolic links with the dawn, the sun and illumination. In China the cock was a funerary emblem warding off evil. In Japan it is a sacred creature. In Islam the cock was seen by Mohammed in the First Heaven. Cocks also symbolize lust.

COCONUT Extensive use in Hindu rituals; "sacrificed" as a replica for the human head and is also associated with Shiva, because its three "eyes" symbolize the eyes of Shiva. Also associated with fertility.

COLUMN/PILLAR Symbols of temporal and spiritual aspiration and power; God appeared to the Israelites in the wilderness as a pillar of fire. Two columns appear outside Masonic temples, representing force and form.

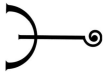

COMB Sacred and protected in Maori tradition.

COMET A change in the heavens; in many cultures a portent of war and disaster. Also a symbol of hope and new beginnings.

COMET Variation.

COMET Variation.

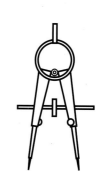

COMPASSES Associated with architecture during the Renaissance; in European art it can symbolize the rational mind. Together with the set square it is one of the most important symbols of Freemasonry.

COMPOSE Alchemistic sign.

CONCH SHELL Buddhists, the Maya and the Aztecs used the conch as a ceremonial horn. Its shape associates it with the symbolism of the spiral. In Hinduism the sound of the conch symbolizes the origin of existence. An emblem of Vishnu.

CONDOR A solar symbol in South America.

CONFERENCE Modern sign, similar to older signs meaning togetherness.

CONFUSED MENTAL STATE Used in modern comic strips.

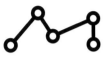

CONSTELLATIONS OF FIXED STARS Chinese.

COPYRIGHT SYMBOL Used to denote lawful ownership of text or images.

CORAL Its red colour links it with blood in many traditions: for Christians it symbolizes Christ's Passion; in Greek myth, it was formed from the drops of Medusa's blood. In ancient Rome, coral necklaces were worn to ward off disease.

CORN In European cultures, associated with summer, harvest and fertility.

CORNUCOPIA Roman horn of plenty that cannot be emptied; it is used to denote abundance and prosperity in Western art, and is a feminine symbol of maternal nourishment and love. Attribute of Dionysus, god of wine, Demeter and Priapus, also of the allegorical figures of Earth, Autumn, Hospitality, Peace, Fortune and Concord in Western art.

COSMIC TREE The "tree of life" reversed so that its roots draw spiritual strength from the sky.

COW Ancient symbol of maternal nourishment, often personified as mother earth, and the moon.

To Hindus and Buddhists the cow's quiet, patient rhythms of life present a parallel with holiness.

COW Hindu, the symbolism of the cow is taken to its highest for Hindus, who view it as sacred. Its image everywhere is one of happiness.

COWRIE SHELL Symbol of wealth and rank in parts of Africa, appearing on costumes and artefacts; Freudian symbol for female sexual organs, also associated with fertility and good luck.

COYOTE A divinatory symbol or culture hero in North America and Africa.

CRADLE Womb symbol; associated with security, protection and safety. Its traditional boat-like shape also links it with travel; a symbol for a safe journey through life.

CRANE Linked by the Chinese to immortality; in Africa with the gift of speech, and widely with the ability to communicate with the gods. Christian symbolism sometimes links it with resurrection.

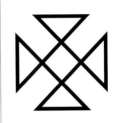

CRICKET Linked with death and resurrection in China; also a good luck symbol.

CROCODILE Major symbol of destructive voracity, bringer of divine punishment, and archetypal devourer. Treated with fearful respect as a creature of primordial and occult power over water, earth and the underworld. The ancient Egyptians had a crocodile fecundity god called Sebek. It has more positive connections in parts of Asia, where it appears as the inventor of the drum and of song.

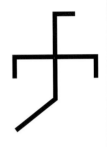

CROSS OF CHRIST.

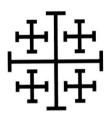

CROSS OF ENDLESSNESS A symbol for eternity.

CROSS OF GOLGOTHA Similar to the cross of the Crusaders.

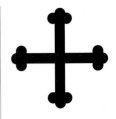

CROSS OF LAZARUS Ancient symbol for holiness and divinity.

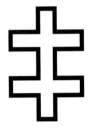

CROSS OF LORAINE Used in heraldry.

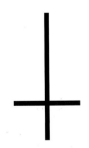

CROSS OF PALESTINE Used as a symbol for the kingdom of Jerusalem after the city was captured by the Crusaders.

CROSS OF PETER An upside-down Latin cross that commemorates the martyrdom of St Peter, who was crucified upside down.

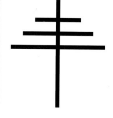

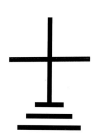

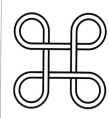
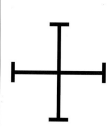

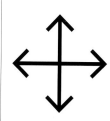

CROSS OF PHILIP
Associated with Nordic countries, some of which use it in their flags.

CROSS OF ST GEORGE

CROSS OF ST ANDREW'S Named after the apostle Andrew, who was crucified on a diagonal cross.

CROSS OF ST HAN/ CROSS OF ST JOHN
Also a magic ideogram from the Viking era, possibly also used in Kabbalism.

CROSS OF ST ANTHONY Named after a hermit in Egypt, who was said to have chased away a pack of demons with a cross of this type. Also known as the Tau cross, T-cross, Egyptian cross, Crux commissa and the robber's cross.

CROSS OF ST JOHN

CROSS OF ST BIRGITTA Set with five precious stones representing the five wounds of Christ.

CROSS OF THE ARCHANGELS Also known as the Golgata cross.

CROSS OF THE ARCHANGELS Variation.

CROSS OF THE EVANGELISTS

CROSS OF THE HOLY CHURCH Also used in alchemy for crucible.

CROSS OF THE PATRIARCH

CROSS OF THE POPE

CROSS OF THE ROBBERS

CROSS, ANCHORED One of the disguised crosses used by early Christians.

CROSS, ANGLED

CROSS, ARROWED Meaning expansion in all directions and for that reason a favoured symbol of fascists.

CROSS, ARROWED Variation.

CROSS, CELTIC

CROSS, CELTIC Variation.

CROSS, COPTIC

CROSS, DIAGONAL Equal-length arms, an extremely old sign found in prehistoric caves. Egyptian hieroglyph meaning divide, count. Signifies multiplication, confrontation, annulment, cancellation, opposition, obstruction, mistake and undecided.

CROSS, DISSIMULATA Variation of the disguised form of the cross used by early Christians.

CROSS, DISSIMULATA Variation, also used on the seal of the Prince of Byblos, a Phoenician city, in the year 2000 BC.

CROSS, EASTERN ORTHODOX

CROSS, EGYPTIAN/ COPTIC

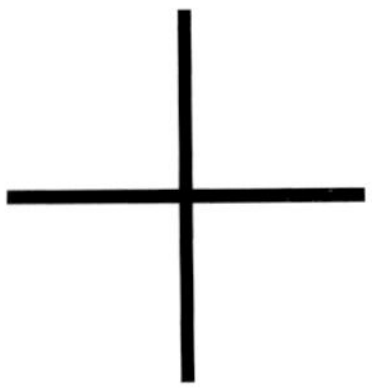

CROSS With equal length arms, an old ideogram from most cultures found in every part of the world, often associated with the four elements. Used in mathematics as the sign for addition.

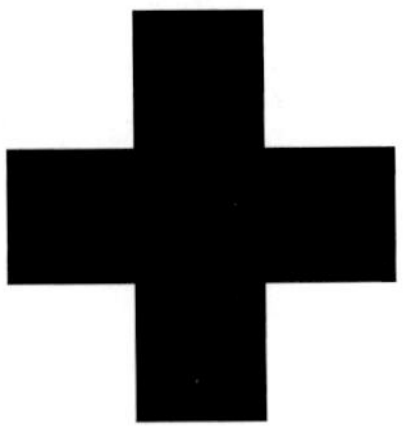

CROSS With filled or closed, short arms, common in ancient Greece, pre-Columbian America and the Near East up to 1000 years before the birth of Christ, associated with the sun and power.

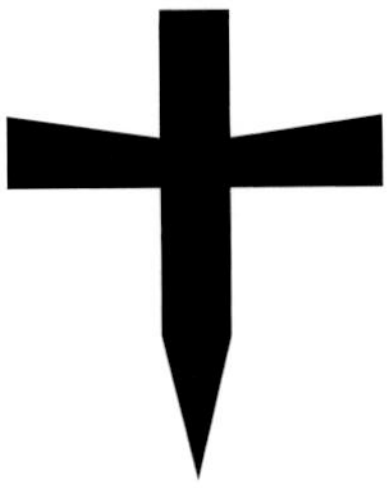

CROSS, FITCHEE Originated in the times of the crusades when knights took crosses with them that could be thrust into the ground during worship in the field of battle or encampment.

CROSS, GREEK

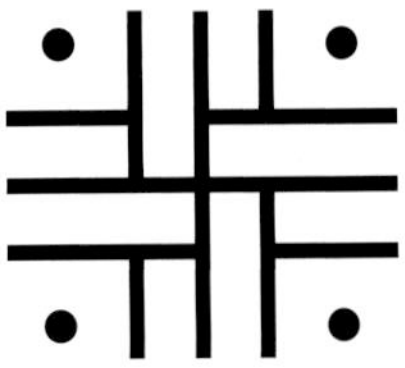

CROSS, HOLY ROMAN Has a swastika in the centre, a possible allusion to the return of Christ.

CROSS, IRON/ MANTUAN CROSS Used as a German order medal.

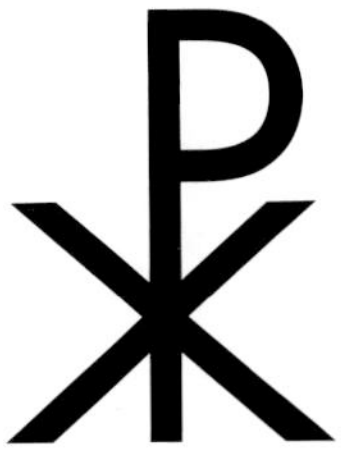

CROSS, LABARUM/ CHI-RHO A monogram formed with the two initial Greek letters of the word Christ.

CROSS, LILY

CROSS, MALTESE Also known as the Cross of Promise. Used as the emblem of the Order of St John, based on old Assyrian symbols.

CROSS, MALTESE Variation.

CROSS Open with closed arms, an ancient symbol that seems to have been linked with the weather, the four winds or the four directions.

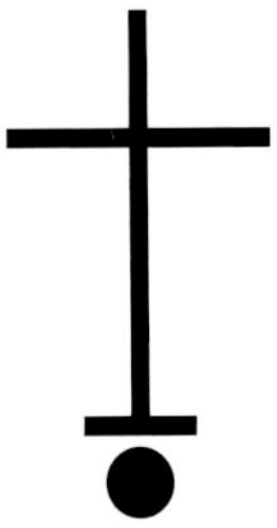

CROSS Sitting over a globe. Sign for world evangelization.

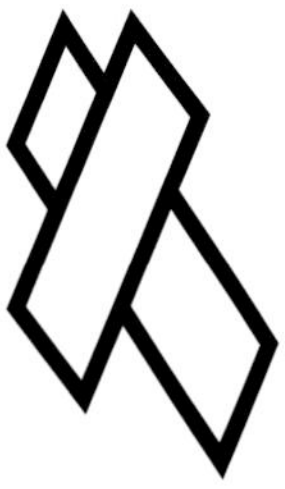

CROSS, PORTALE

CROSS, RESTORATION Used in the 15th century in heraldry and in European coinage. Also used by the Inca as a sign for sun.

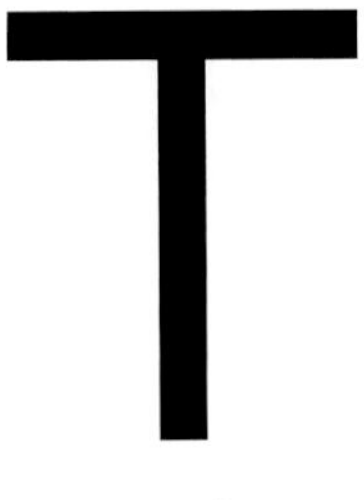

CROSS, TAU/ EGYPTIAN

CROSS, TAU Variation with snake.

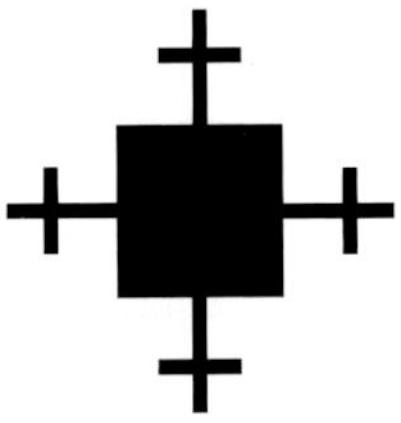

CROSS, SQUARE Representing the Earth with its four corners.

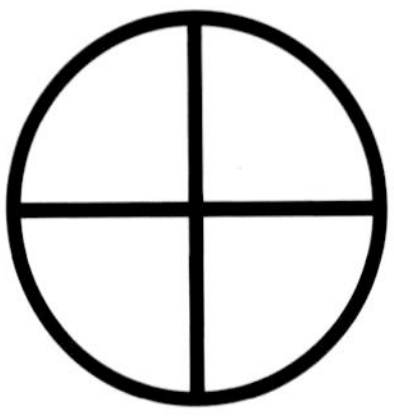

CROSS, WHEEL/SUN CROSS First appeared at the dawn of the Bronze Age, appearing in ancient Egypt, China, pre-Columbian America and the Near East. Associated with the wheel.

CROSS, WHEEL, DIAGONAL Suggests a cancelling or neutralizing characteristic.

CROSS, WITH GARMENT A symbol of the crucifixion.

CROSS, WITH ORB A symbol of the final triumph of Christ over the world.

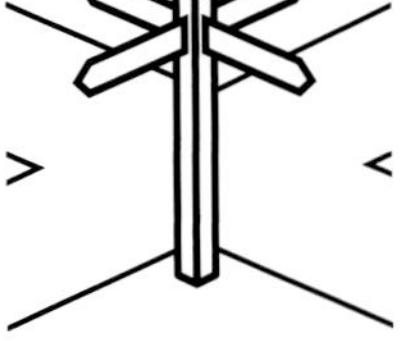

CROSSROADS A symbol of decision-making, life changes and journeys.

CROW Emblem of war, death, solitude, evil and bad luck in Europe and India, but in the Americas and Australia has positive symbolism as a solar bird that is a creative, civilizing bird.

CROWN Identified with power, glory and consecration. Originating as wreaths, crowns draw on the celestial symbolism of the circle – representing perfection and the ring – representing continuity.

CROWN OF THORNS Originally mocking the symbolism of a crown (by the Roman soldiers who crucified Christ) it has now become a symbol in itself of sacrifice and consecration.

CROZIER Originated as a masculine fertility symbol, it implies royal or spiritual power to administer justice. Linked with the sceptre, the staff and the rod. One of the signs of a bishop's religious authority is his crozier.

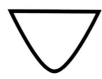

CRUCIBLE OR MELTING POT Alchemistic sign, also old chemistry.

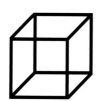

CRUCIBLE Old chemistry, variation.

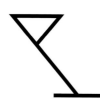

CRUX DISSIMULATA Christian symbol of hope.

CRYSTAL Modern New Age symbol.

CUBE Linked to symbolism of the square, hence associated with the physical manifest world. A symbol of wisdom and perfection; for example in Freemasonry, ashlar (a smooth cube) represents the perfected person; one of Islam's most holy structures, the Ka'ba, is cube-shaped.

CUPID/EROS With his bow and arrows of desire, Cupid is a symbol of love and romance.

CURVED LINE A segment of a circle, appears in many ideographic systems, ancient and modern.

DAISY Christian symbol of innocence associated with the Virgin Mary, and the

rays of the sun; also sacred to Freya, the Germanic sky goddess.

CYPRESS Western symbol of death and mourning, but in Asia and elsewhere a symbol of longevity and endurance.

DAEG Rune for D.

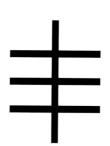

DAGGER/KNIFE Sacred symbol in Buddhist and Sikh religions. For Sikhs, it symbolizes courage and dignity. In Tibetan Buddhism a ritual dagger with a three-sided blade is used to protect sacred buildings. In European traditional lore, daggers are linked to treachery.

DANGER Energy, the symbol for heat combined with an arrow.

DANGER Energy, heat, variation.

DANGER Poisonous, used in botany. Also stands for checkmate in chess.

DAY Rune associated with light, breakthrough and success.

DEATH The moment of/passing out, used in modern comic strips.

DECOCTION Alchemistic sign.

DEER Universally benevolent symbol associated with dawn, light, purity, regeneration, creativity and magic.

DENEB ALGEDI Magical amulet seal.

DENKYEM The crocodile, Ghanaian adinkra symbol meaning ability to adapt to circumstances, just as the crocodile adapts from water to land.

DHARMACHAKRA The Buddhist eight-spoked wheel.

DIED IN BATTLE Military expression, also used on maps to denote a battle site.

DIGGING STICK Aboriginal, traditional tool used to gather roots and vegetables now used in modern art to represent ancestral being.

DISTAFF Used to prepare flax for spinning, a symbol of Athena/Minerva, Greco-Roman goddess of wisdom and inventor of spinning and weaving; also associated with the passing of time.

DISTANCE Modern technical symbol.

DISTILLATION Alchemistic sign.

DISTILLED OIL Alchemistic sign.

DIVINE POWER Ancient Nordic/Anglo Saxon sign; also logo for Mitsubishi Group.

DIVISION Mathematical sign.

DIVISION Mathematical sign, variation.

DIVORCED Genealogy.

DIVORCED Genealogy, variation.

DOG Symbol of loyalty; protective vigilance in Celtic and Christian traditions; in ancient thought associated with the underworld, where it acted as guide and guardian. Dogs are guardian symbols in Japan and China, but in China they also have demonic links.

DOLL Used in religion, ritual and magic as surrogates for people and deities.

DOLLAR SIGN USA currency.

DOLPHIN Widespread symbol of salvation, transformation and love. Emblem of Christ as saviour. In ancient Greek mythology the dolphin is the bearer of the gods, saviour of heroes and carrier of souls to the Islands of the Blessed. Attribute of Poseidon, Aphrodite, Eros, Demeter and Dionysus. Entwined with an anchor, the dolphin can symbolize prudence.

DOME Symbol of the heavens, frequently appearing in sacred or important civic buildings, such as mosques, Byzantine churches or the Roman pantheon.

DONKEY/ASS Well-entrenched modern symbol of foolishness, but earlier connotations were much more positive (humility, poverty and patience), or sinister in both Egyptian and Indian mythology.

DOOR/ENTRANCE A place of transition seen in many cultures as an opportunity for good or evil forces to enter or leave, hence doorways are often guarded.

DOSE OF MEDICINE Large pill or bolus, old pharmacology; also Japanese Buddhism, also in alchemy for orichalcum or dissolvent.

DOT, SINGLE One of the most common ancient Western ideograms in existence since the era of cave paintings and rock carvings.

DOTS, THREE IN TRIANGLE Sign for therefore (modern).

DOTS IN A LINE Sign for something left out (modern). Several dots in a line was the sign for rain for the Anglo Saxons.

221

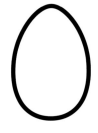

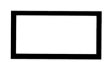

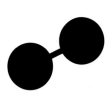

DOVE Universal symbol of peace, particularly when holding an olive branch – this is an allusion to the story of Noah, when the flood began to recede and land became visible. The dove is also a personification of the Holy Spirit and a symbol of baptism.

DOWN WITH! Sign of popular dissent, formed by the sign for "viva!" upside down.

DRAGON Benevolent symbol in the East, malevolent in the West, and containing a wealth of symbolism for each.

DRUM Primeval means of communication, symbol of creative power in India, the voice of Heaven in China, used to promote trance and ecstasy in shamanistic societies. In modern Western symbolism the drum is linked to war and warning.

DUCK Symbol of happiness in Japan and China, with a pair of mandarin ducks symbolizing marriage and domestic harmony.

DWELLING Egyptian hieroglyph.

EAGLE An unambiguous and universal symbol of power, speed and perception. Attribute of the greatest gods, adopted much later as a symbol of imperial power. Also appears in carvings in Christian churches, usually on fonts, pulpits and lecterns, as one of the attributes of St John.

EAR Receptivity; in Africa, ears symbolize humans' animal nature. In the East, long earlobes are a symbol of wisdom and longevity. Ear piercing was traditionally an ancient sign of a pledge.

EARTH Element.

EARTH Element, Kabbalistic.

EARTH The planet, used as early as 500 BC. Used today on maps to signify a chapel. Alchemy sign for antinomy.

EARTH The planet, modern.

EARTH The planet, modern variation.

EARTH The planet, variation.

ECLIPSE OF THE MOON Astronomy.

EGG A universal symbol for creation, often the thing that life sprang from, whether vegetative, godly or elemental. A propitious symbol all over the world symbolizing luck, wealth, health, birth and resurrection. Also associated with spring. In Jewish tradition the egg is a symbol of promise.

EHWAZ Rune for E.

EIGHT Symbol of cosmic equilibrium and renewal. A lucky number in China.

EIGHTH HOUSE Astrology.

ELECTRICITY Thunder, lightning.

ELEPHANT Ancient symbol of sovereign power in India, China and Africa, and by this association linked with dignity, intelligence, prudence, peace. The mount of Indian rulers, and of the thunder and rain god, Indra. Ancient Rome associated the elephant with victory. Medieval Europe believed the male refrained from sex with its mate during her pregnancy, which made it an emblem of chastity, fidelity and love. The white elephant of Burma, Thailand and Cambodia is a symbol of fertility and rainfall.

ELEVENTH HOUSE Astrology.

ELHAZ Rune for Z, meaning an elk.

ELLIPSIS Nothing, zero, absence.

EMPEDOCLES' ELEMENTS, AIR Pre-Socratian ancient Greek geometrical symbols of the elements.

EMPEDOCLES' ELEMENTS, EARTH Pre-Socratian ancient Greek geometrical symbols of the elements.

EMPEDOCLES' ELEMENTS, FIRE Pre-Socratian ancient Greek geometrical symbols of the elements.

EMPEDOCLES' ELEMENTS, WATER Pre-Socratian ancient Greek geometrical symbols of the elements.

EMPEROR Jesus, first, only one, self.

EMU Appears in Australian Aboriginal creation stories; therefore killing an emu is associated with bad luck.

ENCLOSED SPACE Tank or closed room, also buried in genealogy.

ENNEAGRAM Nine-pointed star, Christian, nine gifts of spirit.

ENTRANCE See Door

EOH Rune for Y, meaning yew tree.

EPA Ghanaian adinkra symbol, meaning handcuffs, symbol of slavery and captivity.

ERMINE Heraldry.

ESSENCE Alchemistic sign.

ETHERIC OIL Alchemistic sign.

EVAPORATION Modern.

EXCLAMATION MARK Modern, denoting surprise or emphasis in text.

EYE OF FIRE Ancient Germanic, four elements in alchemy.

EYE OF HORUS Symbol of cosmic wholeness, and of the all-seeing power of the ancient Egyptian god Horus. Also known as the wedjat.

EYE OF THE DRAGON Ancient Germanic sign for threat, danger.

EYE/EYEBROW The ability to see, vision (literal and metaphorical), associated with magic or spiritual power in many traditions. In Chinese Buddhism long eyebrows are a sign of wisdom and old age.

EYE, THE THIRD Also called the "eye of the heart", a symbol of the eye of spiritual perception in Hinduism, and of clairvoyance in Islam. Adopted by the Freemasons as one of their society's signs.

FAITH Early Christian symbol, one of those found inscribed in the catacombs where the Christians hid from Roman persecution. Fish are associated with hope in Hebrew tradition.

FALCON Identical symbolism to the hawk; a solar emblem of victory, superiority, aspiration, spirit, light and liberty. Many Egyptian gods are depicted with the head of a falcon. The eye of a falcon symbolizes sharp vision. In Western tradition the falcon is an emblem of the hunter, and in Nordic mythology of the sky god, Woden.

223

FAMILY A sign combining the sign for woman, the sign for man, and the sign for woman with child.

FE Rune, meaning cattle or livestock, also a Viking symbol for moveable property.

FERN Koru fern, Polynesian.

FIG Symbol of fecundity, also in Buddhism of moral teaching and immortality.

FIRE Masculine symbol of creation, destruction, purification, revelation, transformation, regeneration and spiritual or sexual ardour.

FIRST HOUSE Astrology.

FAN Symbol of goodness (Chinese); an attribute of one of the Japanese Seven Deities of Good Fortune, and of Vishnu (Hindu god). Emblem of kingship in Africa, Asia and the Far East.

FEATHER Symbol of Maat, ancient Egyptian goddess of justice. In Native American traditions, feathers hold the spirit of the bird and are highly prized.

FIAT Corporate emblem of the car manufacturer, derived from the sun cross.

FILTER (VERB) Alchemistic sign.

FIRE Alchemistic sign.

FISH Phallic symbol of sexual happiness and fecundity. In China the fish is an emblem of plenty and good luck. The letters of the Greek word for fish – *icthus* – form an acronym for Jesus Christ, and so the fish became an early secret Christian sign. In Hebrew tradition fish represent the true and faithful. Fish appear as saviours in Hindu myth.

FASCES Pictorial representation of an axe wrapped around with rods and bound with leather, which Roman officials carried as a symbol of their authority. Later the fasces became a Roman punitive emblem of state power, and was later adopted by fascism.

FEMALE

FEOH Rune for F.

FIFTH ELEMENT The quintessence or ether. The best.

FIFTH HOUSE Astrology.

FINGERS/ FINGERNAILS Connection with spiritual power (India), and with the five tenets of Islam. Long fingernails are traditionally a sign of wealth and status; long, claw-like nails are attributes of the kings of the Dahomey in Africa.

FIRE Very old ideogram, also used for lunar halo.

FIRE Kabbalism.

FIREPLACE See Hearth.

FISH A simplified icon that was used by early Christians as the first emblem of Christ.

FIREWORK In the modern world associated with festivals and celebration, the more lavish the spectacle, the bigger the occasion; also associated with other symbolism, for example rocket, wheel, star, spiral.

FAST MOVEMENT Modern.

FISH HOOK Symbol of fishing and helpless entrapment.

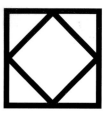

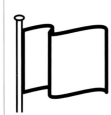

FIVE ELEMENTS OF WESTERN IDEOGRAPHY, THE DOT Almost all Western ideography is based upon five basic shapes, the dot, the line, the semi circle and the two spirals.

FIVE ELEMENTS OF WESTERN IDEOGRAPHY, THE LINE

FIVE ELEMENTS OF WESTERN IDEOGRAPHY, THE SEMI-CIRCLE Also known as the section.

FIVE ELEMENTS OF WESTERN IDEOGRAPHY, THE SPIRAL Also depicted in reverse.

FIVE ELEMENTS OF WESTERN IDEOGRAPHY, THE SPIRAL Variation.

FIVE Associated with the human microcosm and the hand; important symbol of totality in China, Japan and Celtic tradition. Also associated with love, health, sensuality, meditation, analysis, criticism and the heart.

FIXATION Alchemistic.

FLAG Emblem of rulership and identity at many levels (international, national, local); in war, a symbol of military honour, with a white flag representing surrender; a fluttering flag can suggest new beginnings.

FLAMING HEART See Heart of fire.

FLASK/BOTTLE Alchemistic sign for a flask that is not transparent.

FLASK Alchemistic sign for a flask made of glass.

FLEUR-DE-LIS A stylized lily with three flowers used as the emblem of France.

FLOW/MELT Alchemistic sign.

FLOWER Culmination or crowning achievement; feminine beauty; also a sign of impermanence and transience. Specific flowers also have their own symbolism, and, in some cultures, language. Widespread use in rituals all over the world (birth, marriage, death, celebrations).

FLUTE/PAN PIPES Associated with Pan (Greek god of the woods and fields), hence linked with nature and sexuality; bamboo flutes are associated with Zen Buddhist monks.

FLY Associated with sickness, death and the devil in many traditions.

FLY WHISK Symbol of royalty in many cultures, in Polynesia a mark of rank, for Buddhists a sign of compassion.

FOOT Bare feet are often a sign of humility. In the East, foot washing is an act of hospitality and a sign of love; Christ washing the feet of his disciples was a symbolic gesture of his love and service.

FOUNTAIN A source of water and therefore of life. Drinking from a fountain can symbolize spiritual refreshment or immortality. In Islamic tradition fountains represent the connection between humans and God.

FOUR ELEMENTS Medieval.

FOUR EVANGELISTS

FOUR EVANGELISTS Variation.

FOUR Solidity, organization, power, intellect, justice and omnipotence.

FOURTH HOUSE Astrology.

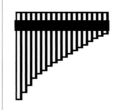

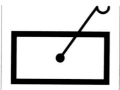

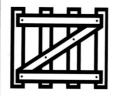

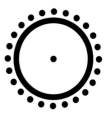

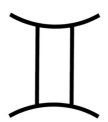

FOX In European traditions, associated with cunning and slyness, appearing in medieval art as a symbol of the devil. In China and Japan the fox is a bringer of wealth.

FROG Foetal symbol especially in Egypt, associated with magic, germination, evolution, the moon's phases, water and rain. Good luck emblem in Japan.

FU Authority, Chinese.

FULFOOT Swedish variation of the swastika.

FUMES Alchemistic.

FUNTUNFUNEFU The Ghanaian adinkra symbol of Siamese crocodiles, who share one stomach but still fight over food. A warning against infighting and tribal conflict.

GARGOYLE A carved waterspout, typically seen on the gutters of church or cathedral parapets. During the Middle Ages gargoyles were mostly grotesque or demonic, symbolizing the power of the Church to wash away evil.

GARLIC Associated with strength and protection from evil spirits in many traditions. In antiquity garlic was associated

with the moon and magic and was regarded as a powerful aphrodisiac.

GATE A transitional symbol marking the movement from one place, time, spiritual or psychological state to another. Gates can also symbolize spiritual and/or secular power.

GEMINI Zodiac sign.

GEOFU Rune for G.

GIANTS An ancient ideogram probably first drawn 10,000 years ago, used in the Nordic runic alphabet

as a sign for giants or Titans. Also used as an expression of power.

GLASS/ARSENIC Alchemistic sign, also unmarried in genealogy.

GLOBE/ORB Power emblem of gods or imperial rulers, symbol of totality.

GLOVE Powerful symbol of rank used as an acknowledgement of superiority or fealty, also as a love pledge.

GOAT Ambiguous symbol meaning virility, lust, cunning and destructiveness in the male, and fecundity and nourishment in the female. Sign for

Capricorn, one of the signs of the zodiac. In Roman myth the cornucopia derives from the horn of the goat, Amaltheia, the revered wet-nurse of the baby Zeus.

GODDESS Of morning or evening, Greek and Byzantium.

GODDESS

GOHEI Sacred wands topped with zigzag streamers of white paper used in Shinto rituals.

GOLD LEAF/GOLD FOIL, Alchemistic sign.

GOLD Alchemistic, variation.

GOLD Alchemistic, variation.

GOLD Alchemistic, variation.

GOLDEN NUMBER 17 From the medieval clog almanacs for calculating the phases of the moon.

GOLDEN NUMBER 18 From the medieval clog almanacs for calculating the phases of the moon.

GONG Widespread use in sacred rituals in China and Japan. In Chinese temples they are beaten to gain the attention of the spirits, while Zen Buddhists use gongs as part of liturgical chanting and meditation. Sounding a gong can indicate arrivals or departures.

GOOSE Medieval bestiaries compared geese to the devout, although white geese were linked to fancy dressing and malicious gossip. The domestic goose is a symbol of the home, women, fidelity and married life. The wild goose is associated with cooperation, interdependence and vigilance. Because wild geese are said to stay with a sick goose, they are also symbols of loyalty.

GORGONS Snake-haired mythological winged women-hybrids of ancient Greece, embodiments of adversarial evil.

GOURD/CALABASH Pre-eminent symbol for many traditional African societies, where it appears in creation myths, representing the world egg or the womb.

GRAIL In European traditions the grail is a sacred object (typically a chalice or stone) whose wondrous powers confer the elixir of life and eternal youth; in medieval legend, particularly linked with King Arthur and his knights, it was believed to be the cup used by Christ at the Last Supper and used to catch his blood at the crucifixion.

GRAIN A central symbol of growth, rebirth and fertility, together with rice, corn, barley and wheat. Often an attribute of earth gods and goddesses. Ancient fertility symbol, used at weddings to sprinkle over the married couple.

GRAPES Complex ancient symbol of natural fecundity and of spiritual life in both pagan and Christian traditions.

GRASS The victory over barrenness, a fertile land; as a dream symbol, can represent new growth, new ideas and new enterprises.

GRAVE Related literally and symbolically to a place of residence for the dead and where the dead can be remembered. As a barrow or tumulus, it may be a symbolic allusion to holy mountains.

GRAVEL/SAND Alchemistic sign.

GRIFFIN Lion-eagle hybrid symbol of dominion over land and sky, evolved from an aggressive emblem of power into a protective symbol.

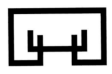

GRIND/CRUSH Alchemistic sign.

GROWING Also rebirth and genesis, Egyptian hieroglyphs for woman and female sex.

GYE NYAME Ubiquitous Ghanaian adinkra symbol, meaning "except for God", which is by far the most popular for use in decoration.

HAGALL Rune for H.

HAGITH Kabbalism.

HAIL Rune associated with accidents and misfortune.

HAIR A complex symbol with many meanings, most associated with the life force; can be a sign of holiness and strength, royal power, freedom, virility, virginity or permissiveness.

HALO Symbol of divinity or sanctity, originally based on the nimbus that surrounds the sun. Used particularly in Christian art, the halo is thought to have been first used on pagan sun gods, such as Mithras. Halos also appear in Buddhist spiritual traditions.

HAMMER As a weapon the hammer is a symbol of male strength, linked with the power of the sun and the gods of war. As a tool the hammer can appear as a symbol of protection or of divine skill.

HAMMER AND SICKLE Symbol of communism's unification of the working classes, combing the sickle as a symbol of agricultural workers, and the hammer, symbol of industrial workers.

HAND Symbol of temporal and spiritual power, action, strength and protection.

HAND OF FATIMA A symbol of the hand of God and of the five fundamentals of Islam: faith, prayer, pilgrimage, fasting and charity. Used extensively in Islamic countries as a protective and good luck charm.

HAPPINESS Rune.

HARE A lunar animal linked with divinity, menstruation and fertility. Because of its links with divinity it has sometimes been a forbidden food.

HARP Widespread use in ritual and sacred ceremony; in the Old Testament associated with Jewish nationhood. The magical harp of the Dagda (Celtic) could play music suitable for every occasion and had the power to send its enemies to sleep. The three-stringed harp used in ancient Egypt symbolized the three seasons of flood, growth and dryness.

HAWK Solar emblem of victory, superiority, aspiration, spirit, light and liberty.

HAZEL Symbol of divinity, wisdom, fertility and rain. A hazel wand was the instrument of northern European magicians and wizards.

HEAD In some traditions the location of the soul, associated with fertility and phallic symbolism, instrument of reason and thought.

HEART An ancient symbol whose original meaning is not known. Graphically related to fire. Signifies love; also appears with religious meaning among the Aztecs, Hindus, Buddhists, Muslims, Jews, Celts and Taoists.

HEART ON FIRE/FLAMING HEART Symbol of an ardent Christian, but also, in art, an attribute of charity and profane passion.

HEARTH/FIREPLACE Symbol of the home, of comfort, security and human community. For the Romans, it was the site of the household guardian spirits (lares), for the Aztecs the sacred place of Ometecuhtli, who was believed to live at the heart of the universe and in the heart of all people.

HEDGEHOG A symbol of wealth in China and Japan; in medieval Europe associated with greed and gluttony. In parts of Central Asia and Africa it is associated with the sun (because of the ray pattern made by its spines) and the invention of fire.

HELMET Symbol of protection, but also linked with invisible power.

HEMESH HAND A Jewish variation of the hand of Fatima with similar protective symbolism.

HEPTAGRAM This star contains all the symbolism of the number 7.

HERALDIC DAGGER Used in printed text as a sign for note.

HERMAPHRODITE Used in botany for double-sexed plants.

HERMES Sign of the god.

HERMES Sign of the god, variation.

HERMES Sign of the god, variation.

HERON Emblem of the morning sun.

HEXAGON Geometric shape, important in Islam as a directional.

HEXAGRAM Based on the triangle, an ancient sign for the Jewish kingdom.

HINDU/HINDUISM

HIPPOPOTAMUS In ancient Egypt, a female hippo was a fertility symbol and worshipped as an upright hippopotamus goddess. In the Old Testament, the hippo is a symbol of brute force.

HIEROGLYPH Symbolizing the unification of Egypt.

HIGH Spiritual dignity.

HNEFATAFL A design for a games board used by the Vikings.

HIJAB An Islamic item of clothing that carries various symbolic interpretations, including liberation and oppression. For many of those who wear it, it is an expression of their love for God.

HOLY SIGN From India around 4,000 years ago. Also found on Japanese Buddha statues from the 8th century.

HOLY SPIRIT According to some sources this Christian sign is derived from a stylized dove. This sign was also used in alchemy to signify the spirit of a substance.

HOLY SPIRIT An early Christian symbol, one of those found inscribed in the catacombs of Roman Palestine in the years of Christian persecution.

HOLLY A symbol of hope and joy.

HOLY TRINITY This shape, denoting the unity of three, is used extensively in the architecture of churches and cathedrals. The sign itself, however, is ancient, and has been found as far back as 3000 BC inscribed on the statue of an Indian priest king.

HOLY TRINITY A triquetras variation.

HOLY TRINITY Another triquetras variation.

HOLY TRINITY Variation.

HOLY TRINITY A Spanish variation.

HOMECOMINGS A sign from the Hopi Indians of Arizona, also symbolizes several returns or tribal migration.

HOMOSEXUAL See Male

HONEY Linked with the gods, purity, inspiration, eloquence and plenty.

HONEY Alchemistic sign.

HONEY Alchemistic, variation.

HONEY Alchemistic, variation.

HOOD Associated with magic and the power to make its wearer invisible. Freudian phallic symbol.

HORN Symbol of power and strength associated with the animals that have them. A bull's horn is a female lunar symbol (the crescent moon is horn-shaped), and associated with fertility; a ram's horn is a male, solar symbol, associated with virility.

HORSE Symbol of animal vitality, velocity and beauty, also associated with the power of wind, storm, fire, waves and running water.

HORSESHOE Ancient protective symbol, with heel uppermost it is used in magic to call on the protection of the moon.

HORUS Ancient Egyptian solar god, symbol of cosmic wholeness.

HOUR Time sign, alchemistic.

HOUR Time sign, alchemistic, representation of hourglass.

HOURGLASS Symbol of time, and its inevitable passing.

HWEMUDUA Measuring stick, Ghanaian adinkra sign, meaning the need to strive for the best quality, whether in production of goods or in human endeavours

HYDRA The many-headed dragon serpent of Greek myth symbolizes the difficulty in conquering our vices.

HYE WON HYE Ghanaian adinkra sign meaning "that which cannot be burnt". This symbol gets its meaning from traditional priests that were able to walk on fire without burning their feet, an inspiration to others to endure and overcome difficulties.

IBIS A sacred symbol of wisdom for the ancient Egyptians.

ICE GRANULES Hail, meteorology

IGLOO Inuit symbol of their culture and way of life.

INFINITE Modern mathematical sign for infinitely great sum or number or indefinite number.

INFINITY Referring to time, distance or numbers.

ING Rune for Ng.

INGZ Rune, associated with fertility.

IRON Alchemistic sign.

IRON Alchemistic sign, variation.

IS Rune for I.

ISHTAR Goddess, queen of the heavens for the Babylonians and Assyrians, also god of childbirth.

ISLAM Made up of the morning star and the morning moon.

ISLAND A symbol of non-celestial heaven, a magical other place set apart from the real world.

ISOMORPH/ CONGRUENT In mathematical and geometrical systems.

IVY Symbol of immortality and also friendship; in the classical world also associated with vegetative abundance and sensuality, hence Dionysus/Bacchus (god of wine) is often depicted wearing an ivy crown.

JACKAL Symbol of destructiveness or evil in India, but in ancient Egypt worshipped as Anubis, god of embalming.

JAGUAR Linked with divination, royalty, magic, the spirit world, the earth, the moon and fertility. An important icon in shamanic traditions.

JARA Rune for J.

JESUS CHRIST

JEUNE BRETAGNE The Celtic separatist movement in Brittany, France. The symbol was originally a Celtic one associated with migration.

JEWELS Symbols of purity, refinement and superiority. In Eastern traditions they embody spiritual knowledge.

JUICE/SAP Alchemistic sign.

JUNO Asteroid.

JUNO Asteroid, archaic variation.

JUNO Asteroid, variation.

JUPITER The planet.

KANGAROO A symbol of modern-day Australia, traditionally associated with powerful mothering instincts (it carries its young in its pouch and is a fierce fighter) and with ancestor spirits.

KAUN Rune meaning boil or pustule.

KEN Rune for K.

KEY Through its power to lock and unlock doors, the key is a symbol of spiritual and secular authority, of access to sacred and temporal wealth. In Christianity for example, Christ gave St Peter the keys to heaven and earth, while in West Africa, a bunch of gold keys on a ring are part of court regalia, symbolizing the wealth of the state. In Japan, the key is a symbol of happiness because of its power to unlock the rice pantry.

KINTINKANTAN Ghanain adinkra sign for puffed-up extravagance.

KITE Used as an oracular device in China and Japan; the Japanese flew kites for good health and to secure a good harvest. Chinese kites decorated with butterflies symbolized prayers for the souls of the dead and the living.

KNOT In art, literature and sacred tradition, knots symbolize the power to bind and to set free; in ancient Egypt the knot of Isis (a type of Ankh with arms folded down) was the emblem of life and immortality. Knots can be used to symbolize love and marriage, A recurring motif in Celtic art, its symbolism linked to the ouroboros, the perpetual moving and joining together of human and cosmic activities. A loose interwoven knot symbolizes infinity or longevity. Tight knots symbolize union, but also blockage or protection.

KU KLUX KLAN The symbol of the racist organization of USA.

LABYRINTH See Maze

LADDER One of the symbolic links to mountains, also a symbol of ascension, aspiration and success.

LADDER OF TRANSMIGRATION Medieval Christian sign for the soul's pilgrimage from earthly existence to paradise.

LAGU Rune for L, meaning water or sea.

LAMB One of the earliest symbols for Christ, emblem of purity, sacrifice, renewal, redemption, innocence and gentleness. Important sacrificial and redemptive symbol for Islam and Judaism.

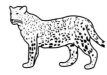

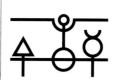

LAMP/LANTERN Symbol of spirit, truth and life. In shrines or on altars symbol of devotion and the presence of divinity. In art personification of vigilance. A Chinese lantern is a fertility symbol, used in Chinese and Japanese festivals to attract the souls of dead ancestors.

LAPIS LAZULI Alchemistic sign.

LAPIS PHILOSOPHORUM Stone of wisdom, alchemistic.

LEAD Alchemistic sign.

LEAD Alchemistic, variation.

"take in God's name". In modern use it is called the hash sign and is used on telephones.

LEAD SULPHATE Alchemistic sign.

LEMON Symbol of bitterness, failure or disappointment, in Christian art can represent faithfulness.

LEOPARD Often associated with wildness, aggression and battle; in antiquity, a symbol of strength and fertility and an attribute of Dionysus; a symbol of the supreme judicial authority of the Kings of Benin (West Africa).

LESBIANISM See Love between women

LIBRA Zodiac sign.

LIGHTNING Modern western sign for lightening made from the two signs for danger, heat together with the arrow sign for directed movement.

LIGHTNING Variation, linked with Fascism, also rune for 's'.

LANCE Associated with Christ's Passion, also with chivalry, symbol of masculine, phallic, earthly power. A broken lance symbolizes the experienced soldier

LAUREL The leaves of the laurel or bay tree were, for the Greco-Roman world, symbols of victory, peace, purification, divination and immortality. Laurel also had talismanic significance in North Africa, and in China it is the tree under which the lunar hare produces the elixir of immortality.

LEAD Early chemistry.

LEAD Old chemists sign.

LEO Zodiac sign.

LIGHTHOUSE Symbol of safety and protection in the face of danger; in Early Christian art, associated with Christ, also the heavenly harbour into which the soul sails after the dangerous journey through life. Freudian phallic symbol.

LILY Identified with Christian piety, purity and innocence. In older traditions associated with fertility and erotic love and the fertility of the Earth Goddess. Symbol of fecundity in ancient Greece and Egypt.

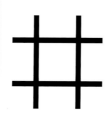

LAND OF EGYPT Associated with symbol for return or homecoming.

LAMP See Lantern

LAUREL LEAF WREATH Linked to Apollo, Greco-Roman victory crown for both warriors and poets.

LEAD Alchemistic, variation also musical notation meaning to raise a half tone. In old pharmacology it was used to mean

LEO Zodiac sign, variation.

LIME Alchemistic.

LIME Early chemistry.

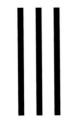

LINE Straight, diagonal, in modern iconography signifies forbidden or cancelled when over another sign.

LINE Straight, horizontal, represents the base, the earth, or land. Can also mean to link, increase or decrease when placed over or under another sign.

LINE Straight, vertical, one of the basic elements in western ideography. Stands for unity, oneness, the self, authority, power. Also symbol for yang, the active, powerful, warm, extrovert and masculine dimensions of the universe.

LINES Three identical parallel and vertical, signifies three units, also active intellect.

LINES Three identical, parallel and horizontal, similarity in one dimension, used in meteorology to indicate mist.

LINES Two identical, parallel and horizontal, equals, a doubling of the uniting and linking quality of a single horizontal line.

LINES Two identical, parallel and vertical, symbol for yin, the passive, receptive, material dimension of the universe.

LINGA A sculpted upright phallus common throughout India. A cult image and sacred symbol of the male, creative principle (Hindu), associated with Shiva, the divine power of creation, and the "world axis". The feminine counterpart of the linga is the yoni.

LION Solar animal invested with divine qualities; symbol of royal power and dominion, military victory, bravery, vigilance and fortitude. Royal emblem of England and Scotland and of British imperial power in the 19th century. In China and Japan the lion is protective.

LIZARD Symbol of evil (Greco-Roman, Christianity, Maori). Among Native American tribes, associated with shamanic powers and vision quests as well as strength (the Plains Dakota). For Aboriginal Australians the

frill-necked lizard (kendi) is a powerful rainmaker. A symbol of a peaceful household for the Babanki (Cameroon).

LOGR Rune for onion or water, stream or sea.

LOOSEN/UNSCREW Modern.

LOTUS FLOWER Ancient and prolific symbol in Egypt, India, China and Japan. Symbol of birth, cosmic life, the divine, human spiritual growth and the soul's potential to achieve perfection.

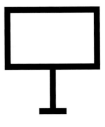

LOTUS FLOWER An ancient Egyptian mystical symbol used to signify the Earth.

LOVE BETWEEN WOMEN Lesbianism, modern ideogram.

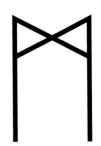

LOZENGE The rhombus or diamond shape – one of Chinese Eight Treasures, representing good fortune.

LUTE In China symbol of the scholar and of harmony in marriage and government. In Renaissance art popular emblem of the lover; if shown with strings broken can be a symbol of discord.

LYE Alchemistic sign.

LYRE Symbol of divine harmony, musical inspiration and divination. Linked with Orpheus. In myth it was invented by Hermes, who gave it to Apollo, whose attribute it became.

MADR Rune for M, meaning, man or human. Also known as mann.

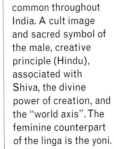

MAGNESIUM Early chemistry.

MALE HOMOSEXUAL LOVE Modern.

MAN/THE MALE There is no one symbol that represents the male principle, but this is a symbolic theme that underlies most of the world's cultures: the principle of the patriarch. Less potent today, it is still important, and carries associations such as the sun, law, authority and the warlike spirit.

MANDRAKE Believed in the Middle Ages to have magical powers; a symbol for sorcery and witchcraft.

MAP OF THE WORLD Ideogram from the Middle Ages, the vertical line signified the Mediterranean sea, the horizontal line to the left was the Nile, that to the right the Don River, the upper right section was Europe, the left Africa, the bottom Asia. The full point in Asia was Jerusalem.

MARCASITE/FOOL'S GOLD Also iron sulphate, alchemistic.

MARS The planet, named after the Roman god of war, in Greece known as Ares. Became the sign for iron (the metal used for weapons) due to Mars' link with war.

MARS The planet, variation, also sign for iron.

MASK Dramatic means of projecting symbolism in religion, ritual and theatre. Symbol of concealment or illusion, in Western art an attribute of deceit personified, of vice and of night.

MAYPOLE European folkloric phallic symbol, spring emblem of fertility and solar renewal, linked to classical spring rites.

MAZE/LABYRINTH Possibly linking back to the cave systems in which humanity once lived; ambivalent symbolism includes protection, initiation, death or rebirth, choices and life direction.

MELTING OVEN/ FORGE Alchemistic.

MENORAH The nine-candelabra of Judaism, symbol of the nation of Israel.

MERCURY Alchemistic.

MERCURY Alchemistic, variation.

MERCURY Alchemistic, variation.

MERCURY Sign of the planet.

MERCURY Sign of the planet, variation; also for mercury, metal, also poison in early chemistry.

MERCURY Sign of the planet, ancient Greek variation.

MERCURY Sign of the planet, variation.

MERCURY Sign of the planet, variation.

MERMAID See Siren

METAL Alchemistic.

234

MIGRATION A Hopi Indian sign centred around the idea of several returns, or homecoming.

MIGRATION Variation, Celtic, more recently adopted by Jeune Bretagne, a French separatist movement.

MIHRAB Islamic, niche in the wall of a mosque indicating the direction of Mecca, decorated with geometric motifs and text from the Qu'ran.

MINARET A slim tower connected to an Islamic mosque. Derived from an Arabic word meaning "to give off light", the minaret acts as a beacon of illumination to the surrounding community – it is from here that the muezzin calls the faithful to prayer.

MIRAGE

MIRROR Symbol of veracity, self-knowledge, purity, enlightenment and divination. Sometimes in Western art seen as symbol of pride, vanity or lust. Linked with magic, especially divination.

MISTLETOE Sacred to the Celtic druids as a fertility and regeneration symbol, has since been attributed with fire, lightning and rebirth. The berries were once credited with healing properties.

MITSUBISHI Corporate emblem of the Japanese firm.

MIX/MIXTURE Alchemistic.

MIX Alchemistic, variation.

MONKEY Its imitative skills make it a symbol of human vanity and other folly.

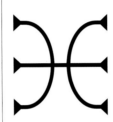

MOON Egyptian hieroglyph.

MOTHER AND CHILD Appears on pre-Columbian engravings and rock

MOON/MONTH Hittite hieroglyphic system.

MOON, NEW In astrology symbolizes human receptivity, instinct, subconscious, emotional life and ability to react. Also used as a symbol for the mother, or women in general. Alchemical sign for silver.

MOON (WANING) Used, together with a star, as the symbol for the Roman province of Illyricum and then for Constantinople. Later it developed into the sign for the Islamic faith.

paintings in Arizona, and on an Etruscan vase from around 550 BC. Also found in medieval churches throughout Europe, and in ancient stone structures in Sweden.

MOUNTAIN Symbol of transcendence, eternity, purity and spiritual ascent. Associated with immortals, heroes, sanctified prophets and gods.

MOUSE Associated with female sexuality, lechery and voracity (Greco-Roman), although a white mouse is a good luck symbol (Roman). Also associated with destructive, dark forces, stealth and cunning (Celtic) in European folklore during the Middle Ages; mice were associated with witches and the souls of the dead; infestations of mice were considered a divine punishment.

MOUTH An open mouth associated with the power of the spirit to speak, the inspiration of the soul; alternatively it can symbolize destructive forces, things being "eaten" and "devoured".

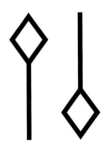

MUSHROOM Symbol of life arising from death, longevity and happiness in China; souls of the reborn in some parts of central Europe and Africa. Folklore links it with the supernatural.

MUSICAL NOTE In the Middle Ages, also (reversed) used as ideogram by the Sumerians around 3000 BC.

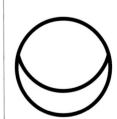

NANNAN Very ancient sign for moon god later known as Sin in the Euphrates-Tigris region. For the Babylonians the sign was linked with Venus and the sun.

NAUDH Rune for N meaning need, misery.

NAVEL The centre of creative and psychic energy, the source of life, linked to fertility.

NAZI SS Logo of the Nazi special police unit known as the Schutz Staffeln, or SS.

NEPTUNE Sign for the planet, rare variation.

NET Symbol of catching and gathering; in the East, deities sometimes shown with a net that they use to draw people closer to them; in Christianity, it is associated with the apostles as "fishers of men". In Jungian psychology, fishing with a net can signify connecting with the unconscious.

NICKEL Calcinated copper, alchemistic.

NIED Rune for N.

NIGHT Time sign, alchemistic.

NIKE Corporate logo.

NINE As the triple triad, nine is a supremely powerful number, the most auspicious Chinese number, the most potent yang number. In mysticism it represents the triple synthesis of mind, body and spirit. Hebrew symbol of truth, Christian symbol of order within order.

NKONSONKONSON Chain links, Ghanaian adinkra symbol meaning strength within unity, used as a reminder to contribute to the community.

NOOSE A masonic symbol of the cord that binds one to life and in initiation rituals, of being born into a new life. As hangman's noose, a symbol of death and the end of life.

NOSE Associated with intuitive discernment, hence expressions such as "sniffing out the truth". In Maori culture, rubbing noses is not only a way of kissing, but symbolizes the gods breathing life into humans and is a sign of peace. In Japan, people point to their nose rather than their heart to indicate themselves.

NSORAN Sorrow or lament, Ghanian adinkra symbol.

NSOROMMA Child of the heavens, Ghanaian adinkra symbol used as a reminder that God is father and watches over all people.

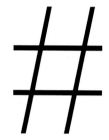

NUMBER In modern Western systems. In musical notation it is called a sharp and is an instruction to raise a half tone. Also used in early chemistry to denote air.

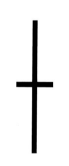

NUMBER 10 From the medieval clog almanacs to calculate the moon's phases.

NUT Highly symbolic in the Jewish tradition, the nut is the symbol of the scholar, and represents virtue in that the beginning and end, seed and fruit are one and the same. The Romans considered the nut a fertility symbol in both humans and animals.

NYAME BIRIBI WO SORO God is in the heavens. Ghanaian adinkra symbol.

NYAME NNWU NA MAWU God never dies, therefore I cannot die. Ghanaian adinkra symbol reminding people of immortality.

OAK Linked with nobility and endurance, sacred to thunder gods of the Celts, Greeks and Germanic tribes, symbol of male potency and wisdom but linked to mother goddesses and the Dryads, oak nymphs.

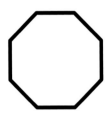

OBELISK Rectangular, tapering pillar, Egyptian symbol of the sun god, Ra, topped by a reflective pyramid that caught the light.

OCTAGON Draws on the symbolism of the number eight, emblem of renewal, and combining the symbolism of the square and the circle.

OCTAGRAM OF CREATION Gnostic, also Nordic invocation of magic and protection.

OIL Alchemistic.

OLYMPIC GAMES Five linked rings symbolizing the five continents of the world that participate in the sporting event.

OM SYMBOL (Aum), the greeting of peace in India. The symbol represents the four states of consciousness: awake, dreaming, sleeping, without dreams and the transcendental state.

OMEGA The last letter of the Greek alphabet.

ONE A symbol of God, emblem of primordial unity, could also stand for the sun or light, and the origin of life. Confucian perfect entity. Symbol of beginning, the self and loneliness.

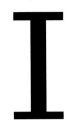

ONE Roman numeral, singular, individual, emperor, Jesus. Used in English speaking world to signify the first person.

OPEL For their corporate logo this car manufacturer used the ancient sign for victory.

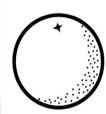

ORANGE Commonly a symbol of fertility

ORB See Globe

OSTRICH In ancient Egypt an ostrich feather was a symbol of justice and truth. The burying of its head in the sand is a modern symbol of avoiding the truth.

OTHEL Rune for O.

OTTER Often associated with lunar symbolism from its periodic nature of diving and rising in water. A Romanian folk song tells of otters guiding the souls of the dead. The otter often also symbolizes laughter, playfulness and mischievousness.

OURBOUROUS A serpent in circular formation with tail in its mouth, symbol of cyclic time, eternity and the indivisible, self-sustaining character of Nature.

OWL Associated with magic, the otherworld, wisdom and prophecy in many traditions.

OX Universally benevolent symbol of strength, patience, submissiveness and steady toil. Christian emblem of sacrificial Christ. Sacrificial animal in the ancient world. Taoist and Buddhist symbol of the sage.

PACHUCO CROSS An identifying sign, often used as a tattoo, by Hispanic-American street gangs.

PAGODA Sacred building in the Buddhist tradition, the diminishing tiers symbolize spiritual ascent.

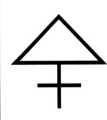

PALLAS Sign of the asteroid.

PANTHER The panther commonly depicts desire and power. However, in ancient Christian symbolism the panther was one of three animals representing chastity. The black panther is a feminine symbol of the night, death and rebirth.

PARASOL/UMBRELLA Symbol for the dome of Heaven in ancient China. The parasol was Vishnu's symbol and also an emblem of the Buddha himself. The parasol is often also a solar symbol suggesting the rank, authority and even the halo of the king who is shaded by it. In an everyday sense the parasol represents protection.

PARROT A symbol of the sun and the coming of the rainy season in Native American lore. In Hinduism, Kama – god of love – rides a parrot across three worlds spreading love and desire.

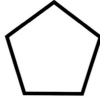

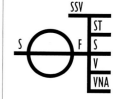

PARZ A very early rune, later came to mean secret, mystery, initiation in Anglo-Saxon literature.

PAWNSHOP Originally part of the Medici family arms, who were rich money lenders.

PEACE Christian.

PEACH A very important symbol in Chinese culture with many meanings; associated with immortality, an emblem of marriage, a fertility symbol.

PEAR The pear is a mother, or love, symbol with erotic associations that are probably due to its shape. Associated with Aphrodite and Hera in classical mythology. A longevity symbol in China.

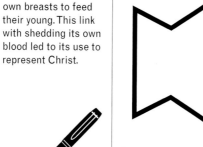

PELICAN Christian symbol of self-sacrificial love, based on the medieval misconception that the birds tore their own breasts to feed their young. This link with shedding its own blood led to its use to represent Christ.

PEN A Freudian phallic symbol, also associated with the executive function and the power of reason. In the Sufi tradition the Supreme Pen represents Universal Intelligence.

PENTAGON Associated with the planet Venus, used in a few established Western ideographic systems.

PENTAGRAM/ PENTACLE Used since 4000 BC with unknown significance, especially by the Sumerians, until Pythagorean mysticism defined it as a symbol of the human being. Known as Solomon's Seal in medieval Jewish mysticism.

PEORTH Rune for P.

PER CENT Modern.

PHALEC Used in Kabbalistic mysticism for the spirit of Mars.

PHILOSOPHER'S STONE Alchemistic.

PHOENIX The legendary bird that renews itself in fire became the most famous of all rebirth symbols, a resurrection emblem and eventually the symbol of the indomitable human spirit.

PIG Ambiguous symbolism of gluttony, selfishness, lust, obstinacy and ignorance, but also motherhood, fertility, prosperity and happiness.

PIPE In Native American culture tobacco was a sacred herb. Smoking shared pipes was a social activity based around religious ceremony or tribal alliances.

PISCES Zodiac sign.

PISCES Zodiac sign, ancient Greek variation.

PLAITED SIGN Nordic design pattern.

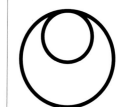

PLATINUM A metal discovered in the mid-1800s, its sign is a combination of those for gold and silver.

PLEIADES Magical amulet seal.

PLIMSOLL MARK Named after its inventor, printed on the sides of cargo ships to give visible checks as to the safety of the cargo's weight, depending on which waters the ship was sailing in.

PLOUGH Symbol of peace, also a male fertility symbol, the male plough entering the female earth. Also a thematic symbol of man's farming activity, pushing back the wilderness and taming it to produce food. Counter-balance to the sword, as an anti-war concept.

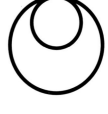

PLUTO Sign of the planet, the most common variation.

PLUTO Sign of the planet, variation.

PLUTO Sign of the planet, variation.

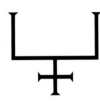

POLARIS Fixed star, magical amulet seal, Kabbalism.

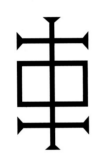

POMEGRANATE Strongly identified with sexual temptation, also with unity, linked to fertility, love and marriage.

POSEIDON Sign of the god.

POTASH Alchemistic.

POTASSIUM CARBONATE Late alchemy and early chemistry.

POUND STERLING British currency.

PRAYER BEADS Used in religious contexts, such as Catholicism and Buddhism, as an aid to remembering specific prayers or sequences of prayers. The number of beads in the string usually has symbolic meaning.

PRAYER STICK An aid to prayer in shamanic traditions, and a link with God.

PRAYER WHEEL Tibetan, an aid to prayer for Buddhists and Hindus that is spun round as the prayer unfolds. Its turning movement therefore is a symbol in itself of the cycles of birth, death and rebirth.

PRECIPITATION Alchemistic.

PROCYON Astrological sign for the star procyon.

PROTECTION An example of several similar structures that were drawn on barns and houses for protection or good fortune.

PUMPKIN In China, and in feng shui the pumpkin symbolizes prosperity and abundance. A pumpkin with a face carved out of it is known as a Jack O' Lantern, which is a symbol of Halloween.

PURIFICATION Alchemistic.

PYRAMID Carrying the same symbolism as the triangle, one of the most powerful and versatile geometric symbols.

QUAIL Chinese symbol of light, also warmth, ardour and courage. In Greek and Hindu traditions the quail is a symbol of renewal of life and return of the sun.

QUESTION MARK Modern, denoting a question in written text.

QUINCUNX Astrology, the inconjunct aspect: a 150-degree angle between planets as seen from Earth.

QUINTESSENCE Alchemistic.

QUINTILE Astrology.

RABBIT Strong moon association and therefore linked with menstruation and fertility in most traditions. Folkloric symbol of harmless guile.

RAD Rune for R.

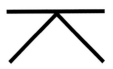

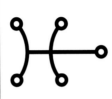

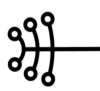
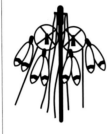

RADIATION Used since antiquity for radiation of light, in modern usage release of energy or radiation, in comic strips fistfights and explosions.

RAIDO Rune associated with raiding, journey.

RAIN Vital symbol of fecundity linked to divine blessings or punishments. Emblem of purity.

RAM Symbol of solar energy, as first sign of the zodiac represents

RAPHAEL Symbol of the archangel.

RAT Symbol of fecundity, also destructiveness and avarice. Generally negative associations but in folkloric traditions it is a symbol of knowingness, and in Asian traditions it is associated with gods of wisdom, success or prosperity.

RATTLE Used in shamanic rituals, and a symbol of the shaman him/herself and their position as a mediator between Earth and the otherworld.

RAVEN A symbol of loss, death and war in western Europe, but venerated elsewhere

renewal of fertility and return of spring. Also symbolizes virility, ardour and obstinacy.

as a solar and oracular symbol; the messenger bird of the god Apollo in the Greek world and linked with the Roman cult of Mithras. In Africa the raven is a guide, and to Native Americans a culture hero. The Inuits have a creator god called the Raven Father, and they believed that killing a raven would bring bad weather.

RECYCLING A modern sign for the recycling of household or industrial waste.

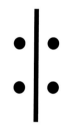

REEDS Japanese and Celtic symbol of purification. Fertility symbol in Mesoamerica. In classical tradition it is an emblem of Pan (he made his pipes from reeds), and in Christian symbolism it is linked to Christ's Passion from the vinegar-soaked sponge that was offered to him on the end of a reed. In Western folklore tradition, reeds were believed to protect from witchcraft.

REGULUS Star, medieval magical amulet seal.

REINDEER In cultures of the far north reindeer have lunar significance as funerary symbols, and are said to be conductors of dead souls. The flight of reindeer associated with Christmas probably originates in the flight of the Lapp shaman.

REPETITION Musical notation.

REVERSED FOUR Ancient and widespread structure found in prehistoric caves in Western Europe, meaning unknown.

RHINOCEROS An astrological symbol of the ancient Indus Calendar (3100 BC), the rhinoceros is one of four animals that surround Brahma, the Hindu god of creation.

RIBBON The symbolism of the ribbon depends more upon colour or context. Ribbons are often worn to indicate the wearer identifies with a particular cause or memory.

RICE Central emblem of growth, rebirth and fertility. Staple food in India and China and therefore has particular significance in these cultures, with links to divine nourishment. In Asia rice is used as a fecundity symbol at Indian weddings and appears in mythology as the gift of the gods to the first humans. In China rice wine was a sacred drink, and grains of rice were placed in the mouths of the dead. The Japanese god, Inari is the god of prosperity and of rice.

RING Circular symbol of eternity and therefore a prime binding symbol, also symbol of completion, continuity, strength and protection. Used as an emblem of authority, occult protective power, and as the sign of a personal pledge.

ROCK The rock commonly symbolizes that which is unchanging, enduring and motionless. In Chinese Taoist thought, rocks, as seen in landscape paintings, are associated with the qualities of the active principle, yang. Similarly in Hindu tradition rocks are embued with this same active principle. Sisyphus' rock is a symbol of the earthly desires of humans.

ROCK SALT Alchemistic.

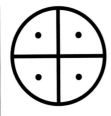

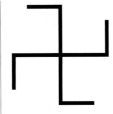

ROD/WAND, ancient symbol of supernatural power associated with the tree, the phallus and the snake.

SAFFRON Alchemistic.

SALT WATER Alchemistic sign.

SATURN Sign for the god.

SAUVASTIKA Reversed swastika, associated with misfortune and bad luck.

SCEPTRE/STAFF Originally a male fertility symbol, implies royal or divine power and has been used as a symbol of imperial or kingly position, especially in Western art.

ROSE Mystic symbol of the heart; centre of the cosmic wheel; of sacred, romantic and sensual love, and of perfection.

SAGITTARIUS Zodiac sign.

SANDAL Removal of sandals represents the connection between the human and the Earth: this is seen in the Masonic ritual of removing sandals, and in Moses making contact with holy ground on Mount Sinai. To the ancient Taoists winged sandals enabled the immortals to move through the air, symbolism seen also in the winged sandals of Hermes and Perseus.

SATURN Sign for the god, variation.

SCALES Common representation of justice, truth, balance and prudence; the weighing up of decisions and actions. In ancient Egyptian mythology, scales were used to weigh the souls of the dead, and in Christian iconography angels are often depicted with scales as the symbol of divine judgement.

SALMON Symbol of virility, fecundity, courage, wisdom and foresight. To the Celts the salmon was linked to transformation and virility. To the people of northern Europe the salmon's migration upriver made it a totem of nature's bounty and wisdom.

SATURN Sign for the planet.

ROSETTE The eight-leaf rosette is an ancient and global symbol representing birth, death and rebirth, specifically in relation to the sun or the planet Venus. In modern times rosettes made from ribbons are used to mark a victory.

SANFOKA Ghanaian adinkra symbol meaning "return and get it", signifying the importance of learning from the past.

SCALLOP SHELL Associated with Aphrodite, and therefore with love.

SCISSORS Ceremonial tool whose action of cutting marks the culmination and opening of a new project, as in the opening of a building. Scissors were associated with Atropos, the Fate who cut the thread of life.

SALT Alchemistic sign.

SAP See Juice

SAUVASTIKA Reversed swastika, Greek variation from around 500 BC.

SCARAB BEETLE Ancient Egyptian solar symbol.

SCORPIO Zodiac sign.

SCORPIO Zodiac sign, variation.

RUBBER Alchemistic.

SCORPIO Zodiac sign, variation.

SEAL OF LOA-TZU Taoist sage.

African myths the rainbow snake links the earth with the heavens; the Aztec bird-snake divinity Quetzalcoatl does the same, and in Egypt the barge that carries the dead to the underworld enters a serpent. The snake also has sexual and agricultural fertility symbolism.

Apollo, Osiris, Mithras and the Buddha. Symbol of perfection for Islam.

SHEAF OF WHEAT Fertility symbol, also associated with abundance, plenty, with daily bread and with harvest time.

SHIELD Symbol of protection and deliverance. In the medieval chivalric period, the shield was part of a knight's badge of honour and identification. In Aboriginal myth, the shield is associated with the moon.

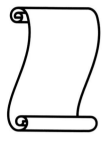

SCROLL Symbol of learning and law.

SEAL OF SOLOMON Also known as the pentagram, and the Star of David.

SEXUAL LOVE Modern, composed of heart sign and the arrow of Eros, one of the most widely used contemporary icons.

SERPENT COILED AROUND EGG Sometimes referred to as the cosmic egg, Greek symbol of the world being protected by a cosmic serpent.

SHEEP Meekness and a helpless need for leadership and protection.

SHOE The shoe is commonly a symbol of possession. It is an Islamic tradition to remove one's shoes when crossing the threshold of another's house, showing one claims no possession of the property. Shoes can also signify that an individual is his or her own master.

SCYTHE Farm implement used for cutting crops, associated with Roman god Saturn. In medieval iconography, an attribute of the Grim Reaper (Death).

SEED OF THE UNIVERSE This is the Tibetan sign for the origins of the universe, also found in the coat of arms of the Aztec god Quetzalcoatl.

SHAMROCK Emblem of Ireland, supposedly from the time when St Patrick, patron saint of Ireland, used the shamrock to explain the three elements of the Holy Trinity to his congregation.

SHEPHERD Symbol of protection and care. Jesus Christ is portrayed in the Bible as the Good Shepherd, and this image has been widely used in Western art.

SHOFAR A symbol of the Jewish faith, a ram's horn that is blown like a trumpet on Jewish new year.

SESA WORUBAN Ghanaian adinkra symbol, meaning the ability to change or transform life.

SHARK Modern associations with terror and violence.

SEA HORSE Can symbolize the male role in the birthing process, as the male animal carries its young within its own body.

SERPENT/SNAKE Most significant and complex animal, symbol of primeval life force and divine self-sufficiency. Often part of creation myths; Vishnu, the Hindu creator god, rests on the coils of a great snake; in

SEVEN Sacred, mystical and magical number; symbol of cosmic and spiritual order; sacred to

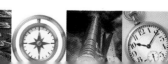

SHOU The Chinese character for long life, used in the decoration of ceramics and textiles.

SICKLE One of the tools of the Grim Reaper, associated with death, also with harvest and agriculture. One of the parts of the sign for communism.

SIEVE Commonly symbolizes the separation of good and evil. The sieve is also used as a sifting tool of divine justice or satanic judgement.

SIGEL Rune for S.

SIGRUNE Rune linked with victory.

SIKHISM Sign of the Sikh faith.

SILVER Alchemistic.

SILVER Alchemistic, variation.

SIREN/MERMAID Seen as the embodiment of the sexual side of the female, symbol of temptation, beauty and otherness.

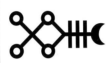

SIRIUS Star, magical amulet seal, Kabbalism.

SIX Symbol of union and equilibrium.

SKULL Potent symbol of death, used as a sign warning that a substance is poison. As part of the skull and crossbones motif is also a symbol of piratism.

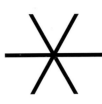

SLING From the biblical story of David and Goliath, the sling has been used as a symbol of the triumph of the weak.

SMA Egyptian, union.

SMOKE An ascension symbol; means of communication on cosmic and mundane level for Native Americans. Also a symbol of concealment.

SNAIL Usually a lunar symbol associated with cyclical or periodic processes in nature. In coming out and returning to its shell the snail is indicative of an eternal homecoming. The snail is also associated with the sexual symbolism of the vulva; the Aztecs considered it to be a symbol of conception, pregnancy and birth.

SNOW Six-pointed crystal; modern sign for freezing.

SOLAR ECLIPSE Symbol of cosmic danger; in ancient cultures was a symbol of fear.

SPACE ROCKET Symbol of human endeavour and soaring ambition.

SPADES Suit of cards, associated with fighting, destiny, logical thinking, and death. Originally iconic sign for sword.

SPEAR As the lance, a symbol of masculine, phallic and earthly power. Associated with chivalry and with the Passion of Christ, from the spear that pierced his side. The broken lance is an attribute of St George, patron saint of England, and symbolizes the experienced soldier.

SPHINX In ancient Egypt, a monument of a human-headed lion, symbol of the sun. In ancient Greece, a riddle-spinning hybrid with wings, female human head and breasts, which Jung saw as a symbol of the devouring mother.

SPICA Sign of the star.

SPIDER Folkloric links with oncoming rain, also with gifts from Heaven.

SPIRAL The clockwise spiral starts from the middle, symbolizes water, power, independent movement and migration. One of the most important and ancient symbols; most common of all decorative motifs throughout cultures. As an open and flowing line it suggests extension, evolution and continuity.

SPIRAL Maori Koru, the Polynesian spiral has sexual symbolism and is based on the uncurling fern leaf. It shows the close link between spiral motifs and natural phenomena.

SPIRAL OF LIFE Found in the Bronze Age in Ireland, this sign is drawn in one single line without beginning or end.

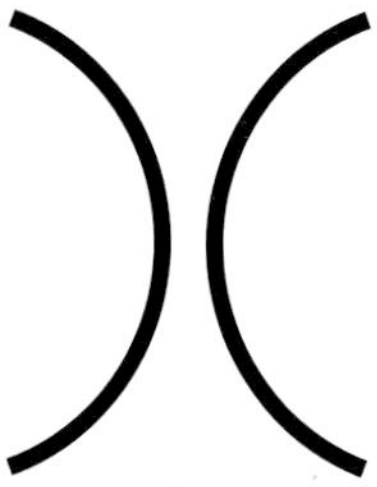

SPLIT/CLEAVE Appears in earliest Chinese and other ancient writing systems.

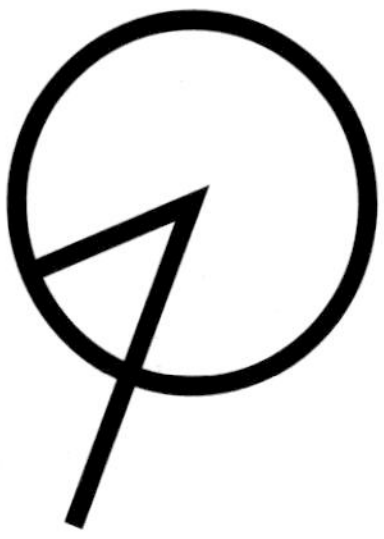

SPRING Time sign, alchemistic.

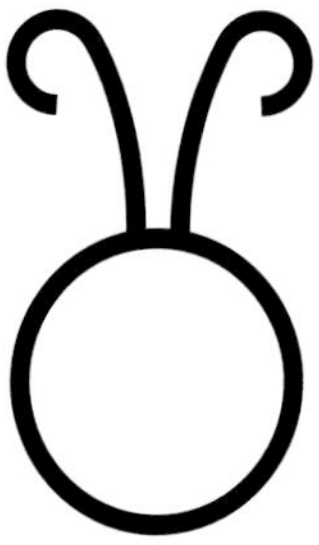

SPRING Time sign, Germanic.

SQUARE An expression of the two dimensions that constitute a surface; symbol of land, field, ground, or the earth element. Thought to mean realization or materialization in Egyptian hieroglyphs.

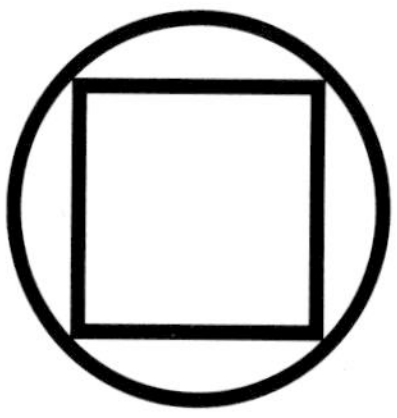

SQUARE WITHIN A CIRCLE In Chinese symbolism this represents Earth. In Beijing the temple of Earth is constructed on this principle, whereas the temple of Heaven is a circle within a square.

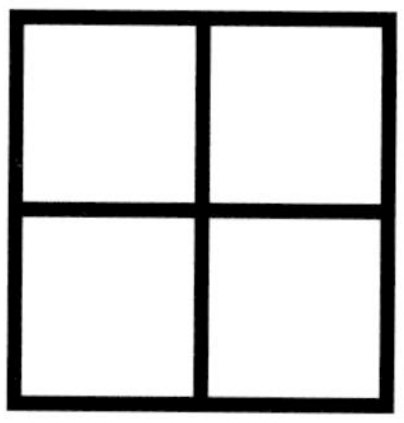

SQUARE, WITH CROSS In China and Japan symbolizes field or ground, not common in Western ideography.

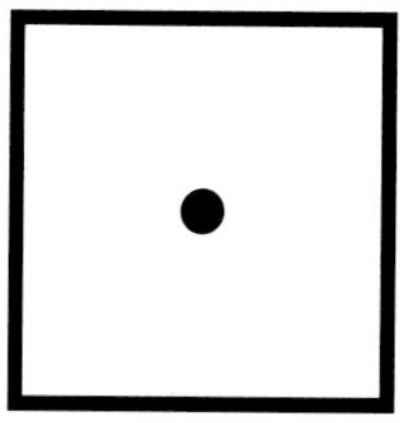

SQUARE, WITH DOT Village in Chinese writing; urine in alchemistic; wet ground in meteorology.

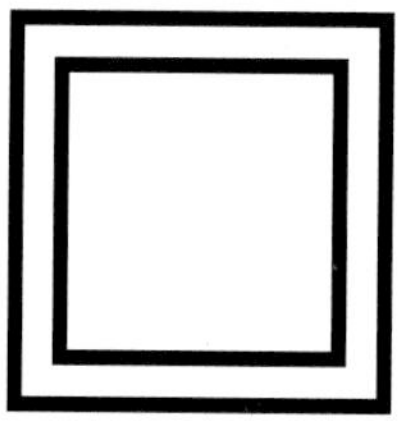

SQUARE, WITHIN A SQUARE Keep, retain, keep inside or close in. Modern sign for manhole.

STAFF See Sceptre

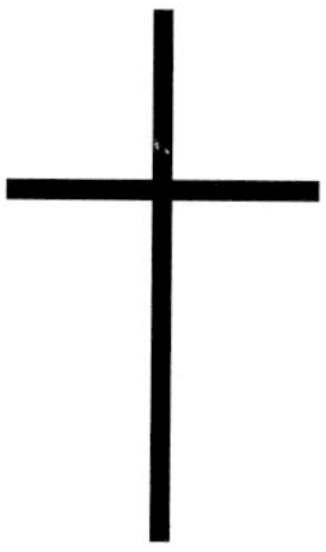

STAFF OF APOLLO Also known as the Latin cross; in pre-Christian times it represented the god Apollo and appeared on ancient coins. Also used in pre-Columbian America and the Euphrates–Tigris region as a sun sign.

STAFF OF THE DEVIL

STAFF OF JUPITER/ZEUS.

STAFF OF ODIN

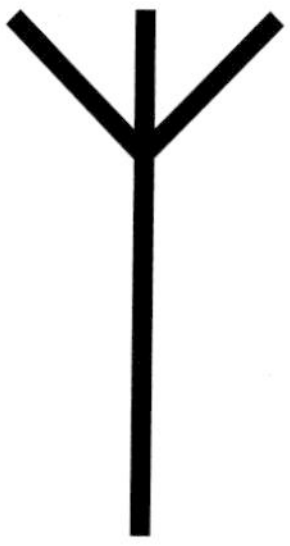

STAFF OF POSEIDON

STAFF Egyptian.

STAFF Phoenician.

STAG Solar emblem of fertility, the antlers symbolize the tree of life, the sun's rays, longevity and rebirth. Antlers have been used as headdresses for dieties; on the Celtic antlered god Cerunnus they represented spring and fecundity.

STAIRCASE Symbol of ascent and descent; in the acquisition of knowledge of the divine when rising, or of the unconscious or the occult when descending

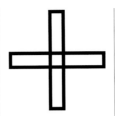

244

STAR Three-pointed, known as an Ethiopian emblem, a rare three-pointed star symbol.

STAR Eight-pointed, an ancient symbol for the goddess, or the planet, Venus, and for the Morning or Evening Star.

STAR OF LAKSHMI

STONES/PEBBLES Alchemistic.

SUCCESS Protection against evil, Sumerian; also Viking.

vitality, passion, courage and eternally renewed youth, knowledge, intellect and truth. Emblem of royalty and imperial splendour.

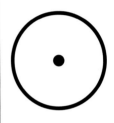

STAR Four-pointed, also known as the sun star, denotes serious and solemn warning.

STAR OF VENUS

SUN Variation, also gold in pre-Christian Greece.

STAR, EASTERN Sign for the planet Venus. Common among tribal peoples in Africa and the Americas.

STORK Symbol of longevity and filial devotion. Sacred to Greek goddess Hera. Linked to purity, piety and resurrection for Christians.

SULPHUR Alchemistic.

STAR OF VENUS Phoenician variation.

SULPHUR Alchemistic, variation.

SUN Most ancient ideogram for the sun, seems to have been used in every cultural sphere on earth.

STAR Five-pointed, one of the most common and important Western ideograms; used on 35 national flags; widely used as a military and law enforcement symbol. Denotes the Bethlehem star. Used to indicate top quality.

STAR Gnostic.

STARFISH With its five-fold symmetry, the starfish is an esoteric symbol associated with five-pointed stars and the spiral of life.

STUPA Graphical representation of a stupa symbolizing the organization of the universe: square for earth, circle for water, triangle for fire, crescent for air and droplet for ether.

SUMMER Time sign, alchemistic.

SUN Bronze Age Nordic, also prehistoric Egyptian.

STAR Six-pointed; rare in Western ideography but used in some United States as a policeman's badge.

STAR OF DAVID Most well known of Jewish symbols, is supposed to be based on the shape of King David's shield, but is almost certainly more modern. Also known as the seal of Solomon, and in mystic traditions as the pentagram.

STEEL Alchemistic.

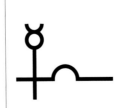

SUBLIMATE Alchemistic.

SUN Dominant symbol of creative energy in most traditions; symbol of

SUN CROSS Danish Bronze age.

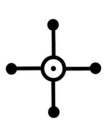

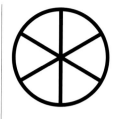

SUN CROSS Variation found in excavation of 4000 year-old Cretan city of Troy.

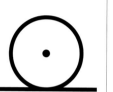
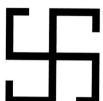

SUN GOD The archetypal ancient Egyptian sign, known as the Eye of Horus, and as the *wedjat*. Symbol of cosmic wholeness, and of the all-seeing power of the god Horus.

SUN/SUNLIGHT/STARS Japanese.

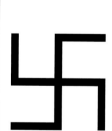

SUN WHEEL Also known as the ring cross; common in the Nordic countries, pre-Columbian America, and throughout the Mediterranean about 3,500 years ago.

SUN WHEEL Used in Gaul, also sign of Taranis, Celtic god of thunder.

SUNRISE New day, earliest Chinese writing systems.

SWAN Romantic and ambiguous symbol of masculine light and feminine beauty in Western music and ballet. Attribute of Aphrodite and Apollo.

SWASTIKA Ancient ideogram first found in Sumeria about 3000 BC. Its name comes from the Sanskrit *su*, "well", and *asti* "being". Used in India, Japan and Southern Europe with various meanings, all of them positive, including as one of the symbols of the Buddha. The swastika is usually associated with sun and power, with the life force and cyclic regeneration – often extended to signify the Supreme Being. In modern times the swastika was monopolized by Hitler as sign of the Nazi party in 1930s.

SWASTIKA Ancient Greek variation.

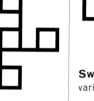

SWASTIKA Celtic variation.

SWASTIKA Christian variation.

SWASTIKA Nazi variation, in which an ancient symbol that for thousands of years had been a positive sign of cosmic regeneration was degraded into a political emblem of repression and violence.

SWASTIKA Pre-Columbian America variation.

SWASTIKA Viking variation.

SWORD Important and ancient symbol of authority, justice, intellect and light. Emblem of magic. Linked to exceptional virtue and cults of the sword, particularly in Japan and in the religious rituals of the crusades. Carries a ceremonial role, especially to confer knighthoods. Symbol of constancy, and wrath personified, in religious thought it is often equated with wisdom and knowledge.

TAMBOURINE/TIMBREL An important ritual object to the Israelites and a Jewish symbol of victory and jubilee.

TAMFOA BEBRE Ghanaian adinkra symbol meaning the importance of learning from the past.

TARGET Modern.

TARTAR Alchemistic, also found on South American rock carvings.

TARTRATE Alchemistic.

TASSELS In 17th-century France the tassel came to represent wealth, prestige and power. As Masonic symbols, the four tassels represent the cardinal virtues. In Catholicism and other religious traditions, the wearing of tassels can symbolize rank.

TAURUS Zodiac sign.

TEARS Symbols of grief or sadness.

TEETH Primordial symbols of aggressive-defensive power.

TEFILLIN Jewish, leather pouch containing quote from the Torah, strapped to the arm and head.

10

TEN Symbol of perfection, especially in Jewish tradition; symbol for whole of creation for Pythagoreans; and for perfect balance for Chinese.

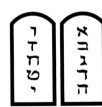

TEN COMMANDMENTS Jewish.

TEST Alchemistic.

TET OF OSIRIS Also known as the Djed Pillar, is a stylized tree, symbolic of the tamarisk tree that held Osiris's body. It symbolizes sturdiness, stability and the ability of the spirit to break from its earthly bonds and rise towards the heavens. It is equated with the backbone, and possibly also with the penis.

יהוה

TETRAGRAMMATON The four Hebrew letters used to represent the name of God, Yahweh, a name that must not be spoken aloud in the Jewish faith.

THEOSOPHICAL SOCIETY A society founded in the 19th century and still in existence today, whose primary objective is Universal Brotherhood based on the idea that life and all its forms is indivisibly One.

THISTLE Symbol of retaliation; also healing or talismanic powers. Emblem of martyrdom and of Scotland.

THORN Commonly associated with blocks and barriers, whether internal or external. Christ's crown of thorns can be understood as a crown of suffering or as a solar symbol with the thorns representing the rays of the sun emanating outwards. Flying thorns in China were weapons that drove out evil. "A land of thorn and thistles" in the Jewish and Christian traditions referred to soil that was untilled and therefore virginal.

THORN Rune for Th.

THREAD A linking symbol that connects many different states of being to one another, and to a unifying origin. Ariadne's thread linked Theseus between the underworld and the everyday world. Puppet strings link the puppet to the puppet master.

3

THREE The most positive number in symbolism, religious thought, legend, mythology and folklore. The lucky three is a very ancient concept. In Christian thought it has central importance as the doctrine of the Trinity, God the Father, God the Son and God the Holy Spirit, a theology that has forerunners in classical, Celtic and Hindu traditions.

THRONE Traditional symbol of kingship, divine authority and power.

THUNDERBOLT Linked with Nazism, and with the rune for yew, Viking.

TIGER In Asia and India the tiger replaces the lion as the symbol of all that is great and terrible in nature.

TOAD Symbol of death; linked to witchcraft in European traditions; a good luck lunar symbol in China; associated with rain and riches.

TODESRUNE Rune of death.

TODESRUNE Rune of death, variation.

TOMAHAWK Pipe tomahawks were used to seal treaties between different Native American groups. The Algonquian tamahak was ceremonial and a symbol of leadership.

TOMATO The Bambara associate tomato juice with blood, and thus the tomato is considered to have the blood of life, and is the bearer of the foetus.

TORCH A symbol of illumination. Its light is born to illuminate passage on a journey. The concept of the flame that is never extinguished is a potent one.

TOTEM POLE A symbolic carved pole representing totem animal and guardian spirits of an individual or clan.

TREASURE Abundant riches, found rather than earned, have always been a symbol of attainment, and feature in mythologies as reward for the just, or the means to punishment for the wrong-doer.

TREE OF LIFE Universal symbol of creation, the tree of life has its roots in the waters of the underworld, its trunk in the earthly world, and its branches in the heavens. Seen as a way of accessing other worlds.

TRIANGLE Equilateral, associated with the divine number three, symbol for power, success, prosperity and safety. The Hittites used it for well, good or healthy.

TRIANGLE Single axis symmetric, variation of equilateral triangle.

TRIANGLE Pythagorean.

TRIANGLE With horizontal line, element of fire in the Middle Ages.

TRIANGLE Upside down, element of water. Also negative spectrum of meaning.

TRIANGLE Upside down, with horizontal line, element of earth in the Middle Ages.

TRIANGLE With a vertical line, in Hittite hieroglyphics this sign represented the king, the vertical line signifying the unique being inside the triangle, which stood for power and divinity.

TRIDENT Symbol of sea power; emblem of Neptune; of ancient Minoan civilization; and later of Britannia.

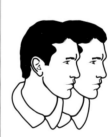

TRIQUETRA A tripartate symbol composed of three interlocked vesica pisces, most commonly used for the Holy Trinity but predates Christianity and was likely a Celtic symbol of the triple goddess or Odin.

TRISKELION Greek word for three-leg, this was found on an Athenian shield used as a competition prize in 500 BC.

TRUMPET Instrument of portent, momentous news or action, used in military, ritualistic and state occasions.

TUDOR ROSE Emblem of the Tudor royal dynasty created by combining the white rose of York with the red rose of Lancaster.

TURTLE/TORTOISE Symbol of the whole universe, its shell representing the heavens, and its flat base, earth. Chinese and Amerindian tradition link penile erection with the way the head emerges from its shell.

TWINS Sign of Gemini, twins are generally symbols of the nature of dualism.

TWO Symbol of duality: division but synthesis, attraction but repulsion, equilibrium but conflict. Thought of as unlucky in China.

TYR Rune for T.

UMBRELLA See Parasol

UNDERWORLD Egyptian hieroglyph.

UNICORN Ultimate symbol of chastity, courtly symbol of sublimated desire, Christian symbol of the incarnation.

UR/URUZ Rune, meaning strength, sacrificial animal.

URANUS The planet.

URANUS The planet, variation, also morning.

URN/VASE Female symbol, often appearing as emblems of eternal life in art or in funeral rituals.

VENUS The planet.

VENUS The planet, variation.

VESCIA PISCIS Also known as the fish bladder or mystical almond, adopted by Christians from pagan sources to symbolize purity and virginity.

VESSEL/BOWL Alchemical; also ancient Germanic time sign for summer.

VICTORY Christian.

VINEGAR Alchemistic.

VIRGIN MARY A symbol used by the Christian Church to represent the mother of Jesus.

VIRGO Zodiac sign.

VISHNU The Hindu god holds this sign in one of his four hands as a symbol of the whole universe.

VITRIOL Alchemistic.

VITRIOL Early chemistry.

VIVA! See Down with!

VOLKSWAGEN Emblem of the car manufacturer.

WALNUT Judeo-Christian symbol of fertility and longevity.

WAND See Rod

WATER Alchemistic, also modern.

WATER In all times and all cultures; among the earliest Egyptian hieroglyphs; also adopted to signify resistence.

WATER Kabbalism.

WATER Early chemistry.

WATER ELEMENT See Triangle, upside down.

WATER Common in ancient Greece as decoration.

WAX Alchemistic.

WEEK Time sign in alchemy.

WELL The symbolism of the well is commonly associated with qualities of the sacred or of the unconscious; wells are places of knowledge; the source of life; places of healing; wishes or good luck.

WHALE Ark or womb symbol of regeneration, linked with initiation in Africa and Polynesia.

WHEEL Solar image of cosmic momentum, ceaseless change and cyclic repetition; later of power and dominion. Linked with the progress of mankind. Hindu and Buddhist emblem of reincarnation. Western image of fortune and fate.

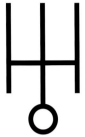

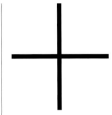

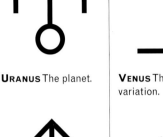

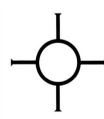

WHIP Symbol of rulership, judgement and fertility; the flail replaced the whip in Egypt, and the fly whisk in Africa, China and India.

WHITE ARSENIC Alchemistic.

WHITE LEAD Early chemistry.

WIND FURNACE Alchemistic.

WINTER Old Germanic time sign.

WOLF Ambivalent symbol of cruelty, cunning and greed but in other cultures of courage, victory or nourishing care (Roman). Sacred to Apollo and Odin.

WOMAN A common sign in both ancient and modern systems.

WOMAN/FEMALE SEX Egyptian hieroglyphs; also found widely in cave art; associated with growing and genesis implying that woman is the originator of life.

WOOD Alchemistic.

WOOD Alchemistic, variation.

WORLD Tibetan.

WOW FORO ADOBE Ghanaian adinkra symbol for persistence and prudence.

WREATH The first crown – symbol of spiritual or temporal authority – drawing on the symbolism of the circle (perfection) and the ring (continuity).

WYNN Rune for W.

YANTRA STRUCTURE Indian, also sorting in computer usage.

YEAR Time sign, alchemistic.

YIN YANG Chinese symbol for the duality of the universe.

YIN YANG Earliest ideogram for yin yang. Ideogram in the West for the number 10 from latin X; also signifies hourglass.

YOKE Symbol of oppression from Roman times.

YONI Buddhist symbol of the vulva.

ZEUS Sign of the god.

ZEUS God, variation.

ZEUS God, variation.

ZIGZAG

ZINC Alchemistic.

ZODIAC Also known as the ecliptic, the via solis or the way of the sun.

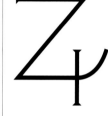
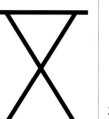
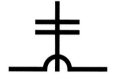

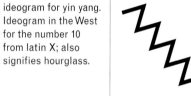

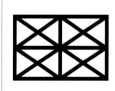

ACKNOWLEDGEMENTS

THE ART ARCHIVE: p1 Warburg Institute London/Eileen Tweedy; p2tl British Library; p2ml Sydney Parkinson, British Library , p4m tomb of Nefertari, Dagli Orti; p10t Musée des Antiquités St Germain en Laye/Dagli Orti; p12t British Museum/Dagli Orti; p12b Musée du Louvre, Paris/Dagli Orti; p13t Musée du Louvre Paris/Dagli Orti; p13m Abbey of Novacella or Neustift/Dagli Orti; p14tm Luxor Museum, Egypt/Dagli Orti; p15b Egyptian Museum Cairo/Dagli Orti; p16b Musée du Louvre Paris/Dagli Orti; p17tl National Archaeological Museum Athens/ Dagli Orti; p19 Chateau de Malmaison, France/Dagli Orti; p21t National Museum of Prague/Dagli Orti; p21b Bibliothèque des Arts Décoratifs Paris/Dagli Orti; p27t Taj Mahal, India, Dagli Orti; p36 from George Catlin's illustrations; p42t Buddha, Musée Guimet, Paris/Dagli Orti; p45t Palatine Library Parma/Dagli Orti; p46tr Museo San Marco Florence/Dagli Orti; p46br Musée des Beaux Arts Tours/Dagli Orti; p48t Turkish and Islamic Art Museum Istanbul/Dagli Orti; p49b British Library; p53tl Palazzo Barberini Rome/ Dagli Orti; p52tr; p54t; p55 Musée des Beaux Arts Nantes/Dagli Orti; p66t British Museum; p72b British Library; p74t Venus of Willendorf; p75 Peggy Guggenheim Collection Venice/Dagli Orti; p83t Palazzo Arco Mantua Italy/Dagli Orti; p86bl Cathedral Museum Ferrara/Dagli Orti; p89t Dagli Orti; p90t (Douce OR.a3 fol 30), Bodleian Library Oxford; p91b Stadelisches Kunstinstitut Frankfurt; p94tr Russian Historical Museum Moscow/Dagli Orti; p96tm Archaeological Museum Aleppo, Syria/Dagli Orti; p97b Old Kingdom Egyptian, Saqqarah, Egypt (B.49) Musée du Louvre Paris/Dagli Orti; p98b Médiathèque François Mitterand, Poitiers/ Dagli Orti; p99bl Warburg Institute London/Eileen Tweedy; p105t Scrovegni Chapel Padua/Dagli Orti; p110br Newgrange, Ireland/Dagli Orti; p116 Musée des Beaux Arts Tours /Dagli Orti; p117t Ragab Papyrus Institute Cairo/Dagli Orti; p119t Galleria Sabauda Turin/Dagli Orti; p120 Queretaro Museum Mexico/ Dagli Orti; p122tl Galleria Sabauda, Turin/ Dagli Orti; p124br Victoria and Albert Museum London/Eileen Tweedy; p125tm British Library; p127t Dagli Orti; p127b British Library; p128t Musée d'Orsay, Paris/Dagli Orti; p128b British Library; p129t Musée des Arts Africains et Océaniens/Dagli Orti; p129b Prehistoric Museum Moesgard Højbjerg, Denmark/ Dagli Orti; p131t Dagli Orti; p131b British Museum/Eileen Tweedy; p132br Victoria and Albert Museum London/Graham Brandon; p133 Museo Civico Padua/Dagli Orti; p135t (Pers b1 Folio 15a)

Farrukhabad, Bodleian Library Oxford; p136t Museo del Prado Madrid/Dagli Orti; p136b Galleria d'Arte Moderna, Rome/ Dagli Orti; p138t Canto XIII, Dante's Divine Comedy, by Gustave Dore; p139tl Musée Condé Chantilly/Dagli Orti; p139tr Ashmole 1511 folio 68r, Bodleian Library Oxford; p140tr Museum Recklinghausen/ Harper Collins Publishers; p141b Mexican National Libary/Mireille Vautier; p150b Lucien Biton Collection Paris/Dagli Orti; p153t Dagli Orti; p155t Musée Thomas Dobrée, Nantes/ Dagli Orti; p155b Palazzo Pitti Florence/Dagli Orti; p156t Tate Gallery London/Eileen Tweedy; p159tr Médiathèque François Mitterand, Poitiers/ Dagli Orti; p160tr National Gallery, London/Eileen Tweedy; p162t National Gallery London/Joseph Martin; p172t Buonconsiglio Castle Trento/Dagli Orti; p178t Burnley Art Gallery/Dagli Orti; p179t British Library; p180t Culver Pictures; p181tl Galleria Borghese, Rome/ Dagli Orti; p186b Museo del Prado, Madrid/Dagli Orti; p187t Dagli Orti; p189t Archaeological Museum Merida Spain/ Dagli Orti; p192t (Arch Bb9 plate 98), Bodleian Library Oxford.

THE BRIDGEMAN ART LIBRARY: p19tl Museo e Gallerie Nazionali di Capodimonte, Naples, Italy; p19b Louvre, Paris, France, Lauros/Giraudon; p20tl Musee des Antiquites Nationales, St. Germain-en-Laye, France; p26t, Nottingham City Museums and Galleries (Nottingham Castle); p30b Museo Nacional de Antropologia, Mexico City, Mexico, Sean Sprague/Mexicolore; p37t Bibliotheque des Arts Decoratifs, Paris, France, Archives Charmet; p38b Bibliotheque Nationale, Paris, France/ Archives Charmet; p40b Private Collection/Ann & Bury Peerless Picture Library; p47 Prado, Madrid, Spain, Giraudon; p50t Freud Museum, London, UK; p51tr Archives Larousse, Paris, France; p52b Fogg Art Museum/Harvard University Art Museums, USA, Bequest of Grenville L. Winthrop; p56 Johnny van Haeften Gallery, London, UK; p57t Prado, Madrid, Spain; p57b Collection Kharbine-Tapabor, Paris, France; p58b Private Collection; p59 Private Collection/Chris

Beetles, London, UK; p70br Private Collection/Chris Beetles, London, UK; p72t Bristol City Museum and Art Gallery, UK; p73t Musee Gustave Moreau, Paris, France; p83b Private Collection/Archives Charmet; p92t Private Collection; p100b The Illustrated London News Picture Library, London, UK; p101tl Private Collection/Paul Freeman; p101tr Institut National des Jeunes Sourds, Paris, France/ Archives Charmet; p102b Museo de America, Madrid, Spain; p104tr Private Collection/Richard Philp, London; p107t Walker Art Gallery, National Museums, Liverpool; p109tr Palazzo Ducale, Urbino, Italy; p111t British Museum, London, UK; p112b Private Collection/The Fine Art Society, London, UK; p113t Private Collection/Christopher Wood Gallery, London, UK; p114t Private Collection; p115tr Leighton House Museum and Art Gallery, London, UK; p126t Private Collection/Lawrence Steigrad Fine Arts, New York; p130 Private Collection; p132bl Bibliotheque de L'Arsenal, Paris, France, Archives Charmet; p134t Musee d'Art Thomas Henry, Cherbourg, France, Giraudon; p134b Nationalmuseum, Stockholm, Sweden; p135 Bibliotheque des Arts Decoratifs, Paris, France, Archives Charmet; p137t Bibliotheque des Arts Decoratifs, Paris, France, Archives Charmet; p138b Royal Asiatic Society, London, UK; p139b The Marsden Archive, UK; p146t Bibliotheque de L'Arsenal, Paris, France/Archives Charmet; p147t/ Private Collection/Stapleton Collection; p147b Private Collection/Stapleton Collection; p148bl Private Collection/ Stapleton Collection; p149 Musee des Beaux-Arts, Rouen, France, Lauros/Giraudon; p152b Ms Add 24189 fol.15 Library, London, UK; p159tl Ashmolean Museum, University of Oxford, UK; p161b Private Collection/Stapleton Collection; p165t Lady Lever Art Gallery, National Museums Liverpool; p169t Trustees of the Watts Gallery, Compton, Surrey, UK; p174b Private Collection/Ann & Bury Peerless Picture Library; p176t Johnny van Haeften Gallery, London, UK; 177t Galleria degli Uffizi, Florence, Italy, Alinari; p182t Archaeological Museum of Heraklion, Crete, Greece; p182b Giraudon; p184t Musee Girodet, Montargis, France/ Peter Willi; p186tr; p190b 28681 f.9 Psalter Map, British Library, London, UK; p191 Hotel Dieu, Beaune, France/Paul Maeyaert; p194b Ms 386 fol.25r Bibliotheque Municipale, Cambrai, France, Giraudon; p196b Palazzo Pitti, Florence, Italy; 197t Louvre, Paris, France; p199t Nationalmuseum, Stockholm, Sweden; p199b Louvre, Paris, France; p201b Private Collection/Index; p202b Private

Collection/Bonhams, London, UK; p203tr Musee de la Chartreuse, France/Giraudon.

CORBIS: p20b Richard T. Nowitz; p22bl; p22br Charles & Josette Lenars; p23t DiMaggio/Kalish; p23m Kevin Fleming; p24 Paul Almasy; p25l Charles & Josette Lenars; p25r Margaret Courtney-Clarke; p28t Wolfgang Kaehler; p28b Chris Rainier; p29t Charles & Josette Lenars; p29bl Michael & Patricia Fogden; p32b; p33t; p34t John Noble; p34b Peter Harholdt; p35b Tiziana and Gianni Baldizzone; p39t Brian A. Vikander; p41t Reuters; p43t Christine Kolisch; p48b Nevada Wier; p52t Close Murray/Corbis Sygma; p53b Elke Stolzenberg; p61b Richard Hamilton Smith; p64t Hulton-Deutsch Collection; p54b David Turnley; p55t Bettmann; p55b Hulton-Deutsch Collection; p66b Archivo Iconografico, S.A.; p67t Anthony Bannister; Gallo Images; p69tl Matthew McKee; Eye Ubiquitous; p69tr; p74m Charles & Josette Lenars; p74b Christie's Images; p76b Murray Andrew/Corbis Sygma; p77b Leonard de Selva; p78b 1661-Drawing of Copernicus' world system, Bettmann; p79t Galileo Galilei before the Inquisition (ca. 1632) by Robert-Fleury, Bettmann; p84t David Muench; p85tl Nik Wheeler; p85tr Dean Conger; p85b Jose Luis Pelaez, Inc.; p86bm Bob Krist; p86br Carl & Ann Purcell; p87t Michael S. Yamashita; p88t Roger Antrobus; p91t Jim Zuckerman; p93t; p94tl Anthony Bannister; Gallo Images; p96tr Carmen Redondo; p99br early print shop workers at their trade, c.1800s, Bettmann; p102t Jeffrey L. Rotman; p103t Bettmann; p103b William Whitehurst; p108t Farrell Grehan; p109tl Penny Tweedie; p120 Greenhalf Photography; p121 Tranquility Base, the Moon: Apollo 11 commander Neil Armstrong takes first step on lunar surface, Bettmann; p123 Matthias Kulka; p142b Tiziana and Gianni Baldizzone; p143t Sheldan Collins; p143m Werner Forman; p145tl Jonathan Blair; p145tr Brian A. Vikander; p145b Michael S. Lewis; p148br; p151t Alison Wright; p151b Bob Krist; p157b Michael Freeman; p164t Rose Hartman; p165bl Adam Woolfitt; p166b Lindsay Hebberd; p167t Mark Cooper; p167b Norbert Schaefer; p168t Lindsay Hebberd; p169b George Huey; p170tl Lindsay Hebberd; p170tr; p174t Fabrizio Bensch; p175b Catherine Karnow; p179 Jim Zuckerman; p181 Lindsay Hebberd; p184b Werner H. Müller; p187b Michael & Patricia Fogden; p188t Archivo Icono-grafico; p189b Reuters; p192b Werner Forman; p195tr Galen Rowell; p198b Hubert Stadler; p203tl Clayton J. Price.

THE KOBAL COLLECTION: p76t Warner Bros/The Kobal Collection

Index

"A" 96, 206
abscesses 210
Acropolis 16, 17
active intellect 206
Adam and Eve 117
adinkra 25, 162
adoni 206
adrinkrahene 206
advertising 76–7
aeroplanes 206
afterlife 71
agal 23
age 64
Ahriman 22
Ahura Mazda 22
air 198–9, 206, 222
aircraft 89
akoben 206
akokonan 206
akoma ntoso 206
albedo 147
alchemy 146–7, 206
alcohol 206
alcoves 85
alembic 206
Algol 206
Algorab 206
alinea 206
all is well 206
alligators 31, 182
almonds 206
Alpha 99, 116, 206
alphabets 96–9, 107, 112
Alphecca 206
altars 144
alum 206
amalgam 206
amalgamation 207
ampersand 207
amulets 15, 24, 143, 153
anacondas 187
Anansi 71
anarchism 207
anchored cross 217
anchors 68, 207
Andrew, St, cross of 217
angakok 34
angels 47, 49, 111, 132–3, 134, 200, 207
angled cross 217
anima 50
animal familiars 67
animalia 207
animals 1, 11, 28, 29, 37, 67, 71, 116, 178–9
animus 50
ankh 15, 108, 109, 143, 207
anointing 94
ansur 207
Antares 207
antelopes 207
anthems 54
anthills 184
Anthony, St, cross of 217
anti-clockwise spiral 207
anti-nuclear 100, 207

antimony 207
antlers 20
ants 207
Anubis 130
anvils 207
apes 67, 207
Aphrodite 207
Apis bull 179
Apollo 16, 17, 207
    staff of 243
apples 67, 117, 123, 160, 162, 171, 176, 177, 207
approximately equal to 207
apricots 177, 207
aqua regia 207
Aquarius 125, 207
aquatic creatures 182–3
aquila 19
Arathron 207
archangels 133
    cross of 217
archers 125
arches 208
archtypes 52
Arcturus 208
Ares 208
Aries 124, 208
Ark of the Covenant 44, 208
arks 208
armour 208
arms 208
arrow heads 208
arrowed cross 217
arrows 103, 123, 161, 162, 163, 208
arsenic 208, 225, 249
art 74–5
asaba 23
Asclepius 18
ash tree 170
Ashtar 13
asphodel 159
Ass (god) 208
asses 220
Astarte 13
asterisks 208
Athene 18
atomic explosions 51
atoms 208
attics 85
Audi 208
augury 153
auroch 208
autumn 189, 208
axes 109, 148, 199, 209

Baal 199
baboons 179
Babylon 13
badgers 209
badges 54
ball game 31
balls 209
bamboo 175, 209
bananas 50, 176, 209
banners 68
banyan trees 170
baptism 159, 164–5
barber's pole 68
bards 72
barges 159
basements 85
basil 173
basilisk 137, 209
baskets 92–3, 209
bass clef 209
baths 209
bats 52, 209
beads 142, 163
beans 209
beards 209
bears 32, 34, 55, 143, 179, 209
bedrooms 85
beehives 209
bees 161, 184–5, 209
beetles 15
Behemoth 138
Bellerophon 137
bells 164, 165, 209
belts 209
beorc 209
Bethor 209
bile 157
bindu 106
biohazards 209
birch 209
birds 153, 158, 162, 170, 180–1,
    of power 139
    of prey 180
Birgitta, St, cross of 217
birth 158–9, 209, 135
birthdays 164
bison 10, 11, 32, 160, 179, 210
bjarkan 210
black 114, 115, 165
black knights 55
black sun 119
blankets 167
blessed sign 210
blessings 210
blind 155, 169, 210
blindfold 210
blood 67, 117, 156, 158, 179
bloomers 64
blue 114, 115, 161, 163
blue moon 120
BMW 210
boars 21, 210
boasso 35
boats 88–9, 159, 208, 210
bodhisattvas 42, 43
body art 102–3

body language 100–1
body painting 102
body piercing 102–3
boil (verb) 210
boils (abscess) 210
bones 117, 210
bonfires 200
books 98, 210
boots 88
borax 210
bottles 224
bowls 92, 93, 248
bows 123, 160, 162, 202, 210
boxes 50, 210
bracelets 111, 210
Brahman 40
brass 210
bread 45, 47, 164, 210
breath 117, 156, 198, 199
Brer Rabbit 71
bricks 84–5
bridesmaids 165
bridges 202, 210
bridles 211
Brigid 20
broom flowers 175
brooms 92, 211
brushes 98
bubbles 211
buckle of Isis 211
Buddha 42, 75, 150, 211
Buddhism 42–3
buffalo 32, 160, 179, 210
buildings 31, 52, 84–5 145
bull roarers 211
bulls 11, 13, 19, 22, 41, 124, 179, 196, 211
burglars 52
burial 151, 159, 165
burning bush 200
buses 89
butterflies 158, 184, 185, 211

caduceus 110, 187, 203, 211
caged bears 55
cakes 164, 165
calabashes 25, 226
calcinations 211
calendars 30, 106, 188, 189
caltrap 211
calves 211
camellias 175, 211
camels 22, 211
canals 26
Cancer 124, 211
candelabra 143
candles 144, 164, 200, 211
candytufts 175
cannabis 173, 211
cannons 211
canoes 28, 88–9
canopies 211
capes 95
Capricorn 125, 211–12
cardamom pods 173
cards 212

Tarot 107, 152, 153, 169
carnations 175
carp 182, 212
carpets 23, 93, 212
cars 52, 76, 77, 89, 95
castles 212
caterpillars 212
Catherine wheel 168
cats 178–9, 212
cauldrons 20, 92, 157, 212
caves 50, 84–5, 157, 212
    cave art 10–11
cavik 34
cedar 212
ceiba tree 171
Celtic alphabet 97
Celtic bards 72
Celtic clans 163
Celtic cross 108, 151, 217
Celtic harp 212
Celtic knots 212
Celtic wheel of the year 189
centaurs 71, 125, 136, 137, 212
Cerberus 212
ceremonial dress 95
Ceres 17, 53, 212
chai 212
chains 142, 162, 212
chairs 93, 95, 212
chakras 40, 157, 168
chalices 135, 212
chariots 52, 88, 119, 213
charms 24
chastity 160, 161
chef's hat 68
chemical symbols 79
cher 213
cherries 176, 213
cherry blossom 75, 176
cherubim 133
cherubs 213
chess 167
chestnuts 161
chevrons 213
Chi-Rho 46, 218
chickens 213
childbirth 213
childhood 166–7
chimera 136, 137, 213
chimneys 213
China 213
Chiron 136
Christ 213
    cross of 109, 216
Christianity 46–7
Christmas trees 171
Chronos 189, 213

chrysalises 158
chrysanthemums 26, 175, 213
Chrysler 214
Chukwa 183
churches 47, 164, 193, 214
cigarettes 64
cinnabar 214
circle and arrow 214
circles 32, 108, 110–11, 113, 118, 119, 124, 150–1, 168, 188, 200, 202, 208, 210, 214, 223, 233, 236, 243, 245
    semi circles 224
Citroen 214
clans, Celtic 163
clay 215
cledon 153
cliff edges 55
cloaks 47, 215
clocks 60, 78, 188, 215
clothes 64, 102
clouds 75, 150, 198–9, 215
clover 175
cloves 173, 215
clowns 53
    sacred 166–7
clubs 40, 215
coagulate 215
coats of arms 69
cobras 71, 215
cockatiel 28
cockerels 198
cocks 215
coconuts 215
codes 99
coffins 159
coins 94–5
Colosseum 18, 19
colours 114–15, 161, 163, 202
columns 107, 215
combs 215
comets 215
communication 96–9
compasses 192–3, 215
compose 215
computers 95
    computer games 166
conch shells 40, 183, 215
condors 215
cones 127
conference 215
confetti 165
confused mental state 216
congruent 229
constellations 124
    of fixed stars 216
containers 92
cooking vessels 92
Coptic cross 217, 218
copyright symbol 216
coral 183, 216
corn 33, 189, 216
corn dollies 160–1
cornucopia 161, 162, 176, 216
corporate identity 76
cosmic tree 170–1, 216
cosmology 116–17
counting sticks 106
court jesters 53
cowrie shells 183, 216
cows 11, 41, 67, 179, 216
coyotes 71, 178, 216

crabs 124, 183
cradles 216
cranes 181, 216
creation 116–17
creativity 166
cremation 159, 165
crescent moon 48, 121
crickets 185, 216
crocodiles 29, 182, 216
cross of the archangels 217
cross of Christ 109, 216
cross of endlessness 216
cross of the Evangelists 217
cross of Golgotha 216
cross of the Holy Church 217
cross of Lazarus 216
cross of Loraine 109, 216
cross of Palestine 216
cross of the Patriarch 217
cross of Peter 216
cross of Philip 217
cross of the Pope 217
cross of the robbers 217
cross of St Andrew's 217
cross of St Anthony 217
cross of St Birgitta 217
cross of St George 217
cross of St Han 217
cross of St John 217
crosses 46, 47, 108–9, 218
    anchored 217
    angled 217
    arrowed 217
    Celtic 108, 151, 217
    Chi-Rho 46, 218
    Coptic 217, 218
    diagonal 217
    dissimulata 217
    Eastern Orthodox 217
    Egyptian 218
    fitchee 218
    with garment 218
    Greek 108, 218
    iron 218
    labarum 46, 218
    Latin 109
    lily 218
    Maltese 218
    Mantuan 218
    with orb 218
    pachuco 103, 236
    portale 218
    restoration 218
    Roman holy 218
    square 218
    square with cross 108, 243
    sun 218, 244
    Tau 109, 218
    wheel 218
crossroads 89, 218
crown of thorns 46, 219
crowns 14, 95, 111, 154, 163, 219
crows 129, 180, 219
croziers 46, 219
crucibles 157, 219
crucifix 109
crush 226
crux dissimulata 219
crystals 195, 219
cubes 113, 219
cuneiform 12

Cupid 162, 163, 219
cups 153, 212
curtains 93, 248
curved lines 219
cypress trees 171
cypresses 159, 219

daeg 219
daffodils 175
Dagda 20
daggers 219
daimones 132
daisies 219
dakini 133
daleth 86
dances 111, 119
danger 219
date palms 177
dates 177
dawn 55, 189
day 219
day lilies 175
Dead Sea 196
death 103, 117, 158, 159, 165, 187, 219
death's head 31
death's head sphinx moth 158
decoction 219
deer 31, 219
delta 112
Demeter 17, 53, 160, 175, 194
demons 103, 132–3
deneb algedi 219
denkyem 220
deserts 195
Deshret 14
devas 133
devil, staff of 243
dharmachakra 105, 220
diagonal cross 217
diamonds 163
died in battle 220
digging sticks 220
discus 40
dissimulata cross 217
distaffs 220
distance 220
distillation 220
distilled oil 220
divination 107, 152–3, 167
divine figures 11
divine power 220
Divine Proportion 123
division 220
divorced 220
Dodona oak 153
does 11
dogs 31, 67, 158, 178, 220
dollar sign 220
dolls 220
dolphins 103, 182, 220
domes 43, 50, 220
donkeys 220
doors 50, 85, 86–7, 220
dose of medicine 220
dots 106, 107, 224
    in a line 220
    single 220
    square with 243
    three in triangle 220
Double Crown 14
double signals 101

double spirals 110
doves 47, 129, 161, 162, 180, 221
down with! 221
dragon, eye of 222
dragonflies 184
dragons 26, 139, 140, 192, 221
drawers 50
dream figures 55
dreams 58–9, 79
Dreamtime 28
dreidel 167
dress 102
    ceremonial 95
    codes 68
drums 35, 37, 221
dryads 134–5
ducks 162, 189, 221
dusk 55
dvarapala 86
dwellings 84–5, 221

eagles 19, 31, 32–3, 37, 47, 69, 103, 118, 138–9, 180, 186, 221
    double-headed 180
ear of wheat 17
ears 221
earth 37, 78, 190–1, 221, 222
earth lights 135
earthquakes 194
east 193, 198
Eastern Orthodox cross 217
eclipse, 119, 221, 242
Eden 90
edge 55
Edshu 53
eggs 221
eglantine 174
Egypt, land of 231
Egyptian cross 218
ehwaz 221
eight 105, 221
eight-pointed star 123
eighth house 221
El Dorado 196
elders 53
electricity 221
elemental beasts 136
elementals 135
elements
    Empedocles' 222
    fifth 223
    four 224
elephants 43, 128, 179, 221
Eleusis 17
eleventh house 221
elhaz 222
ellipsis 222
Empedocles' elements 222
emperors 26, 119, 222
emus 222
Enata 28
enclosed space 222
endlessness, cross of 216
energy body 157
enneagram 222
entrances 220
eoh 222
epa 222
Epidaurus 18
ermine 95, 161, 222
Eros 116, 162, 219

essence 222
etheric oil 222
Etua 28
Eucharist 47
Evangelists
    cross of 217
    four 224
evaporation 222
Eve 73
Evening Star 122–3
evergreen trees 171
exclamation mark 222
eye of the dragon 222
eye of fire 222
Eye of Horus 15, 118, 143, 155, 222, 244
eyebright 172
eyebrows 222
eyes 155, 162, 197, 222, 101
    third eye 222

fairies 134–5, 167
faith 222
falcons 180, 222
family 223
fans 223
fantastic creatures 136–9
fantasy 167
faravahar 22
fasces 69, 223
fast food 63
fast movement 223
fasting 49
Fatima, hand of 227
fawns 11
fe 223
feasts 164
feathers 181, 223
feet 156, 162, 198, 224
female 223
female sex 249
feng shui 84–5
feoh 223
ferns 223
fertility symbols 160–1
fetish 24, 67
Fiat 223
fifth element 223
fifth house 223
figs 50, 160, 176, 177, 223
figurines 74
filter 223
fingernails 223
fingers 198, 223
fire 10, 11, 147, 159, 165, 169, 200–1, 222, 223
    fire spirits 135
    fire temples 200
fireplaces 227
fireworks 200, 223
first floors 51
first house 223

fish 46, 121, 125, 160, 182, 186, 223
fish hooks 223
fitchee cross 218
five 105, 108, 122, 224
five elements of Western ideography 224
five-pointed star 122, 123
fix 215
fixation 224
flags 54, 68–9, 164, 194, 224
  prayer 142–3
flames 150, 165
flaming heart 227
flasks 224
flat Earth 190
fleur -de-lys 68, 69
fleur-de-lis 224
flies 184, 224
flint knives 31
floods 194, 197
flow 224
flowers 31, 50, 148, 162, 165, 172, 174–5, 224
flutes 224
fly whisks 224
fog 54
food 11, 63, 164, 165
fools 53
fool's gold 233
footprints 42, 43
forest edge 55
forges 233
fortresses 212
Fortuna 169
fountains 91, 224
four 105, 108, 112, 224
four elements 224
four evangelists 224
fourth house 224
foxes 121, 225
foxglove 172
frankincense 23
Freya 21, 129
Freyr 21
Frô 21
frogs 182–3, 225
fruit 50, 63, 67, 117, 176–7
fu 225
Fuji, Mount 144, 195
fulfoot 225
fumes 225
funtunfunefu 225
furniture 93

gaddha 40
Gaia 191
Galahad 52
gall 157
games 166–7
Ganesh 40
Ganges, river 41, 196–7

gardens 26, 47, 90–1
Garduda 71
gargoyles 225
garlic 173, 225
Garuda 139
gates and gateways 47, 86-7, 225
geese 181, 226
Gehenna 131
Gemini 124, 225
gender 64
  taboos 66
gentians 175
geofu 225
George, St, cross of 217
gestures 100
giants 136, 167, 225
Gilgamesh 73
girdle of Isis 143
girdles 111, 160, 161, 162, 209
gladiatorial fights 19
glasses 225
globes 95, 116, 225
gloves 225
gnomes 135
goats 83, 125, 225
God 191
gods and goddesses 11, 126–9, 225
gohei 225
gold 94, 114, 118, 225
gold leaf/gold foil 225
Golden Mean 123
golden number 17 225
golden number 18 225
Golgata cross 217
Golgotha, cross of 216
Goma fire ceremonies 200
gongs 226
gorgons 138, 226
gourds 50, 226
grail 226
grain 160, 226
grapes 177, 226
graphics 104–13
grass 31, 75, 226
gravel 91, 226
graves 55, 193, 226
gravestones 159
graveyards 161
Great Goddess 126–7
Great Wall of China 26, 27
Greek cross 108, 218
green 69, 114–15
Green Man 115, 135, 137
grey 115
griffins 138, 139, 226
grim reaper 159
grind 226
ground floors 51
groups 68–9
  group identity 69
growing 226
guardians 56
guns 211
gye name 25, 226
Gymea lilies 174–5

Hades 17, 130–1
hagall 226
Hagith 226
hail 226

hair 117, 128, 154, 155, 165, 226
haloes 47, 119, 226
hammer and sickle 69, 226
hammers 199, 226
Han, St, cross of 217
hand axes 11
hand of Fatima 49, 227
hands 156, 163, 165, 198, 227
  gestures 100
handshakes 101
Hanuman 40
happiness 227
hares 21, 71, 121, 179, 189, 227
harmless 210
harpies 138
harps 20, 227
  Celtic 212
harvest festivals 189
hawks 180, 227
hawthorn 161, 175
hazel 227
head 154, 227
  gestures 100
headdresses 68, 95
healing 187
heart 155, 163
heart on fire 227
heart shape 227
hearths 92, 227
hearts 103, 113
Heaven 78, 86, 130–1, 191
hedgehogs 227
Hei-matau 28
Heket 183
Hell 86, 130–1
Helm of Awe 21
helmets 227
helpers 56
Hemesh hand 227
Hengist 21
henna, body painting 102
Hephaestus 189
heptagrams 227
heraldic daggers 227
herbs 172–3
hermaphrodites 147, 161, 227
Hermes 17, 227
Hermes Trismegistus 146
Hermetic philosophy 146
heroes 52, 56–7, 72, 119, 167
herons 227
hexagons 105, 113, 227
hexagrams 107, 152, 228
hieroglyphs 228
high 228
hijab 228
hills 50, 51
Hindu/Hinduism 40–1, 228
hippopotamuses 228
hnefatafl 228
holes 195
holly 87, 228
hollyhocks 175
Holy Ark 44, 208
Holy Church, cross of 217
Holy Grail 20, 52, 72–3, 92
holy sign 228
Holy Spirit 228
Holy Trinity 47, 228
homecomings 228
homes 84–5, 92–3
honey 165, 184–5, 228

honeysuckle 174
hoods 228
horizon 106–7, 193
horizontal lines 106–7
horns 188, 194, 228
Horsa 21
horses 21, 88, 89, 179, 196, 228
horseshoes 229
Horus 14, 229
  eye of 118, 143, 155, 222, 244
hour 229
hourglasses 159, 229
houses 31, 52, 84–5
huacas 31
human body 154–7
human sacrifices 31
humours, four 157
hunting 10, 11
hurricanes 199
hwemudua 229
Hydra 137, 229
hye won hye 229

"I" 107
I Ching 107, 152
ibheqe 163
ibis 229
ice granules 229
igloos 34–5, 229
ikebana 174, 175
imps 132
Inanna 13, 130
incense 23, 144
incest 66
infertility 161
infinite 229
infinity 229
ing 229
ingz 229
initiation 56, 164
ink 98
innua 34
inscriptions 96–7
insects 184–5
intercourse 160, 161, 194,
inuksuk 35
inverted tree 171
irises 161
iron 229
iron cross 218
is 229
Ischtar 229
Ishtar 13, 160
Isis 13, 127, 160
  girdle of 143
Islam 49–50, 229
islands 229
isomorphs 229
Itzamna 30
ivy 229

jackals 229
jade 31, 39, 87, 94
Jade Emperor 39
jaguars 30, 31, 119, 121, 178, 229
jara 229
jars 92
jasmine 162, 163
Jerusalem 13
jesters 53
Jesus Christ 230
Jeune Bretagne 230
jewellery 11, 94
jewels 230
John, St, cross of 217
journeys 88–9
  sacred 193
Judaism 44–5
juice 230
Juno 230
Jupiter 17, 230
  staff of 243

Ka'aba 49
kadomatsu 87
Kailas, Mount 150, 193, 195
Kairos 189
Kali 41, 53
Kama 162
kangaroos 230
kata 35
kaun 230
Kemet 14
ken 230
kepun 34
Kernunnos 20
keys 87, 230
kings 119, 147, 167
kinship 163
kintinkantan 230
kitchens 85
kites 230
knives 31, 35, 219
knots 14, 230, 212
Koi carp 26
koru 28, 29
Ku Klux Klan 230
kut 166–7
labarum cross 46, 218
labrys 148
labyrinths 148–9, 151, 233
lace 163
ladders 230
lagu 230
Lakshmi 40
lamassu 13, 86
lambs 46, 178, 189, 230
lamps 45, 231
lances 231
land 194–5
landscapes 75
lanterns 231
Lao-tzu 38, 39
lapis lazuli 231
lapis philosophorum 231
Lapiths 137
Latin cross 109
laurel 231
  wreaths 16, 17, 18, 162, 231
lava 200
Lazarus, cross of 216
lead 231, 249

lead sulphate 231
leaves 27
lemon 231
Leo 124, 231
leopards 231
letters 96–9
Leviathan 138
Libra 125, 231
lichees 177
life force 82
light 41
lighthouses 231
lightning 198, 199, 231
lilies 47, 161, 174–5, 231
lily cross 218
lime 232
lines 106–7, 108, 232
    curved 219
linga 40, 157, 232
lion-dogs 138
lions 13, 47, 69, 71, 118, 124,
    138, 178, 232
lizards 31, 232
Loa-Tzu, seal of 241
locusts 185
logr 232
longships 21
loosen 232
Loraine, cross of 109, 216
lotus 15, 27, 40, 105, 128, 174,
    232
love 128, 162–3
    between women 232
lovebirds 162
lozenges 232
lunar calendar 106, 188
Lung (dragon) 141
lungs 15
lutes 232
lye 232
lyres 232

maat 14
machines 78
Madonna lilies 47, 174
madr 232
magicians 11
magnesium 232
magpies 158, 181
maidens 189
maize 33
make-up 102
male 233
Maltese cross 218
man 233
mana 28
mandalas 106, 150
mandrake 172, 233
mangoes 177
mangrove trees 159
mann 233
Mantuan cross 218
map of the world 233
mappa mundi 192
maps 190, 192–3
marcasite 233
mark of the bustard 95
marriage 162, 163, 165
    sacred 147
Mars 233
Mary, Virgin 47, 53, 191, 248
masks 24–5, 28, 29, 31, 74, 233

masquerade 24–5
mathematical signs 79
matzah 45
Maya calendar 189
Maya fire ceremonies 200
maypoles 161, 170, 233
mazes 148, 151, 233
mead 185
meander patterns 107
medicine 24
    dose of 220
medicine bundles 143
medicine wheels 32, 108, 164,
    168, 169
melons 50
melt 224
melting ovens 233
melting pot 219
Menorah 143, 233
menstruation 67
mercury (element) 17, 146,
    147, 233
Mercury (planet) 233
mermaids 7, 70, 71, 136, 138,
    242
mermen 138
Meru, Mount 195
metal 233
Metatron 133
mezuzah 45
mice 234
midwives 158
migration 234
mihrab 234
milk 159, 165
Mimi 129
minarets 48, 234
minotaur 137, 149
mirages 234
mirrors 47, 60, 92, 93, 95, 234
mist 54
mistletoe 87, 173, 234
mists 75
Mithras 19
Mitsubishi 234
mix/mixture 234
Mjölnir 199
mobile phones 95
money 94–5
monkeys 31, 67, 179, 234
monsters 167
months 234
Moon 11, 37, 39, 47, 118, 120–1,
    122, 127, 147, 162, 168, 189,
    221, 234
    new 121, 234
    waning 121, 234
    waxing 121
moon goddess 13
Morning Star 122–3
Morrigan 20, 129
mosques 48–9, 164, 193

moss 91
Mother Earth 190–1
Mother Goddess 126–7
mothers 53, 189
    mother and child 234
moths 158, 199
motion 31
mountains 50, 52, 111, 145,
    150, 193, 194–5, 234
mouse 32
mouths 155, 234
mudras 101
mulberry trees 171
mummies 15
mushrooms 234
musical notes 234
myrrh 23
mythical creatures 136–9
myths 71

Naga 139, 186
namaste 100
Nandi 41
nannan 234
Nataraja 40
nature spirits 134–5
naudh 235
navel 156, 174, 235
navel-stone 16
Nazca lines 31
Nazi SS 235
necklaces 111
needfires 84–5
Neptune 235
nets 235
nickel 235
nied 235
night 235
nigredo 147
Nike 18–19, 235
Nile, River 14, 144
nine 105, 163, 235
nine hells 130
nixies 135
nkonsonkonson 235
Noah's ark 70, 197
noon 189
noose 235
Norns 21
north 193, 198
nose rings 102
noses 235
nsoran 235
nsoromma 235
number 10 235
numbers 104–5, 235
Nut (goddess) 53
nuts 235
nyame biribi wo soro 235
nyame nnwu na mawu 235

oak trees 20, 153, 170, 173, 235
oats 27
obelisks 236
oceans 196
ochre 114, 159, 165
octagons 236
octagram of creation 236
octopuses 183
oculi, spiral 110
Odin 21
    staff of 243

offerings 11
Ogham alphabet 97
oil 236
    anointing 94
    distilled 220
    etheric 222
old men 189
old woman 189
olive branches 162, 180
olive oil 165
olives 162
Olympic Games 17, 236
om symbol 41, 236
Omega 99, 116, 236
omphalos 17, 156, 195
one 104, 107, 236
Opel 236
opposition 82
oracles 152–3
orange blossom 177
orange (colour) 114, 118
oranges (fruit) 177, 236
orbs 95, 225
orchids 175
orientation 193
Osiris 14, 15, 130, 160
    Tet of 246
ostriches 236
othel 236
otters 236
ourbourous 236
ovens 147
owls 17, 158, 181, 236
oxen 47, 236
oxslips 174
oyster shells 183

pachuco cross 103, 236
padma 40
pagodas 236
Palestine, cross of 216
Pallas 236
palm trees 170
Pan 83
pan pipes 224
Pandora 73
pansies 174
panthers 103, 236
paper 98
papyrus plant 15
paradise gardens 90–1
parallel lines 107
parasols 236
Paravati 41
parrots 236
parz 237
passionflowers 175
Patriarch, cross of 217
patterns 104–13
pawnbroker's balls 68, 237
peace 237
peach blossom 165, 177
peaches 171, 177, 237
peacocks 180, 181
pearls 183
pears 237
pebbles 244
Pegasus 137, 138
pelicans 237
pens 50, 98, 237
pentacles 123, 153, 237
pentagons 113, 237

pentagrams 105, 123, 237
peonies 162
peorth 237
peppercorns 173
peppermint 173
per cent 237
Persephone 17, 160, 175
personal space 101
Pesach 45
Peter, cross of 216
Peter Pan 166
phalec 237
phallic symbols 104, 107, 157,
    161, 195, 197
pharaoh 15
Philip, cross of 217
philosopher's stone 146–7, 237
phlegm 157
phoenix 139, 200, 237
pictographs 98
pigeons 162
pigs 29, 67, 237
pilgrimages 193
pillars 48, 107, 127, 215
pink 69, 114
pipes 237
Pisces 125, 237
placenta 158
places, sacred 144–5, 193
plaited sign 237
planetary system 7
plants 37, 116, 170–5
platinum 237
play 166–7
pleasure gardens 90
Pleiades 188, 237
plimsoll mark 237
ploughs 194, 237
plums 175, 176–7
plus sign 79
Pluto 17, 237–8
Polaris 238
polarity 82
Pole Star 35, 123
pomegranates 117, 177, 238
pools 91
Pope, cross of 217
poppies 159, 175
portale cross 218
Poseidon 196, 238
    staff of 243
post-partum blood 67
potash 238
potassium carbonate 238
pots 92
potter's wheels 169
pound sterling 238
prayer beads 238
prayer sticks 238
prayer strings 142
prayer wheels 43, 142, 238
precious stones 163, 195